Handbook of Computer Games Technology

Volume I

Handbook of Computer Games Technology
Volume I

Edited by **Akira Hanako**

CLANRYE INTERNATIONAL

New Jersey

Published by Clanrye International,
55 Van Reypen Street,
Jersey City, NJ 07306, USA
www.clanryeinternational.com

Handbook of Computer Games Technology: Volume I
Edited by Akira Hanako

International Standard Book Number: 978-1-63240-260-8 (Hardback)

Printed in the United States of America.

Contents

Preface

Computer games once were simple programs. But now, they have transformed into a complex programming technology. From simple flash games, this computer based technology has reached new heights, where one can play games by becoming the character itself. The action of performance in real world can now be converted into the gaming experience. Computer games are software development techniques which use artificial intelligence (AI), graphics of computer, multimedia programming, laws of physics, database designing, automata theory, database designing, input-output, and simulations. Games being developed these days can be categorised into Action, Action-adventure, Adventure, Role-playing, Simulation, Strategy, Vehicle Simulation etc.

The use of motion controllers, 3D tree models, Petri net models and adaptive-AR models are important technical models applied in advancing computer games technology.

This book provides a guideline for game development based learning. It also offers framework for adaptive game presenters with emotions and social comments. Some of the technical as well as conceptual aspects of game development and computer game technologies are discussed in this book.

I would like to express my sincere appreciation to the authors of this book for their excellent contributions and for their efforts involved in the publication process. I do believe that the contents in this book will be helpful to many researchers in this field around the world. Lastly, I would like to thank my family for being a constant source of support.

Editor

A Guideline for Game Development-Based Learning: A Literature Review

Bian Wu and Alf Inge Wang

Norwegian University of Science and Technology, 7491 Trondheim, Norway

Correspondence should be addressed to Bian Wu, oscar.wubian@gmail.com

Academic Editor: Zhigang Deng

This study aims at reviewing the published scientific literature on the topics of a game development-based learning (GDBL) method using game development frameworks (GDFs) with the perspective of (a) summarizing a guideline for using GDBL in a curriculum, (b) identifying relevant features of GDFs, and (c) presenting a synthesis of impact factors with empirical evidence on the educational effectiveness of the GDBL method. After systematically going through the available literature on the topic, 34 relevant articles were selected for the final study. We analyzed the articles from three perspectives: (1) pedagogical context and teaching process, (2) selection of GDFs, and (3) evaluation of the GDBL method. The findings from the 34 articles suggest that GDFs have many potential benefits as an aid to teach computer science, software engineering, art design, and other fields and that such GDFs combined with the motivation from games can improve the students' knowledge, skills, attitudes, and behaviors in contrast to the traditional classroom teaching. Furthermore, based on the results of the literature review, we extract a guideline of how to apply the GDBL method in education. The empirical evidence of current findings gives a positive overall picture and can provide a useful reference to educators, practitioners, and researchers in the area of game-based learning.

1. Introduction

Computer games and video games have become very popular in children and adolescents' life and play a prominent role in the culture of young people [1]. Games can now be played everywhere in technology-rich environments equipped with laptops, smart phones, game consoles (mobile and stationary), set-top, boxes and other digital devices. From this phenomenon, it is believed that the intrinsic motivation that young people shows towards games can be combined with educational content and objectives into what Prensky calls "digital game based learning" [2].

Besides of an abundant appearance of games in young students life, game development technology has matured and became more advanced than before [3]. Based on various existing game development software, the whole duty of game development process can be divided into several domains and roles such as game programmers, 3D model creators, game designers, musicians, animators, and play writers. Under this situation, some web resources and game engines can simplify the game development process. For instance, Microsoft's XNA game development kit provides the game loop function to draw and update the game contents, and it also provides convenient game development components to load the different format of graphics, audio, and videos. This makes it possible for students to modify existing games or develop their own new games with or without programming. They can design and implement their own game concepts with these game creation tools, learn the developing skills and relevant knowledge, and accumulate related practical experience.

In this context, not only can a game be used for learning, but also the game development tools be used for studying relevant topics within computer science, software engineering (SE), or game programming through motivating assignments. Generally, games can be integrated in education in three ways [4, 5]. First, games can be used instead of traditional exercises motivating students to put extra effort in doing the exercises and giving the teacher and/or teaching assistants an opportunity to monitor how the students work with the exercises in real time, for example, [6, 7]. Second, games can be played within lectures to improve the participation and motivation of students, for example, [8, 9]. Third, the students are required to modify or develop a game as a part of a course using a game development framework (GDF) to learn skills within computer science and SE, for example, [10]. And we label this third as game development-based learning (GDBL). And the GDFs denote the toolkits that can be used to develop or modify games, for example, game engine, game editors, or game (simulation) platforms, or even any integrated development environment (IDE), like Visual C++, Eclipse, J2ME, and Android SDK since all of them can be used to build games. This paper focuses on using the GDBL method in education, where GDFs are used in student exercises to learn skills, extending the use of GDFs as a teaching aid. The motivation for teaching through game development is to utilize the students' enthusiasm for games. This GDBL method is not new. The earliest similar application of learning through programming in a game-like environment was in early 1970s. The logo [11], the turtle graphics, is one of the oldest libraries that was used to introduce computing concepts to beginners. The concept was based on a "turtle" that could be moved across a 2D screen with a pen, which could be positioned on or off the screen and, thus, may leave a trace of the turtle's movements. Programming the turtle to draw different patterns can be used to introduce general computing skill, such as procedural operations, iteration, and recursion. Further, in 1987, Micco presented the usage of writing a tic-tac-toe game for learning [12]. After several years of development, we believe that GDBL methods have been improved through the development of technology. Thus, we investigate how GDFs are being used in education through a literature survey and investigate how traditional lectures can become more dynamic, collaborative, and attractive to the students utilizing the current technology rich environment. However, this assertion needs to be further supported by relevant theory, application experiences, evaluation results, and empirical evidence. Nevertheless, to the best of the authors' knowledge, there does not exist any comprehensive literature reviews on the application of the GDBL method so far.

The aim of the study is to review the recently published literature on the use of GDFs in education to

(a) summarize a guideline for how to use GDBL in a curriculum,

(b) identify the features of GDFs related to GDBL,

(c) present a synthesis of impact factors with the empirical evidence on the educational effectiveness of the GDBL method.

The study is unique in that it presents an overview of the recently published literature on the use of GDFs in education, while taking into account both game engines and relevant toolkits to create/modify games or game-like systems (e.g., simulators). The study can provide useful guidance to teachers at different educational levels or areas, as well as to educators, practitioners, and researchers in the areas of game-based education.

The paper is organized as follows. Section 2 describes the method used for carrying out the systematic review of articles, Section 3 presents the results from the literature review, Section 4 extracts a guideline for GDBL according to the existing literature, and finally Section 5 concludes the paper.

2. Method

Informed by the established method of systematic review [13, 14], the review was undertaken in distinct stages: the development of review protocol, the identification of inclusion and exclusion criteria, a search for relevant studies, critical appraisal, data extraction, and synthesis.

2.1. Protocol Development. We developed a protocol for the systematic review by following the guidelines, procedures and policies of the Campbell Collaboration (http://www.campbellcollaboration.org/), the Cochrane Handbook for Systematic Reviews of Interventions [13], the University of York's Centre for Reviews and Dissemination's guidance for those carrying out or commissioning reviews [14], and also refer to reviews on serious game research [15, 16]. This protocol specified the research aim, search strategy, inclusion, exclusion criteria, data extraction, and methods of synthesis.

2.2. Data Source and Search Strategy. For the purpose of the study, a literature search was undertaken in December 2010 in the following international online bibliographic databases: (a) ACM portal, (b) IEEE Xplore, (c) Springer, (d) Science direct. The search string used was ("Game") AND ("Learning" OR "Teaching") AND ("Lecture" OR "Curriculum" OR "Lesson" OR "Course" OR "Exercise"). And "education" was not included in the keyword list since we considered that education was a quite general word and did not help minimize the searching scope. Searches were limited to titles and abstracts of articles published in journals and conference proceedings (some are book chapters), in English, from 2000 and onwards. The latter limitation was posed due to the rapid changes in ICT (Information and Communications Technology) in general, and in computer game development technologies in particular.

2.3. Data Extraction with Inclusion and Exclusion Criteria. Figure 1 shows the complete process of the data extraction. The first step was to identify relevant studies. A number of journal and proceedings articles about GDBL were located during searches in the afore-mentioned databases. The articles were examined and the search resulted in 1155 articles. In step 2, from abstracts of each article, we distinguished learning through game play or game development. And most of the excluded articles were using games directly in the classroom to motivate the students' interest and attendance rate and using game play instead of traditional exercises to study or review the course content. For instance, these were

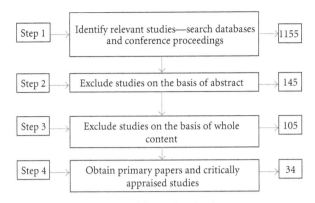

Step 1	→	Identify relevant studies—search databases and conference proceedings	→	1155
Step 2	→	Exclude studies on the basis of abstract	→	145
Step 3	→	Exclude studies on the basis of whole content	→	105
Step 4	→	Obtain primary papers and critically appraised studies	→	34

FIGURE 1: Steps of the study selection process.

articles generally addressing using virtual online multiplayer game environments to provide a collaborative learning style, for example, [17, 18], articles which referred to games used in the classroom to motivate attendance and to review the course knowledge, for example, [8]. In addition, the articles related to the economics terms "game theory" and "business game" used as business terms were also excluded from this category. Besides, we excluded articles that depicted novel game concepts that were not computer or video games but physical game activities without any technology support for the lecture. For instance, the article in [19] used a self-made table card game in SE education. Mainly based on these three criteria, a total of 1010 articles were excluded after this step.

In step 3, the whole content of the articles was checked. The inclusion criteria were further limited to the scope: a case study or several case studies in the article to describe GDBL. In particular, it required (a) a relatively detailed description of the lecture design process. The articles without a detailed description of their teaching design or exercise process made it impossible to validate their process of how to integrate GDFs in lectures or exercises. According to this requirement, posters, tutorial presentations, and some short papers without detailed description on teaching process were excluded since they could not provide valuable data for our research aim and made it impossible to validate the effectiveness of the method, for example, [20–25]. This was also a measure to ensure the inclusion of the high quality literature in the review. (b) Articles using development toolkits in the curriculums but did not aim to develop games were also excluded, for example, [26]. (c) Articles emphasizing on other aspects apart from GDBL were excluded as it was difficult to validate how game development was integrated in class, for example, learning in an interactive e-lab [27]. Similarly, articles that presented the development of an educational game framework but did not mention how it was integrated in a specific curriculum were excluded, for example, [28–31]. (d) Articles, which focused on changing the controller of the software or hardware, but without elements of computer game development, were also excluded, for example, [32, 33]. Most of them focus on creating a robot controller to learn algorithms or changing some component of a robot to learn artificial intelligence (AI). In contrast, we included learning from modifying parts

of a simulator to create the game elements or a game-like system, for example, [34, 35]. Finally, a total of 105 articles were remaining after this step.

In step 4, we carefully looked through the remaining articles and compared their topics, methods, teaching process, and evaluation quality from the presentation of their concepts. After the comparison, the following studies criteria were included: (1) articles that had collected data from assignments or scores after using the GDBL method; (2) articles that had questionnaires with quantitative data and interviews or feedback with qualitative data; and (3) detailed discussion of the collected data and conclusion. In addition, diverse and innovative articles were not neglected, in order to show the various ways to integrate GDFs in education. However, articles reporting on the use of hardware tools to create game or game-like system, such as real robot hand [34], Wii remote [36], Microsoft surface [37], and a projector-camera system [38] to support teaching or learning environment were not included. Finally, a total of 34 articles were included in the review. And we believe these articles were sufficient to get a complete guideline to explain how to integrate the GDBL method in the curriculums.

2.4. Synthesis of Findings. A typology to categorize the 34 articles has to be devised. The classification scheme proposed by [39] in their review of the general instructional gaming literature was adopted for the needs of the present study. This scheme, which was also used in [40], defines the following five categories [39]: (a) research (systematic approaches in the study of gaming targeted at explaining, predicting or controlling particular phenomena or variables), (b) theory (articles explaining the basic concepts or aspects or derived outcomes of gaming), (c) reviews (syntheses of articles concerning general or specific aspects of gaming), (d) discussion (articles stating or describing experiences or opinions with no empirical or systematically presented evidence), and (e) development (articles discussing the design or development of games or projects involving gaming).

Specifically, for the categorization of the articles, the following criteria were applied in this study. Articles comprising empirical research related to GDBL were assigned to the "Research" category. Articles comprising theoretical analyses of concepts, aspects, or outcomes of GDBL were placed in the "Theory" category. Articles presenting syntheses of articles concerning GDBL conducted according to explicit methodology were placed in the "Review" category. Articles reporting on opinions and experiences regarding GDFs used in teaching, with no empirical or systematically presented evidence, were assigned to the "Discussion" category. Finally, articles mainly reporting on the design or development of GDFs used in the GDBL method were assigned to the "Development" category. The articles were grouped into these five categories according to their primary focus. Of the 34 articles found after step 4, 20 were placed in the "Research" category, 1 in the "Theory" category, 7 in the "Discussion" category, and 6 in the "Development" category, whereas no articles fit the "Review" category, which highlights the usefulness and originality of the present study.

Like results from other literature reviews on instructional games [40, 41], in this study there were fewer articles in the "Theory" categories than in the "Research," "Discussion," and "Development" categories. This can be explained by the fact that instructional games, including GDBL are a relatively new domain of educational technology.

3. Results

This section presents an overview of the studies of the GDBL method based on the results after step 3 and step 4 in Figure 1.

3.1. Overview of the Study after Step 3. In order to have a complete overview of GDBL, we chose the results from step 3 mainly due to the following: (a) they covered a more complete variation of types of GDFs and contained more information than the 34 articles from step 4. (b) They provided more cases in the diversity of GDFs methods used in teaching, which also presents the potential advantages of using GDF in education. (c) They showed the development tendency of GDF related to other factors (e.g., times and technology). We had a study of 105 articles from step 3 representing the use of GDBL method spanning over 11 years. Figure 2 presents the distribution of these articles related to the publishing year after step 3. The result after step 4 is also presented for reference.

The types of GDF are classified as (a) Game engines: it mainly covers the commercial game engines and mature and well-known toolkits mainly to create games. (b) Self-made GDF: it mainly includes the game development frameworks that were made by the authors of the articles for usage in a specific course. (c) Games or game editors: it mainly contains editors or platforms that can be used to modify games. (d) Simulation platform: it mainly includes controllers to create a game-like system for robots or other simulation platforms. (e) Hardware platform: it mainly includes both game hardware and related software to build games (laptops and computers are excluded), like Wii remotes, windows surface with XNA, robotic hand. (f) Others are general IDEs, like Visual C++, J2ME, or unspecified game creation toolkits with no specific requirement for learning. For some articles that covers more than one attribute like self-made GDF and simulation platform, we choose priority adhering the following sequence: game engine, self-made GDF, game editor, simulation platform, hardware, and others. Figure 3 shows distribution of types of GDFs applied in GDBL articles in percentage. Further, the top five in game engine subcategory are XNA (9 articles), First Person Shooter (FPS) game engines (unreal: 2 articles, Torque: 2 articles, half-life: 1 article), Flash (4 articles), Alice (4 articles), and Scratch (3 articles).

From statistics shown in Figures 2 and 3, we discovered the following clues.

(1) Tendency of Popularity. Figures 2(a) and 2(b) present the tendency of increasing the number of publications of GDBL articles from 2000, especially from 2006. Between 2006 and 2009, the number of GDBL publications grew with 3–7 articles per year, up to max of 25 articles in Figure 2(a). Figure 3 shows the distribution of the types of GDFs. From the statistics, game engines are most frequently used in GDBL method. We can infer that the continuous development and improvement of game engines will drive the GDBL's development further in the near future.

(2) Technology Changes the Ways of Learning. After 2006, there was a rapid increase in the number of GDBL articles published. We have analyzed possible reasons concerning this phenomenon from three perspectives: (a) frequent release of new commercial GDFs free of charge, like XNA (2007), Android SDK (2008), and evolution of software development environments, like Flash (acquired by Adobe in 2007) made game development easier than before. Technology changes or enriches the ways of learning and teaching. (b) Cross-disciplinary curriculum started to be used after 2006, for example, [42, 43]. It provides the possibility to use game development in these topics. (c) The upgrowing generation of students is a part of a game accepting culture where the public has an open mind towards games. This culture does not only focus on negative effects of video games such as violence and sex but embraces the positive aspects of games such as social integration, various improved skills, and usage of games for educational purposes, such as Sim-city and Civilization. Furthermore, students that grew up with games have become teachers in schools and may use games in their teaching. They show how technology changes the learning style. Whether it has positive and negative impact on learning depends on how we adopt the technology (game) and how it is used in teaching and learning.

3.2. Overview of the Study after Step 4. In terms of the classification method used in e-learning literature [44], a subcategory was iteratively developed based on the thematic topics found in the articles. Each subcategory was labeled with the disciplinary area-programming, SE, art, and other topic areas. As already mentioned in the introduction, the intended target audiences of the present study are educators, practitioners, researchers, and game designers who use GDFs in learning. The thematic subcategories should help the readers review teaching design, benefits, empirical findings, and future research topics in their own topic of interest. A similar thematic subcategorization of research articles was also performed in review of the general instructional games literature [41]. The overview of 34 articles after step 4 is shown in Table 1 grouped in four categories and labeled with course topics.

These articles present various GDFs used in GDBL and the covered course topics are summarized in Figure 4. The article T28 in Table 1 presents a study for using mobile game development as a motivational tool and a learning context in the computing curriculums. From their survey, the game development process can be used in the study of AI, database, computer networks, SE, human-computer interaction, computer graphics, algorithms, programming, computer architectures, and operating systems.

TABLE 1: Overview of articles.

Category	Item	Article	Major topics	Course topic
Research	R1	[55]	Students develop games on Torque game engine to learn game development	Game development
	R2	[56]	Undergraduate and graduate build games by adding code in Spacewar simulator to learn artificial intelligence	AI
	R3	[57]	Undergraduates develop games on XNACS1Lib framework to learn programming	Programming
	R4	[58]	Students develop games on Scratch to learn basic programming	Programming
	R5	[59]	Students develop games on Game Maker platform to learn software engineering	SE
	R6	[60]	Students develop games using Greenfoot to learn programming	Programming
	R7	[61]	Students build games by adding code in Wu's Castle to learn programming	Programming
	R8	[42]	Students build 3D movies on First Person Shooting game engine, Maya, and Photoshop to learn digital character production and machinima	Art
	R9	[10]	Students develop or modify Warcraft3 game editor, unreal game engine, and so forth, to learn software development, programming, project management, artistic concepts, and so forth	Mixed topics
	R10	[43]	Undergraduates develop games to learn outsourcing and software engineering	SE
	R11	[62]	Students develop games on self-made toolsets to learn programming	Programming
	R12	[63]	Students develop games on GameMaker to learn programming	Programming
	R13	[64]	Undergraduates develop Critical Mass board game on the web-based platform to learn data structure	Data structure
	R14	[65]	Undergraduates develop games to learn programming	Programming
	R15	[5]	Undergraduates develop minigames on XNA to learn programming	Programming
	R16	[66]	Graduates develop games on XNA to learn software architecture	SE
	R17	[67]	Students build games on Scratch to learn the Boolean logic	Boolean logic
	R18	[68]	Pupils build games by adding quiz to a web-based game shell platform to learn literacy	Literacy
	R19	[69]	Students build games by adding a code to a board game RoboRally, to learn artificial intelligence	AI
	R20	[70]	Middle school students build games on Storytelling Alice to learn information technology	Mixed topics
Discussion	D21	[4]	Graduate Students develop games on XNA to learn software architecture	SE
	D22	[71]	Middle school students build games on adding code in StarLogo TNG to learn 3D programming	3D programming
	D23	[72]	Art design students develop games on Flash to learn programming	Programming
	D24	[73]	Electronics design field students build a game-like system to learn programming, distributed system, and so forth	Mixed topics
	D25	[74]	Undergraduate students develop games to learn programming	Programming
	D26	[75]	Pupils develop games on NeverWinter Night toolsets to learn basic ICT curriculum	Mixed topics
	D27	[76]	Students build games by adding code to Bomberman game to learn programming	Programming
Theory	T28	[77]	Survey of mobile game development for different learning purposes	Mixed topics
Development	Dev29	[78]	Develop MUPPETS that students could use for game development to learn programming	Programming
	Dev30	[79]	Develop XQUEST based on XNA that graduate could use for game development to learning software architecture	SE
	Dev31	[80]	Develop Sheep based on Android that graduate could use for game development to learn software architecture	SE
	Dev32	[81]	Design and develop SIMPLE framework that students could use for game development to learn programming	Programming
	Dev33	[82]	Develop BiMIP framework that undergraduate could use for game development to learn programming	Programming
	Dev34	[83]	Develop JGOMAS framework that undergraduate could use for game development to learn artificial intelligence	AI

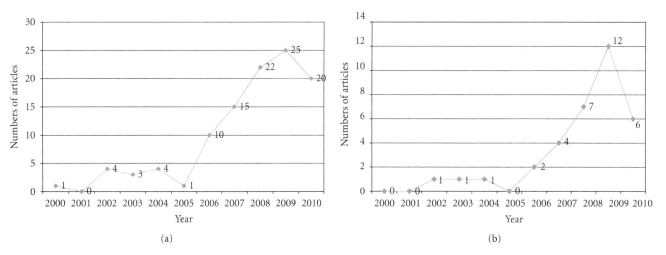

FIGURE 2: (a) Study of each year on using GDBL method (step 3) and (b) study of each year on using GDBL method (step 4).

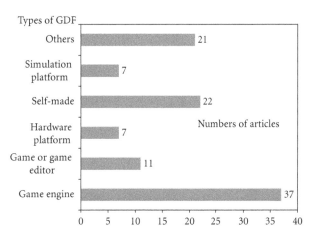

FIGURE 3: Study about types of GDF.

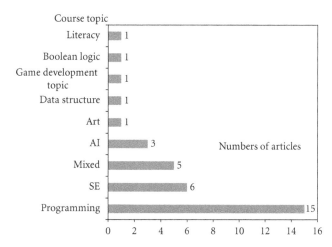

FIGURE 4: Distribution of the course topic.

Both the data from Figure 4 and article T28 can validate that the GDBL method can be used to teach various topics. Most applications are in the field of computer science, electronic, and basic IT learning. However, there are some innovative examples of other applications as well. Article R18 presents how a web-based game-shell platform is used to create a quiz game to teach pupils literacy with no programming requirement. Article R8 presents how Maya and Photoshop are used to create the digital character and movies that could be used as a video inside of a game.

From Table 1, it also shows that GDBL not only can be used in higher education, but also for basic IT education for kids in middle schools. The article D26 presents how pupils are taught basic ICT (Information and Communications Technology) curriculum by creating games. And the articles R20 and D22 describe how middle school students are taught IT and basic 3D programming by building games. The common GDFs used in the primary and middle schools are some GDFs that do not require much programming experiences for pupils, for example, the game editor. This will be further discussed in Section 4.

4. Findings

The articles collected after step 4 are further discussed in this section to serve the purpose of helping to identify and extract the significant elements to meet our aims, like elements to be used to guide the teaching design process when using GDFs in education. Findings are further presented as three aspects: (1) pedagogical context and teaching process, (2) technical aspects, and (3) evaluation results in relation to the aims of this study.

4.1. Pedagogical Context and Teaching Process. This section focuses on the current design process of integrating GDFs in courses or exercises to make the traditional teaching style become more engaging and diversified. This section also provides the detailed steps of how pedagogical theory can be used to guide the teaching design as well as strategies to aid the teaching.

The articles collected in this section are mainly from "Discussion" part in Table 1, and the rest is from the

"Research" and "Development" categories. The "Discussion" articles usually have a more complete description than the articles of other categories and include students background, GDF analysis, course setting and background, and teaching design with strategies. We are also concerned with the diversity and flexibility of using GDBL. The diversity shows not only that standard game engines or game frameworks are used in teaching, for example, XNA, but also that GDFs that are adapted or extended for teaching, for example, in article Dev31 they developed an extended library for the Android platform as a GDF for a specific course. Flexibility shows that (a) the same GDF can be used in different situations, for example, article D22 use XNA to teach software architecture and article R15 use XNA to teach programming, (b) the teaching process can be flexible to include other strategies than just integrating GDFs in the learning. For instance, article R13 adds the competition in game development for the assignments.

4.1.1. Pedagogical Context. Integrating game developments in a course study can provide increased motivation and attractiveness for the students. What is behind this motivation and can any theoretical context explain why GDBL can support learning? We investigated this question in the literature review, mainly focusing on (a) why apply the GDBL method in education and (b) how to apply it in a course in the first place. We found it was common to present the teaching design using a GDF in articles from the perspective of a teacher's experiences from the course, not thinking this process from a learning theory perspective.

Apart from the fact that games motivate for learning, we do not have strong evidence from the pedagogical theory to explain why it is a good idea to apply game development in education yet. However, there exists literature that explains game development, opposed to game play, as a pedagogical activity in the classroom. El-Nasr and Smith mentioned that Seymour Papert presented a relevant conclusion that programming is one example of the constructionism learning theory [10]. Constructionism involves two activities [45]. The *first* is the mental construction of knowledge that occurs with world experiences, a view borrowed from Jean Piaget's constructivist theories of learning and development. The *second* is a more controversial belief that new knowledge can be constructed with particular effectiveness when people engage in constructing products that are personally meaningful. The important issue is that the design and implementation of products are meaningful to those creating them and that learning becomes active and self-directed through the construction of artifacts. In the GDBL method, creating games with GDFs could be this artifact. This could be the fundamental concept to explain the pedagogical context of the GDBL. We can find support for this view from the articles in Table 1. For instance, article R9 considers the learning activity—modifying/creating a game using GDFs as a design activity that has educational benefits such as learning content, skills, and strategies [46]. Design activities are meaningful and engaging to students for exploring skills (analysis, synthesis, evaluation, revision,

planning, and monitoring) and concepts to understand how they can be applied in the real world. Further, GDBL can be considered as a variant of several available construction activities. Similarly, for "learning by design," the article D23 presents using Flash for students from aspect of "learning by doing"—Dewey's theory [47, 48]. The article D26 uses "learning by making" to learn basic ICT (Information and Communications Technology) knowledge by making games, and it describes that "game making" has the potential to be a powerful learning environment according to attributes identified by Smeets [49]. These contexts are the evidence to explain the GDBL method as a constructionism activity from a theoretical aspect.

Based on Seymour Papert's opinion, another question pops up: how to use the pedagogical theory to support the design? A positive response is the article Dev31. It presents a case study on the use of double stimulation [50] to guide the exercise design. It considers that using a GDF in education could be a knowledge construction process and describes how to use double stimulus to guide a teaching activity. In schools, learners face a challenge, a problem, or a task that has been designed for a particular pedagogical purpose or they face situations that are likely to appear in work and public life. In both cases, the purpose of exploiting tools is for the learners to respond to such challenges. Based on constructionism, it constructs the relationship between the educational tasks and the material artifacts. This relationship is at the heart of Vygotskij's notion of double stimulation [50], a method for studying cognitive processes and not just results. In a school setting, typically the first stimulus would be the problem or challenge to which learners are expected to respond to. The second stimulus would be the available mediating tools, like GDFs. Similarly, other pedagogical strategies are also found to support for the GDBL's teaching design. Problem-based learning (PBL) presented in the articles R6, R14, D25, and Dev33 are also considered as theoretical reference when using GDBL methods. PBL is a pedagogical model that emphasizes the role of a real-life problem and a collaborative discovery process in learning [51]. Within a typical PBL setting, students are first given a challenging but realistic problem of significant size, relevant to the learning objectives of a given course. They are then encouraged to solve the problem in a group throughout the semester as independently as possible with minimum help from the instructor of the course. Even further, article D25 classified the process into the inception phase of PBL by giving game development requirements; the elaboration phase of PBL by building a rapid game prototype; the construction phase of PBL by implementing a game in a project; and the transition phase of PBL by a results evaluation. Apart from the traditional lecture-oriented teaching approach, PBL puts more emphasis on the instructor's role as a facilitator to prepare meaningful and interesting problems and to create and organize course materials in a manner that students have a just right dose of information in each class to incrementally develop a final solution based on a GDF to the primary problem of the semester. In addition, the articles R12 and Dev29 proposed to use collaborative learning together with the game creation process, and article D24 proposed using "old model of Aristotle" [52] in the teaching design. All of them are of helpful support for the understanding of the teaching process.

The collections of the above results explain the validity of using a GDF in education from a pedagogical angle. Basically, it explains that applying the course content on GDFs by creating games fits well into a knowledge construction process, and it can be integrated with the pedagogical theory supports, like double stimulus or PBL to achieve an improved learning process and outcome. For instance, when we choose double stimulus as a pedagogical theory support, the learning design can be decomposed into two main elements: one is a problem, task, or goal that is designed by the teacher and the other is a responding learning activity that is implemented by students. From the double stimulus perspective, the first stimulus is tasks or assignments and second stimulus can be chosen as a corresponding tool based on the first stimulus. Its outcome depends on teachers' capacity to keep the two elements match each other. A good task (first stimulus) with inappropriate GDF (second stimulus) will not optimize the output. With this double stimulus support in mind, teachers should find an appropriate match between tasks and GDFs instead of just focusing on one aspect more than the other, like over focus on the design of task but neglect the effort of selecting the GDF. This is not a correct way for applying double stimulus. Further, if the selected GDF always conflicts with the tasks, we should reconsider changing the tasks or GDFs, or even apply a nongame tool. It implies that double stimulus can support learning activity for both GDBL and non-GDBL methods. The teachers should realize it and analyze which tool is better for the course aim and for the students when they apply double stimulus in teaching.

The number of case studies shows that only 30% of 34 articles include both pedagogical and technological design when applying GDBL. This phenomenon reminds us to improve the teaching process with relevant theoretical support. We believe our analysis points to the necessity for further pedagogical and technological codesign to better facilitate awareness of GDBL, thus better conduct the teaching process.

4.1.2. Teaching Process. How to integrate GDFs in teaching and exercises is a very important process when applying GDBL. This section analyzes the teaching process and exercise designs on various GDFs to achieve learning by implementing/modifying a game using GDFs. From our survey, we found necessary and common steps for the integration of GDFs in a course from the selected articles.

The *first step* is to identify explicit course aims. Figures 3 and 4 show relationships between GDBL and other fields and provides the case studies of how to integrate GDBL into different courses. After the course aim is clear, a common way to integrate GDBL in the course is that the teacher can design an assignment asking to develop a game. The students should then find a solution to this assignment that is in alignment with the course content. When facing such situation, the

teacher should find an entry point in how to integrate GDBL with the course and exercises. If this is not possible, we recommend reading articles about similar courses from the selected examples in Table 1 and getting some inspiration. The *second step* is the exercise design and selection of GDFs. When applying a GDF in a certain course, the selection usually depends on the course content and exercise types, and so forth. We have recognized three types of exercises: one type is to modify the game or adding component to game platform or simulation platform to achieve a complete game, like in the articles D26 or Dev29. The second type is to create a simple game as an exercise to study or practice one or two concepts from the course content, like in the article R9. The third type is to do a complete game development project applying all concepts from the course. Usually, the first and second types can be used in the beginning of a course as a transition period when students are not familiar with the GDF environment, while the third type exercise can be used as a final exercise. However, there are other special cases, like in article R2 where only one type exercise was selected and applied in the whole process. The main driver of exercise design depends on the course aim and students' background. Selection of GDFs is separately discussed in Section 4.2. The *third step* is to do a tutorial lecture where the GDF is introduced to the students. The *fourth step* is to run an initial exercise, which should be easy to do and let the students get familiar with the development environment. The *fifth* and *final step* is to do exercises that include implementation of a game. Usually, it is accompanied with some suggestions that were applied in most of the literature: (a) collaborative learning: the student groups range from 2 to 6 students in our statistics; further article R12 has some discussions about how to locate student members in groups such as regular meetings with instructors and flexible meetings among group members. It is important to keep instant communication with the exercise requirements, which would be positive to the students' learning towards the GDBL method. For each group member, it would be a tradeoff between cooperative and individual work during the work duty allocation. Further, a workshop is suggested to be held at the end of the course. (b) Support: technical support to help students overcome the technical difficulties they face. It is helpful to give examples in the beginning such as to provide optional examples codes and exercise examples to explain the exercise's complexity. Also there are other strategies like conducting a pilot study before the formal application of GDBL. This approach only appeared in two articles. After the whole teaching process is completed, usually a survey to evaluate both the teaching process and the used strategies is conducted and a more detailed analysis is performed considering the impact factors described in Section 4.3 based on the evaluation from the literature.

4.2. Technical Solution. The technical aspect of the GDBL method is mainly about GDFs' features described in the 34 articles. And this section will not go into technical details of development of GDFs due to that it is out of the scope of this paper. On contrary, we mainly analyze the GFDs features in the context of GDBL based on our aim of this study.

4.2.1. GDFs Survey. In order to provide a guide to choose a GDF for GDBL, we classify GDFs into two categories: GDFs for novices and GDFs for developers. The main focus of GDFs for novices, including nonprogrammers, is to provide visual methods for customizing game templates and to allow creating or designing games with little or no programming skills. The main focus of GDFs for developers is to offer toolkits that support development of high quality 2D/3D rendering, special effects, physics, animations, sound playback, and network communication in common programming languages, such as C++, C#, and Java. The 34 articles are classified into Tables 2 and 3 according to the GDFs used in the study. The unspecified GDFs or general SDK have been excluded, for example, the articles R10, R11, R14, D24, D25, and T28.

In addition, one mature GDF selected from step 3 in Figure 1 could be a backup for novices—CeeBot Series (http://www.ceebot.com/ceebot/family-e.php) [35]. The programming language in CeeBot is very similar to Java, C++, and C#. It has been developed especially to make learning programming easier. "CeeBots4 School" is a programming course for middle and high school.

4.2.2. Criteria for Selection of Suitable GDFs. Choosing a GDF is considered to be an important procedure during the preparation work for teaching. This process can be described by the following steps: (a) finding various GDF candidates, (b) analyze each GDF's features, (c) make criteria to filter GDF candidates, and choose one or more GDFs that fit best with the course content. Although our literature survey shows that different course aims have different requirements for the selection of the GDFs, there are still some common points to share. The article D21 presents a general criteria to choose a suitable GDF for the education in terms of theory— "What makes learning to be fun" by Thomas [53]: for example, easy to learn, allow rapid development, and provide an open development environment to attract students' curiosity. R1 presents that the GDFs should be chosen based on its cost and license, quality, difficulty, textbooks for guidance, and its main functionality. The article D26 explains that their students were not to become experts in programming, and thus they chose GDFs for novices. The article D27 introduces their self-made GDF and assess their own GDF by comparing it with other GDFs in terms of interactive, amusement, easy to use, using official program language, combine with teaching materials, evolutionary learning mode, census analysis, and storylines. The article Dev31 chose the GDF based on analysis of development environment, tutorial documents, emulator, programming language requirements, test devices, interface of the GDF, and possible ways to share games. Further both articles R3 and Dev31 developed a library for the GDF to make it more suitable for the course context. If we face the condition of only one choice, article D22 presents their effort to improve the only GDF. The article D23 presents how they compared different versions of same GDF and made a choice between the newest version with powerful functions or old version but more stable.

To summarize, there are common and essential guidelines when selecting the GDFs: (a) *technical environment and inexpensive (low costs) to use and acquire*: the technical environment requirements include required operating system and hardware, what tools are provided, are third-party tools supported, and how difficult it is to install GDF. A typical problem can be, for example, that XNA runs only on Windows and many students now have PCs running Linux or Mac OS X. The technical requirements might also be an economical issue, as the choice of GDF might force hardware upgrades or paying for licenses. (b) *Sufficient documentation to guide the usage of the GDF*. Students need to explore the GDF as an extra task before they start game development on the GDF. If the resources and materials are sufficient and easy to acquire for beginners, it will help them shorten the time spent on learning the technical environment. Time is an important factor during the whole teaching process, which will be further discussed in Section 4.3. (c) *Meets the students programming technique contexts*. The GDF must be easy to learn and allow rapid development. This issue is also driven by time constraints. Usually, if learning the GDF is not the major educational goal in the course and only an aid to learn something else, learning a new GDF will steal time from the course schedule. An easy and friendly environment is welcomed in order to save time for the students and to keep the focus on the course content and less on the GDF. (d) *Not in conflict with the educational goals of the course, flexibility to combine a GDF with teaching materials, and possible to add/change libraries that can be used within the GDF*. All GDFs have constraints related to the course content in how they have been designed or how they are released. One example is in SE education where open source GDFs make it possible to do white-box testing on the GDF, while the source code for other GDFs might not be available. Further, some GDFs might have constraints on how you can design your games, what design and architectural patterns you can use, how event-handling must be managed, the freedom of expanding the GDFs functionality, and more. These constraints must be integrated in the SE teaching to introduce the students to the real world where software rarely is built from scratch. In addition, if GDFs are not easy to use, and not strongly relevant to the course content, we can add/change a library with a user guide to apply course content in the GDF. (e) *Using an official programming language*. Conditionally, it applies to the types of GDFs for developers using a commercial game engine with widely known programming languages, like C#, Java, and C++, which are familiar to the students. But for the types of GDF for novices, if the course just lets students know the data structure, an official language is not really needed. But special programming languages are not widely accepted and as useful as official programming languages in a long run if the students will do more software programming in the future. (f) *Amusement and interactive*. The GDF should provide a visual and stable development environment to attract the students' curiosity and engagement. A game development assignment in a user-friendly game development environment could be a good motivation for the students compared to traditional

TABLE 2: Study of GDFs for novices.

GDFs	Features description	Origin
Alice (http://alice.org/)	Alice provides a point-and-click programming interface allowing the creation of simple 3D games and animations. It is a tool for teaching object-oriented programming through creating simple games or animations	R20
Scratch (http://scratch.mit.edu/)	Scratch provides a point-and-click programming interface to create media-rich games, animations, and applications for the Web. Scratch is suitable for teaching children basic programming (variables, arrays, logic, and user interface), and for creating simple 2D quick-and-dirty applications	R4, R17
Greenfoot (http://www.greenfoot.org/)	Greenfoot is a solid tool that provides many of the needed constructs for creating 2D computer games at a level that is especially appropriate and fun for novice programmers	R6
Maya/Photoshop/Flash	They are mainly used for art design to create digital characters and animations for games. Flash could also create Flash games	R8, D23
Game maker (http://www.yoyogames.com/)	Game Maker is a rapid-application development tool for young people at home and in schools to create two-dimensional and isometric games	R5, R12
StarLogo TNG	StarLogo TNG is designed upon the basic framework of Logo. The programming is done with programming blocks instead of text commands and moved programming from abstract to visual	D22
Game editor: Warcraft3 Editors/NeverWinter Night toolsets	The editor provides a simple GUI for customizing game templates and requires little or no programming skills to create interesting game designs. The editors are implemented as visual programming tools that allow users to visually customize game behavior, including character behavior, game map, and game play	R9, D26
Game platforms: Bomberman/Wu's Castle/Critical Mass board game/quiz-based web game shell	These are concrete games, but provide visual interface for the users to modify or add a basic code to change the game scenarios	R7, R13, R18, D27

TABLE 3: Study of GDFs for developers.

GDFs	Features description	Origin
FPS game engine: Torque game engine/Unreal Engine	These are original commercial game engines and already have applied in commercial and popular games. They are usually not free and provide with some edit tools. And more complex than a concrete game editor	R1, R8, R9,
XNA (http://www.xna.com/)/ XNACS1Lib framework/XQUEST/BiMIP	These are game development tools based on MFC and DirectX from windows platform and have the same structure on game loop concept. BiMIP is a self-Made similar to XNA. And XNA is a GDF to develop cross-platform games for the Windows PC, Windows mobile phone, XBOX, and the Zune platform using the C#. XNA features a set of high-level APIs targeted for 2D and 3D games. It consists of an integrated development environment (IDE) along with several tools for managing audio and graphics. XQUEST and XNACS1Lib are game library for XNA that contains convenient game components	R3, R15, R16, D21, Dev30, Dev33
Android/Sheep (http://www.android.com/)	The Android mobile platform is a mobile application development platform issued by Google. And Sheep framework is an extended game library for Android	Dev31
Simulation platforms: Spacewar simulator/RoboRally/JGOMAS MUPPETS/SIMPLE framework	There are self-made simulation game or simulator that provides the controller for the users to modify the parameters and control the avatar in these simulation platforms; they are usually to teach the programming and AI field	R2, R19, Dev29, Dev32, Dev34

assignments. For example, most students think it is more interesting to work on a game project than, for example, a system for a bank. (g) *Ability to develop games in a cross-platform environment.* Conditionally, it applies to the types of GDFs for developers. One good example is XNA where the students can choose developing their games either in PC, mobile (Windows Phone 7), and/or console (Xbox360). Other game engines such as Unity3D also allow developing the game in multiplatform. The advantages are the following. (1) Provide students degrees of freedom in developing their

games for the platform of their choice and (2) learn about the strengths and constraints of different platforms (e.g., user interface, viewing screen size, resolutions, resources such as memory and processor power, storage for saving/loading the game, and, etc.) in game development.

We consider the above to be the most important criteria to guide the teachers in selecting one or more GDFs for their courses. And some criteria could be changed according to the specific context of the teaching environments. For instance, the target students are middle school pupils and the course goal is to let students familiarize themselves with information technology, it is not necessary to choose (e). In principle, the course aims and students context are the two fundamental and prioritized attributes to decide the selection of GDFs.

4.3. Evaluation. Besides the pedagogical analysis and the GDFs' analysis in GDBL, this section summarizes the evaluation data from the articles mainly in the "Research" category. Furthermore, we hope to find empirical evidence to support the effectiveness of GDBL. Specifically, in order to approach the third aim of the study, the following information was drawn from each article (if provided in the article): (a) major empirical findings related to the actual effectiveness of GDFs used as an aid in teaching and (b) factors that impact the teaching outcome in terms of the experiment data from the articles are also posed. It is not a simple process to assess the effectiveness of GDBL and it covers at least two aspects: teachers' and students' satisfaction of using this method. The teachers' concerns are the researcher's understands of the course (not applied where the researchers and the teachers are the same), the GDFs' features, matching between the selected GDFs and the course content, and teachers' expertise on games. The students' concerns involve having interesting exercises and the difficulty of learning extra content—the GDF. Our literature review focuses on these aspects and Table 4 shows a summary of the evaluation process of GDBL in each article. Comparing the students' and teachers' satisfaction, students' satisfaction could be the most important result since it directly relates to teaching effectiveness. And the following results are extracted from the literature and used to validate the effectiveness of GDBL and the impact factors related to it. The results in Table 4 are mainly shown in three categories: (a) experiment data that describes the collected data and materials for the measurement of the effectiveness of the results, (b) conclusion of effectiveness of GDBL, and (c) impact factor that describes the elements that effect outcomes and is classified into positive, neutral, and negative categories based on the articles' data and conclusions.

From evaluation data in Table 4, the common expressions of measurements are (a) students' grade or score on the course exam, (b) project results, including analysis of project size and classes they used in game programming; obtaining certain requirements of exercises by percentage; length of codes; percentage completed of the projects and time spent on the projects or the GDF, and so forth, (c) questionnaire surveys to measure the following aspects: students' satisfaction about the exercise, course and GDF; students background; students' interest in game development topic; course, and exercise learned and open questions to get suggestions for the improvement of a course, and so forth, and (d) observation and feedback to perceive the fluency of the teaching process and interaction between students and the teacher.

From Table 4, the effectiveness of each article is collected. Generally, 22 of 23 articles have a positive conclusion about using game development in a course in most of aspects, for example, student motivation, engagement in lectures, and

exercises. Only the article R5 presents that learning by game design did not have the expected outcome and that the time constraint was a critical issue. Students indicated that they needed more time than two weeks to write a satisfactory 2D game. And finally, it explained that they did not have an adequate number of participants to have an accurate picture about the effects of game design on students' motivation and attitudes.

Apart from validating the effectiveness of using GDBL methods, the impact factors that could cause a positive or negative outcome deserve to be analyzed. From Table 4, we have summarized what should be noticed when applying GDBL. The following items are the most common issues that appeared repeatedly in our survey.

(1) Communication between the Researcher and Teacher towards the Understanding of the Course Content. This item is not applied to the condition where the teacher and the researcher is the same person. If the researcher designs the method and the researcher invites the teachers to adopt it in schools, good communication and mutual trust between them are crucial to achieving the desired effect. The article R15 states that the teachers should become comfortable with using GDBL and spend a bit more time on it compared to traditional method in a certain course, otherwise it may cause a misunderstanding or bias against GDBL. Another aspect is that the researcher may worry about the teacher and not totally understands the game effectiveness in education, and how game motivation can be successfully used to improve the course design, which is mentioned in the articles R3, R6, R15, and R18. This indicates that the researchers should help teachers in gaining self-confidence and provide constant support while the decision is made to apply GDBL in the curriculum.

(2) Teamwork. This factor could have both positive and negative effects on the teaching results if students work in groups. First, the team size and working environment must be considered in advance. For instance, it was found in article R10 that a big team size could have positive impact on outsourcing course teaching, and article R1 claims that lab environment with teamwork could help improving the effectiveness of cooperative learning. On contrary, as the team gets larger, it becomes more difficult to set the time for general meetings and joint work hours. Further, it also means complex relations in a large group. A serious issue— bottleneck—could happen in the game development process. If one member of the team does not perform, then the entire game development process slows down. Second, the instant communication in a team has a significant impact. Article R2 mentions that the group work can help weaker students. Article R12 also agrees with this statement, but it describes that unexpected situations can occur during the teamwork to hinder the instant communication which the teacher should take care of. Third, the R14 article concludes that students need more experience in working effectively in teams. Most of the case studies found in the articles provide the evidence that teamwork can be used together with GDBL and the

TABLE 4: Evaluation data collection and impact factor.

Title	Sample	Comparison	Experiment data	Conclusion of effectiveness	Outcome of impact factor
R1	22 students	No	Quantitative data (1) Questionnaire of students background (2) Survey project results of students' game play preferences (3) Questionnaire on students satisfactory (4) Questionnaire on interest level in game development careers (5) Questionnaire on students assessment of gains (6) Questionnaire on helpful course elements (7) Students peer-evaluation	Students generally satisfied the elements in the course and resources (including teamwork)	Positive (1) Lab environment and teamwork helped to archive the effectiveness of cooperative learning (2) Teaching game development required a shift from teacher-centered to student-centered learning environment (3) GDFs provided an environment that students could integrate wide variety of skills and knowledge (4) Motivation factor: competition Negative (5) Poor textbook for GDF provided negative effect
R2	33 students (28 undergraduates and 5 graduate)	No	Quantitative data (1) General questionnaire Qualitative data (2) Students feedback about the course	Generally, students enjoyed the project and it fulfilled all of the criteria of a successful project outlined at the beginning plan	Positive (1) Flexible and interactive simulation platform (2) Providing examples for the difficulty part in the project that was out of the course aim (3) Group project and discussion helped weaker students Neutral (4) Difficulties at first year, but smoothed out by get more teaching experiences and previous evaluation for the improvement
R3	21 undergraduates	No	Quantitative data (1) General questionnaire Qualitative data (2) Video recording about course process (3) Faculty feedback	The GDF was an excellent catalyst, enabling faculty to begin exploring teaching with game topics and help students to be more engaged	Positive (1) Because of the immediate interactive graphical feedback, students were engaged and motivated to experiment with the programs Neutral (2) Instructor's attitude toward the interest in GDF Negative (3) Visual feedback, although a powerful learning tool, could also be a source of distraction for students (4) Time spending should not involve the reading of background material in class (better before class) (5) Limited classroom time was challenging for students
R4	35 female students from both preschool and university	No	Quantitative data (1) Questionnaire: students' opinions about GDF (2) Questionnaire: effect of students familiarization with Scratch in using of ICT education (3) Questionnaire (pre- and post-test) attitudes against Internet in education and application development	Scratch was user friendly and satisfied by the students, and it also has a rather positive effect on students' opinions and attitudes towards computer programming and ICT educational value in education	Positive Scratch helped to setup confidence of students in exploration of ICT in education.

TABLE 4: Continued.

Title	Sample	Comparison	Experiment data	Conclusion of effectiveness	Outcome of impact factor
R5	20 undergraduates	No	Quantitative data Questionnaire: Likert's scale (pre- and post-survey in game design course)	Game design had both positive and negative impact on students' attitudes about computer science, game design, and further development of programming skills	Positive (1) Students who had prior programming experience can express interest in game design Negative (2) Time constraints: assignment might be better received and increase students' interest if students were given more time and equal emphasis on other phases (3) Game design topic course had a negative impact on students' interest in pursuing a CS degree (4) Not adequate number of participants to have an accurate picture of true effects of game design on students' motivation and attitudes
R6	26 high school students and 8 teachers	Yes	Quantitative data (1) Questionnaire assignment survey (2) Questionnaire with pre- and post-survey: self-assessment on art and design (3) Questionnaire survey on teachers' attitude	It showed great promise for engaging high school students programming and increasing interest in computer related fields of study. Both teachers and students felt a significant improvement in computer programming and self-confidence	Positive (1) Researchers trained both students and teachers by applying GDBL Neutral (2) Teacher attitudes and self-confidence about GDBL's effect the teaching process
R7	26 students in experimental group. 29 in control group	Yes	Quantitative data (1) Each phase of study (2) Pre- and posttest score (3) Learning difference between groups and subgroups (4) Game statistics (5) Questionnaire survey of each task	Students in the game-first group felt they spent less time on assignments and all students preferred the learning game to the program	Positive "Wu castle" was more effective than a traditional programming assignment for learning and could help prepare students to create deeper, more robust understanding of computing concepts and improving their perceptions of homework
R8	—	No	Quantitative data (1) Questionnaire to survey students feedback (2) Compared with whole school average score	Students got higher score in this course than school's average score	Positive Assessing the GDF in the starting
R9	26 students	No	Quantitative data (1) Questionnaire to survey assignment difficulty with Likert's scale Qualitative data (2) Observation of students progress	Using game development motivated students to learn and allowing them to apply and visualize the utility and application of the concepts	Positive (1) GDBL could learn several subjects and concepts Neutral (2) Different game engines implicitly stressed the use and development of certain skills
R10	40 undergraduate students	No	Quantitative data (1) Pre- and posttest questionnaire to survey Changed perception of outsourcing concept (2) Questionnaire: SE outcomes Qualitative data (3) Observation: discoveries in communications	Students improved their understanding of outsourcing, developed better appreciation for the importance of SE techniques, and created ad hoc communication protocols between teams	Neutral Enlarging the teams' sizes to other universities to create an inclusive teaching environment, which had limitation that only applied in outsourcing teaching

TABLE 4: Continued.

Title	Sample	Comparison	Experiment data	Conclusion of effectiveness	Outcome of impact factor
R11	38 students (19 teams)	No	Quantitative data (1) Length of codes according to grade (2) Project size and classes (3) Methods used in programming (4) Weekly working hours (5) Proportion of work discussion, coding, thinking, graphics, and audio (6) Object-oriented skills applied in code	Positive experience had been gained in teaching the topic by using game framework	Neutral (1) To keep the students motivated and teachers tailored the course for each student (2) Using game development to achieve depth of objects and object interactions training
R12	124 students	No	Quantitative data (1) Grade (2) Questionnaire to survey students attitude	Learning by creating game was able to improve the student grades largely	Positive (1) Object-oriented programming concept became easier to understand after seeing object design visually in the GDF (2) Students felt happy with using cooperative learning system, games development, and visual design Negative (3) The group members' communication was hindered by the in front of computers (4) GDBL could help with the passing rate, but still have improving space for graduation aim
R13	55 students'	No	Quantitative data (1) User survey of game project percentage completed (2) Login times (3) Questionnaire with Likert's scale: student satisfaction (4) Questionnaire with Likert's scale: tournament features	Combination of game development and friendly student competition was a significant motivator for the increased student performance	Positive (1) Tournament could increase students' participation and motivation Negative (2) Students' common complaint of not having adequate time to complete the project
R14	—	No	Quantitative data (1) Individual and group creativity levels perceived by students (2) Students' perception of abilities developed at intermediate or high levels Qualitative data (3) Future career survey	Game project development with collaborative learning was manageable and effective for increasing students' teamwork capability and increase the employability confidence	Positive (1) Project (game project development) based learning motivated their team collaboration Negative (2) Teacher attitudes: initial resistance for problems that students' teams faced could be discouraging to faculty members who did not expect it (3) Teamwork: students were not born knowing how to work effectively in teams. A flawed team-based instructional model had negative effect
R15	CS1: 22 in GTA and 10 in Console CS2: 18 in GTA and 9 in Console	Yes	Quantitative data: (1) Success rate (Passing rate) (2) Assignment score (3) Self-reported time spent on assignment (4) Post Assignment Survey (5) Pre and Post course survey Qualitative data: (6) Feedback from faculty	Interactive graphical assignments could be a good tool for teaching CS1 students. The success of GDBL hinged on the instructor's expertise and enthusiasm	Positive (1) GDF feature: interactive graphical application supported experimentation and visualization Negative (2) Teacher's background and attitudes towards the games impacted the output of a lecture, faculty "dropped" GDBL in the end at first experiment, but became more comfortable later

TABLE 4: Continued.

Title	Sample	Comparison	Experiment data	Conclusion of effectiveness	Outcome of impact factor
R16	46 students	No	Quantitative data Questionnaire about learning process, tradeoff between technical and architecture problems, integration of game development and course, learning outcome	GDF was easy to use and did not conflict with course aim. A good GDF could save development time	Neutral GDF selection influenced learning process and extra technical issues, but students could learn a lot through a game project.
R17	27 in control group, 43 in experimental group	Yes	Quantitative data score of the pre- and posttest by a test sheet	Results showed that the proposed game development activity could have higher learning achievements compared to the traditional lecturing	Positive: (1) GDF issues: choosing modifying game according to course topic with simple scenario. And tutorials for GDF were prepared well. Understanding game topic could make engage learning Negative (2) Game was additive for students
R18	125 experimental students and 186 control group students	Yes	Quantitative data (1) GRADE test scores (pretest, posttest) Qualitative data (2) Interviews on teacher's feedback	Game development helped to improve the student content retention and so forth	Positive (1) Optimum amount of time to spend at a sitting on game development activities was about 45 min by observation Negative (2) Too little time allotted to the development of game and insufficient gaps between each game creation activities
R19	33 undergraduate	No	Quantitative data Questionnaire with Likert in general	Using GDBL indicated that the motivation of the students was higher and they understand complex problems easier and exercise could be done more rapidly	Positive GDF was searched and chose based on the requirements
R20	22 middle schoolers	No	Quantitative data (1) Questionnaire: pre- and post-surveys of participants information (2) Programs analysis Qualitative data (3) Daily log (4) Interviews on students	Findings suggested the middle school students could use Alice to make games to build information technology fluency	Neutral (1) To provide a proper challenge in class (2) Difficulty in using GDF to finish the assignment
T28	NA	No	Quantitative data (1) Survey of students background (2) Relevant application about Mobile GDBL	Mobile game development could be successfully integrated into computer science education	Positive Students' background: student lived in game environment and game development exercise could be a good motivation
Dev30	19 graduate	No	Quantitative data Questionnaire survey with Likert's scale and system usability scale survey	XQUEST enhanced XNA in suitability as a teaching aid in SE learning	Positive To design the XQUEST from the previous assessment experiences
Dev32	57 in group1, 45 in group2	Yes	Quantitative data (1) Questionnaire result of students' user experience (2) Score for pre/posttest	SIMPLE improved both learning motivation and programming skills for the students	Positive Use GQM approach in developing game metrics for students' exercise.

nature of teamwork is suitable for cooperative learning and teacher should take care of the issues that may happen during teamwork. However, most of articles did not mention the strategy of competitive learning in GDBL. Only the articles R1 and R13 apply both cooperative and competitive learning in the exercises with a positive feedback in both cases.

(3) GDF Relevance. The most mentioned aspects related to GDFs that impact the outcome are (a) the articles R2, R3, R12, and R15 present the advantages of using interactive graphical GDFs. It shows that visual graphics can provide instant feedback, making student engaged in programs, (b) the articles R3 and R4 describe how a GDF can improve students' confidence in programming tasks, and (c) the articles R1, R8, R9 R17, and R19 emphasize the need to analyze the GDF's features in the light the course content, and detailed GDF tutorials should be conducted before it is used in the later exercises.

(4) Students' Background. In the article T28 surveys, the students' background was that most of them had played games as they were growing up. This is a suitable prerequisite to apply GDBL. But a negative aspect is the addictiveness to games, as mentioned in the articles R16 and R17. Some students may focus too much on the game and game development thus losing focus on what they shall learn in the course. This means that the design of the course and the project must be carried out in such a way that the students are forced to learn and use course content. From the articles R5 and R11, it was also noticed that the diversity of student background causes some difficulty of using GDBL. For instance, the programming experience of the students strongly affects the choice of GDF between the ones for novices and the ones for developers. For instance, to use XNA/XQUEST or Android/Sheep from Table 3 for developers, the students must know object-oriented (OO) programming well and be familiar with OO design patterns and OO principles. And some other GDFs require learning a specialized and simplified programming language for game creation, which is more suitable for students without programming experiences.

(5) Teachers' Requirements. Teachers' attitude of applying the GDBL method in the course is an essential aspect in a teaching process. The articles R3, R6, and R15 suggest that the faculty should have relevant technical background about the applied GDFs. The article R14 also mentions that they should prepare and solve the anticipated problems they may face during teaching. It is essential that the course staff have technical experience in the selected GDF to provide help for students and to avoid the focus shifting from the course content to technical matters.

(6) Time Constraints and Workload. This problem has been stressed repeatedly in several articles. Most of articles found that the time was limited. For instance, the article R5 mentions that time constraint caused to cut down the time in beginning phase. The article R13 reports that some students complain about insufficient time to complete the project. So there are some advices correspondingly, like the article R18 proposes some suggestions on the time consumption, and the article R3 suggests reading the background material better before the class in order to save class time for students. To help with the time management, a comprehensive time schedule should be prepared in advance for both the teacher and the students. Specifically, a series countermeasures can be the following: (1) make sure that the students learn, understand, and apply the GDBL-project process; (2) force students to set a mandatory rule for teams to create the schedule (strict milestones and deadlines); (3) get involved with the students early to make sure that they make a realistic goal; (4) teacher continuously monitor their progress and guide them to make adjustments, if needed, in order for them to complete their projects.

Other atypical factors could be found in Table 4. Further, Section 4.3 also provides a reference of how to assess the GDBL method. This indicates that future evaluation data of using GDBL is also beneficial, for example, [54]. As it does not only reveal the efficiency of using the framework along with how much the students actually learn from game projects, but also the social relationships' investigation of learner-learner, learner-teacher, and teacher-researcher.

5. Conclusions

From the above findings, we summarize a guideline for integrating a GDF in learning with teaching strategies. Figure 5 shows a simplified diagram that gives an overview of the design process of applying GDBL (adapted from article D21 and Section 4.1.2). It contains four elements (course aim, pedagogical theory support, GDF resource pool, and impact factor), two methods (learning by creating and learning by modifying games), and six steps in the teaching process and two subjects (students and teachers).

Basically, the course aim has the fundamental effects on the selection of GDF. And the pedagogical theory (Section 4.1.1) could support the teaching design. The GDF resource pool (Section 4.2.2) could be the reference for the selection of GDFs. Usually, during steps A to B in the teaching process in Figure 5, the pedagogical theory support and GDF resource pool play important roles in these two initial steps. Impact factors concern the whole process, but we suggest considering them at beginning as well. In terms of the course aim, pedagogical theory support and GDFs resource pool, the teaching process (Section 4.1.2) starts with designing the lectures and exercises with the selected GDF. After the lectures and tutorials, the course delivery starts and students begin the design and implementation of their projects. For the evaluation framework (Section 4.3), teachers/researchers are suggested to collect data using surveys. Based on the analysis of collected and teaching experiences, they can improve the teaching process framework. Here, we use a compact case to explain how each element in Figure 5 works in a certain course if the GDBL method is applied. The assumption is that the course aim is to teach basic programming rules for beginners. The choice could be made between "learning by

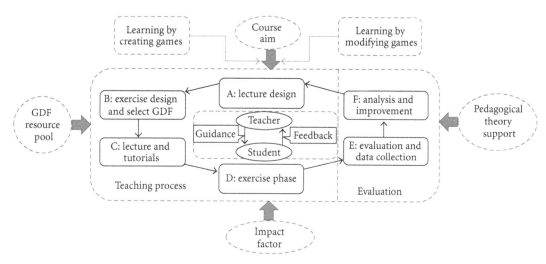

FIGURE 5: A guideline for technical and pedagogical codesign of GDBL.

modifying games" using a game editor with scripting, or "learning by creating games" using a GDF for novices. Then, we should consider the relationships between the problems and tools from the perspective of double stimulus or use other pedagogical theories to construct the learning process, for example, PBL. With this in mind and according to the criteria in Section 4.2.2, commonly used tools can be selected from the GDF resource pool—GDFs for novice in Table 2 or use another GDF if no suitable GDF is found in Table 2. After finishing steps of A to B in teaching process we start the lecture and the introduction of both exercises and GDFs. Later, students commence the implementation individually or in groups. During the whole teaching process from A to D, the impact factors are relevant but optional. For instance, we can choose a graphical interactive GDF and estimate time to be spent on lectures and exercises. Applying the impact factors in the teaching process depends on the courses' situations. That is why we have the evaluation and analysis steps E and F in Figure 5. The feedback data can help to validate the choice in each step—whether we choose a right task or a suitable GDF or focus on the most relevant impact factors in a course. In addition, since many elements interact in GDBL, which makes the real situation more complex to analyze and evaluate. Thus, an effective evaluation helps to validate the whole teaching process, and it is not only judged by teachers' own experiences, but also get opinions from students' aspect.

From the experience of accomplishing this paper, we still have the following limitation: (a) the scope of data search and collection from four scientific search engines is relatively limited; (b) due to the game research field is younger than other traditional research fields, the amount of articles with empirical data is still limited in our the survey, it maybe cause the pitfall of the evaluation results, for example, generalization; (c) some topics deserve further discussion. Cross-disciplinary courses, like game development course in article R1 covers programming and art design, and machinima course in article R8 have 3D animation and movie creation. Both of them could be further discussed

since GDFs plays different roles—the main tool in article R1 and an innovative auxiliary in article R8.

This study has shown that GDBL do have the potential power to help students to learn different curriculums. We hope that the study will provide useful guidance to educators, practitioners, and researchers in the area of GDBL, as well as to GDF designers, and that it will inform their future professional practices and research.

References

[1] S. M. Dorman, "Video and computer games: effect on children and implications for health education," *Journal of School Health*, vol. 67, no. 4, pp. 133–138, 1997.

[2] M. Prensky, "Digital game-based learning," *Computers in Entertainment*, vol. 1, no. 1, pp. 21–24, 2003.

[3] J. Blow, "Game development: harder than you think," *Queue*, vol. 1, no. 10, pp. 28–37, 2004.

[4] A. I. Wang and B. Wu, "An application of a game development framework in higher education," *International Journal of Computer Games Technology*, vol. 2009, Article ID 693267, 12 pages, 2009.

[5] K. Sung, C. Hillyard, R. L. Angotti, M. W. Panitz, D. S. Goldstein, and J. Nordlinger, "Game-themed programming assignment modules: a pathway for gradual integration of gaming context into existing introductory programming courses," *IEEE Transactions on Education*, vol. 54, no. 3, pp. 416–427, 2010.

[6] G. Sindre, L. Natvig, and M. Jahre, "Experimental validation of the learning effect for a pedagogical game on computer fundamentals," *IEEE Transactions on Education*, vol. 52, no. 1, pp. 10–18, 2009.

[7] B. A. Foss and T. I. Eikaas, "Game play in engineering education—concept and experimental results," *International Journal of Engineering Education*, vol. 22, no. 5, pp. 1043–1052, 2006.

[8] A. I. Wang, T. Øfsdahl, and O. K. Mørch-Storstein, "Lecture quiz—a mobile game concept for lectures," in *Proceedings of the 11th IASTED International Conference on Software Engineering and Application (SEA '07)*, pp. 305–310, 2007.

[9] A. I. Wang, T. Øfsdahl, and O. K. Mørch-Storstein-Storstein, "An evaluation of a mobile game concept for lectures," in *Proceedings of the IEEE 21st Conference on Software Engineering Education and Training*, pp. 197–204, 2008.

[10] M. S. El-Nasr and B. K. Smith, "Learning through game modding," *Computers in Entertainment*, vol. 4, no. 1, pp. 45–64, 2006.

[11] G. Lukas, "Uses of the LOGO programming language in undergraduate instruction," in *Proceedings of the Association for Computing Machinery Annual Conference (ACM '72)*, vol. 2, pp. 1130–1136, Boston, Mass, USA, 1972.

[12] M. Micco, "An undergraduate curriculum in expert systems design or knowledge engineering," in *Proceedings of the 15th Annual Conference on Computer Science (CSC '87)*, pp. 36–39, St. Louis, Mo, USA, 1987.

[13] J. P. Higgins and S. Green, *Front Matter*, John Wiley & Sons, New York, NY, USA, 2008.

[14] K. S. Khan et al., *Undertaking Systematic Reviews of Research on Effectiveness: CRD'S Guidance For Carrying Out or Commissioning Reviews: CRD Report*, Number 4, NHS centre for revies and lissemination, University of York, 2nd edition, 2001.

[15] M. Papastergiou, "Exploring the potential of computer and video games for health and physical education: a literature review," *Computers and Education*, vol. 53, no. 3, pp. 603–622, 2009.

[16] J. Kirriemuir and A. McFarlane, "Literature review in games and learning," Tech. Rep. 8, 2004.

[17] E. Ye, C. Liu, and J. A. Polack-Wahl, "Enhancing software engineering education using teaching aids in 3-D online virtual worlds," in *Proceedings of the 37th Annual Frontiers In Education Conference—Global Engineering: Knowledge Without Borders, Opportunities Without Passports (FIE' 07)*, pp. T1E-8–T1E-13, Milwaukee, Wis, USA, October 2007.

[18] B. Wu, A. I. Wang, and Y. Zhang, "Experiences from implementing an educational MMORPG," in *Proceedings of the 2nd International IEEE Consumer Electronic Society's Games Innovation Conference (GIC '10)*, pp. 1–8, December 2010.

[19] A. Baker, E. O. Navarro, and A. van der Hoek, "Problems and programmers: an educational software engineering card game," in *Proceedings of the 25th International Conference on Software Engineering*, pp. 614–619, May 2003.

[20] F. McCown, "Teaching a game programming class for the first time: tutorial presentation," *Journal of Computing Sciences in Colleges*, vol. 25, no. 5, pp. 131–132, 2010.

[21] C. Leska and J. Rabung, "Learning O-O concepts in CS I using game projects," in *Proceedings of the 9th Annual SIGCSE Conference on Innovation and Technology in Computer Science Education*, vol. 36, p. 237, June 2004.

[22] E. Ferguson, B. Rockhold, and B. Heck, "Video game development using XNA game studio and C#.Net," *Journal of Computing Sciences in Colleges*, vol. 23, no. 4, pp. 186–188, 2008.

[23] R. H. Seidman, "Alice first: 3D interactive game programming," *ACM SIGCSE Bulletin*, vol. 41, no. 3, p. 345, 2009.

[24] X. Fu, S. Doboli, and J. Impagliazzo, "Work in progress—a sandbox model for teaching entrepreneurship," in *Proceedings of the 40th IEEE Annual Frontiers in Education Conference (FIE '10)*, pp. F2C-1–F2C-2.

[25] M. Kolling, "Greenfoot: introduction to Java with games and simulations," *Journal of Computing Sciences in Colleges*, vol. 25, no. 3, p. 117, 2010.

[26] A. Azemi and L. L. Pauley, "Teaching the introductory computer programming course for engineers using Matlab," in *Proceedings of the 38th Annual Frontiers in Education Conference (FIE '08)*, pp. T3B-1–T3B-23, October 2008.

[27] A. Pardo and C. D. Kloos, "Deploying interactive e-labs for a course on operating systems," in *Proceedings of the 6th Conference on Information Technology Education*, pp. 71–78, Newark, NJ, USA, 2005.

[28] P. Rooney, K. C. O'Rourke, G. Burke, B. Mac Namee, and C. Igbrude, "Cross-disciplinary approaches for developing serious games in higher education: frameworks for food safety and environmental health education," in *Proceedings of the Conference in Games and Virtual Worlds for Serious Applications (VS-GAMES '09)*, pp. 161–165, March 2009.

[29] A. W. B. Furtado, G. D. de Andrade, A. R. G. do Amaral Leitão et al., "Cegadef: a collaborative educational game development framework," in *Proceedings of the Conference on Interaction Design and Children*, Preston, UK, 2003.

[30] H. C. Yang, "A general framework for automatically creating games for learning," in *Proceedings of the 5th IEEE International Conference on Advanced Learning Technologies (ICALT '05)*, pp. 28–29, July 2005.

[31] K. Kardan, "Computer role-playing games as a vehicle for teaching history, culture, and language," in *Proceedings of the Association for Computing Machinery's Special Interest Group on Computer Graphics and Interactive Techniques Symposium on Videogames*, pp. 91–93, Boston, Mass, USA, July 2006.

[32] S. Arakawa and S. Yukita, "An effective agile teaching environment for java programming courses," in *Proceedings of 36th Annual Frontiers in Education Conference*, pp. 13–18, October 2006.

[33] W. W. Y. Lau, G. Ngai, S. C. F. Chan, and J. C. Y. Cheung, "Learning programming through fashion and design: a pilot summer course in wearable computing for middle school students," *SIGCSE Bulletin Inroads*, vol. 41, no. 1, pp. 504–508, 2009.

[34] S. V. Delden, "Industrial robotic game playing: an AI course," *Journal of Computing Sciences in Colleges*, vol. 25, no. 3, pp. 134–142, 2010.

[35] P. H. Tan, C. Y. Ting, and S. W. Ling, "Learning difficulties in programming courses: undergraduates' perspective and perception," in *Proceedings of the International Conference on Computer Technology and Development (ICCTD '09)*, pp. 42–46, November 2009.

[36] T. E. Daniels, "Integrating engagement and first year problem solving using game controller technology," in *Proceedings of the 39th IEEE Annual Frontiers in Education Conference (FIE '09)*, pp. 1–6, October 2009.

[37] A. Striegel and D. van Bruggen, "Work in progress—development of a HCI course on the microsoft surface," in *Proceedings of the 40th Annual Frontiers in Education Conference (FIE '10)*, pp. S3F-1–S3F-6, October 2010.

[38] A. Wang, "Interactive game development with a projector-camera system," in *Proceedings of the 3rd International Conference on Technologies for E-Learning and Digital Entertainment*, pp. 535–543, Springer, 2008.

[39] J. Dempsey, K. Rasmussen, and B. Lucassen, "The instructional gaming literature: implications and 99 sources," Tech. Rep. 96-1, University of South Alabama, College of Education, 1996.

[40] J. Dempsey, B. Lucassen, W. Gilley et al., "Since Malone's theory of intrinsically motivating instruction: what's the score in the gaming literature?" *Journal of Educational Technology Systems*, vol. 22, no. 2, pp. 173–183, 1993-1994.

[41] R. Hays, "The effectiveness of instructional games: a literature review and discussion," Tech. Rep. 2005-004, Naval Air Warfare Center, Training Systems Division, Orlando, Fla, USA, 2005.

[42] M. C. V. Langeveld and R. Kessler, "Two in the middle: digital character production and machinima courses," *SIGCSE Bulletin Inroads*, vol. 41, no. 1, pp. 463–467, 2009.

[43] W. L. Honig and T. Prasad, "A classroom outsourcing experience for software engineering learning," *SIGCSE Bulletin Inroads*, vol. 39, pp. 181–185, 2007.

[44] S. Hrastinski, "What is online learner participation? A literature review," *Computers and Education*, vol. 51, no. 4, pp. 1755–1765, 2008.

[45] S. Papert, *Mindstorms: Children, Computers, and Powerful Ideas*, Basic Books, New York, NY, USA, 1980.

[46] S. Puntambekar and J. L. Kolodner, "Toward implementing distributed scaffolding: helping students learn science from design," *Journal of Research in Science Teaching*, vol. 42, no. 2, pp. 185–217, 2005.

[47] J. Dewey, *Democracy and Education: An Introduction to the Philosophy of Education*, 2005.

[48] J. Dewey, *Experience and Education*, Simon and Schuster, New York, NY, USA, 1997.

[49] E. Smeets, "Does ICT contribute to powerful learning environments in primary education?" *Computers and Education*, vol. 44, no. 3, pp. 343–355, 2005.

[50] L. S. Vygotskij, *Mind in Society: The Development of Higher Psychological Processes*, Harvard University Press, Cambridge, Mass, USA, 1978.

[51] H. S. Barrows, "A taxonomy of problem-based learning methods," *Medical Education*, vol. 20, no. 6, pp. 481–486, 1986.

[52] B. Lennartsson and E. Sundin, "Fronesis—the third dimension of knowledge, learning, and evaluation," in *Proceedings of the 31st Annual Frontiers in Education Conference*, vol. 1, pp. T2B/14–T2B/19, October 2001.

[53] W. M. Thomas, "What makes things fun to learn? Heuristics for designing instructional computer games," in *Proceedings of the 3rd ACM SIGSMALL Symposium and the 1st SIGPC Symposium on Small Systems*, Palo Alto, Calif, USA, 1980.

[54] A. I. Wang, "Extensive evaluation of using a game project in a software architecture course," *ACM Transactions on Computing Education*, vol. 11, no. 1, article 5, 2011.

[55] A. D. Ritzhaupt, "creating a game development course with limited resources: an evaluation study," *ACM Transactions on Computing Education*, vol. 9, no. 1, pp. 1–16, 2009.

[56] A. McGovern and J. Fager, "Creating significant learning experiences in introductory artificial intelligence," *SIGCSE Bulletin Inroads*, vol. 39, pp. 39–43, 2007.

[57] R. Angotti, C. Hillyard, M. Panitz, K. Sung, and K. Marino, "Game-themed instructional modules: a video case study," in *Proceedings of the 5th International Conference on the Foundations of Digital Games (FDG '10)*, pp. 9–16, Monterey, Calif, USA, June 2010.

[58] G. Fesakis and K. Serafeim, "Influence of the familiarization with "scratch" on future teachers' opinions and attitudes about programming and ICT in education," in *Proceedings of the 14th Annual ACM SIGCSE Conference on Innovation and Technology in Computer Science Education (ITiCSE '09)*, pp. 258–262, Paris, France, July 2009.

[59] Y. Rankin, A. Gooch, and B. Gooch, "The impact of game design on students' interest in CS," in *Proceedings of the 3rd International Conference on Game Development in Computer Science Education (GDCSE '08)*, pp. 31–35, Miami, Fla, USA, March 2008.

[60] M. Al-Bow, D. Austin, J. Edgington et al., "Using game creation for teaching computer programming to high school students and teachers," *ACM SIGCSE Bulletin*, vol. 41, pp. 104–108, 2009.

[61] M. Eagle and T. Barnes, "Experimental evaluation of an educational game for improved learning in introductory computing," *SIGCSE Bulletin Inroads*, vol. 41, no. 1, pp. 321–325, 2009.

[62] W. K. Chen and Y. C. Cheng, "Teaching object-oriented programming laboratory with computer game programming," *IEEE Transactions on Education*, vol. 50, no. 3, pp. 197–203, 2007.

[63] Yulia and R. Adipranata, "Teaching object oriented programming course using cooperative learning method based on game design and visual object oriented environment," in *Proceedings of the 2nd International Conference on Education Technology and Computer (ICETC '10)*, pp. V2-355–V2-359, June 2010.

[64] R. Lawrence, "Teaching data structures using competitive games," *IEEE Transactions on Education*, vol. 47, no. 4, pp. 459–466, 2004.

[65] J. Huang, "Improving undergraduates' teamwork skills by adapting project-based learning methodology," in *Proceedings of the 5th International Conference on Computer Science and Education (ICCSE '10)*, pp. 652–655, August 2010.

[66] B. Wu, A. I. Wang, J. E. Strøm, and T. B. Kvamme, "An evaluation of using a game development framework in higher education," in *Proceedings of the 22nd Conference on Software Engineering Education and Training (CSEET '09)*, pp. 41–44, February 2009.

[67] J.-F. Weng, S.-S. Tseng, and T.-J. Lee, "Teaching boolean logic through game Rule tuning," *IEEE Transactions on Learning Technologies*, vol. 3, no. 4, pp. 319–328, 2010.

[68] R. Owston, H. Wideman, N. S. Ronda, and C. Brown, "Computer game development as a literacy activity," *Computers and Education*, vol. 53, no. 3, pp. 977–989, 2009.

[69] I. J. Timm, T. Bogon, A. D. Lattner, and R. Schumann, "Teaching distributed artificial intelligence with RoboRally," in *Multiagent System Technologies*, vol. 5244, pp. 171–182, Springer, Berlin, Germany, 2008.

[70] L. Werner, J. Denner, M. Bliesner, and P. Rex, "Can middle-schoolers use Storytelling Alice to make games? Results of a pilot study," in *Proceedings of the 4th International Conference on the Foundations of Digital Games (ICFDG '09)*, pp. 207–214, Orlando, Fla, USA, April 2009.

[71] K. Wang, C. McCaffrey, D. Wendel, and E. Klopfer, "3D game design with programming blocks in StarLogo TNG," in *Proceedings of the 7th International Conference on Learning Sciences*, pp. 1008–1009, Bloomington, Ind, USA, 2006.

[72] C. H. Huang, P. C. Ho, and S. M. Chung, "Computer game programming course for art design students by using flash software," in *Proceedings of the International Conference on Cyberworlds (CW '08)*, pp. 710–713, September 2008.

[73] B. Lennartsson and E. Sundin, "Experience from a course aiming at understanding system development with focus on system design and integration," in *Proceedings of the 32nd Annual Frontiers in Education*, vol. 1, pp. T3G-1–T3G-6, November 2002.

[74] J. Ryoo, F. Fonseca, and D. S. Janzen, "Teaching object-oriented software engineering through problem-based learning in the context of game design," in *Proceedings of the 21st*

Conference on Software Engineering Education and Training (CSEET '08), pp. 137–144, April 2008.

[75] J. Robertson and C. Howells, "Computer game design: opportunities for successful learning," *Computers and Education*, vol. 50, no. 2, pp. 559–578, 2008.

[76] W.-C. Chang and Y.-M. Chou, "Introductory C programming language learning with game-based digital learning," *Advances in Web Based Learning*, vol. 5145, pp. 221–231, 2008.

[77] S. Kurkovsky, "Can mobile game development foster student interest in computer science?" in *Proceedings of the 1st International IEEE Consumer Electronic Society's Games Innovation Conference (ICE-GIC '09)*, pp. 92–100, August 2009.

[78] K. J. Bierre and A. M. Phelps, "The use of MUPPETS in an introductory java programming course," in *Proceedings of the 5th Conference on Information Technology Education (CITC5 '04)*, pp. 122–127, Salt Lake City, Utah, USA, October 2004.

[79] B. Wu, A. I. Wang, J. E. Strøm, and T. B. Kvamme, "XQUEST used in software architecture education," in *Proceedings of the 1st International IEEE Consumer Electronic Society's Games Innovation Conference (ICE-GIC '09)*, pp. 70–77, August 2009.

[80] B. Wu, A. I. Wang, A. H. Ruud, and W. Z. Zhang, "Extending google android's application as an educational tool," in *Proceedings of the 3rd IEEE International Conference on Digital Game and Intelligent Toy Enhanced Learning (DIGITEL '10)*, pp. 23–30, April 2010.

[81] H. C. Jiau, J. C. Chen, and K. F. Ssu, "Enhancing self-motivation in learning programming using game-based simulation and metrics," *IEEE Transactions on Education*, vol. 52, no. 4, pp. 555–562, 2009.

[82] A. Garrido, J. Martinez-Baena, R. Rodriguez-Sanchez, J. Fdez-Valdivia, and J. A. Garcia, "Using graphics: motivating students in a C++ programming introductory course," in *Proceedings of the 20th European Association for Education in Electrical and Information Engineering Annual Conference (EAEEIE '09)*, pp. 1–6, June 2009.

[83] A. Barella, S. Valero, and C. Carrascosa, "JGOMAS: new approach to AI teaching," *IEEE Transactions on Education*, vol. 52, no. 2, pp. 228–235, 2009.

2

Single- versus Multiobjective Optimization for Evolution of Neural Controllers in Ms. Pac-Man

Tse Guan Tan, Jason Teo, and Kim On Chin

Evolutionary Computing Laboratory, School of Engineering and Information Technology, Universiti Malaysia, Jalan (UMS), 88400 Kota Kinabalu, Sabah, Malaysia

Correspondence should be addressed to Tse Guan Tan; tseguantan@gmail.com

Academic Editor: Abdennour El Rhalibi

The objective of this study is to focus on the automatic generation of game artificial intelligence (AI) controllers for Ms. Pac-Man agent by using artificial neural network (ANN) and multiobjective artificial evolution. The Pareto Archived Evolution Strategy (PAES) is used to generate a Pareto optimal set of ANNs that optimize the conflicting objectives of maximizing Ms. Pac-Man scores (screen-capture mode) and minimizing neural network complexity. This proposed algorithm is called Pareto Archived Evolution Strategy Neural Network or PAESNet. Three different architectures of PAESNet were investigated, namely, PAESNet with fixed number of hidden neurons (PAESNet_F), PAESNet with varied number of hidden neurons (PAESNet_V), and the PAESNet with multiobjective techniques (PAESNet_M). A comparison between the single- versus multiobjective optimization is conducted in both training and testing processes. In general, therefore, it seems that PAESNet_F yielded better results in training phase. But the PAESNet_M successfully reduces the runtime operation and complexity of ANN by minimizing the number of hidden neurons needed in hidden layer and also it provides better generalization capability for controlling the game agent in a nondeterministic and dynamic environment.

1. Introduction

A number of optimization solution techniques have been introduced for solving Multi-Objective Problems (MOPs) [1]. An MOP has a set of conflicting objective functions subject to certain constraints which are to be minimized or maximized [2]. Among these techniques, Evolutionary Algorithms (EAs) are particularly suited for handling MOPs [3, 4] because of its population approach that can help in finding a set of trade-off solutions in single simulation run, instead of having to perform a series of separate runs such as in the case of traditional optimization techniques. Moreover, EAs have been successfully used in solving complex problems such as discontinuities, multimodality, disjoint feasible spaces, and noisy function evaluations [5]. A large range of practical applications of Multi-Objective Evolutionary Algorithms (MOEAs) to real-life problems across a host of different disciplines can be found in the reference texts by Deb [6] and Coello et al. [3]. There are several types of effective MOEAs such as Pareto Archived Evolution Strategy

(PAES) [7], Strength Pareto Evolutionary Algorithm 2 [8], Nondominated Sorting Genetic Algorithm II [9], and Pareto-frontier Differential Evolution [10].

Generally, MOEAs are able to solve separate distinct varied dimensional optimization problems. In other words, MOEAs outperformed single-objective EAs without combining and resorting those multiple problems into single weighted-sum objective. Such weighted-sum methods are disadvantageous in obtaining suitable mode for combining different objectives into a single-objective function, which caused high-cost effective [6]. Furthermore, each evolutionary run generates single solution; the second solution will only be generated after the weights are changed; these processes will be repeated for obtaining other solutions [11, 12]. Another distinct advantage of MOEAs is its capability in generating a complete set of Pareto optimal solutions in a single run with provides users a choice of solutions for trade-off between different objectives.

On the other hand, the disadvantages of MOEAs [6, 11, 12] are (i) as the number of objectives increases, the coverage of the Pareto front sparser and become unable to provide a comprehensive set of solutions over multiple dimensions, (ii) problematic in maintaining good spread diverse solutions along the Pareto front, and (iii) the difficulty of fitness sharing decision making in MOEAs which utilize multiple populations. This open research question provides the motivation for the work in this paper. In other words, "Is a single-objective optimization technique better than multiobjective optimization in real-life problems?"

Games are one of the common used platforms for answering research question by allowing the testing and comparison of new and experimental approaches on a challenging but well-defined problem [13–17]. In this research, Ms. Pac-man has been chosen as the test-bed due to its ease of use in comparing the performances of the single-objective optimization and multiobjective optimization techniques.

In this study, a feed-forward artificial neural network (FFNN) is used and later evolved with PAES, a well-known and simple MOEA, for computer-based players to learn and optimally play Ms. Pac-man game. There are two distinct objectives to be optimized: (i) maximize the Ms. Pac-man's game scores and (ii) minimize the number of hidden neurons used in the FFNN architecture.

A comparative empirical experiment will be conducted in order to verify the performances for the methods used.

(1) Single-objective optimization: the first experiment uses fixed number of hidden neurons in the FFNN and only maximizes Ms. Pac-man game scores, namely, PAESNet_F.

(2) Single-objective optimization: the second experiment is using variable number of hidden neurons in the FFNN and only maximizes Ms. Pac-man game scores, namely, PAESNet_V.

(3) Multiobjective optimization: the third experiment maximizes the game scores as well as minimizes the hidden neurons in the FFNN, namely, PAESNet_M.

The main contribution of these proposed algorithms is to create computer-based agent that not only is able to make intelligent decisions like human players in the dynamic game environments, but also is highly beneficial to the real-world problems with the successful application of these techniques, such as in the application of robotics and other complex systems.

2. Other Related Researches

Basically, most studies in the game of Ms. Pac-man have only focussed on hand-coded rule-based (RB) approaches or other specific methods [18–21]. Although these methods can achieve quite high scores, they are associated with some limitations. Firstly, game domains contain highly complex solution spaces that require a large number of rules in order to represent a set of all possible situations and corresponding actions in game environments. For instance, Szita and Lorincz [21] list 42 rules of a very basic hand-coded RB agent used in Ms. Pac-man game from the lists of action modules and observations to control the behaviour of agent. Secondly,

the computation time required to exhaustively explore the search space is very expensive indeed if large sets of rules are used by the search strategies. Thirdly, there is a lack of generalization across different game domains or platforms because they would only apply in that particular game or genre of game.

The intention of this research is to create game controllers capable of general intelligent action without requiring any domain-dependent solution and also trying to be proficient in other games by just changing the input and output values of ANN. Thus, the experimental results will be compared to an appropriate reference system created by Lucas [22]. Lucas used general methods in designing the game controller which evolves ANN by using evolutionary strategy to play Ms. Pac-man. The input of the network is a handcrafted feature vector that consists of the distance to each normal ghost, distance to each edible ghost, location of current node, distance to nearest pill, the distance to nearest power pill, and distance to nearest junction, whereas the calculated output is a score for every possible next location given the agent's current location. ES is applied to evolve ANN connection weights. The best evolved agent with $(10 + 10)$-ES had an average score of 4781 over 100 runs of the nondeterministic game.

3. Methods and Parameter Setting

This investigation has two modes of operation: training and testing as shown in Figure 1. In the training mode, the FFNNs are trained using evolution-based algorithm. The agents will learn to play many games in order to optimize weights, biases, and number of hidden neurons in FFNN architecture, as an effective mode for training. After the training process, the neural network is tested for generalization using the optimized networks.

3.1. Pareto Archived Evolution Strategy. The $(1 + 1)$-PAES for a two-membered PAES has been applied for simultaneously optimizing network parameters and architecture to solve single, and multiobjective optimization problems. The resulting algorithm is referred to as the PAESNet. Figure 2 shows the flowchart of PAESNet and fitness evaluation process. The strengths of PAES are listed as follows:

(1) simple structure;

(2) easy to implement;

(3) $(1 + 1)$-PAES and $(1 + \lambda)$-PAES are based on local search method with lower computational effort required compared to population-based MOEAs.

(4) a small number of parameters are needed;

(5) the simplest possible nontrivial algorithm capable of generating diverse solutions in the Pareto optimal set [23].

3.2. Single Objective: PAESNet with Fixed Number of Hidden Neurons and PAESNet with Varied Number of Hidden Neurons. Two systems are discussed in this section, which are the PAESNet with fixed number of hidden neuron (PAESNet_F) and PAESNet with varied number of hidden neurons

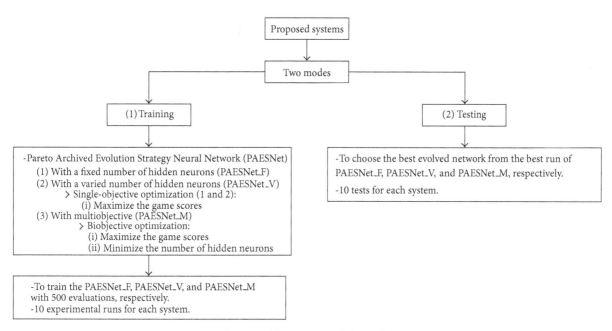

FIGURE 1: The overview of the study.

(PAESNet_V). The default number of hidden neurons is set to 20. In the initialization phase, the ANN weights and biases are encoded into a chromosome from uniform distribution with range $[-1, 1]$ to act as parent and its fitness is evaluated. Subsequently, polynomial mutation operator is used with distribution index = 20.0 to create an offspring from the parent and the fitness is evaluated. After that, the fitnesses of the offspring and parent are compared. If the offspring performs better than the parent, then the parent is replaced by the offspring as a new parent for the next evaluation. Otherwise the offspring is eliminated and a new mutated offspring is generated. If the parent and the offspring are incomparable, the offspring is compared with a set of previously nondominated individuals in the archive. Below is the description of the archiving process in PAESNet.

There are three possible situations that can occur between the comparison of the offspring and archive [7, 24, 25]. First, if the offspring is dominated by a member of the archive, then the offspring is discarded and a new mutated offspring is created from the parent. Second, if the offspring dominates some members of the archive, then the set of dominated members is removed from the archive. The offspring will then be added to the archive and it also becomes the parent of the next generation. Third, if the offspring and the archive members do not dominate each other, then the archive will be maintained depending on the archive size. If the archive is not full, the offspring will be directly copied to the archive. Otherwise, in the scenario that the archive is full, a neighborhood density measure is used to ensure that a well-spread distribution is maintained in the archive. If the offspring has succeeded to increase the archive diversity, it will replace the archive member in the most crowded grid location in order to maintain the maximum archive size. Note that in this third situation, the offspring and the parent are the nondominated members of the archive. The neighborhood

density measure is also applied for parent selection of the next generation from both of them. If the offspring resides in the less crowded area than the parent, then the offspring is selected.

3.3. Multiobjective: PAESNet with Multiobjective (PAESNet_M). The structure of this proposed algorithm is similar to the algorithms in Section 3.2 except for the architecture of the ANN. In this proposed algorithms, two objectives are involved. The first objective is to maximize the game scores while the second objective is to minimize the number of neurons in the FFNN. The initial value of hidden neurons is set to 20.

3.4. Feed-Forward ANN. The typical FFNN is composed of three layers: input, hidden, and output layers [26]. The following is used to describe the feed-forward ANN architecture:

(1) I, H, and O are the numbers of input neurons, hidden neurons, and output neurons, respectively;

(2) ω_{ih} and ω_{ho} are the weights connecting input unit i, $i = 1, \ldots, I$, to hidden unit h, $h = 1, \ldots, H$, and from hidden unit to output unit o, $o = 1, \ldots, O$;

(3) x_i is the input signal.

The net input of a neuron is calculated using the weighted sum of inputs from all neurons in the previous layer, as follows:

$$\sum_{i=0}^{I} \omega_{ih} x_i. \tag{1}$$

Log-sigmoid (logsig) is used as the activation function in the hidden and output layers. Based on [27], logsig has been identified as suitable activation function in ANN for creating neural-based Ms. Pac-man agent.

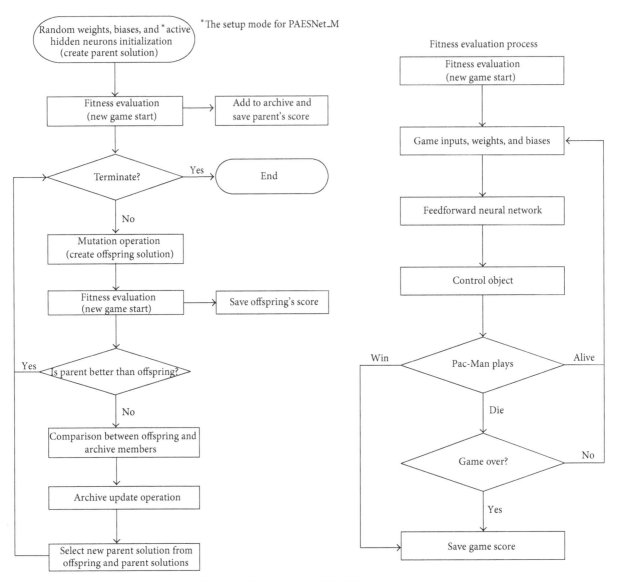

FIGURE 2: The flowchart of PAESNet optimizer.

3.5. Experimental Setting. The FFNN architecture of this model has a 5-20-1 structure, which consists of 5 inputs and 1 output together with one hidden layer of 20 neurons. This number of hidden neurons was suggested by Lucas [22]. The Euclidean distance is applied to calculate the distance in the maze as the inputs of the network were obtained based on the following information:

(1) the closest distance from agent to a pill;

(2) the closest distance from agent to a power pill;

(3) the closest distance from agent to a ghost;

(4) the closest distance from agent to an edible ghost;

(5) the closest distance from agent to a fruit.

4. Experimental Results and Discussions

The results obtained from the analysis of training and testing performances can be compared in the tables and figures below.

4.1. Training Results. Table 1 presents the training results of mean, standard deviation (SD), minimum (Min) and maximum (Max) values obtained from the best game scores, and number of hidden neurons in each run. The statistics (mean of scores, mean of hidden neurons) for PAESNet_F, PAESNet_V, and PAESNet_M were (7161, 20), (5935, 9.7), and (5734, 8), respectively. According to the mean values of scores, the results showed that PAESNet_F has the highest average score. However, the best scores are comparable across all three approaches (7430 in PAESNet_F, 7190 in PAESNet_V, and 7170 in PAESNet_M). On the other hand, taking the mean

TABLE 1: The training results.

Run	PAESNet_F		PAESNet_V		PAESNet_M	
	Score	Neurons	Score	Neurons	Score	Neurons
1	6710	20	7190	13	7170	7
2	7050	20	5810	11	5690	10
3	7290	20	6260	11	6400	8
4	7190	20	5450	6	4940	5
5	7430	20	5190	8	4670	9
6	6930	20	5520	6	5990	6
7	7080	20	6650	11	5280	9
8	7280	20	5980	9	5260	9
9	7320	20	5500	12	6120	8
10	7330	20	5800	10	5820	9
Min	6710	20	5190	6	4670	5
Max	7430	20	7190	13	7170	10
Mean	7161	20	5935	9.7	5734	8
SD	219.47	0	612.78	2.41	739.58	1.56

Score: best score; Neurons: number of hidden neurons.

TABLE 2: Win rates for training results across all 10 runs.

Proposed algorithm	PAESNet_F	PAESNet_V	PAESNet_M
PAESNet_F	—	90%	90%
PAESNet_V	10%	—	60%
PAESNet_M	10%	40%	—

(A versus B) + (B versus A) = 100%.

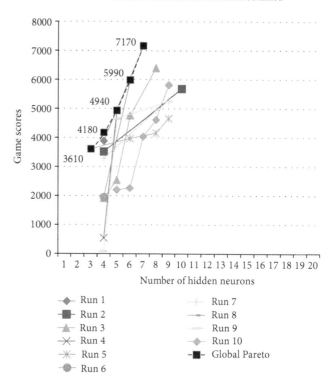

Global Pareto-frontier solutions obtained

FIGURE 3: The global Pareto-frontier solutions obtained across all 10 runs using multiobjective optimization.

values of hidden neurons, we observed that the PAESNet_M reduces the number of hidden neurons from 20 to 8 which is around 60% improvement. This emphasizes the advantages of MOEA approach in terms of computational complexity in FFNN.

Additionally, the average scores of all the proposed algorithms, PAESNet_F (7161), PAESNet_V (5935), and PAES-Net_M (5734), are relatively higher when compared to Lucas (4781) [22] for training to play the Ms. Pac-man. Hence, this is further a proof that the proposed systems with PAES are able to usefully and automatically generate Ms. Pac-Man agents that display some intelligent playing behavior.

Table 2 lists the win rates (WR) for each comparison, which is the number of runs an artificial controller wins per total number of runs as shown in (2). Firstly, for PAESNet_F versus PAESNet_V, WR = 90%, PAESNet_F won 9 out of 10 runs compared to PAESNet_V except Run 1, and the result is same for PAESNet_F versus PAESNet_M. Subsequently, for PAESNet_V versus PAESNet_M, WR = 60%, PAESNet_V won 6 out of 10 runs compared to PAESNet_M except Run 3, Run 6, Run 9 and Run 10. The results clearly show that PAES-Net_F outperformed the other two competing approaches. This result may be explained by the fact that PAESNet_F is concerned with a single-objective of maximizing the game scores, while that of the PAESNet_M is to find the set of trade-off solutions between the scores and number of hidden neurons. The acceptance of trade-off solutions is due to convergence performance and diversity preservation in Pareto

optimal front. Due to these two criteria, the multiobjective optimization is harder than single-objective optimization. Another possible explanation for this is that multiobjective optimization is dealing with two search spaces, which are decision variable space and objective space compared to single-objective optimization just involving one search space (decision variable space). This factor may influence the performance of PAESNet_M:

$$WR = \frac{runs\ won}{total\ of\ runs\ played} * 100\%. \qquad (2)$$

The global Pareto-frontier solutions obtained with the goal of maximizing scores and minimizing hidden neurons across all 10 runs using multiobjective optimization are illustrated in Figure 3. The global Pareto solutions are shown by the dotted line. As can be seen from the figure, the PAESNet_M reported significantly decreases the number of hidden neurons needed from 20 to the range of 3 to 7 nodes in the hidden layer as the optimized networks and the game scores achieved were 3610, 4180, 4940, 5990, and 7170.

4.2. Testing Results. After the training phase, the best evolved networks were used to test the generalization ability of the models in order to score as high as possible. The selected best numbers of neurons in the hidden layer are 20, 13, and 7 for PAESNet_F, PAESNet_V, and PAESNet_M, respectively, as the optimum networks, as shown in Table 3.

TABLE 3: The best evolved networks from proposed algorithms.

Proposed algorithm	Number of hidden neurons
PAESNet_F	20
PAESNet_V	13
PAESNet_M	7

TABLE 4: The testing results.

Run	PAESNet_F	PAESNet_V	PAESNet_M
1	3090	4160	4250
2	2720	2740	2700
3	2020	2590	2890
4	4170	2100	5360
5	2500	2280	2510
6	2580	1080	2760
7	2780	4020	2860
8	1990	4820	2080
9	2090	2290	3130
10	4360	4880	3950
Min	1990	1080	2080
Max	4360	4880	5360
Mean	2830	3096	3249
SD	836.62	1286.48	983.04

TABLE 5: Win rates for testing results across all 10 runs.

Proposed algorithm	PAESNet_F	PAESNet_V	PAESNet_M
PAESNet_F	—	30%	20%
PAESNet_V	70%	—	40%
PAESNet_M	80%	60%	—

(A versus B) + (B versus A) = 100%.

Table 4 presents the testing results of the three proposed algorithms. We can observe that both of the max and mean scores in PAESNet_M (5360, 3249) were higher than PAESNet_F (4360, 2830) and PAESNet_V (4880, 3096). Based on mean values, PAESNet_M was shown to have better performance compared to PAESNet_F and PAESNet_V.

Table 5 lists the win rates for each comparison. Firstly, for PAESNet_F versus PAESNet_V, WR = 70% and PAESNet_V won 7 out of 10 runs compared to PAESNet_F, except Run 4, Run 5, and Run 6. Next, for PAESNet_F versus PAESNet_M, WR = 80% PAESNet_M won 8 out of 10 runs compared to PAESNet_F, except Run 2 and Run 10. Lastly, for PAESNet_V versus PAESNet_M, WR = 60% and PAESNet_M won 6 out of 10 runs compared to PAESNet_V, except Run 2, Run 7, Run 8, and Run 10. From this data, we can see that PAESNet_M resulted in the highest value of win rate compared to the two algorithms. The PAESNet_M successfully found the appropriate network architecture and parameters by maximizing the game scores and minimizing the hidden neurons. Overall, the testing results have shown that FFNNs and PAES have strong potential for controlling game agents in the game world.

5. Conclusions

In this study, the FFNN is evolved with the PAES MOEA for the computer player to automatically learn and optimally play the game of Ms. Pac-man which is called PAESNet. Three forms of PAESNet, PAESNet_F, PAESNet_V, and PAESNet_M, were introduced to solve single- and multiobjective optimization problems and compared to each other in the training and testing processes. The Pareto optimal front resulted from each MOEA run provided a set of NNs which maximized the scores of Ms. Pac-man and at the same time minimized the size of the controller. In the training process, PAESNet_F outperformed PAESNet_V and PAESNet_M. However, in the testing process, PAESNet_M outperformed the other two algorithms. One of the most significant findings to emerge from this study is that the generalization performance of the neural networks could improve significantly by evolving the architecture and connection weights (including biases) synchronously via a MOEA approach as opposed to fixing the network architecture and optimizing the scoring component only using a single-objective optimization approach.

Acknowledgment

This research is funded under the Science Fund Project SCF52-ICT-3/2008 granted by the Ministry of Science, Technology and Innovation, Malaysia.

References

[1] C. Zheng and P. Wang, "Application of flow and transport optimization codes to groundwater pump-and-treat systems: Umatilla Army Depot, Oregon," Tech. Rep., University of Alabama, Tuscaloosa, Ala, USA, 2001.

[2] C. A. C. Coello, "Evolutionary multi-objective optimization: a critical review," in Evolutionary Optimization, R. Sarker, M. Mohammadian, and X. Yao, Eds., pp. 117–146, Kluwer Academic, Boston, Mass, USA, 2002.

[3] C. A. C. Coello, G. B. Lamont, and D. A. van Veldhuizen, Evolutionary Algorithms for Solving Multi-Objective Problems, Springer, New York, NY, USA, 2007.

[4] W. Q. Ying, Y. X. Li, C. Y. S. Phillip, Y. Wu, and F. H. Yu, "Geometric thermodynamicalselection for evolutionary multiobjective optimization," Chinese Journal of Computers, vol. 33, no. 4, pp. 755–767, 2010.

[5] C. M. Fonseca and P. J. Fleming, "An overview of evolutionary algorithms in multiobjective optimization," Evolutionary Computation, vol. 3, pp. 1–16, 1995.

[6] K. Deb, Multi-Objective Optimization Using Evolutionary Algorithms, Wiley, New York, NY, USA, 2001.

[7] J. D. Knowles and D. W. Corne, "The Pareto archived evolution strategy: a new baseline algorithm for Pareto multiobjective optimisation," in Proceedings of the IEEE Congress on Evolutionary Computation (CEC '99), pp. 98–105, Washington, DC, USA, July, 1999.

[8] E. Zitzler, M. Laumanns, and L. Thiele, "SPEA2: improving the strength Pareto evolutionary algorithm," Tech. Rep. 103, Computer Engineering and Network Laboratory (TIK), Swiss Federal Institute of Technology (ETH), Zurich, Switzerland, 2001.

[9] K. Deb, A. Pratap, S. Agarwal, and T. Meyarivan, "A fast and elitist multiobjective genetic algorithm: NSGA-II," *IEEE Transactions on Evolutionary Computation*, vol. 6, no. 2, pp. 182–197, 2002.

[10] H. A. Abbass, R. Sarker, and C. Newton, "PDE: a Pareto-frontier differential evolution approach for multi-objective optimization problems," in *Proceedings of the IEEE Conference on Evolutionary Computation*, pp. 971–978, May 2001.

[11] C. A. C. Coello, G. T. Pulido, and E. M. Montes, "Current and future research trends in evolutionary multiobjective optimization," in *Information Processing with Evolutionary Algorithms: From Industrial Applications to Academic Speculations*, M. Grana, R. Duro, A. d'Anjou, and P. P. Wang, Eds., pp. 213–231, Springer, London, UK, 2005.

[12] C. A. C. Coello, "Recent trends in evolutionary multiobjective optimization," in *Evolutionary Multiobjective Optimization: Theoretical Advances and Applications*, A. Abraham, L. Jain, and R. Goldberg, Eds., pp. 7–32, Springer, London, UK, 2005.

[13] K. T. Chang, K. O. Chin, J. Teo, and A. M. Jilui-Kiring, "Evolving neural controllers using GA for warcraft 3-real time strategy game," in *Proceedings of the IEEE 6th International Conference on Bio-Inspired Computing: Theories and Applications*, pp. 15–20, September 2011.

[14] K. T. Chang, J. H. Ong, J. Teo, and K. O. Chin, "The evolution of gamebots for 3D first person shooter (FPS)," in *Proceedings of the IEEE 6th International Conference on Bio-Inspired Computing: Theories and Applications*, pp. 21–26, September 2011.

[15] K. T. Chang, J. Teo, K. O. Chin, and B. L. Chua, "Automatic generation of real time strategy tournament units using differential evolution," in *Proceedings of the IEEE Conference on Sustainable Utilization and Development in Engineering and Technology*, pp. 101–106, October 2011.

[16] C. H. Ng, S. H. Niew, K. O. Chin, and J. Teo, "Infinite mario bross AI using genetic algorithm," in *Proceedings of the IEEE Conference on Sustainable Utilization and Development in Engineering and Technology*, pp. 85–89, October 2011.

[17] J. H. Ong, J. Teo, and K. O. Chin, "Interactive evolutionary programming for mobile games rules generation," in *Proceedings of the IEEE Conference on Sustainable Utilization and Development in Engineering and Technology*, pp. 95–100, Semenyih, Malaysia, October 2011.

[18] A. Fitzgerald and C. B. Congdon, "RAMP: a rule-based agent for Ms. Pac-man," in *Proceedings of the IEEE Congress on Evolutionary Computation (CEC '09)*, pp. 2646–2653, Trondheim, Norway, May 2009.

[19] E. Galván-López, J. M. Swafford, M. O'Neill, and A. Brabazon, "Evolving a Ms. Pacman controller using grammatical evolution," in *Proceedings of the Applications of Evolutionary Computation, EvoApplicatons: EvoCOMPLEX, EvoGAMES, EvoIASP, EvoINTELLIGENCE, EvoNUM, and EvoSTOC*, pp. 161–170, Istanbul, Turkey, April 2010.

[20] D. Robles and S. M. Lucas, "A simple tree search method for playing Ms. Pac-man," in *Proceedings of the IEEE Symposium on Computational Intelligence and Games (CIG '09)*, pp. 249–255, September 2009.

[21] I. Szita and A. Lorincz, "Learning to play using low-complexity rule-based policies: illustrations through Ms. Pac-man," *Journal of Artificial Intelligence Research*, vol. 30, pp. 659–684, 2007.

[22] S. M. Lucas, "Evolving a neural network location evaluator to play Ms. Pac-man," in *Proceedings of the IEEE Symposium on Computational Intelligence and Games*, pp. 203–210, Essex, UK, April 2005.

[23] J. D. Knowles and D. W. Corne, "Approximating the nondominated front using the Pareto Archived Evolution Strategy," *Evolutionary Computation*, vol. 8, no. 2, pp. 149–172, 2000.

[24] L. T. Bui and S. Alam, "An introduction to multi-objective optimization," in *Multi-Objective Optimization in Computational Intelligence: Theory and Practice*, L. T. Bui and S. Alam, Eds., pp. 1–19, IGI Global, Hershey, Pa, USA, 2008.

[25] T. Wong, P. Bigras, and K. Khayati, "Causality assignment using multi-objective evolutionary algorithms," in *Proceedings of the IEEE International Conference on Systems, Man and Cybernetics*, pp. 36–41, October 2002.

[26] D. Svozil, V. Kvasnička, and J. Pospíchal, "Tutorial: introduction to multi-layer feed-forward neural networks," *Chemometrics and Intelligent Laboratory Systems*, vol. 39, no. 1, pp. 43–62, 1997.

[27] T. G. Tan, J. Teo, and P. Anthony, "Comparative investigation of non-linear activation functions in neural controllers for search-based game AI engineering," *Artificial Intelligence Review*, 2011.

3

Development of Embedded CAPTCHA Elements for Bot Prevention in Fischer Random Chess

Ryan McDaniel and Roman V. Yampolskiy

Computer Engineering and Computer Science, University of Louisville, Louisville, KY 40292, USA

Correspondence should be addressed to Ryan McDaniel, rcmcda01@louisville.edu

Academic Editor: Narendra Chaudhari

Cheating in chess can take many forms and has existed almost as long as the game itself. The advent of computers has introduced a new form of cheating into the game. Thanks to the computational power of modern-day computers, a player can use a program to calculate thousands of moves for him or her, and determine the best possible scenario for each move and countermove. These programs are often referred to as "bots," and can even play the game without any user interaction. In this paper, we describe a methodology aimed at preventing bots from participating in online chess games. The proposed approach is based on the integration of a CAPTCHA protocol into a game scenario, and the subsequent inability of bots to accurately track the game states. This is achieved by rotating the images of the individual chess pieces and adjusting their resolution in an attempt to render them unreadable by a bot. Feedback from users during testing shows that there is minimal impact on their ability to play the game. Players rated the difficulty of reading the pieces on a scale of one to ten, with an average rank of 6.5. However, the average number of moves to adjust to the distorted pieces was only 3.75. This tells us that, although it is difficult to read the pieces at first, it is easy to adjust quickly to the new image.

1. Introduction

Chess programs have been designed and implemented on computers since the 1950s. In 1950, Shannon published "Programming a computer for playing chess," in which he presented a chess computer as possible proof of artificial intelligence [1]. At first, these chess programs were created only to test the waters of what computing could do to enhance the game. However, over the years, programs such as Rybka have become very powerful [2]. In 1997, a computer built by IBM, called Deep Blue, even beat then-world champion Garry Kasparov, marking the first time a computer was able to beat a reigning world champion [3]. Some of the chess programs available today include databases of past games and provide numerous ways for players to learn the game and improve their skills. These aspects are certainly positive; however, there are other forms of computer-assisted chess which are not. While cheating in chess can take many forms and has existed almost as long as the game itself, the advent of computers has introduced a new form of cheating

into the game. Robots, or "bots," are computer programs that can read a chessboard and the pieces, determine the best possible move to make, and either recommend the move to a player or make the move for them [4]. These bots are easily accessible and can be very difficult to detect. Chess is not the only game plagued by bots, however. These technology cheats are very common in online games today, from traditional games such as poker and chess, all the way up to complex Massively Multiplayer Online Roleplaying Games (MMORPGs) like Blizzard Entertainment's World of Warcraft [5]. Keeping bots from ruining the game for honest players requires a constant effort, since whenever a game update to eliminate bots is implemented, the bot creators update their bot to circumvent the latest fix [6]. Cheating in online gaming can have far-reaching impact on honest players. For example, online poker is played for money. If someone is cheating with a bot, then they are having a direct impact on the other players by taking money from them [7]. Poker is gambling, however, and whenever money is involved, you can expect dishonesty as well. Chess, on the other hand, has traditionally been about the spirit of the game. Quintessentially, chess is a war campaign, with two players battling it out, planning their short-term and long-term strategies, and utilizing either an offensive or defensive game plan. Inevitably, some plans end in defeat, some in victory, and yet still some end with a draw. In this regard, it is easy to see how one player planning his moves with a computer has a very unfair advantage over the other. The game is not intended to be played this way, so the chess-playing community gets frustrated with cheating players. Unknowingly playing a game of chess against a bot may have varied repercussions. Some players may just brush off the loss, attributing it to a stronger opponent, and trying to learn from it; they may or may not be suspicious that cheating was involved. Others may get so frustrated that they quit playing chess altogether after a few encounters [8]. It is the latter group that makes preventing cheating so very important. Quickly and accurately identifying a bots' presence in an online game is crucial; false positives cannot be tolerated.

2. Related Work

A popular method of ensuring the players involved in a game are, in fact, human players is "Completely Automated Public Turing test to tell Computers and Humans Apart" (CAPTCHA). A typical CAPTCHA test will present the player with distorted text and then require them to type that text into a box in order to continue. A computer program will be unable to read the text and respond correctly, preventing the bot from continuing beyond that point [4].

There are, however, ways to beat a CAPTCHA test. A bug in the CAPTCHA may be exploited to bypass the CAPTCHA test completely, for example, reusing the session ID of an image that is known to have passed the test.

Also, Optical Character Recognition (OCR) software is improving, allowing the bot to "read" the CAPTCHA text. CAPTCHA breaking algorithms have been designed with alarmingly high success rates as high as 70% on some websites [9].

Finally, the bot may present the CAPTCHA to the player as a part of the program. Due to the limitations of a CAPTCHA test, it is not an ideal solution for bot prevention; the test can be easily defeated if it is presented at the beginning of the game, and the test becomes an inconvenience to the player if it is presented during the game [10].

Research on bot detection and prevention in online games has expanded over the past few years, with methodologies ranging from direct impact on the player's game experience, to total transparency, with varying degrees of success. Input devices could be used as a type of hardware-based CAPTCHA; for example, a joystick could be used as a CAPTCHA device, or a specially designed keypad could be used to input a series of characters at certain points during a game. This method would require the output of the device to be authenticated by a game server or console, as well as making the device itself secure to avoid tampering [10]. The cost associated with tamper-proofing devices and the incompatibilities that would exist with legacy hardware limit

FIGURE 1: Embedding CAPTCHA by altering the appearance of a bishop.

the usefulness of this approach. Requiring special hardware and keying in characters on a keypad would have a direct negative impact on the game also, as it draws the players' attention away.

Embedding a CAPTCHA into the game itself is a clever idea (see Figure 1). However, it can be difficult to implement properly. Randomizing certain aspects of the game can make it much more difficult for a bot to participate. Randomization creates a noninteractive CAPTCHA type of test, as the bot will have to analyze options; however, it is not a particularly powerful deterrent since it can be solved. A more formal test could be presented to a player as well, in the form of a simple text-based or image-based CAPTCHA, in order to allow access to various aspects of the game [11]. This type of test would at least force some human interaction, adding only minor disruption to the playing experience, ensuring that a bot cannot operate completely autonomously.

Server-side bot detection is a method that is concealed to users and typically focuses on the behavioral patterns of game clients. For example, the movement pattern of a character can be analyzed for overly repetitious actions to determine whether a bot or a human is in control [5].

Also, input data from devices such as a mouse or keyboard could be analyzed for button-press-length and interval to determine if a bot is controlling a character [6]. Server-side bot detection requires some resources to analyze the data that is collected, however, and could possibly be circumvented by a bot program [12]. Once a bot is removed from the game, the bot creator can easily change the program to avoid the behavior that resulted in detection.

3. Behavior of a Bot

A robot or "bot," for the purposes of this research, can be described as an artificially intelligent program, with either partial or full autonomy, which assists a player in an online game [4]. One must understand how a bot works before one can discuss how to combat it. A typical bot program will go through three basic steps, the first of which is collecting data for the input. The second step is the heart of the program, where the collected data will be used to create a course of action, predicated by the bots' purpose and design. For example, in this step, a poker bot would determine the action a player should take, while a chess bot would determine which piece should be moved. In step three, the bot will output the desired action to the player, or even perform that action for the player, in the case of a fully autonomous bot. Bots commonly collect input data in one of two ways. A chess server may give the location of pieces in a log file, possibly even in real time, making it very easy to gather the information needed for a bot to process the locations and determine a move. If the data is not available via a log file, a second data collection option is called screen scraping [13]. In the case of chess, the bot will compare the images on the board with images in its database. The bot can then essentially know which piece is a king, which is a queen, and so forth. The position of each piece is also easily determined, since the board is an image as well. As a result, the bot can look at the board, identify each piece, and its respective location, and process that information to determine the best move to make.

4. Procedure

Written in C#, the software contains menu, grid, and options elements. The grid consists of sixty-four separate panels, each representing a single space on a chess board. Each 100×100 pixel panel is added to a two-dimensional array, arranged in an 8 panel $\times$ 8 panel square. This layout makes it simple to place a chess board image behind the panels, allowing the panels themselves to contain the chess piece images. While standard functions are used to determine the movability of pieces, it is the resolution, rotation, and randomization which provide additional ammunition to prevent bot play, and protect the players who simply wish to pursue a challenging game of chess against another human opponent.

The algorithm is based on two morphing functions:

Rotate Image Function

   (i) Accepts image data type as argument.

   (ii) Generate random number between −35 and +35.

   (iii) Create new bitmap from image passed in.

   (iv) Create new graphics object from bitmap and rotate.

   (v) Draw image back to bitmap form and return it.

Reduce Resolution Function

   (i) Accepts image and integer data types as arguments.

   (ii) Returns the image to its original resolution if percentage = 0.

   (iii) Pass image to Rotate Image Function.

   (iv) Create a temporary image from the rotated image.

   (v) Create new bitmap from temporary image with new size based on input.

As shown in Figure 2, functions to adjust the resolution and rotation of the chess pieces have been added to the user interface, using a text box on the right-hand side of the form to accept entry of an integer between zero and ninety-nine. Once a valid number is input into the text box and the adjacent "Ok" button is pressed, the resolution of all

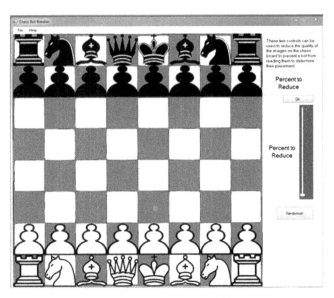

FIGURE 2: Standard chess board layout.

pieces is decreased by the value entered, as a percentage, and a rotation between −35 degrees and +35 degrees is applied to each piece individually. This will result in all pieces having the same resolution reduction, but a different rotation for each piece (see Figure 3).

Track Bar Function

   (i) Track bar minimum is 0, maximum is 5, increments by 1.

   (ii) Generate random number between 5 and 10 and multiply it by track bar value.

   (iii) Pass image and random number to Resolution Reduction Function.

   (iv) Repeat steps 2 and 3 for each image to give every piece a different rotation and reduction.

Below the text box is a track bar that can be used to increment the distortion of the pieces in a slightly different way. The track bar consists of six values, starting with zero at the bottom and incrementing by one to five at the very top notch. The track bar starts at zero by default. When incremented, the track bar value is multiplied by a random number, labeled randNum, between five and ten, and passed on to the resolution reduction function. A new random number is generated for each chess piece, giving a certain amount of randomness to the resolution reduction of each individual piece. Incrementing the track bar increases the value to be multiplied by the random number, somewhat guaranteeing an increase in distortion as the track bar is incremented.

As illustrated in Figure 4, when the "Randomize!" button below the track bar is selected, the program rearranges the back row of both team's pieces according to the rules set forth for Fischer Random Chess. Another function, RandomResolution, is called to distort the images as well.

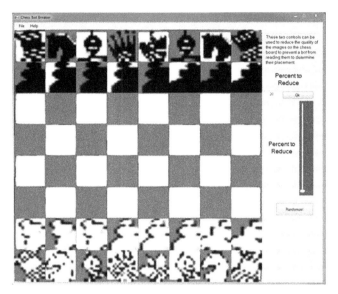

FIGURE 3: Distortion using the text box.

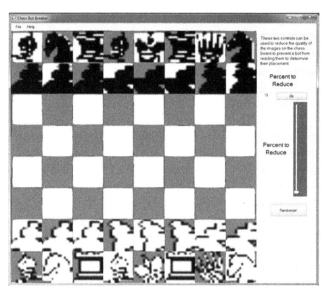

FIGURE 4: Fischer Random Chess.

A random value, between five and thirty percent, is chosen for resolution reduction and applied to every piece on the board. Rotation is again applied to each piece individually. The "Randomize!" button may be pressed as many times as desired; however, once a piece has been moved, the game is officially started and the button is disabled. Distortion of the pieces can still be controlled via the other two methods at any point during the game.

Fischer Random Chess Function

(i) Assign const integers to pieces (example: EMPTY = 0, KING = 1, QUEEN = 2, etc.).

(ii) Create two lists to keep track of empty spaces in the back row, one for odd and one for even spaces.

(iii) Create an array to hold piece positions in the back row.

(iv) Generate a random number between 1 and 6 to place the KING.

(v) Place KING into back row array at index just generated.

(vi) Generate 2 random numbers for placing ROOK. These must be between 0 and KING index, KING index and 7.

(vii) Place ROOK into back row array, 1 at each index just generated.

(viii) Update even and odd lists so no pieces are placed on occupied spaces.

(ix) Generate random number between 0 and even list size.

(x) Place BISHOP into back row array at index just generated.

(xi) Generate random number between 0 and odd list size.

(xii) Place BISHOP into back row array at index just generated.

(xiii) Update odd and even lists.

(xiv) Consolidate odd and even lists into 1 empty spaces list since no remaining pieces have an odd or even requirement.

(xv) Generate random number between 0 and empty spaces list size.

(xvi) Place QUEEN into back row array at index just generated.

(xvii) Update empty spaces list.

(xviii) Place KNIGHT into back row array at last 2 remaining indices.

5. Results

Each user filled out a feedback form during testing, as seen in Table 1, and the results were consistent. The form was used to collect some background information from 11 players to get an idea of their skill level at chess and determine how long it took them to adjust to the distorted pieces. Adjusting to the altered appearance of the pieces took most users a few seconds regardless of their skill level; after an average of four moves, none of the players had any trouble differentiating between pieces. Very few mistakes were made by the players. Some users did mention that additional changes could be implemented to make distinguishing pieces easier. For example, a letter representing the piece could be added to the image in a distorted way as well.

Humans are much better than computers at identifying patterns in an image [14]. Most modern text-based CAPTCHAs rely on letters which have been distorted. Therefore, distorting and rotating an image should prove very difficult for a bot to recognize. Including additional distortion effects will increase the difficulty of programming

TABLE 1: Feedback form embedded non-interactive CAPTCHA for Fischer Random Chess. Adjust the distortion to desired level. Try playing the game for at least 5–10 minutes. Feedback form used to gather information about the difficulty of the CAPTCHA tests.

What level of distortion was applied? (e.g., 17% or trackbar tick number 2)			
Your gender	☐ Male	☐ Female	
Your age			
Chess skill (beginner, intermediate, advanced)	☐ Beginner	☐ Intermediate	☐ Advanced
How many times have you played online chess?	☐ 0	☐ <10	☐ >10
How recently have you played online chess?	☐ Less than a month ago	☐ 1–6 months ago	☐ >6 months ago
On a scale of 1–10, with 10 being very difficult, how difficult was it to recognize pieces after distortion?			
Approximately how long did it take to get used to the look of the distorted pieces?	☐ Less than 3 moves	☐ 4–7 moves	☐ >8 moves
Have you ever played Fischer Random Chess?	☐ Yes	☐ No	
Comments			

a bot to read the pieces. For example, a skewing function would further help to prevent recognition. Adding background noise to each individual image would also provide more distortion for a bot to overcome, as well as changing the size of each piece slightly.

However, there are weaknesses to this approach to bot prevention. If there is only one available set of images for the chess pieces, then a bot simply has to compare the known images to distorted ones and make a guess based on similarity. This method could be fairly accurate, so it would be important to include multiple sets of images that can be used. Tracking piece movements could also give a bot clues as to what the pieces are; the bot may be fooled at the start, but as the game progresses, the movement trail left by the opponent may allow the bot to identify the pieces and resume control of the board.

The feedback, gathered from players with skill levels ranging from beginner to advanced, is promising. Players rated the difficulty of reading the pieces on a scale of one to ten, with an average rank of 6.5. However, the average number of moves to adjust to the distorted pieces was only 3.75, indicating that although this approach has a direct impact on the game experience, the user's ability to play the game is not hindered. The relatively high level of difficulty to read the pieces can be seen as a good indicator that a bot will have a hard time determining what the pieces are as well. The low number of moves to adjust to the distortion is a good sign that the player's experience will not be affected a great deal.

6. Conclusion

The program is designed to prevent a bot's ability to read a chess board, which renders the bot harmless and unable to suggest or make moves for the opposing player. This is accomplished by altering the visual aspects of the chess pieces on the board via user-controlled changes in resolution and/or rotation of the pieces; this skewing makes the pieces unrecognizable by a bot, while allowing human players to identify the pieces. With the added ability to play the game using the rules of Fischer Random Chess, a bot's inability to read the piece positions would prevent unfair advantages.

Additional research into bot prevention is clearly needed. One path may be further altering the area of CAPTCHA tests. For example, added altering of visual elements—such as skewing or stretching—could be tested. Other user-interface changes could include multiple image sets for swapping. These options continually evolve as standard CAPTCHA research moves forward. Additionally, although distorted audio or program-initiated questioning are alternatives to standard CAPTCHA tests, those methods could not be used with chess pieces. However, some of these methods are very creative; it is possible future research could find a way to incorporate an alternative method into the game of chess.

Breaking down a CAPTCHA is not always considered a total loss, as there are some positives that arise from it. For one, a weakness in the CAPTCHA has to be exposed, which can be fixed to strengthen the test in future revisions. Also, it is important to note that programming a bot to break a CAPTCHA test can be considered an advancement in Artificial Intelligence, as a bot has to try to emulate how a human would think in order to pass the test. This kind of competition is very important for promoting advancement in the fields of both artificial intelligence and security.

References

[1] C. E. Shannon, "Programming a computer for playing chess," *Philosophical Magazine*, 1950.

[2] Rybka, for the serious chess player, http://rybkachess.com/.

[3] IBM Research, Deep Blue. 1997, http://www.research.ibm.com/deepblue.

[4] R. V. Yampolskiy and V. Govindaraju, "Embedded noninteractive continuous bot detection," *Computers in Entertainment*, vol. 5, no. 4, article no. 7, 2008.

[5] S. Mitterhofer, C. Kruegel, E. Kirda, and C. Platzer, "Server-side bot detection in massively multiplayer online games," *IEEE Security and Privacy*, vol. 7, no. 3, pp. 29–36, 2009.

[6] S. Gianvecchio, Z. Wu, M. Xie, and H. Wang, "Battle of Botcraft: Fighting bots in online games with human observational proofs," in *Proceedings of the 16th ACM Conference on Computer and Communications Security (CCS '09)*, pp. 256–268, November 2009.

[7] D. Kushner, "On the Internet, nobody knows you're a Bot," *Wired Magazine*, p. 13, 2005.

[8] Ethical cheating in online chess. 2007, http://amirbagheri.virtuaboard.com/t34-ethical-cheating-in-online-chess.

[9] E. Bursztein, M. Matthieu, and J. Mitchell, "Text-based CAPTCHA strengths and weaknesses," in *ACM Computer and Communicatino Security*, Chicago, Ill, USA, 2011.

[10] P. Golle and N. Ducheneaut, "Preventing Bots from playing online games," *ACM Computers in Entertainment*, vol. 3, no. 3, 2005.

[11] D. Bushell, "In search of the perfect CAPTCHA," *Smashing Magazine*, 2011.

[12] D. Bethea, R. Cochran, and M. Reite, "Server-Side verification of client behavior in online games," in *Proceedings of the 17th Annual Network and Distributed System Security Symposium of the Internet Society*, San Diego, Calif, USA, 2010.

[13] J. Devlin, "How I built a working poker Bot," Part 1. 2008, http://www.codingthewheel.com/archives/how-i-built-a-working-poker-bot.

[14] J. Strickland, "How CAPTCHA works," 2011, http://computer.howstuffworks.com/captcha.htm/printable.

4

Comparison of Learning Software Architecture by Developing Social Applications versus Games on the Android Platform

Bian Wu and Alf Inge Wang

Department of Computer Science, Norwegian University of Science and Technology, 7491 Trondheim, Norway

Correspondence should be addressed to Bian Wu, bian@idi.ntnu.no

Academic Editor: Daniel Thalmann

This paper describes an empirical study where the focus was on discovering differences and similarities in students working on development of social applications versus students working on development of games using the same Android development platform. In 2010-2011, students attending the software architecture course at the Norwegian University of Science and Technology (NTNU) could choose between four types of projects. Independently of the chosen type of project, all students had to go through the same phases, produce the same documents based on the same templates, and follow exactly the same process. This study focuses on one of projects—Android project, to see how much the application domain affects the course project independently of the chosen technology. Our results revealed some positive effects for the students doing game development compared to social application development to learn software architecture, like motivated to work with games, a better focus on quality attributes such as modifiability and testability during the development, production of software architectures of higher complexity, and more productive coding working for the project. However, we did not find significant differences in awarded grade between students choosing the two different domains.

1. Introduction

Computer games and video games have become very popular for children and youths and play a prominent role in the culture of young people [1]. Games can now be played everywhere in technology-rich environments equipped with laptops, smart phones, game consoles (mobile and stationary), set-top boxes, and other digital devices. From this phenomenon, it is believed that the intrinsic motivation that young people show towards games could be combined with educational content and objectives into what Prensky calls "digital game based learning" [2].

Besides an abundant appearance of games in young students life, game development technology has matured and become more advanced [3]. Based on various existing game development environments, the whole duty of game development process can be divided into several expert domains and roles such as game programmer, 3D model creator, game designer, musician, animator, and play writer, and so forth. The process of integrating game content with technology

can be simplified through the usage of game engines and available information on the web from various user and expert communities. For instance, Microsoft's XNA game development kit provides the game loop function to draw and update the game contents, and it also provides convenient game development components to load the different format of graphics, audio, and videos. This makes it possible for game fans such as students with or without programming background to modify existing games or develop new games. They can design and implement their own game concepts with these game creation tools, learn the developing skills and relevant knowledge, and accumulate related practical experience.

In this context, not only can games be used for learning but also the game development tools can be used for studying relevant topics within computer science (CS), software engineering (SE), and game programming through motivating assignments. Generally, games can be integrated in education in three ways [4, 5]. First, games can be used instead of traditional exercises motivating students to put extra effort in doing the exercises and giving the teacher and/or teaching assistants an opportunity to monitor how the students work with the exercises in real time, for example [6, 7]. Second, games can be played as a part of a lecture to improve the participation and motivation of students, for example [8, 9]. Third, the students are asked to modify or develop a game as a part of a course using a Game Development Framework (GDF) to learn skills within CS and SE, for example [10]. We label the latter learning approach Game Development-Based Learning (GDBL). And the GDF denotes the toolkits that can be used to develop or modify games, for example, game engine, game editors, or game (simulation) platforms, or even any Integrated Development Environment (IDE), like Visual C++, Eclipse, J2ME, and Android SDK since all of them can be used to develop games.

This paper focuses on an evaluation where we wanted to discover similarities and differences between making students learn software architecture through game development versus social application development (e.g., weather Forecast, chatting software) using the Android platform. The motivation for bringing game development into a CS or SE course is to exploit the students' fascination for games and game development to stimulate them to work more and better with course material through the project.

2. Related Works

This section describes the research context and previous results about using GDBL method in software engineering field.

2.1. Research Contexts. The earliest similar application of learning by programming in a game-like environment was in early 1970s. The Logo [11], the turtle graphics, is one of the oldest libraries that was used to introduce computing concepts to beginners. The concept was based on a "turtle" that could be moved across a 2D screen with a pen, which could be positioned on or off the screen, and, thus, may leave a trace of the turtle's movements. Programming the turtle to draw different patterns could be used to introduce general computing skill, such as procedural operations, iteration, and recursion. Further, in 1987, Micco presented the usage of writing a tic-tac-toe game for learning [12]. Afterwards, other studies have been conducted using specialist game programming toolkits such as Stage Cast Creator [13], Gamemaker [14], Alice [15], and Neverwinter Nights [16]. Besides, article [17] presents an investigation for using mobile game development as a motivational tool and a learning context in computing curriculum. From their survey, it shows the relation between game programming and other computer science fields—Game development can be used in study of Artificial intelligence (AI), database, computer networks, SE, human-computer interaction, computer graphics, algorithms, programming, computer architecture, and operating system.

These studies indicate that making games is motivating and develops storytelling as well as technical programming skills. The nature of the task of making games is slightly different in purpose-built environments and the balance of

the roles assumed by the learner shifts accordingly. More recent game programming toolkits tend to have a stronger visual aspect than Logo, either in the sense that they enable designers to easily create graphical games or because they have a visual programming language, or both. This shifts the emphasis away from low-level programming, enabling learners to focus on the other roles as designers or writers. Thus, we investigate how GDFs are used in education through an experiment study and explore the evolution of the traditional lecture to be dynamic, collaborative, and attractive to the students under current technology-rich environment. However, this assertion needs to be further supported by relevant theory, application experiences, evaluation results, and empirical evidence. This is one motivation for sharing our experiences and empirical results in field of GDBL on using Android in a software architecture course.

2.2. Course and Project Setting. The software architecture course at Norwegian University of Science and Technology (NTNU) (course code TDT4240) is taught in a different way than at most other universities, as the students also have to implement their designed architecture in a project. The motivation for doing so is to make the students understand the relationship between the architecture and the implementation and to be able to perform a real evaluation of whether the architecture and the resulting implementation fulfill the quality requirements specified for the application. The architecture project in the course has similarities with projects in other software engineering courses, but everything in the project is carried out from a software architecture perspective. Throughout the project, the students have to use software architecture techniques, methods, and tools to succeed according to the specified project.

The software architecture project consists of the following phases.

(i) COTS (Commercial Off-the-Shelf) exercise: learn the technology to be used through developing a simple game.

(ii) Design pattern: learn how to use and apply design pattern by making changes in an existing system.

(iii) Requirements and architecture: list functional and quality requirements and design the software architecture for a game.

(iv) Architecture evaluation: use the Architecture Trade-off Analysis Method (ATAM) [18–20] evaluation method to evaluate the software architecture of project in regards to the quality requirements.

(v) Implementation: do a detailed design and implement the game based on the created architecture and on the changes from the evaluation.

(vi) Project evaluation: evaluate the project as a whole using a Postmortem Analysis (PMA) method [21].

In the first two phases of the project, the students work on their own or in pairs. For phases 3–6, the students work in self-selected teams of 4-5 students. Meantime, students have one fixed primary assigned quality attribute to focus on during the project. For the secondary quality attribute, students can choose the quality attribute they like. The students spend most time in the implementation phase (six weeks), and they are also encouraged to start the implementation in earlier phases to test their architectural choices (incremental development). During the implementation phase, the students continually extend, refine, and evolve the software architecture through several iterations.

2.3. Previous Results. Previously, the goal of the project has been to develop a robot controller for the WSU Khepera robot simulator (Robot) in Java [22] with emphasis on an assigned quality attribute such as availability, performance, modifiability, or testability. The students were asked to program the robot controller to move a robot around in a maze, collect four balls, and bring them to a light source in the maze. In 2008, the students were allowed to choose between a robot controller project and a game development project. The process, the deliverables, and the evaluation of the project were the same for both types of projects—only the domain was different. In the Game project, the students were asked to develop a game using the Microsoft XNA framework and C#. Finally, an evaluation about software architecture course is conducted [23, 24]. The evaluation is based on data from a project survey, the project deliverables from the students, and other accessible course information. The main conclusion from study was that game development projects can successfully be used to teach software architecture if we consider Robot as an evaluation benchmark.

Integrating our experiences on running of game project in software architecture course in 2008, we conducted a new option to add one more COTS-Android in software architecture course project during 2010-2011. The students could now in addition to the Java Robot project and the XNA Game project choose to develop a social application or a game in Android. Independently of the COTS and the domain chosen, the students had to focus on the same software architecture issues during the project and follow the same templates. The introduction of game and social Android projects allowed us to compare how the domain the students work on in the project affects the learning and the project experiences independently of the COTS. A detailed description was in following sections.

3. Method

This section describes the research method to get the relevant data for our experiment of using Android development in software architecture projects.

3.1. Aim. This paper focuses on using the same COTS but with different development domains to investigate whether the different domains produce different output. In our previous research, the effectiveness of GDBL conclusion was based on the different COTS-Robot and XNA. This paper excludes game developed in XNA and robot controller developed in Java and only focuses on the Android platform and development of social application versus game application. Our evaluation covers five topics: distribution of chosen domain, students' perception of the project, project deliveries and code quality and complexity, students' effort, and awarded project grades.

3.2. GQM Approach. The comparison of the social and game project should help to discover the differences and reveal the effects of introducing a project on the Android platform. This evaluation is a quasiexperiment, not a controlled experiment. The research method used is based on the Goal, Question Metrics (GQM) approach [25] where we first define a research goal (conceptual level), then define a set of research questions (operational level), and finally describe a set of metrics to answer the defined research questions (quantitative level). In our case, the metrics used to give answers to the research questions are a mixture of quantitative and qualitative data. Table 1 shows the GQM approach used to analyze game development project in software architecture course.

3.3. Procedures. When students start the project and follow the projects phases, they should report the time they spend on each phase of the project. The first two phases allow the students individually or in pairs to get familiar with the COTS and architectural and design patterns. The main work of the project is carried out in the phases 3–5 and includes requirement specification, architectural design, architectural evaluation, implementation, and testing. The students produce a delivery for each phase, which is evaluated by the course staff, and feedback is given to improve before the final delivery. At the end of phase 5, the students will produce a final delivery, which is evaluated and graded by the course staff. After completing phase 5, the students have to answer a questionnaire that focuses on how the students perceive the project. In phases 6, the students must carry out a postmortem analysis of their project as a whole to reflect on their successes and their challenges.

4. Results

In 2010 and 2011, the students could choose to do the project using three COTS: Robot (Java), XNA (C#), and Android (Java). The students' selection of COTS is shown in Figure 1, where 36 students chose Khepera robot (19%), 55 students chose XNA (27%), and 102 students (54%) chose Android. Of the students that chose Android, 58 students (57%) chose social application versus 44 students (43%) game. If we look at the domains the students chose we see that 51% chose game development, 30% chose social applications, and 19% chose robot controller.

The statistics of Figure 1 clearly reveal that the majority of students prefer game development compared to other domains. And Android is the most popular COTS by far, and we believe this is due to its openness for developers, development in Java, attractive devices, innovative features and development, and a new way of sharing developed applications through Android marked.

In the first phase of the project, the students were asked to fill in a questionnaire on the reasons to choose the COTS and

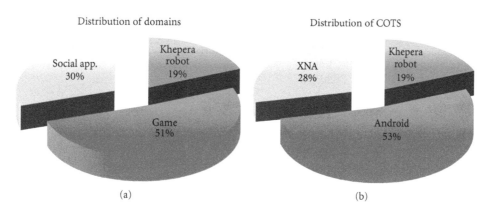

FIGURE 1: Distribution of selection of type of software architecture projects.

TABLE 1: GQM table.

Goal	Analyze	Software development project		
	For the purpose of	Comparing social application versus game application domain on same COTS		
	With respect to	Difference and effectiveness of two domains of the projects		
	From the point of view of	Researcher and educator		
	In context of	Students in software architecture course		
Questions	Q1: Are there any differences in how the students perceive the project for students choosing an Android game project versus students choosing an Android social project?	Q2: Are there any differences in the software architectures designed by students doing an Android game project versus students doing an Android social project?	Q3: Are there any differences in the implementation effort in the project by students doing an Android game project versus students doing an Android social project?	Q4: Are there any differences in the performance of students doing an Android game project versus students doing an Android social project?
Metric	M1: Number of students choosing game project versus social project.	M3: Project reports	M4: Source code files	M6: Project score
	M2: Questionnaire survey with 5-Level Likert Scale: Strong disagree (1), Disagree (2), Neutral (3), Agree (4), Strong Agree (5)		M5: Time spent	

domain. The top reasons list was: (1) programming reason (familiar with Java or C#) (70.7%), (2) to learn about the COTS (Robot, XNA, Android) (59.5%), (3) games motivation or amusement reasons (40.1%), (4) social application motivation (39.5%), (5) to learn about the domain (robot, game, social) (34.2%), (6) hardware motivation, running games on Android phone, Zuneplayer (33%), and (7) make games for Android Market or XNA club (24.5%). From above data, we found that the game domain has advantages in drawing students' attention and its attractive peripherals, like hardware or software markets, and so does android social domain. This was not the case for the Robot domain.

The following subsections focus on the analysis of whether the domain game versus social causes any significant different output in the following four aspects: (1) students perception of the project, (2) the design complexity of software architectures, (3) students' implementation effort in the project, and (4) students' score in projects.

4.1. Differences in How Students Perceived the Project. A project survey was conducted one week after the students completed their software architecture project. The goal of this survey was to reveal possible differences in the students' perception of the project between teams working with social projects versus teams working with game projects on the same COTS—the Android platform. Statements in the survey made the students reflect on how the project helped them to learn software architecture.

The hypothesis defined for this survey was the following.

H_0: There is no difference in how students doing game project and social project on the same COTS-Android perceive the software architecture project.

To test hypothesis we used Kruskal-Wallis Test [26] since it is a nonparametric method for testing equality of population medians among groups [24]. This test is usually for (1) users cannot assume a normal population and (2) the

TABLE 2: Wilcoxon Test of the statements PS1-PS11.

Statement	COTS	Average	Median	Standard deviation	P
PS1: I found it difficult to evaluate the other group's architecture in the ATAM?	Game	3.45	4	1.06	0.178
	Social	3.77	4	0.91	
PS2: I found it difficult to focus on our assigned quality attributes	Game	3.05	3	1.09	**0.024**
	Social	3.57	4	0.85	
PS3: I found it easy to integrate known architectural or design patterns	Game	3.21	3	0.93	0.332
	Social	2.94	3	1.03	
PS4: I spent more time on technical matters than on architectural matters	Game	3.71	4	1.20	0.175
	Social	4.06	4	1.03	
PS5: I have learned a lot about software architecture during the project	Game	3.50	4	0.86	0.552
	Social	3.31	4	0.99	
PS6: I would have chosen another project if I could go back in time	Game	1.13	1	0.34	0.289
	Social	1.20	1	0.41	

sample sizes of the two groups are different. Table 2 shows the results of Kruskal-Wallis Test on the statements PS1–PS6. 38 of 44 game project students replied while 35 out of 58 social project students replied the questionnaire. Each item in the questionnaire is responded to by assigning a scale value from 1 to 5, where 1 indicates strong disagreement and 5 indicates strong agreement.

From the test results, the lowest significant difference ($P \le 0.05$) in questionnaire's response is PS2 ($P = 0.024$). We conclude that the Android game and Android social have significant difference on the students perceiving the difficulty to focus on the assigned quality attributes in the project. The median of Likert scale score is 3 for android game, but 4 for android social. It indicates that android game project students were neutral on this PS5, but social project students have a tendency on the agreement of PS5. One possible explanation is that quality attribute, like termsmodifiability or testability linked to a game concept, is easier to imagine and catch the students' attention to look into it. But social applications may have more fixed impression in students' life and cause less deep effect than games to motivate students to think. Others statement have no significant difference from students perception.

Further, even there is no significant difference for the two other low P values, the average value of PS1 and PS4 still indicates that students from game project found it less difficult to evaluate the other group's architecture in the ATAM and spent less time on technical matters than the students from social projects. In addition, PS6: the students had to answer whether they would have chosen another project if they could go back in time. Figure 2 shows more detailed statistics for it.

Figure 2 shows that there is a higher percentage of the social project students that would have chosen another project (20%) compared to the game project students (13%).

As an overall, the survey reveals one significant difference that students from game projects have a better focus on quality attributes. Statements got low P values (P1, P2, P4) that revealed the tendency that game teams receive more positive feedback than the social teams on how they perceived the project.

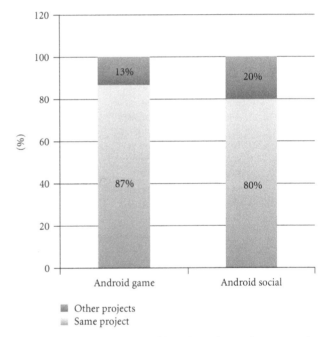

FIGURE 2: Reponses to PS6: would you have chosen the same project if you could go back in time.

4.2. Differences in the Design of Software Architecture. It is difficult to evaluate software architectures empirically, but we have chosen to do so by comparing the number of design patterns the students used, the number of main modules/classes identified in the logical view of the software architecture, and the number of hierarchical levels in the architecture. We admit that that there are many sources of errors in this comparison, as the two domains are so different. However, the emphasis in this course is on using software design patterns and presenting the different views of the software architecture in sufficient detail with emphasis on the logical view. The empirical data should highlight the differences between the two types of projects if any. The empirical data has been collected by reading through and analyzing the final project reports from 12 game project teams and 16 social project teams.

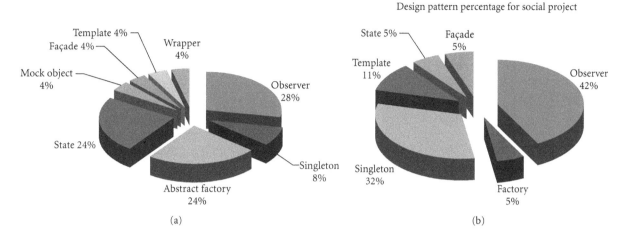

FIGURE 3: Distribution of usage of design patterns for game and social projects.

TABLE 3: Number of design patterns used.

		Average	Standard deviation	Max	Min
Design Patterns	Game	2.67	1.92	7	1
	Social	1.56	0.73	3	1

4.2.1. Use of Design Patterns. Table 3 presents the descriptive statistics of the number of architectural and design patterns used in the Social and the Game projects. The results in Table 3 indicate that there are some differences in how patterns are used in the two types of projects.

Table 4 presents Kruskal-Wallis Test results and shows that there are no statistically significant differences in the number of design patterns produced by the two different project types.

Table 4 indicates no statistically significant difference for the number of design pattern used for the two types of projects. From reading through the projects reports, Figure 3 presents the distribution of design patterns used by social teams and by game teams. The charts show that the Observer was the most popular for both types of project. Further, the Abstract Factory and State pattern was among the top three for Game teams, singleton and template pattern was among the top three for social teams. The Game projects had more diversity in applying architecture and design patterns than social project. For instance, game projects used eight design patterns compared to six design patterns in social projects as shown in Figure 3.

Even there is no significant difference, but the low P value is close to 0.1. The median in Table 4 implies that game teams used more design patterns in their projects, it may cause that game projects used more types of patterns than social projects in an overall statistics shown in Figure 3.

4.2.2. Software Architecture Complexity. Two metrics were chosen to indicate the complexity of the software architecture [24]: (1) the number of main modules or main classes described in the logical view of the software architecture and (2) the number of hierarchical levels in the model presented in the logical view of the software architecture. The reason the logical view was chosen for computing complexity is that the logical view is the main one that gives the best overview of the designed architecture. Table 5 lists the measurements of the number of main modules/classes and the number of hierarchical levels in the logical view of the software architecture for social and game projects.

Table 5 shows that the game project teams on average have almost four more main modules/classes (28%) than the social teams, and the standard deviation is lower. Further, the number of levels in the architecture in game projects can be decomposed into almost twice as many levels compared to social projects.

Table 6 gives the results from Kruskal-Wallis Test on a number of main modules/classes and numbers of levels in the architecture. Both of the tests give low P values ($P < 0.05$). Specifically, the tests show that there is statistically significant difference on the number of main classes and levels in architecture. From this result, it implies game project has more complexity in architecture levels than social projects; it may be due to the fact that they used more patterns to implement their game projects that cause this difference.

4.3. Differences in the Effort Put into the Project. To evaluate the effort of each project that students put into it, two indicators are used as the measurement criteria: (1) time spent on the project and (2) structure and size of project files and number of lines of code.

4.3.1. Time Spent. We have asked students to estimate on how many hours the project teams worked in the software

TABLE 4: Hypothesis tests on number of design patterns used.

Hypothesis	COTS	N	Median	P
No difference in number of used design patterns	Game	12	2	0.111
	Social	16	1	

TABLE 5: Measurement of software architecture complexity.

	Numbers of main modules/classes		Number of levels in architecture	
	Game	Social	Game	Social
Average	14	9.7	3	1.75
Standard deviation	4.9	6.6	0.6	0.77
Max	21	28	4	3
Min	7	3	2	1

TABLE 6: Hypothesis tests on architectural complexity.

Hypothesis	COTS	N	Median	P
No difference in number of main modules/classes	Game	12	14	0.021
	Social	16	7	
No difference in number of levels in architecture	Game	12	3	0.000
	Social	16	2	

TABLE 7: Time spent on the project for each team.

Time per team (hours)	Game	Social
Average	334	338
Standard deviation	133.7	114.7
Max	520	535
Min	110	183

architecture project during the phases 3–5 (core phases of the project). Table 7 shows the estimated number of hours given by each team.

Based on each team's time effort, we ran the Kruskal-Wallis Test on the difference on hours spending in the project for each team.

From previous results, there is no statistically significant difference on time spent on the project for game teams and social teams. On contrary, the time spending distribution in both projects is quite similar.

4.3.2. Project Analysis. Further, we chose to look at metrics from the implementation to give an estimate on how much was produced during the project. It can give a good indication of the complexity of the software architecture and the resulting implementation of the application [24]. Since both types of teams used Android and the domains are comparable in terms of complexity, we expected to find difference in productivity. During the development process, they were free to use online resource or other open source libraries for Android to save coding time for the software architecture design.

The following metrics were chosen to compute the effort of the student teams: (1) number of source Files (NoF); (2)

number of comments in code (NoC); (3) lines of source code not counting empty lines or comments (LoC).

Table 9 presents a comparison of the implementation metrics for the game projects and social projects, only java code files to be counted in the table, and the external library code files and resource files are excluded.

Table 10 shows the results from Kruskal-Wallis Test on the difference in the number of files and the number of lines of code produced by the two different types of project.

The results from the Kruskal-Wallis Test indicate that there is no statistically significant difference in LoC between the two types of project. But the low P value is close to 0.1. The average value from Table 9 indicates game teams put more effort on the implementation, like coding, making comments, structure codes into more files during the project.

From the Tables 7, 8, 9, and 10, we can find the game project teams have produced on average almost one third as much code (133% more) in similar time spending (334 versus 338). It implies that game project teams are more productive to put effort in coding, comments to construct a complex game software architecture in similar time spending than social project teams.

4.4. Difference in the Project Grades. The project score is between 0 and 30 points and takes 30% of the final grade. The project grades intervals are classified as: A: score $\geq 90\%$; B: score $\geq 80\%$ and score $<90\%$; C: score $\geq 60\%$ and score $<80\%$; D: score $\geq 50\%$ and score $<60\%$; E: score $\geq 40\%$ and score $<50\%$; F: score $<40\%$ (fail).

In order to investigate if there were any differences in how the group scored (0–30 points) on the project for students that has chosen game and social projects on Android, the Kruskal-Wallis Test was used to test this hypothesis, as we cannot assume a normal population and the sample size of

TABLE 8: Hypothesis on hours spending.

Hypothesis	COTS	N	Median	P
No difference in time spending for each team	Game	12	362	
	Social	16	334	0.889

TABLE 9: Implementation metrics from the architecture projects.

	NoF		NoC		LoC	
	Game	Social	Game	Social	Game	Social
Average	37	24	1016	536	2585	1949
Standard deviation	13	13	807	755	1172	1368
Max	54	45	2571	2886	4173	5082
Min	15	5	206	37	844	390

TABLE 10: Hypothesis tests on project implementation codes.

Hypothesis		N	Median	P
No difference in number of lines of code	Game	12	2672	
	Social	16	1523	0.114

the two groups is different. Table 11 presents the results of the Kruskal-Wallis Test on the difference in project grades for each game and social student.

There is no significant difference in the project score using same COTS for development. We run the social project in 2010 and game project in 2011 separately. The project implementation requirements and templates are keeping the same from phase 3 to 6 in two years, and evaluation process and persons are the same; we can identify that students accomplished both projects under the same conditions. It reflects the difficulty could be similar. So, we only make a conclusion on the project score has no significant difference. In order to get an overview of the scores, Figure 4 gives the distribution of grades on the project for the two types of projects (game versus social).

5. Validity Threats

We now turn to what are considered to be the most important threats to the validity of this evaluation.

5.1. Internal Validity. The internal validity of an experiment concerns "the validity of inferences about whether observed covariation between A (the presumed treatment) and B (the presumed outcome) reflects a causal relationship from A to B as those variables were manipulated or measured" [27]. If changes in B have causes other than the manipulation of A, there is a threat to internal validity.

There are two main internal validity threats to this evaluation. The first internal threat is that the sample of two groups used in the evaluation is not randomized. The students were allowed to choose either an Android game or an Android social project. We do not believe that one specific type of student chose one project over the other, thus harming the evaluation results. The second internal

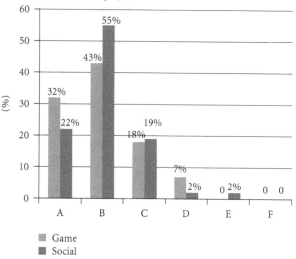

FIGURE 4: Grades distribution on project.

threat is if there were any differences, how the students had to perform the project independently of the domain chosen. Independently of doing a social or a game project, the students had to go through exactly the same phases in the project and deliver exactly the same documents based on the same document templates in both 2010 and 2011. We have identified one difference in how the two types of projects were carried out. The 1-2 phases of the project phase were different for the game and social projects students. These two phases are not a part of inclusive data and material used to evaluate the project. We do not believe that these differences have had any major impact in the way the students did or performed in their projects since it is the preparation phases, that we noticed and excluded of them.

TABLE 11: Kruskal-Wallis Test on different in project score.

Hypothesis	COTS	N	Median	P
No difference in project score groups get from doing Game versus Social project	Game	44	26	0.997
	Social	58	26	

5.2. Construct Validity. Construct validity concerns the degree to which inferences are warranted, from (1) the observed persons, settings, and cause- and effect-operations included in a study to (2) the constructs that these instances might represent. The question, therefore, is whether the sampling particulars of a study can be defended as measures of general constructs [27].

In the evaluation of using Android project in a software architecture course our research goal was to investigate the difference and similarity of game project and social project on Android platform. The GQM approach was chosen to detail this goal into four research questions with supporting metrics. In order to give answers to these four research questions the data sources and metrics available from our software architecture course were chosen. It cannot be claimed that the selected data sources and metrics in our evaluation give evidence for all the conclusions, but they are all strong indicators contributing to a picture that describes the differences between the two project types. Through the evaluation we have used various methods for comparing the results. The choice of methods is based on the best way of describing and visualizing the differences between the two groups using the available data.

5.3. External Validity. The issue of external validity concerns whether a causal relationship holds (1) for variations in persons, settings, treatments, and outcomes that were in the experiment and (2) for persons, settings, treatments, and outcomes that were not in the experiment [27].

The results reported in this paper are most relevant for other teachers thinking of introducing game projects as a part of their software architecture course. Further, the results are also relevant for teachers that want to introduce game projects in SE and CS courses, as many of these courses have similar characteristics. A limitation of this study is that the subjects in the evaluation are CS or SE students who have completed their first three years. It is not evident that the results are valid for students without any or less than three-year background in CS or SE.

6. Conclusions

Based on our previous experiment of using XNA and current experiment of using Android in software architecture, we found game motivation and surrounding interesting peripherals are one of the most attractive factors. Besides the introduction of a new COTS-Android in a software architecture course, the goal of this paper is to identify the difference output of same COTS and get evaluation result to answer the four research questions.

The first research question asked is if there are any differences in how students choosing Android game versus Android social projects perceived the software architecture project (RQ1). The statistically significant finding is that social project students found it more difficult to focus on the assigned quality attributes than game project ($P = 0.024$). Other data from lower P value also reflect that game teams have more positive attitudes towards project requirements than the social team. In addition, the results show that 20% of the students doing an Android social project would have chosen the other projects if they had to do the project again, which is more than the android game project students.

The second research question asked is if there are any differences in how students choosing Android game versus social projects designed their software architectures (RQ2). Even the analysis of the project reports concludes that no significant difference on the used design patterns, but the low P value close to 0.1 reveals that game teams applied more diverse patterns in their projects than social team. Further, the statistically significant difference shows that the software architectures produced in game projects were on average more complex than the architectures produced in social projects ($P < 0.05$).

The third research question asked is if there were any differences in the effort the students put into the project when they worked with an Android game or an Android social project (RQ3). The results show that in similar time spending, teams working with game projects produced on average almost 133% as much code as teams working with Android social projects, and game project students had customs to make twice detailed comments on the codes and organized codes into more files than social projects students.

The fourth and final research question asked is if there are any differences in the performance of students doing a Game project versus students doing a Social project (RQ4). The comparison of the two types of projects showed that there was no statistically significant difference in the project.

According to the previous conclusion and compared with previous research on XNA and Robot project used in software architecture course [24], we found that there exist quite similar conclusions for both game domain (XNA and Android game) in respect to (1) stable popularity of game domain; (2) better perception of project from students aspect (3) more design patterns used and high complexity of software architecture (4) same output in project score as social project.

Referring to Android COTS specifically, the main differences from Android game projects could be used as an interesting and effective tool in software architecture teaching aspect to motivate students on design of complex architecture with applying more patterns and more productive coding work than Android social projects. Further, compared to XNA and Robot simulator, Android is an attractive platform to the students from the students' survey, that encourages us to conduct more practices on improvement of using Android as a development tool in software engineering practices and inspires us the possibility to bring more choices, like iPhone SDK into COTS domains.

References

[1] S. M. Dorman, "Video and computer games: effect on children and implications for health education," *Journal of School Health*, vol. 67, no. 4, pp. 133–138, 1997.

[2] M. Prensky, "Digital game-based learning," *Computers in Entertainment*, vol. 1, pp. 21–24, 2003.

[3] J. Blow, "Game development: harder than you think," *Queue*, vol. 1, pp. 28–37, 2004.

[4] K. Sung, C. Hillyard, R. L. Angotti, M. W. Panitz, D. S. Goldstein, and J. Nordlinger, "Game-Themed Programming Assignment Modules: a pathway for gradual integration of gaming context into existing introductory Programming Courses," *IEEE Transactions on Education*, vol. 54, no. 3, pp. 416–427, 2010.

[5] A. I. Wang and B. Wu, "An application of a game development framework in higher education," *International Journal of Computer Games Technology*, vol. 2009, no. 1, Article ID 693267, 12 pages, 2009.

[6] B. A. Foss and T. I. Eikaas, "Game play in engineering education—concept and experimental results," *International Journal of Engineering Education*, vol. 22, no. 5, pp. 1043–1052, 2006.

[7] G. Sindre, L. Natvig, and M. Jahre, "Experimental validation of the learning effect for a pedagogical game on computer fundamentals," *IEEE Transactions on Education*, vol. 52, no. 1, pp. 10–18, 2009.

[8] A. I. Wang, "An evaluation of a mobile game concept for lectures," in *Proceedings of the IEEE 21st Conference on Software Engineering Education and Training*, 2008.

[9] A. I. Wang, T. Øfsdahl, and O. K. Mørch-Storstein, "LECTURE QUIZ—a mobile game concept for lectures," in *Proceedings of the 11th IASTED International Conference on Software Engineering and Application (SEA '07)*, 2007.

[10] M. S. El-Nasr and B. K. Smith, "Learning through game modding," *Computers in Entertainment*, vol. 4, no. 1, pp. 45–64, 2006.

[11] G. Lukas, "Uses of the LOGO programming language in undergraduate instruction," in *Proceedings of the ACM Annual Conference*, vol. 2, Boston, Mass, USA, 1972.

[12] M. Micco, "An undergraduate curriculum in expert systems design or knowledge engineering," in *Proceedings of the 15th Annual Conference on Computer Science*, St. Louis, Mo, USA, 1987.

[13] M. Habgood, S. Ainsworth, and S. Benford, "The educational and motivational content of digital games made by children," in *Proceedings of the Virtual Learning (CAL '05)*, Bristol, UK, 2005.

[14] Yulia and R. Adipranata, "Teaching object oriented programming course using cooperative learning method based on game design and visual object oriented environment," in *Proceedings of the 2nd International Conference on Education Technology and Computer (ICETC '10)*, pp. V2355–V2359, June 2010.

[15] L. Werner, J. Denner, M. Bliesner, and P. Rex, "Can middle-schoolers use Storytelling Alice to make games? Results of a pilot study," in *Proceedings of the 4th International Conference on the Foundations of Digital Games (ICFDG '09)*, pp. 207–214, Orlando, Fla, USA, April 2009.

[16] J. Robertson and C. Howells, "Computer game design: opportunities for successful learning," *Computers and Education*, vol. 50, no. 2, pp. 559–578, 2008.

[17] S. Kurkovsky, "Can mobile game development foster student interest in computer science?" in *Proceedings of the 1st International IEEE Consumer Electronic Society's Games Innovation Conference (ICE-GiC '09)*, pp. 92–100, August 2009.

[18] B. Ahmed and M. Steve, "Using ATAM to evaluate a game-based architecture," in *Proceedings of the 20th European Conference on Object-Oriented Programming ECOOP, Workshop on Architecture-Centric Evolution (ACE '06)*, Nantes, France, 2006.

[19] L. Bass, P. Clements, R. Kazman et al., *Software Architecture in Practice*, Addison-Wesley Professional, 2nd edition, 2003.

[20] R. Kazman, M. Klein, M. Barbacci, T. Longstaff, H. Lipson, J. Carriere et al., "The architecture tradeoff analysis method," in *Proceedings of the 4th IEEE International Conference on Engineering of Complex Computer Systems (ICECCS '98)*, pp. 68–78, 1998.

[21] A. I. Wang and T. Stålhane, "Using post mortem analysis to evaluate software architecture student projects," in *Proceedings of the 18th Conference on Software Engineering Education and Training (CSEE & T '05)*, pp. 43–50, April 2005.

[22] WSU, Download WSU_KSuite_1.1.2., 2009.

[23] B. Wu, A. I. Wang, J. E. Strøm, and T. B. Kvamme, "An evaluation of using a Game Development Framework in higher education," in *Proceedings of the 22nd Conference on Software Engineering Education and Training (CSEET '09)*, pp. 41–44, February 2009.

[24] A. I. Wang, "Extensive evaluation of using a game project in a software architecture course," *ACM Transactions on Computing Education*, vol. 11, no. 1, article 5, 2011.

[25] V. Basili, "Software modeling and measurement: the Goal/Question/Metric paradigm," 1992.

[26] W. H. Kruskal and W. A. Wallis, "Use of ranks in one-criterion variance analysis," *Journal of the American Statistical Association*, vol. 47, pp. 583–621, 1952.

[27] W. R. Shadish, T. D. Cook, and D. T. Campbell, *Experimental and Quasi-Experimental Designs for Generalized Causal Inference*, Houghton, Mifflin and Company, Boston, Mass, USA, 2002.

5

The Brigade Renderer: A Path Tracer for Real-Time Games

Jacco Bikker and Jeroen van Schijndel

ADE/IGAD, NHTV Breda University of Applied Sciences, Monseigneur Hopmansstraat 1, 4817 JT Breda, The Netherlands

Correspondence should be addressed to Jacco Bikker; bikker.j@gmail.com

Academic Editor: Yiyu Cai

We present the Brigade renderer: an efficient system that uses the path tracing algorithm to produce images for real-time games. We describe the architecture of the Brigade renderer, and provide implementation details. We describe two games that have been created using Brigade.

1. Background

Historically, games have been an important driving force in the advance of graphics hardware and rendering algorithms. Effort has evolved from striving for abstract, visually pleasing results, to more plausible realistic rendering. In the former, a distinct visual style is chosen, which does not necessarily require realism. Instead, over-the-top animation styles and matching graphics are used. Examples of this approach are most early 2D computer games, but there are also more recent titles such as Super Mario Galaxy [1] and Okami [2] (Figure 1).

Many modern games strive for realistic graphics, where the goal is to convince the player that the result is (or could be) realistic. Examples are racing games such as the Gran Turismo series [3] and flight simulators such as Tom Clancy's H.A.W.X. [4] (Figure 2), which use rasterization-based renderers, augmented with various algorithms to add secondary effects such as shadows, reflections, and indirect illumination.

Recently, efforts are being made towards physically correct results. For static scenery and a static light configuration, this can be achieved by precalculating global illumination, or by coarsely calculating radiosity. Examples of this are games based on the Unreal 3 engine [5] (Figure 3). Games using the Frostbite 2 engine [6] support ray tracing of coarse level geometry for glossy reflections. The Unreal 4 engine [7] supports approximate global illumination using cone tracing [8].

Physically based rendering of virtual worlds has strong advantages. The obvious advantage is image fidelity (Figure 4). Perhaps of equal importance, however, is production efficiency. Whereas lighting for a scene in a rasterization-based engine typically requires a designer to work around technical limitations of the renderer to make the lighting look right, physically based rendering naturally leads to correct lighting. This limits the design effort to a creative process alone.

Of the available physically based rendering algorithms, stochastic ray-tracing based methods (path tracing and derived methods) are favored over finite element methods, due to their elegance and efficient handling of large scenes. Unlike rasterization-based approaches, path tracing scales up to photo realism with minimal algorithmic complexity: the only dependencies are compute power and memory bandwidth. Both increase over time. Moore's law states that the number of transistors that can be placed inexpensively on an integrated circuit rises exponentially over time [9]. Although the link between transistor count and application performance is complex, the latter follows the same pattern, with compute power increasing at 71% per year on average, and DRAM bandwidth at 25% per year [10].

Assuming that all other factors remain constant (e.g., scene complexity, screen resolution), it can thus be assumed

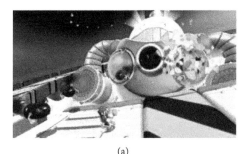

(a)

(b)

FIGURE 1: Two examples of modern games that use a nonrealistic visual style. (a) Super Mario Galaxy, (b) Okami.

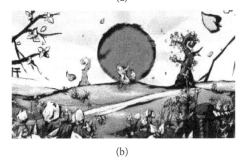

(a)

(b)

FIGURE 2: Two examples of modern games that aim for a high level of realism. (a) Tom Clancy's H.A.W.X., (b) Gran Turismo 5.

that there will be a point where physically based rendering is feasible on consumer hardware.

2. Previous Work

Recently, Whitted-style ray tracing and distribution ray tracing have been shown to run in real-time, or at least at interactive frame rates, on CPUs (see e.g., [12–15] and

GPUs [16–19], as well as the streaming processors of modern consoles [20, 21]).

Interactive path tracing was first mentioned in 1999 by Walter et al. as a possible application of their Render Cache system [22]. Using their system and a sixty-core machine, a scene can be navigated at interactive frame rates. During camera movement, samples are cached and reprojected to construct an approximation for the new camera view point. New samples are created for pixels with a relatively large error. The image converges to the correct solution when the camera is stationary.

Sadeghi et al. use ray packets for their path tracer [23]. Coherence between rays on the paths of block of pixels is obtained by using the same random numbers for all pixels in the block. This introduces structural noise but remains unbiased. The system is CPU based and achieves about 1.2 M rays per second per core of an Intel Core 2 Quad running at 2.83 Ghz.

In their 2009 paper, Aila and Laine evaluate the performance of various ray traversal kernels on the GPU [19]. Although they did not aim to implement a full path tracer, their measurements include a diffuse bounce, for which they report nearly 50 M rays per second on an NVidia GTX285, not including shading.

More recently, Novák et al. used GPU path tracing with path regeneration to double the performance of the path tracing algorithm on stream processors [24]. Their system is able to render interactive previews on commodity hardware, achieving 13 M rays per second on an NVidia GTX285 on moderately complex scenes, and is claimed to be "the first efficient (bidirectional) path tracer on the GPU." Van Antwerpen proposed a generic streaming approach for GPU path tracing algorithms and used this to implement three streaming GPU-only unbiased rendering algorithms: a path tracer, a bidirectional path tracer, and an energy redistribution path tracer [25].

Outside academia, several applications implement interactive path tracing. Examples are octane [26], smallpt [27], tokaspt [28], smallluxgpu [29], and nvidia's Design Garage demo [30].

3. Efficient GPU Path Tracing

The unbiased path tracing algorithm with russian roulette is shown in Algorithm 1. The algorithm aims to find a number of paths that connect the camera to light sources, via zero or more scene surfaces, by performing a random walk. The expected value of the average energy transported via these paths is the solution to the rendering equation [31]. To reduce the variance of the estimate, two extensions are commonly used. Russian Roulette is used to reduce the number of very long paths (which generally contribute little to the final image), and at each nonspecular surface interaction, direct light is explicitly sampled.

The path tracing algorithm can be efficiently implemented as on the GPU, using a single kernel per pixel. The kernel loops over the samples for a pixel and outputs the final color. This limits memory access to read-only scene

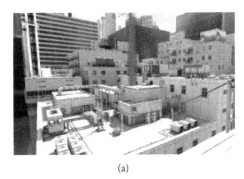

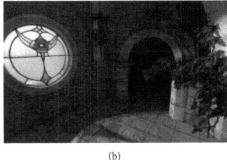

(a)   (b)

FIGURE 3: Precalculated global illumination, calculated using Unreal technology. (a) Mirror's edge, lit by Beäst. (b) Scene lit by Lightmass.

(a)   (b)

FIGURE 4: Ray tracing versus path tracing. (a) was rendered using the Arauna ray tracer [9], which supports direct illumination from point lights only. (b) uses path tracing for direct and indirect illumination of area light sources.

FIGURE 5: Scene from Kayija's paper, rendered using our CUDA path tracing algorithm.

access, and a single write for the final pixel color. CUDA code for this is provided in Appendix Section. Example output is shown in Figure 5. For this scene, ray/scene intersection uses a hardcoded scene consisting of axis aligned rectangular cuboids, spheres, and ellipsoids. Materials are limited to diffuse and dielectric. Using this setup, a single NVidia

GTX580 achieves 750 M rays per second, which results in an almost converged image at real-time frame rates.

For more general scenes, we can replace the hardcoded ray/scene intersection by the BVH traversal code proposed by Aila and Laine [19].

4. The Brigade System

A renderer for games has specific requirements, which differ significantly from other applications. Of these, the requirement of real-time performance probably has the greatest overall impact on the design of a renderer. A modern game runs at 60 fps or more. For certain genres, a lower frame rate is acceptable. For the game Doom 4, a fixed frame rate of 30 fps is enforced by the renderer [32].

Frame rate translates to a strict millisecond budget, which must be divided over all subsystems. Note that if we chose to run the subsystems in order, the budget available to rendering decreases. If, on the other hand, we run the subsystems and rendering in parallel, we introduce input lag: in a worst-case scenario, user input that occurred at the beginning of frame N will be rendered in frame $N + 1$ and presented to the user just before frame $N + 2$ starts.

```
for each pass
    for each pixel
        c_rgb ← 0, scale_rgb ← 1
        hitDiffuse ← false
        D⃗,O ←ray_through_pixel()
        do
            // find material, distance and normal along ray
            m, I, N⃗ ← find nearest(O, D⃗)
            if (isempty(m))
                break //path left scene
            else if (is_light(m))
                if not hitDiffuse
                    c_rgb ← c_rgb + scale_rgb * getEmissive(m)
                break // path hit light
            else
                O ← I
                if is_diffuse(m)
                    c_rgb ← c_rgb + sampleDirect()
                    hitDiffuse←true
                D⃗, scale_rgb ← evalBRDF(m, I, D⃗, N⃗)
                p ← RR(m)
                if rnd() < p break // russian roulette
                    scale_rgb ← scale_rgb * (1 − p)
        while (true)
        pixel[x, y] ← pixel[x, y] + c_rgb
    endfor
endfor
```

ALGORITHM 1: The path tracing algorithm with Russian roulette and explicit light sampling, in a format suitable for sequential execution. The final image is scaled by 1/passes.

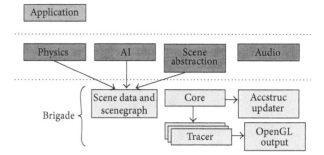

FIGURE 6: Functional overview of the Brigade renderer, combined with a generic game engine.

illuminated using emissive surfaces, of which an unlimited amount may be present.

The rendering system achieves high performance by fully utilizing all compute devices in a heterogeneous architecture (Section 4.2). It implements a synchronization-free balancing scheme to divide the workload over these compute devices (Section 4.3). Adaptive converging (Section 4.5) and dynamic workload scaling (Section 4.7) are used to ensure a real-time frame rate at high-definition resolutions.

4.1. Functional Overview. Figure 6 provides a functional overview of the Brigade renderer. In a typical setup, Brigade is combined with a game engine that provides components not specific to the rendering algorithm, such as artificial intelligence and physics libraries. In terms of abstraction, the functionality provided by Brigade is thus similar to the functionality implemented by OpenGL and DirectX.

The main components of Brigade are as follows.

4.1.1. Scene Graph. The scene and hierarchical scene graph contain all data required for rendering. This includes the object hierarchy, mesh data, materials, textures, cameras, and lights. The object decomposition represented by the scene graph is used to steer acceleration structure construction, which makes the scene graph an essential data structure within the system. For convenience, the scene graph object implements keyframe and bone animation.

4.1.2. Core. The core implements the Render () method, initiates acceleration structure updates, synchronizes scene data changes with the compute devices, and divides work over the tracers, if there is more than one.

4.1.3. Acceleration Structure Updater. The acceleration structure updater maintains the BVH, by selectively rebuilding parts of the acceleration structure based on changes in the scene graph.

4.1.4. Tracers. A tracer is an abstract representation of a compute device or group of similar compute devices. A "compute device" in this context can be a GPU, the set of available CPU cores, or a compute device connected over a network. The tracer holds a copy of the scene data and the acceleration

Apart from real-time performance, rendering for games requires dynamic scenery. Scene elements may undergo complex movement due to physics as well as hand-crafted animations and procedural effects such as explosions. Contrary to popular belief, global changes to scenery are uncommon in games. Typically, large portions of the scenery are static, to avoid game states in which the user cannot progress.

Tightly coupled to the real-time requirement is the fact that games are interactive applications. The renderer must produce correct results for all possible user input and cannot predict any scenery changes that depend on user interaction.

On top of the generic requirements, there are requirements that evolve over time, most notably rendering resolution and scene complexity. At the time of writing, a typical game renders at a resolution of at least 1280 × 720 (HD 720). A typical scene consists of hundreds of thousands of polygons.

The Brigade rendering system is designed specifically for games and applies and encapsulates the technology of Section 3 in this context. Brigade renders scenes consisting of static and dynamic geometry, consisting of millions of triangles. It uses a fixed-function shading pipeline and supports diffuse and specular surfaces with textures and normal maps, as well as dielectrics with absorption. The animation system supports rigid animation and skinned meshes. Scenes are

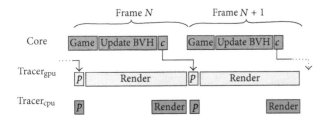

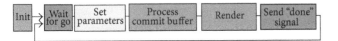

FIGURE 7: Double buffering the BVH. The CPU updates the BVH and sends changes to the tracers. Each tracer processes the changes in a commit buffer before rendering the next frame.

| Init | → | Wait for go | Set parameters | Process commit buffer | Render | Send "done" signal |

FIGURE 8: Tracer thread initialization and main loop.

structure and implements the path tracing algorithm with the next event estimation and multiple importance sampling. Tracers are assumed to produce identical output for identical input (except for nondeterministic aspects of the rendering algorithm).

The acceleration structure used by the tracers is the only cached data structure that is derived from scene data. All other data can be modified on-the-fly. This includes (all properties of) materials and lights.

In this system, the governing processes run on the CPU, and tracers (which in a typical setup primarily run on the GPUs) function as workers.

4.2. Rendering on a Heterogeneous System.

A modern PC is a heterogeneous architecture, which typically consists of a CPU with multiple cores, and at least one GPU.

To efficiently use the available compute power, several options are available.

(1) The rendering algorithm is implemented completely on either the CPU or the GPU.

(2) The rendering algorithm is implemented on both the CPU and the GPU.

(3) Tasks are divided over CPU and GPU.

Each of these options has advantages and disadvantages. A renderer that runs entirely on the CPU or GPU may result in underutilization of the other compute device. An algorithm that is implemented on both the CPU and the GPU will use all resources but requires a greater implementation effort. Dividing tasks over CPU and GPU seems the most attractive option. This is, however, only efficient when CPU and GPU spend equal amounts of time on their assigned tasks.

A fourth option is to use a hybrid solution, where the CPU has specific tasks and uses the frame time that remains to assist the GPU. This is the approach implemented in our system. The CPU is responsible for game logic and acceleration structure maintenance, while the tracers perform the actual rendering. Assuming a CPU tracer is available, this system is

able to keep compute devices fully occupied. The process is illustrated in Figure 7.

For each frame, the CPU updates the game state. The resulting changes to the scene graph are then used to update the BVH. The changes to the BVH, as well as any other scene changes, are sent to the tracers, where they are placed in a commit buffer, which the tracers use to iteratively update a local copy of the scene.

Parallel to these activities, the tracers render using the data that was prepared in the previous frame. A tracer starts a frame by processing the changes in the commit buffer, and then renders a part of the frame. CPU tracers are handled slightly differently than GPU tracers, by postponing rendering until the acceleration structure has been updated. This prevents rendering interferes with acceleration structure maintenance.

When no CPU tracer is available, the CPU can execute game code that does not affect the scene graph after copying scene changes to the commit buffers of the tracers.

4.3. Workload Balancing.

The tracer flow is shown in Figure 8. Upon instantiation, the tracer spawns a thread that executes the worker loop. This loop waits for a signal from the core, renders a number of pixels, and signals the core, before going to sleep until the next frame.

When more than a single tracer is available, the core estimates an optimal workload division prior to rendering each frame. The advantage of this approach is that no communication between the tracers and the core is required once rendering has commenced, which greatly reduces communication overhead for GPU and network tracers. Dividing the work is nontrivial; however, not every compute device may have the same rendering capacity, and not every line of pixels has the same rendering cost (see Figure 10).

In a game, a typical camera moves in a somewhat smooth fashion. A good workload division for one frame will thus be at least reasonable for the next frame. We exploit this by adjusting the workload balance in an iterative manner.

We implemented four schemes to divide work over the tracers.

4.3.1. Do Not Balance.

In this naive scheme, all workers are assigned an equal share of the screen pixels; no balancing is performed. This scheme is included for reference.

4.3.2. Robin Hood.

This scheme starts with an equal distribution of the work for each tracer. After completing each frame, the tracer that finished last passes one work unit (one work unit equals four rows of pixels) to the tracer that finished first. When the work is poorly distributed, it may take a large number of frames to properly balance.

4.3.3. Perfect.

Calculates the exact amount of work a tracer can handle based on the previous frame, but without considering differences in cost between lines of pixels. This may result in hickups, when many expensive lines are assigned to a tracer at once. The perfect balancer uses the following

Average percentage of summed rendering time for all GPUs spent idling due to early completion, for the four balancing schemes, over 128 frames, for a slow and a faster moving camera. Measured for the Aztec scene.

	2 GPUs		3 GPUs	
	Slow	Fast	Slow	Fast
None	46.4	30.2	45.1	47.2
Robin Hood	2.1	8.2	4.9	20.7
Perfect	2.8	2.4	12.2	8.0
Perfect Smooth	1.4	3.4	2.8	6.2

formula to determine the workload for worker w for frame $i + 1$ based on the unit count and render time of frame i:

$$P_{w,i+1} = \frac{\text{units}_{w,i}\, \text{time}_{w,i}^{-1}}{\sum \left(\text{units}_i\, \text{time}_i^{-1}\right)}. \tag{1}$$

Perfect Smooth. Same as "Perfect", but this time, the workload per tracer is smoothed over multiple frames, using the following formula:

$$S_{w,i+1} = \alpha P_{w,i} + (1 - \alpha) S_{w,i}, \tag{2}$$

where $\alpha \in (0, 1)$.

Figure 9 shows the efficiency of the four schemes, for a spinning camera in the Aztec scene. For a slow moving camera, the workload in two subsequent frames is similar. All schemes except the overcompensating Perfect balancer work well. The Robin Hood balancer exhibits poor efficiency for the first frames. For a faster camera, Robin Hood is not able to keep up. For this situation, the aggressive Perfect balancer outperforms even the Perfect Smooth balancer. When more GPUs are used, Perfect Smooth is clearly the optimal scheme.

Table 1 shows the average efficiency of the four balancers over 128 frames, for a slow and a faster moving camera. This table confirms that the Perfect and Perfect Smooth schemes are similar in terms of average efficiency. The table does not, however, show the spikes that are visible in the graphs.

4.4. Double-Buffering Scene Data. For acceleration structure maintenance, we use the following assumptions.

(1) A game world may consist of millions of polygons.

(2) A small portion of these polygons is dynamic.

(3) Several tracers will use the same acceleration structure.

Based on these assumptions, a full rebuild of the BVH for each frame is neither required nor desired, as it would put a cap on maximum scene complexity, even when very few changes occur. We reuse the system described by Bikker [13], where each scene graph node has its own BVH, and a top-level BVH is constructed per frame over these BVHs. Each changed scene graph node is updated, using either full reconstruction or refitting.

Brigade uses a double-buffered approach for BVH maintenance. During a single frame, the CPU updates the BVH based on modifications of the scene graph. The resulting changes to the BVH are sent to the tracers, where they are placed in a commit buffer. At the start of the next frame, the commit buffer is processed, which results in an up-to-date BVH for each of the tracers. This process is illustrated in Figure 7.

Each frame is thus rendered using the BVH constructed during the previous frame. Acceleration maintenance construction thus only becomes a bottleneck when the time it requires exceeds the duration of a frame.

4.5. Converging. To reduce the noise in the final rendered image, several frames can be blended. Each pixel of the final image is calculated as $C_{\text{final}} = (1 - f)C_{\text{prev}} + f C_{\text{new}}$, where $f \in (0, 1]$. Value f is chosen either manually, or automatically, for example, based on camera speed. For stationary views, this approach results in a higher number of samples per pixel. For nonstationary views, this results in an incorrect image. The result can be improved by linking f to camera movement. For a stationary camera, a small value of f allows the renderer to blend many frames. For a moving camera, a value of f close to 1 minimizes ghosting.

Note that even though the camera may be static, objects in the scene may not be. It is therefore important to limit the minimum value of f to keep the ghosting for dynamic objects within acceptable bounds.

4.6. CPU Single Ray Queries. Brigade exposes a CPU-based synchronous single ray query that uses the BVH from the previous frame, to provide the game engine with a fast single-ray query. This query is useful for a number of typical game situations, such as line-of-sight queries for weapons and AI, collision queries for physics, and general object picking. The single-ray query uses the full detailed scene (rather than, e.g., a coarse collision mesh), including animated objects.

4.7. Dynamically Scaling Workload. Maintaining a sufficient frame rate is of paramount importance to a game application. In this subsection, we propose several approaches to scale the workload.

4.7.1. Adjusting Samples per Pixel. The relation between frames per second and samples per pixel is almost linear. Brigade adjusts the rendered number of samples per pixel when the frame rate drops below a specified minimum and increases this value when the frame rate exceeds a specified maximum.

4.7.2. Balancing Primary Rays and Secondary Rays. By balancing the ratio of primary and secondary rays, the quality of antialiasing and depth of field blurring can be traded for secondary effects. The primary rays are faster; increasing their ratio will also improve frame rate.

4.7.3. Scale Russian Roulette Termination Probability. Changing the termination probability of Russian roulette does not introduce bias, although it may increase variance [33]. Altering the termination probability affects the number of deeper path segments, and thus frame rate. Unlike the

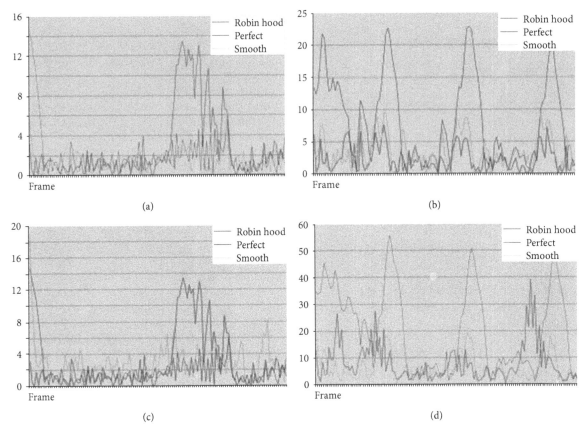

FIGURE 9: Efficiency of three workload balancing schemes, for two GPUs ((a)-(b)) and three GPUs ((c)-(d)), small camera movements ((a)–(c)) and larger camera movements ((b)–(d)). Values are percentages of rendering time spent idling due to early completion. Measured for the Aztec scene.

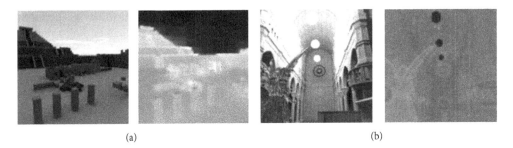

FIGURE 10: Render cost visualized: pixels representing the sky dome or light sources have a significant lower cost than other pixels. Cost is represented by greyscale values (brighter is higher cost), per 32 pixels (a full warp). Measured using a tracer implemented in NVidia's CUDA [11] for two scenes: Aztec (a) and Sibenik Cathedral (b).

previous approach, scaling the termination probability using a factor which is based on frame rate does not distinguish between primary and secondary rays and allows smooth scaling of performance.

Alternatively, the workload can be reduced by reducing rendering resolution, or limiting trace depth. Limiting the maximum recursion depth of the path tracer introduces bias but also improves performance. In practice, due to Russian roulette, deep rays are rare, which limits the effect of a recursion depth cap on performance.

For game development, the scalability of a renderer based on path tracing is an attractive characteristic. A relatively slow system is able to run the path tracer at an acceptable frame rate, albeit perhaps not at an acceptable level of variance. Faster systems benefit from the additional performance by producing more samples per pixel, and thus a smoother image.

5. Discussion

The rendering system described in the previous section is relatively simple. To a large extend, this simplicity is the result of the chosen rendering algorithm. The path tracer does not rely on any precalculated data, which greatly reduces

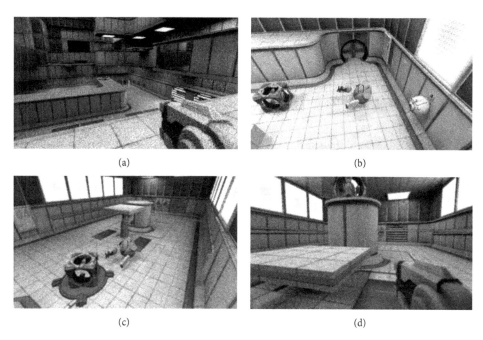

(a)   (b)

(c)   (d)

FIGURE 11: Two views from the "Reflect" game, rendered at 448 × 576 pixels using 16 spp, scaled up to 896 × 576.

data dependencies. There are two exceptions, and these are also the most complex parts of the system. The first is the acceleration structure, which is cached and updated iteratively, in a double-buffered fashion. As a result, games cannot make arbitrary changes to the scene graph. The second is the data synchronization between the renderer core and the tracers, which generally run on the GPU(s). Using a commit buffer system, Brigade makes this virtually invisible to the application, and few restrictions apply.

Apart from the tracers, Brigade is a platform-independent system. The tracers abstract away vendor-specific APIs for GPGPU and allow the implementation of networked tracers and CPU-based tracers. When using a CPU tracer, the system is able to achieve full system utilization, with little overhead.

6. Applied

To validate our results, we have applied the renderer to two-student game projects. Both games have been produced in approximately 14 working days.

6.1. Demo Project "Reflect". The Reflect game application is a student game that was developed using an early version of the Brigade engine. The game scenery is designed to simulate actual requirements for game development, and purposely mimics the graphical style of a well-known modern game (Portal 2 [34]).

The scenery has the following characteristics:

(i) scenery consists of approximately 250 k triangles, divided over multiple, separated rooms;

(ii) the scene is illuminated by thousands of area light sources, many of which are dynamic;

(iii) the game world is populated by dozens of dynamic objects.

Art assets for the game were created in Alias Wavefront Maya 2011 and were directly imported into the game.

Like Portal 2, Reflect is a puzzle game, where the player advances by activating triggers that in turn open doors or activate elevators. A "mirror gun" is available to the player to transform flat and curved wall sections into mirrors. These mirrors, as well as glass cube objects, can be used to divert lasers that block the way.

Configuration. Reflect was developed for a dual-CPU/dual-GPU machine (2 hexacore Intel Xeon processors, 2 NVidia GTX470 GPUs). We implemented a CPU tracer as well as a CUDA GPU tracer. For performance reasons, we limited the path tracers to a single diffuse bounce.

Game-Specific Optimizations. The scenery of the game consists of many rooms, separated by doors. A common optimization in rasterization-based renderers is to disable geometry that is known to be invisible. For a path tracer this does not significantly improve performance. We did find, however, that turning off lights in those rooms reduces variance, as the path tracer will no longer sample those light sources. This optimization is implemented at the application level: a system of triggers in the scene enables and disables sets of lights.

Performance and Variance. Figure 11 shows two scenes from the game running on a dual-CPU/dual GPU machine. At 16 spp, the game runs at 10–12 fps. At this sample count, brightly lit scenes are close to acceptable. Darker regions, such as the area under the platform in the right image, show significant temporal noise. Careful level layout helps to reduce objectionable noise levels. To the visual artist, this is

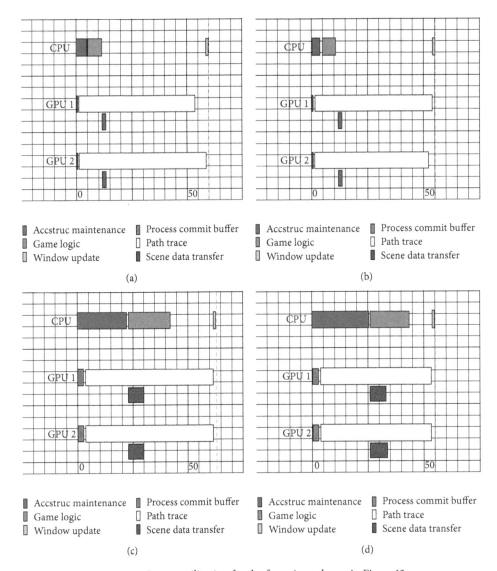

FIGURE 12: System utilization for the four views shown in Figure 13.

counter-intuitive, where rasterization-based renderers tend to use small amounts of point light sources, a path tracer benefits from large area lights, and incurs no slowdown when those lights are animated.

Materials in the levels are deliberately simple. Although specular surfaces are supported by this version of the renderer, specularity significantly increases noise, making this impractical in most situations.

Observations. The Reflect game struggles to achieve an acceptable frame rate, at a low resolution, on a high-end system. The project does, however, show the potential of path tracing for games. The art for this game was produced in Maya 2011 and was directly imported into the game, leading to very short development cycles, and usable art on the second day of the project. Within the same time span, the programmers implemented a basic physics engine using ray queries that allowed them to navigate the rooms.

The freedom in lighting setup led to a final level that contains approximately 10 k light emitting polygons. Direct

and indirect illumination simply works and results in subtle global illumination, both for static and dynamic objects.

The CPU tracer that was implemented for this project proved to be problematic: keeping the CPU and GPU tracers in sync required significant engineering effort, while the overall contribution of the CPU is quite small.

6.2. Demo Project "It's About Time". The student game "It's About Time" was created using a recent version of the Brigade renderer. Four views from the game are shown in Figure 13.

"It's About Time" is a third-person puzzle game that takes place in deserted Aztec ruins. The player must collect a number of artifacts by solving a number of puzzles, located in several areas in an open outdoor world.

6.2.1. Configuration. "It's About Time" is designed to run on a typical high-end system, using a single hexacore CPU and one or more current-generation NVidia or AMD GPUs. The game renders to standard HD resolution. This resolution can

(a)

(b)

(c)

(d)

FIGURE 13: Four views from "It's About Time."

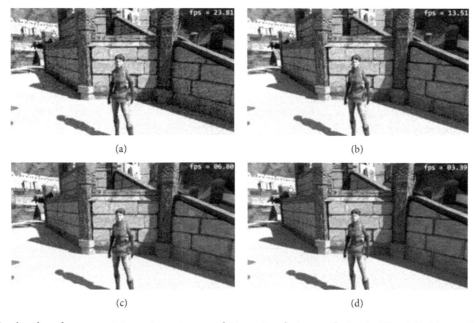

(a)

(b)

(c)

(d)

FIGURE 14: Noise level and performance at 2 spp, 4 spp, 8 spp, and 16 spp. Rendering resolution is 640 × 360. Measured on a system with a 6-core CPU and two NVidia GTX470 GPUs.

be halved to improve frame rate. We developed an updated CUDA tracer that roughly doubles the performance of the first iteration (as used in Reflect), as well as an OpenCL tracer, which produces identical images. A CPU tracer was not developed; the CPU is reserved for acceleration structure maintenance and game logic. The implemented path tracers are unbiased.

6.2.2. Project-Specific Features. One of the puzzles features an animated water surface that responds to the player, consisting

of tens of thousands of polygons. For the player character, a detailed set of skinned animations is used. The puzzles make extensive use of rigid animation. As a result, acceleration structure maintenance requires considerable processing. A detailed day-night cycle and an animated cloud system (with shadowing) were implemented to emphasize the strength of the path tracer for dynamic lighting. A standard physics engine was integrated to provide high quality physics simulation. The level is detailed and consists of 1.4 M triangles. The artists used a small set of sand stones to construct most of the buildings and ruins.

6.2.3. Game-Specific Optimizations. The game world is illuminated by a sun (or the moon), and some smaller light sources. To reduce variance, we modified the path tracer to always sample two light sources per diffuse surface interaction. One of these rays always probes the primary light source. This significantly reduces variance in most areas. Adaptive converging is used to improve image quality when the camera is (almost) stationary. These application-specific optimizations where implemented in the GPU tracer code.

6.2.4. System Utilization. Figure 12 shows system utilization for the four views of Figure 13, rendered at 4 spp.

For the first two views, the CPU is underutilized, as both acceleration structure maintenance and game logic require little processing time. For the other two views, the camera is near a simulated water surface that consists of 18 k polygons. Both the simulation itself and the resulting acceleration structure maintenance require considerable processing time. This also affects the GPU tracers, which use more time to transfer and process the modified scene data.

6.2.5. Memory Use. The Brigade renderer is an in-core rendering system, which stores multiple copies of the scenery. The host system stores a full copy of the scene and synchronizes this data with each of the tracers.

For the 1.4 M triangle scene of "It's About Time," memory use is 737 MB, which consists of 175 MB triangle data, 42 MB for the acceleration structure, and 520 MB texture data. The size of other data structures is negligible, except for the commit buffer, which must be large enough to store per-frame changes to scene data and the acceleration structure. For "It's About Time," we used a 2 MB commit buffer.

6.2.6. Performance and Variance. Figure 14 shows a single scene from the game, rendered using varying sample counts. As in Reflect, areas that are directly illuminated converge quickly, while shadowed areas exhibit more noise. For the outdoor scenery of "It's About Time," an acceptable quality for most camera views is obtained with 8 or 16 spp. On a system with two NVidia GTX470 GPUs, we achieve 2 to 4 spp at real-time frame rates, at a quarter of 720p HD resolution (640×360). This lets us quantify the remaining performance gap: real-time frame rates at 720p require 8 to 16 times the achieved performance.

7. Conclusions and Future Work

We have investigated the feasibility of using physically based rendering in the context of real-time graphics for games. We implemented a renderer based on the path tracing algorithm, and used this to develop two proof-of-concept games. We have shown that real-time path tracing is feasible on current

generation hardware, although careful light setup is required to keep variance levels acceptable.

The development of a game using path tracing for rendering simplifies game development. This affects both software engineering and art asset development. Since Brigade does not distinguish static and dynamic light sources and does not impose any limitations on the number or size of light sources, lighting design requires little knowledge beyond discipline-specific skills. The fact that polygon counts and material properties have only a small impact on rendering performance provides level designers and graphical artists with a high level of freedom in the design of the game. This reduces the number of iterations level art goes through, and allows a team to have game assets in the engine early on in the project.

Despite these positive experiences, real-time path tracing in commercial games is not feasible yet on current generation high-end hardware. Acceptable variance at HD resolution and real-time frame rates requires 8x to 16x the performance that can be achieved on our test system. Without further algorithmic improvements, this level may be reached in a few years. We do believe this can be accelerated. Already GPU ray tracing performance is benefiting from architectural improvements, on top of steady performance improvements. Another way to partially solve the rendering performance problem is to use cloud rendering, where dedicated servers are used for rendering images, which are then transferred over the internet to the client. At the time of writing, the Brigade system is being integrated into the OTOY cloud service, specifically for this purpose. The cloud rendering service will be made available to indie game developers in the near future and will allow them to use path tracing without the need of owning sufficiently powerful hardware.

Apart from raw performance, we should address the issue of variance. While low sample rates already result in reasonably converged images in our experiments, this will not be sufficient for more complex materials. Techniques like bidirectional path tracing (BDPT) and energy redistribution path tracing (ERPT) may solve this to some extent. However, not all of these techniques produce acceptable images at low sample rates; therefore, a minimum performance level is required before this can be considered for real-time graphics.

A temporary solution to the rendering performance problem is to use postprocessing on the path traced image. Although some work has been conducted in this area, it typically does not consider all the data that is available in a path tracer, which leaves room for improvement. Note that any form of postprocessing will introduce bias in the rendered image. For the intended purpose, this is, however, not an objection.

Appendix

Efficient CUDA implementation of the path tracing algorithm, using a single kernel per pixel (see Algorithm 2).

```
extern "C" _global_void TracePixelReference()
{
  // setup path
  int numRays = context.width * context.height;
  int idx0 = threadIdx.y + blockDim.y *
    (blockIdx.x + gridDim.x * blockIdx.y) +
    ((context.firstline * context.width) >> 5);
  int tx = threadIdx.x & 7, ty = threadIdx.x >> 3;
  int tilesperline = context.width >> 3;
  int xt = idx0 % tilesperline;
  int yt = idx0/tilesperline;
  int px = (xt << 3) + tx, py = (yt << 2) + ty;
  int pidx = numRays -1 -
    (px + py * context.width);
  RNG genrand(pidx, (clock() * pidx *
    8191) ^140167);
  int spp = context.SampleCount;
  float rcpw = 1.0f/context.width;
  float u = (float)px * rcpw -0.5f;
  floatv = (float)(py + (context.width -
    context.height) * 0.5f) * rcpw -0.5f;
  float3 E = make_float3(0, 0, 0);
  // trace path
  for(int sample = 0; sample < spp; sample++)
  {
    // construct primary ray
    float3 O, D;
    CreatePrimaryRay(O, D);
    // trace path
    float3 throughput = make_float3(1, 1, 1);
    int depth = 0;
    while (1)
    {
      int prim = 0;
      float2 BC, UV = make_float2(0, 0);
      float dist = 1000000;
      bool backfaced = false;
      intersect(O, D, dist, BC, prim, backfaced);
      O += D * dist;
      if (prim == -1)
      {
        E += throughput * GetSkySample(D);
        break;
      }
      Triangle& tri = context.Triangles[prim];
      TracerMaterial mat =
        context.Materials[tri.GetMaterialIdx()];
      if (mat.flags & Material::EMITTER) // light
      {
        E += throughput * mat.EmissiveColor;
        break;
      }
      else // diffuse reflection
      {
        float3 matcol = tri.GetMaterialColor(
          mat, BC, UV);
        float3 N = tri.GetNormal(mat, BC, UV) *
          (backfaced ? -1: 1);
```

ALGORITHM 2: Continued.

```
            D = normalize(RandomReflection(
                genrand, N) );
            throughput *= matcol * dot(D, N);
          }
          O += D * EPSILON;
          depth++;
          if (depth > 3)
          {
            if (genrand() > 0.5f) break;
            throughput *= 2.0f;
          }
        }
      }
      context.RenderTarget[pidx] =
        make_float4(E/(float)spp, 1);
  }
```

ALGORITHM 2: Path tracing implemented in CUDA.

Acknowledgments

Several scenes used in this paper were modeled by students of the IGAD program of the NHTV Breda University of Applied Sciences. The original of the scene shown in scene 4 was modeled by Jim Kajiya. The author wishes to thank Erik Jansen and the anonymous reviewers for proofreading and useful suggestions.

References

[1] S. Miyamoto, *Super Mario Galaxy*, Nintendo, 2007.

[2] H. Kamiya and A. O. Inaba, "Okami," 2006.

[3] K. Yamauchi, Gran Tourismo Series, 1997.

[4] T. Simon, Tom Clancy's H.A.W.X., 2009.

[5] T. Sweeny, Unreal Engine 3, 2008.

[6] J. Andersson, *Frostbite 2 Engine*, Nvidia, 2011.

[7] M. Mittring, *The Technology behind the "Unreal Engine 4 Elemental Demo"*, Epic Games, Inc., 2012.

[8] C. Crassin, F. Neyret, M. Sainz, S. Green, and E. Eisemann, "Interactive indirect illumination using voxel-based cone tracing: an insight," in *Proceedings of the ACM International Conference on Computer Graphics and Interactive Techniques (SIGGRAPH '11)*, Vancouver, Canada, August 2011.

[9] G. E. Moore, "Cramming more components onto integrated circuits," *Electronics*, vol. 38, no. 8, pp. 114–117, 1965.

[10] J. Owens, "Streaming architectures and technology trends," in *GPU Gems 2*, Addison-Wesley, 2005.

[11] NVidia, *Fermi: NVidia's Next Generation CUDA Compute Architecture*, NVidia, Santa Clara, Calif, USA, 2009.

[12] I. Wald and P. Slusallek, "State of the art in interactive ray tracing," in *State of the Art Reports, Eurographics*, pp. 21–42, Manchester, UK, 2001.

[13] J. Bikker, "Real-time ray tracing through the eyes of a game developer," in *Proceedings of the IEEE Symposium on Interactive Ray Tracing (RT '07)*, pp. 1–10, IEEE Computer Society, Ulm, Germany, September 2007.

[14] S. Boulos, D. Edwards, J. D. Lacewell et al., "Packet-based whitted and distribution ray tracing," in *Proceedings of the Graphics Interface (GI '07)*, pp. 177–184, ACM, Montreal, Canada, 2007.

[15] R. Overbeck, R. Ramamoorthi, and W. R. Mark, "Large ray packets for real-time whitted ray tracing," in *Proceedings of the IEEE/EG Symposium on Interactive Ray Tracing (RT '08)*, pp. 41–48, August 2008.

[16] T. J. Purcell, I. Buck, W. R. Mark, and P. Hanrahan, "Ray tracing on programmable graphics hardware," *ACM Transactions on Graphics*, vol. 21, no. 3, pp. 703–712, 2002.

[17] T. Foley and J. Sugerman, "KD-tree acceleration structures for a GPU raytracer," in *Proceedings of the ACM SIG-GRAPH/EUROGRAPHICS Conference on Graphics Hardware (HWWS '05)*, pp. 15–22, ACM, Los Angeles, Calif, USA, 2005.

[18] D. R. Horn, J. Sugerman, M. Houston, and P. Hanrahan, "Interactive k-D tree GPU raytracing," in *Proceedings of the Symposium on Interactive 3D Graphics and Games (I3D '07)*, pp. 167–174, ACM, Seattle, Wash, USA, 2007.

[19] T. Aila and S. Laine, "Understanding the efficiency of ray traversal on GPUs," in *Proceedings of the Conference on High-Performance Graphics (HPG '09)*, pp. 145–150, ACM, New Orleans, La, USA, August 2009.

[20] C. Benthin, *Realtime ray tracing on current CPU architectures [Ph.D. thesis]*, Saarland University, Saarbrücken, Germany, 2006.

[21] J. Sugerman, T. Foley, S. Yoshioka, and P. Hanrahan, "Ray tracing on a cell processor with software caching," in *Proceedings of the IEEE Symposium on Interactive Ray Tracing (RT '06)*, September 2006.

[22] B. Walter, G. Drettakis, and S. Parker, "Interactive rendering using the render cache," in *Rendering Techniques '99 (Proceedings of the 10th Eurographics Workshop on Rendering)*, D. Lischinski and G. W. Larson, Eds., vol. 10, pp. 235–246, Springer, New York, NY, USA, 1999.

[23] I. Sadeghi, B. Chen, and H. W. Jensen, "Coherent path tracing," *Journal of Graphics, GPU, and Game Tools*, vol. 14, no. 2, pp. 33–43, 2009.

[24] J. Novák, V. Havran, and C. Daschbacher, "Path regeneration for interactive path tracing," in *The European Association for Computer Graphics 28th Annual Conference: EUROGRAPHICS 2007, Short Papers*, pp. 61–64, The European Association for Computer Graphics, 2010.

[25] D. Van Antwerpen, *Unbiased physically based rendering on the GPU [M.S. thesis]*, Technical University Delft, Delft, The Netherlands, 2011.

[26] Refractive, Octane Renderer, 2010, http://www.refractive-software.com/.

[27] K. Beason, SmallPT, 2007, http://www.kevinbeason.com/.

[28] T. Berger-Perrin, "The Once Known As SmallPT," 2009, http://code.google.com/p/tokaspt/.

[29] Jromang, SmallLuxGPU, 2009, http://www.luxrender.net/wiki/SLG.

[30] NVidia, Design Garage, 2010, http://www.nvidia.com/.

[31] J. T. Kajiya, "The rendering equation," in *Proceedings of the 13th Annual Conference on Computer Graphics and Interactive Techniques (SIGGRAPH '86)*, pp. 143–150, ACM, Dallas, Tex, USA, 1986.

[32] T. Bramwell, "Doom 4 "three times" Rage visual quality," 2011, http://www.eurogamer.net/articles/doom-4-three-times-rage-visual-quality.

[33] L. Szirmay-Kalos, G. Antal, and M. Sbert, "Go with the winners strategy in path tracing," in *Proceedings of the International Conference in Central Europe on Computer Graphics and Visualization (WSCG '05)*, pp. 49–56, 2005.

[34] G. Newell and J. Weier, Portal 2. Valve Corporation, 2011.

6

Pose Space Surface Manipulation

Yusuke Yoshiyasu[1] and Nobutoshi Yamazaki[2]

[1] School of Science and Technology, Keio University, Kanagawa 223-8522, Japan
[2] Department of Mechanical Engineering, Keio University, Kanagawa 223-8522, Japan

Correspondence should be addressed to Yusuke Yoshiyasu, yusuke_2_ax_es@z6.keio.jp

Academic Editor: Alexander Pasko

Example-based mesh deformation techniques produce natural and realistic shapes by learning the space of deformations from examples. However, skeleton-based methods cannot manipulate a global mesh structure naturally, whereas the mesh-based approaches based on a translational control do not allow the user to edit a local mesh structure intuitively. This paper presents an example-driven mesh editing framework that achieves both global and local pose manipulations. The proposed system is built with a surface deformation method based on a two-step linear optimization technique and achieves direct manipulations of a model surface using translational and rotational controls. With the translational control, the user can create a model in natural poses easily. The rotational control can adjust the local pose intuitively by bending and twisting. We encode example deformations with a rotation-invariant mesh representation which handles large rotations in examples. To incorporate example deformations, we infer a pose from the handle translations/rotations and perform pose space interpolation, thereby avoiding involved nonlinear optimization. With the two-step linear approach combined with the proposed multiresolution deformation method, we can edit models at interactive rates without losing important deformation effects such as muscle bulging.

1. Introduction

Editing and animation of character models is an important task in computer graphics. The user, in general, demands the editing procedure to be interactive and intuitive. However, the ability to pose a model naturally and realistically is equally important for a character modeling system. Example-based techniques are a promising approach to improve the realism of interactive editing techniques. Pose space deformation (PSD) [1] is a skeleton-based approach which animates the model using skeletons and then corrects the resulting surface to conform to example shapes. In PSD, corrective displacements, the differences between a skinning surface and examples, are interpolated in pose space formed by joint angles. These displacements are then added to the skinning surface. While this method can model deformation effects such as muscle bulging, editing the pose of the model naturally is difficult and tedious as the number of joints increases.

In contrast, the mesh-based inverse kinematics (MeshIK) technique [2, 3] can pose a model meaningfully by just translating a few vertices of the mesh. Instead of interpolating

corrective displacements, MeshIK interpolates local deformations called deformation gradients. It automatically determines interpolation weights from the user-specified position constraints through nonlinear optimization. Because of this iterative process, it is time consuming for this method to edit a large model. Moreover, while MeshIK can edit the global pose naturally, it is counterintuitive to manipulate the local pose via translation; bending and twisting are more intuitive in this case.

In this paper, we present an example-driven mesh deformation technique that allows us not only to edit a global pose naturally but also to adjust a local pose precisely. Our system provides both translational and rotational controls to deform a model. By translating handle vertices, the user can produce a model in natural poses easily. By applying rotations to handle triangles, the user can bend and twist the model as if manipulating a joint. To this end, we formulate the problem by inferring a pose from handle translations/rotations and using a two-step linear surface optimization technique that is based on a linear rotation-invariant mesh representation. The benefits of this formulation are as follows: (1) it is straightforward to incorporate translational and rotational constraints; (2) it achieves rotation invariance and thus is applicable to examples that involves large deformations (rotations and bending); (3) it avoids time-consuming nonlinear optimization. In combination with the proposed multiresolution approach, we can edit high-resolution meshes at interactive rates while retaining important deformation effects such as muscle bulging.

The rest of the paper is organized as follows. In Section 2, we briefly review-related work. We provide an overview of our system in Section 3. We then describe our basic deformation framework in Section 4. In Section 5, we explain our PSD technique. Section 6 shows our multiresolution method. We demonstrate our method and show our results in Section 7. Finally, we conclude our work in Section 8.

2. Related Work

Pose Space Deformation. Pose space deformation (PSD) [1] is an example-based deformation method that corrects the artifacts of skeletal subspace deformation (SSD) and models subtle surface deformation, such as muscle bulging. This method is thought of as a combination of SSD and shape interpolation (morphing). In PSD, an initial mesh is first computed by SSD. This is then corrected by adding corrective displacements. These displacements, regarded as differences between SSD and examples, are interpolated such that they can properly correct the SSD surface in an arbitrary pose. Kry et al. [4] compressed corrective displacements using PCA to make them more compact. Kurihara and Miyata [5] introduced weighted pose space deformation to achieve PSD from a limited number of examples. Weber et al. [6] showed that the use of differential surface deformation in the PSD framework improves the quality of the result. They represented corrections with rotations and integrated them by solving a Poisson system. Wang et al. [7] introduced a similar method to [6] using a regression model.

Incorporating Real Dataset. To create realistic animation, some methods [8–11] use range scanned data as examples. Allen et al. [8] captured 3D shapes of body parts in different poses and animated them using a k-nearest neighbor approach. Anguelov et al. [9] and Hasler et al. [10] developed statistical human models that can create new human models with different body shapes and poses.

Linear Surface Deformation. Linear differential surface deformation methods (see, e.g., [12–14] and a well-organized survey [15]) deform a mesh by manipulating handle points or triangles, which provide position or transformation constraints, while preserving original details. The problem with these methods is the deformation of the model must be known beforehand to obtain the deformed vertex positions. Therefore, explicit methods [14, 16, 17] propagate user-specified transformations to other regions of the mesh. The problem of this approach is the translation-insensitivity: this approach cannot avoid shearing distortions when pure translations are applied, because there is no change in orientation. On the other hand, implicit methods [13] linearly approximate transformations. This approach fails when handles are moved largely, because, in 3D, the approximation is only valid for small rotation angles. In 2D, however, we can completely determine transformations linearly. Igarashi et al. [18] exploits this fact and proposed a 2D deformation method that works for large translations, based on a two-step as-rigid-as possible deformation framework. Two-step optimization methods in 3D, based on a linear rotation-invariant mesh representation [10, 12, 19], optimize transformations first and then optimize positions. Because these methods optimize rotations and positions separately, they are also translation insensitive.

Nonlinear Surface Deformation. In contrast, nonlinear methods solve these problems by iteratively optimizing both positions and transformations and thus work for large deformations at the cost of additional computations [20–22]. The main criteria for optimizing vertex positions are rigidity, smoothness, and user-specified position constraints. The optimization problem is solved either using the Gauss-Newton method [23] or through a local/global approach [22, 24]. Kilian et al. [25], in contrast, introduced an interesting approach that formulates the optimization as a path problem instead of deforming the reference shape. To improve performance, recent methods [23, 24, 26–29] incorporate skeleton/space deformation to form a subspace. These methods are, therefore, scalable in mesh size, that is, the computational cost does not depend on the number of vertices. Consequently, they can edit a large model in real time. Our method also utilizes a subspace method, but we not only increase the speed but also compress example deformations.

Mesh-Based Inverse Kinematics. The mesh-based inverse kinematics (MeshIK) system edits a mesh by manipulating handle points while constraining deformation in example space [2]. Although this method can pose a mesh meaningfully only by moving a few handles, it is expensive to edit a large mesh due to the nonlinear optimization it solves. The computational performance of MeshIK can be improved with the use of the reduced deformable model [3], but it loses deformation effects, for example, muscle bulging. In addition, because the feature vector used in MeshIK is not rotation invariant, there is the risk of producing erroneous results if the orientations and poses of examples differ significantly, as shown in Figure 4.

Deformation Transfer. Deformation transfer [30] is another related class of techniques that literally transfers deformation of one model to another to change the pose. In fact, as pointed out by Botsch et al. [31], this method solves exactly the same Poisson system as the deformation method of [14]. Semantic deformation transfer [32] allows the transfer to drastically different characters that move in unique ways. Like our method, they interpolate a rotation-invariant mesh representation, but the interpolation weights come from the projection of a new model to the example space. In contrast, our method manipulates a surface with handle translations/rotations and computes interpolation weights from them.

Our method is most similar to the variational PSD proposed by Weber et al. [6] and MeshIK proposed by Sumner et al. [2] in the sense that it formulates an example-based deformation technique using differential surface representation. However, we use the rotation-invariant mesh representation. Thus, our method can handle large rotations robustly. In addition, we allow the user to specify both translational and rotational constraints to deform a model. This enables us to edit both global and local poses of the model.

3. Overview

Our goal is to develop a mesh editing system that can manipulate a pose of the model both globally and locally. An overview of our method is depicted in Figure 1. We provide a translational control to achieve global pose editing (Figure 1(a)) and a rotational control for local pose editing (Figure 1(b)).

Our method is based on pose space interpolation and a two-step surface optimization method. The workflow is depicted in Figure 1(c). Prior to deformation, examples are encoded and stored as the rotation-invariant mesh representation. To achieve deformation, the user selects a set of vertices or triangles called handles. If a certain region on the mesh should be kept fixed, the user specifies the fixed region (blue), which is not affected by the examples. From handle translations or rotations, we infer a pose of a model (Section 5.1). When editing with the translational control, the user specifies a coordinate frame and handle vertices on the mesh. The pose is evaluated as relative positions of handles in the local coordinate frame. When editing with the rotational control, the user places a pair of handle triangles called *virtual joint*. The pose is evaluated as relative rotations between them. Once we have the pose, we then interpolate example deformations in pose space (Section 5.2). The deformed vertex coordinates are obtained using a two-step optimization approach. First, we optimize transformations (Section 4.2.1). Next, we optimize vertex positions from the resulting transformations. Finally, we perform multiresolution deformation to edit high resolution meshes (Section 6).

3.1. Notations. Inputs to our system are the base mesh and example meshes. The base mesh $\mathcal{M}^{(0)} = \{\mathcal{V}^{(0)}, \mathcal{T}\}$ is in the rest pose, and the example meshes are provided in the form of N additional geometries $\mathcal{V}^{(1)} \cdots \mathcal{V}^{(N)}$ (the connectivity $\mathcal{T}$ is shared with all the examples). Each mesh consists of n vertices and m triangles. We denote the indices of a vertex and a triangle as $p \in \{1 \cdots n\}$ and $i \in \{1 \cdots m\}$, respectively. We denote the index of an edge between triangle i and j by $e \in \{1 \cdots l\}$, where l is the number of triangle pairs. The vertex position is defined by $\mathbf{v}_p \in \mathbb{R}^3$, and it is concatenated into an $n \times 3$ matrix, $\mathbf{v} = [\mathbf{v}_1 \cdots \mathbf{v}_n]^T$. Also, we denote vertices by $\tilde{\mathbf{v}}$ after deformation.

4. Basic Deformation Framework

Our system is based on the pose space deformation framework that is thought of as a combination of surface deformation and shape interpolation. To integrate these two effectively, we use a two-step optimization method based on a rotation-invariant mesh representation similar to those proposed in [12, 19]. This formulation makes it straightforward to incorporate both translational and rotational constraints. We refer to our rotation-invariant representation as rotation-invariant encoding that is computed from a local deformation called the deformation gradient. In this section, we first describe derivations of these representations. Next, we explain the reconstruction process of vertex positions from these representations. Finally, we introduce surface manipulation tools: handle-based surface deformation and shape interpolation.

4.1. Basic Shape Representation

4.1.1. Deformation Gradient. Consider triangle i with its three vertices before and after deformation: $[\mathbf{v}_{i1}, \mathbf{v}_{i2}, \mathbf{v}_{i3}]$ and $[\tilde{\mathbf{v}}_{i1}, \tilde{\mathbf{v}}_{i2}, \tilde{\mathbf{v}}_{i3}]$. Given edge vectors before and after deformation, $\mathbf{V}_i = [\mathbf{v}_{i2} - \mathbf{v}_{i1}, \mathbf{v}_{i3} - \mathbf{v}_{i1}]$ and $\tilde{\mathbf{V}}_i = [\tilde{\mathbf{v}}_{i2} - \tilde{\mathbf{v}}_{i1}, \tilde{\mathbf{v}}_{i3} - \tilde{\mathbf{v}}_{i1}]$, we can approximate the deformation gradient by

$$\mathbf{T}_i = \tilde{\mathbf{V}}_i \mathbf{V}_i^+, \tag{1}$$

where $\mathbf{V}_i^+$ is the pseudoinverse of edge vectors before deformation. Thus, the computation of deformation gradients $\mathbf{T} = [\mathbf{T}_1 \cdots \mathbf{T}_m]^T$ can be achieved linearly from vertex positions after deformation $\tilde{\mathbf{v}} = [\tilde{\mathbf{v}}_1 \cdots \tilde{\mathbf{v}}_n]^T$. Using a $3m \times n$ deformation gradient operator $\mathbf{G}$, which contains the pseudoinverses of the edge vectors before deformation, we can compute $\mathbf{T}$ by

$$\mathbf{T} = \mathbf{G}\tilde{\mathbf{v}}. \tag{2}$$

4.1.2. Rotation-Invariant Encoding. The deformation gradient is translation invariant but not rotation invariant, which means that it is affected by global rotations. To address this issue, we first decompose the deformation gradient into rotation and scale/shear components by polar decomposition, that is, $\mathbf{T}_i = \mathbf{R}_i \mathbf{S}_i$ (Figure 2). Note that the scale/shear component $\mathbf{S}_i$ is already rotation invariant, but $\mathbf{R}_i$ is not. To achieve rotation invariance, we compute the relative rotation from the absolute rotations of two adjacent triangles, $\mathbf{R}_i$ and $\mathbf{R}_j$, as follows:

$$\mathbf{Q}_{ij} = \left(\mathbf{R}_j\right)^{-1} \mathbf{R}_i. \tag{3}$$

We call $\mathbf{Q}_{ij}$ and $\mathbf{S}_i$ rotation-invariant encoding because they encode changes in surface details and are invariant under the global rotation.

4.2. Reconstruction. To reconstruct vertex positions from rotation-invariant encodings, we solve two sparse linear systems. We use the penalty method [33] to enforce rotation/position constraints. Although the use of the penalty method can only provide approximate constraint satisfaction, it can produce sufficiently close results to the exact method by setting the penalty weight sufficiently high [33]. On the other

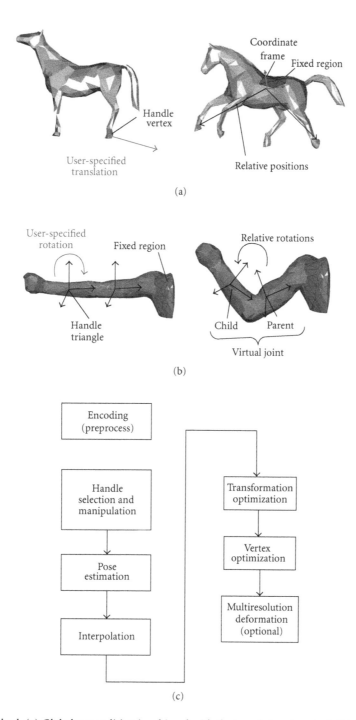

FIGURE 1: Overview of our method. (a) Global pose editing is achieved with the translational control. (b) Local pose editing is done using the rotational control. (c) Flow of deformation.

hand, if we use small values for penalty weights, the deformed mesh does not necessarily conform to handle positions. This flexibility is useful in our pose space surface deformation framework such that the user can adjust deformations to satisfy position constraints exactly or to conform to example deformations. Using a small weight, we can avoid local distortions around handles, caused by the deviation of the pose from the interpolation range.

4.2.1. Rotation Optimization.
To compute the new absolute rotation $\widetilde{\mathbf{R}}_i$ from the relative encoding $\mathbf{Q}_{ij}$, we rewrite (3) as follows:

$$\mathbf{Q}_{ij}^T \widetilde{\mathbf{R}}_j^T - \widetilde{\mathbf{R}}_i^T = 0. \qquad (4)$$

By gathering this equation for all the triangle pairs in the mesh, we can write this with a sparse linear system in the following form:

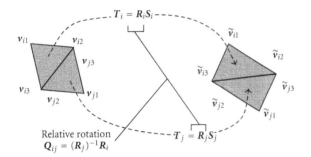

FIGURE 2: Rotation-invariant encoding. We first compute the deformation gradients. We then decompose these into absolute rotations and scale/shear components. While the scale/shear components are rotation invariant, the absolute rotations are not. Thus, we compute a relative rotation of two adjacent triangles to remove a global rotation.

$$\mathbf{H}\widetilde{\mathbf{R}} = \begin{bmatrix} \cdots - \mathbf{I} \cdots \mathbf{Q}_{ij}^T \cdots \end{bmatrix} \begin{bmatrix} \vdots \\ \widetilde{\mathbf{R}}_i^T \\ \vdots \\ \widetilde{\mathbf{R}}_j^T \\ \vdots \end{bmatrix} = 0, \qquad (5)$$

where $\mathbf{I}$ is a 3×3 identity matrix and the size of $\mathbf{H}$ is $3l \times 3m$. When achieving surface deformation, rotation constraints are applied to the set of triangles that include $\mathcal{R} \subseteq \{1 \cdots m\}$. Thus, the absolute rotations are optimized such that they satisfy both (5) and the rotation constraints. In general, there is no exact solution for this, and thus we need a least-squares approximation, that is, (5) becomes $\mathbf{H}^T\mathbf{H}\widetilde{\mathbf{R}} = 0$. Using the penalty method [33], the problem is formulated as follows:

$$\left(\mathbf{H}^T\mathbf{H} + \omega^R\mathbf{C}^R\right)\widetilde{\mathbf{R}} = \omega^R\mathbf{R}^C, \qquad (6)$$

where ω^R is the weight of rotation constraints; $\mathbf{R}^C$ is a $3m \times 3$ matrix of rotation constraints containing transposed target rotations at $3i-2$ to $3i$ rows if $i \in \mathcal{R}$, and otherwise 0; $\mathbf{C}^R$ is a $3m \times 3m$ diagonal matrix containing 1 at $3i-2$ to $3i$ rows if $i \in \mathcal{R}$, and otherwise 0. With $\mathbf{C}^R$, we can choose actual rotations that can be constrained to target rotations as follows:

$$\mathbf{C}^R\widetilde{\mathbf{R}} = \begin{bmatrix} \cdots \mathbf{I} \cdots \end{bmatrix} \begin{bmatrix} \vdots \\ \widetilde{\mathbf{R}}_i^T \\ \vdots \end{bmatrix}, \qquad (7)$$

where $\mathbf{I}$ is a 3×3 identity matrix. Note that $\mathbf{H}^T\mathbf{H} + \omega^R\mathbf{C}^R$ must be constructed and factorized once for every frame, which is somewhat costly for a large mesh.

Having obtained $\widetilde{\mathbf{R}}$, we perform matrix orthonormalization using SVD to factor out undesired shears. We then compute the new deformation gradient by $\widetilde{\mathbf{T}}_i = \widetilde{\mathbf{R}}_i\widetilde{\mathbf{S}}_i$. Note that we do not allow the user to use scale constraints in our method. Thus, $\widetilde{\mathbf{S}}_i$ comes only from the result of shape interpolation (Section 4.3.2). For a detail-preserving deformation, $\widetilde{\mathbf{S}}_i$ is omitted (Section 4.3.1).

4.2.2. Vertex Optimization. Once the deformation gradients $\widetilde{\mathbf{T}}$ are obtained, we can reconstruct vertex coordinates $\widetilde{\mathbf{v}}$ by solving (2). Equation (2) is solved in a weighted least-square sense: $\mathbf{G}^T\mathbf{D}\mathbf{G}\widetilde{\mathbf{v}} = \mathbf{G}^T\mathbf{D}\widetilde{\mathbf{T}}$ where $\mathbf{D}$ is a $3m \times 3m$ diagonal weight matrix containing the areas of the triangles [15]. As indicated by Botsch et al. [31], $\mathbf{G}^T\mathbf{D}\mathbf{G}$ is equivalent to the Laplace Bertrami operator $\mathbf{L}$, which can be computed directly from the cotangent weights [34]. In contrast to $\mathbf{H}^T\mathbf{H}$, $\mathbf{L}$ is factorized once for all the frames, which requires only back substitution and is, therefore, very efficient. When a set of position constraints, $\mathcal{P} \subseteq \{1 \cdots n\}$, is provided, this is solved via the penalty method, which leads to the following system:

$$\left(\mathbf{G}^T\mathbf{D}\mathbf{G} + \omega^P\mathbf{C}^P\right)\widetilde{\mathbf{v}} = \mathbf{G}^T\mathbf{D}\widetilde{\mathbf{T}} + \omega^P\mathbf{v}^C, \qquad (8)$$

where ω^P is the weight for position constraints; $\mathbf{v}^C$ is a $n \times 3$ matrix containing target positions at row p if $p \in \mathcal{P}$, and otherwise 0; $\mathbf{C}^P$ is a $n \times n$ diagonal matrix having 1 at row p if $p \in \mathcal{P}$, and otherwise 0. Like $\mathbf{C}^R$, we can choose vertices that should be constrained to the target positions using $\mathbf{C}^P$ as follows:

$$\mathbf{C}^P\widetilde{\mathbf{v}} = \begin{bmatrix} \cdots \mathbf{1} \cdots \end{bmatrix} \begin{bmatrix} \vdots \\ \widetilde{\mathbf{v}}_p \\ \vdots \end{bmatrix}. \qquad (9)$$

4.3. Surface Manipulation Tools. In this section, we introduce two basic surface manipulation tools for formulating our pose space deformation.

4.3.1. Handle-Based Surface Deformation. To deform a surface, we specify handle vertices/triangles on the mesh and apply translations/rotations to them (Figure 3). In addition, if a certain region on the mesh should be kept fixed, the user specifies the fixed region. To obtain the deformed vertices $\widetilde{\mathbf{v}}$, we solve sparse linear systems (6) and (8). Note that, because we optimize rotations and vertices separately, rotation constraints and translation constraints should be compatible with each other, otherwise, it produces distortions.

4.3.2. Shape Interpolation. The advantage of performing interpolation using the rotation-invariant encoding is that it is robust to large rotations. However, when simply interpolating the components of $\mathbf{Q}_{ij}$, it leads to the artifacts which can be seen in the linear blend skinning. One practical way to correctly interpolating rotations is to map them to so(3) using the matrix logarithm, interpolate linearly in so(3), and map back to $\mathbf{SO}(3)$ using the matrix exponential [2, 7, 10, 17, 32].

FIGURE 3: Handle-based surface deformation. We manipulate handle vertices/triangles on the surface by applying translations/rotations to them. The mesh deforms according to handle movements while preserving the original details. Note that, because we optimize rotations and vertices separately, rotation constraints and translation constraints should be compatible with each other, otherwise, it produces distortions. Without incorporating examples, our method deforms the model smoothly regardless of anatomical structures.

$\mathcal{M}^{(1)}$ $\mathcal{M}^{(2)}$ Def Grad   Rot Inv

FIGURE 4: Comparison of interpolation results. We perform interpolation on two meshes in different orientations: $\mathcal{M}^{(1)}$ and $\mathcal{M}^{(2)}$. The interpolation result using deformation gradients (Def Grad) is distorted because there is an ambiguity for interpolation if the orientations of the triangles differ by more than 180 degrees. The result obtained using the rotation-invariant encoding (Rot Inv) does not suffer from this ambiguity.

To achieve this, we use Rodrigues' formula and convert $\mathbf{Q}_{ij} \in \mathbb{R}^{3\times3}$ into an axis angle representation (rotation vector) $\mathbf{q}_{ij} \in \mathbb{R}^3$ which is a compact form of $\log\mathbf{Q}_{ij} \cdot \mathbf{S}_i$, however, can be interpolated directly. Note that, when linearly interpolating matrix logarithms, the interpolation path is not the shortest path, which introduces error. This error is minimal when the rotation is small, that is, the rotation is close to the identity. Therefore, we encode deformation gradients and rotation-invariant encodings relative to the rest pose [6, 32]. As a result, when we encode the rest pose, $\mathbf{Q}_{ij}$ is the identity for all triangle pairs.

We concatenate $\mathbf{q}_{ij}$ into a $3 \times l$ matrix, $\mathbf{q}$. Likewise, a symmetric matrix $\mathbf{S}_i \in \mathbb{R}^{3\times3}$ is flattened to $\mathbf{s}_i \in \mathbb{R}^6$ and concatenated into a $6 \times m$ matrix, $\mathbf{s}$. Interpolation of the rotation-invariant encodings of N meshes is achieved with a simple weighted combination. The interpolated values $\tilde{\mathbf{s}}$ and $\tilde{\mathbf{q}}$ are obtained from the following:

$$\tilde{\mathbf{s}} = \sum_{P=1}^{N} \alpha^{(P)}\mathbf{s}^{(P)},$$
$$\tilde{\mathbf{q}} = \sum_{P=1}^{N} \alpha^{(P)}\mathbf{q}^{(P)}, \tag{10}$$

where $\alpha^{(P)}$ is the weight for example P, which satisfies $\sum_{P=1}^{N} \alpha^{(P)} = 1$. After converting $\tilde{\mathbf{s}}$ and $\tilde{\mathbf{q}}$ to matrix form, the deformed vertex positions $\tilde{\mathbf{v}}$ are obtained by solving (6) and (8). We constrain one of the rotations to an identity matrix when solving (6) and fix one of the positions when solving (8).

Interpolation Properties. The rotation-invariant encoding is robust-to-extreme orientation differences of input models [12, 19, 32]. To show this, we compared the interpolation results using rotation-invariant encodings and using deformation gradients (Figure 4). Given two meshes, $\mathcal{M}^{(1)}$ and $\mathcal{M}^{(2)}$, which are in extremely different orientations, we create the intermediate steps between them. Let $\mathbf{s}^{(1)}$, $\mathbf{q}^{(1)}$, and $\mathbf{s}^{(2)}$, $\mathbf{q}^{(2)}$ be rotation-invariant encodings of two meshes. Then, we can perform interpolation with $\tilde{\mathbf{s}} = \alpha^{(1)}\mathbf{s}^{(1)} + (1-\alpha^{(1)})\mathbf{s}^{(2)}$ and

$\tilde{\mathbf{q}} = \alpha^{(1)}\mathbf{q}^{(1)} + (1-\alpha^{(1)})\mathbf{q}^{(2)}$. The interpolation of deformation gradients is performed in the same manner except that the rotations are represented in absolute world coordinates. If triangle orientations differ by more than 180 degrees, there is ambiguity in interpolating deformation gradients. Because of this ambiguity, the result using deformation gradients is distorted around the foot, as shown in Figure 4. Shape interpolation using rotation-invariant encodings does not suffer from this ambiguity and produces a natural result.

5. Pose Space Surface Manipulation

Now, we are ready to formulate our pose space surface manipulation technique by unifying the handle-based surface deformation and shape interpolation methods described in the previous section. To integrate these two, rotation-invariant encodings must be altered according to handle movements, that is, a technique to associate handle translations/rotations with interpolation weights must be developed.

5.1. Pose Estimation. To obtain interpolation weights, the original MeshIK [2] solves nonlinear optimization to determine the weights from handle positions. We, in turn, compute interpolation weights from the handle translations/rotations based on pose space interpolation. This allows us to avoid involved nonlinear optimization and to incorporate both translational/rotational controls.

To evaluate the pose of the model, we need the measure that is rotation invariant. To this end, we compute relative positions and rotations from handles (Figure 5).

When editing with the translational control, the user places a coordinate frame and handle vertices on the mesh. The frame is placed on a triangle that exists around the trunk of the model and is used to form a local coordinate to compute relative positions of handles. This way, we can eliminate the effect of global rotations and can evaluate the pose successfully. In addition, our system allows the user to manipulate global orientation and position of the model by rotating and translating the frame.

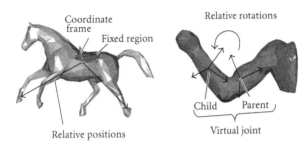

FIGURE 5: We infer a pose of a model from relative positions and rotations computed from handle translations/rotations.

When editing with the rotational control, the user places a pair of handle triangles called *virtual joint*. The virtual joint consists of *parent*, which is placed on the proximal segment, and *child*, which is placed on the distal segment. The user applies rotations to the child triangle whereas the parent triangle is not manipulated. To apply rotations, the user places a frame on a triangle that exists near the actual joint center in order to use its centroid as a rotation center. By rotating the frame, we can achieve twisting easily. By dragging the child triangle around the frame, bending is achieved. The pose is evaluated as a relative rotation between the virtual joint, which is represented as Euler angles.

5.2. Pose Space Deformation. Next, we compute the interpolation weights from the pose using a scattered data interpolation method. The interpolation weights are obtained by evaluating the pose computed from handle translations/rotations, in the pose space formed by example poses. We would like to compute the interpolation weights such that they satisfy the following criteria.

(1) At an example point, the weight for that example must be one, and all other weights must be zero.

(2) The weights must add up to 1.

(3) The weight must change continuously to produce smooth animation.

(4) The absolute value of the weight must be small to avoid excessive exaggeration of deformation.

For this task, we use k-nearest-neighbors interpolation [8] because it satisfies all of the above criteria and returns the weights within the range [0–1]. This method chooses the k closest example points and assigns weights based on the proximity (distance). All other example points are assigned a weight of zero. Before normalization, the weights for each examples are computed as

$$\alpha^{(P)} = \left(1 - \frac{d^{(P)}}{d_{\max}}\right)^2.$$ (11)

This is then normalized to sum to one. $d^{(P)}$ is the distance to the Pth example and the $d_{\max}$ is the distance to the $k + 1$ nearest point. We use $k = 6$ in this paper.

Let $K \in \{1 \cdots M\}$ be the index of handle vertex or virtual joint. Then, the pose is defined by a $3M \times 1$ vector, $\mathbf{f}$, that contains relative positions or relative rotations. The distance between an arbitrary pose and example P is defined as follows:

$$d^{(P)} = \left(\left\|\mathbf{f}^{(P)} - \mathbf{f}\right\|^2\right)^{1/2},$$ (12)

where $\mathbf{f}^{(P)}$ is a pose of example P.

After computing interpolation weights, we use (10) to obtain new rotation-invariant encodings. The new vertices are calculated by solving (6) and (8). When editing with translational controls, we constrain the rotation of triangle where the frame is placed, to the frame orientation relative to the rest pose. When editing with rotational controls, at least one vertex must be fixed to provide position constraints.

6. Multiresolution Deformation

By incorporating examples, our method can edit the model naturally and capture deformation effects such as muscle bulging. However, solving two large linear systems is still relatively time consuming, mainly due to the rotation optimization, which requires performing factorization for every frame. In addition, it requires a relatively large memory space ($3l$ for $\mathbf{q}$ and $6m$ for $\mathbf{s}$). To make our representation more compact and to speed up the computation, we use a multiresolution approach.

Our observation is that, if we layer a surface with a coarse mesh and fine details, then deformation induced by pose changes mainly affects the underlying coarse mesh and has little effect on the fine details. In fact, Weber et al. [6] reported that deformation behaviors of a character tend to have a low-frequency nature. They then used this fact to make example deformations more compact using a method similar to the geometry compression proposed in [35]. We, in turn, take a multiresolution approach using coarse meshes to compress example deformations. We compute rotation-invariant encodings from coarse meshes and perform PSD with them. We then add original fine details to the deformed coarse mesh to obtain a dense output model.

Inspired by Sumner et al. [23], we employ linear blend skinning to decouple a dense mesh into a coarse mesh and fine-details. Here, we represent the vertex position of the coarse mesh by $\mathbf{v}_k$, an affine transformation by $\mathbf{T}_k \in \mathbb{R}^{3 \times 3}$, and a translation vector by $\mathbf{b}_k \in \mathbb{R}^3$. The deformed vertex $\tilde{\mathbf{v}}_p$ is obtained as follows:

$$\tilde{\mathbf{v}}_p = \sum_{k=1}^{c} w_p^{(k)} \left[\mathbf{T}_k\left(\mathbf{v}_p - \mathbf{v}_k\right) + \mathbf{v}_k + \mathbf{b}_k\right],$$ (13)

where c is the number of vertices in the coarse mesh, and $w_p^{(k)}$ is a weight for vertex p. $w_p^{(k)}$ represents the extent to which $\mathbf{v}_p$ is influenced by $\mathbf{v}_k$.

To compute the weight $w_p^{(k)}$, we use harmonic interpolation [16] as opposed the Euclid distance-based weighting method [23]. This eliminates distortions caused by assigning large weights to the vertices that are geodesically distant. As

(a)   (b)

FIGURE 6: Editing a horse (1k triangles) with translations and rotations. By translating the handles on the feet, we can pose the horse naturally (a). Once the overall pose is determined, the user edit the pose locally with the rotational control, if required (b). The blue region is frozen so that deformations remain local.

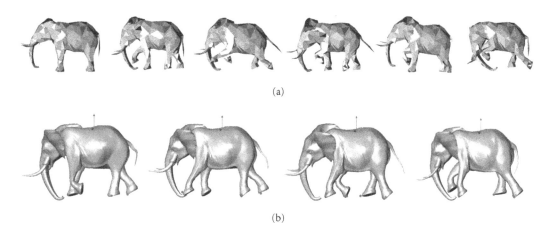

(a)

(b)

FIGURE 7: With 6 coarse examples (1k triangles) (a), we can create walking elephant (30k triangles) by translating handles on the feet (b).

for the boundary condition, vertex k is assigned the value $\mathbf{w}_p^{(k)} = 1$, and all other vertices in the coarse mesh are assigned the value $\mathbf{w}_p^{(k)} = 0$. If the harmonic value is $\mathbf{w}_p^{(k)} < 0.01$, then we replace it with 0 so that we can reduce memory space. The values are then normalized such that their sum is 1.

To construct a coarse mesh, we use a variant of the quadratic mesh simplification method (Qslim) [36]. Because Qslim only considers a static shape, the resulting coarse mesh is not suitable for deformation. For example, if we apply Qslim to a character model with its knee extended, then we would lose vertices around the knee. This loss would be a problem when we want to bend the knee. To solve this problem, we modify Qslim slightly by computing the error metric using all the examples. This method is similar to that proposed in [37], but we do not move the vertices during edge collapse; thus, we can easily specify boundary conditions of harmonic interpolation.

Incorporating the above technique into the pose space surface manipulation framework is straightforward. We prepare coarse examples and store their rotation-invariant encodings. We also store harmonic weights and fine details that are the vectors emanating from the vertex of a coarse mesh to that of a dense mesh, $\mathbf{v}_p - \mathbf{v}_k$. We then perform PSD using those values. Once the result using coarse meshes is obtained, fine details are added using (13). Unlike [23], who place them on the dense mesh, we place handles directly on the coarse mesh. However, we found that the manipulation

of handles on a coarse mesh of around 1k triangles retains sufficient freedom for interactive mesh editing.

7. Results

We implemented the pose space surface manipulation technique on an Intel Core2 Quad Q9400 2.66 GHz machine. We used the sparse Cholesky solver provided with the CHOLMOD [38] library. We found that the range $\omega^R = [10^4–10^8]$ worked well for all the examples presented in this paper. In contrast, we provide a wider range of $\omega^P = [10^{-2}–10^8]$.

Interactive Editing. In the accompanying video, we show use cases of the pose space surface manipulation framework for interactive editing of mesh models. Figure 6 demonstrates how our method edits a model using both translational and rotational control. By translating the handles on the feet, we can pose the horse (1k triangles) naturally (Figure 6(a)). Once the overall pose is determined, the user manipulates the part of the model with the rotational control (Figure 6(b)). The blue region is frozen so that deformations remain local.

Using our translational editing method, we can create animation sequences. As shown in Figure 7, we can create walking elephant (30k triangles) from 6 coarse examples (1k triangles) by translating handles on the feet. We can also pose the performer (dense: 20k triangles, coarse: 1k triangles)

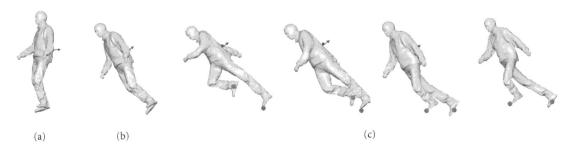

FIGURE 8: Posing of the performer model (dense: 20k triangles, coarse: 1k triangles). We place a frame on the back and handles on the feet (a). We first adjust the global orientation of the performer (b). We can pose the performer in a running sequence by translating the handles (c).

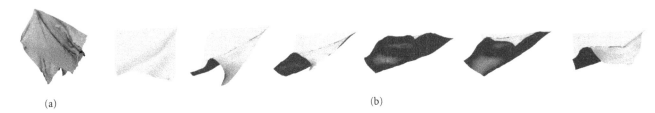

FIGURE 9: Editing of highly nonrigid objects. (a) We provide 14 examples (1k triangles) to edit a cloth. (b) By just dragging the lower right corner of the model to apply translations, we can animate the cloth realistically.

in a running sequence by moving the handles on the feet (Figure 8).

Figure 9 demonstrates the applicability of our method to highly nonrigid objects such as a cloth. We used 14 examples (1k triangles) created by a simulation. We fixed the top edge of a model and placed a frame on the top-left corner. By just dragging the handle on the bottom right corner, we can animate the cloth realistically.

Figure 10 demonstrates the ability of our method to accomplish twisting. We placed handle triangles on the upper arm and shoulder blade. We manipulate the frame placed on the triangle which is near the joint center. The rotational control is more intuitive for controlling shoulder movements than the translational control. Even for these challenging cases involving twisting and bending, our method can produce natural results.

Handle Locations and Sizes. In Figure 11, we evaluated the sensitivity of our method to the locations of triangles. Our method works when the handle triangle is distally or proximally placed in the segment (Figure 11(b) and 11(c)). Even when the handle is placed on the region where it is deformed by muscle bulging, pose space interpolation was successfully achieved (Figure 11(d)). Although we recommend placing the triangles in the middle of the segments, our method works robustly as long as child and parent triangles are placed on different segments. Our method works even when the triangle is placed far from the virtual joint. However, it is somewhat difficult for the user to manipulate the triangle in this case; because joints exist between the triangle and the virtual joint, the distance between the triangle and the

virtual joint changes during dragging and the model will deform unexpectedly. In this case, the translational control is more suitable and easy to use. In addition, the size of the triangle is also important. If the size of the triangle is so small and its orientation changes drastically with high-frequency deformations, then the pose space interpolation will probably introduce large approximation errors. For the examples presented in this paper, however, pose space interpolation is successfully achieved because we manipulate relatively large triangles that is on a coarse mesh with around 1k triangles.

Comparisons. In Figure 12, we compare our method using rotational controls with the transformation propagation approach of Zayer et al. [16]. As expected, our method is more realistic where the elbow bends sharply, and the biceps bulges naturally, whereas the transformation propagation method just deforms the model smoothly. In Figure 13, we compared our method with the material modulation approach [17]. Although material modulation exploits the examples, it is difficult to control details precisely because it only computes a weight per vertex from all examples and does not account for pose changes. The result of our method looks nearly identical to the ground truth. We also quantitatively compared our method with [17]. We measured the error defined by the mean distance between the deformed model and the ground truth, which was normalized by the bounding box diagonal. Our method is more accurate than [17] where the error of our method is approximately 1.5% of the bounding box diagonal whereas that of [17] is 5.8%.

(a)

(b)

FIGURE 10: Twisting of the shoulder. We provide 9 examples (a) and are able to obtain natural results using the rotational control (b). The rotational control is more intuitive for controlling shoulder movements than the translational control.

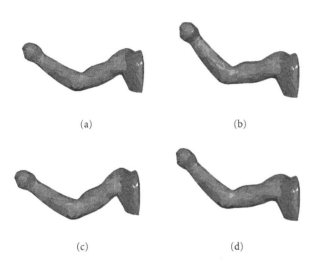

(a)

(b)

(c)

(d)

FIGURE 11: Locations of triangles. Our method works even when the handle triangle is placed distally (b), proximally (c), or on the region where a muscle bulges (d).

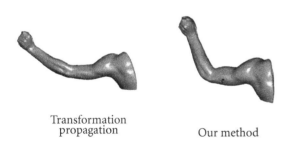

Transformation propagation

Our method

FIGURE 12: Comparison with the transformation propagation approach [16]. Our method produces a more realistic result because the elbow bends sharply and the biceps bulges naturally. In contrast, the transformation propagation method deforms the model smoothly.

Next, we compared our method using translational controls with MeshIK [2]. When the pose is in the example space, our method is on par with MeshIK (compare Figure 14 of this paper and Figure 5 of [2]). As with MeshIK, our method fails when the pose is outside of the example space (Figure 14(a)). The advantage of our method is the applicability to the examples with large bending (Figure 15); this is, important when editing models that have tails, tentacles, and

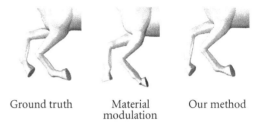

Ground truth

Material modulation

Our method

FIGURE 13: Comparison with the material modulation method [17]. Although material modulation produces a plausible result, it is still difficult to control details precisely. Our method is nearly identical to the ground truth.

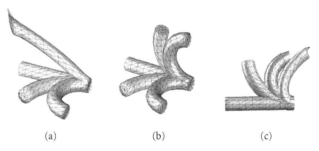

(a)

(b)

(c)

FIGURE 14: Edits of a bar model with the translational control. (a) We first provide two examples (gray). The shape in-between can be created meaningfully. However, it causes shearing distortions when we deform the bar in the vertical direction. (b) By providing another example in this direction, we can produce a natural result. (c) Because the distance-based interpolation method lacks the extrapolation capability, local distortions around handles occur when the pose is outside of the interpolation range.

so forth. Since MeshIK uses deformation gradient (Def Grad) as its basic representation, which is defined in the absolute world coordinate, it results in the discontinuity artifact (Figure 15 top right). Our method based on a rotation-invariant mesh representation naturally deforms the model using the examples that involve large rotations and bending (Figure 15 bottom). The downside of our method is the lack of extrapolation capability due to the use of the distance-based interpolation method, which violates the smoothness around handles (Figure 14(c)). This can be avoided by incorporating an adequate number of example poses with extreme poses, since our method accepts examples with large

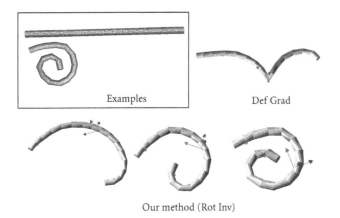

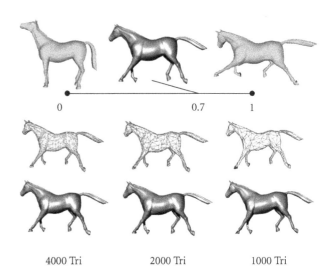

FIGURE 15: If we use deformation gradient (Def Grad) that was used in MeshIK [2], our method results in the discontinuity artifact because Def Grad is defined in the absolute world coordinate (top right). Our method based on a rotation-invariant mesh representation (Rot Inv) naturally deforms the model using the examples that involve large rotations and bending (bottom).

FIGURE 17: Interpolation results using coarse meshes. We perform interpolation on several mesh resolutions. Top: interpolation of the original model (17k triangles). Middle: the interpolation results of coarse meshes (4k, 2k and 1k triangles). Bottom: comparison of the dense results. The results are nearly identical for all the resolutions.

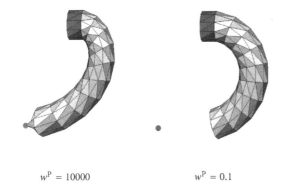

FIGURE 16: The effect of using a small weight for position constraints. Using a small value for w^P, we can avoid violating the smoothness around the handle.

bending. Another way to solve this problem is to use a small value for w^P such that the deformed model conforms to example deformations by not obeying handle positions exactly (Figure 16).

Memory Consumptions. Storing rotation-invariant encodings requires a relatively large amount of memory. To solve this problem, we propose a multiresolution approach. In Figure 17, we show the morphing results of Horse in several mesh resolutions. With only 1k triangles, we can generate a result that is nearly identical to that of the original resolution (17k triangles). Using our multiresolution technique, the memory consumptions in this case can be reduced to at least 6% of the original without degrading the quality of the output.

Performance. In Table 1, we show the performance results. The most time consuming processes in our method are the

rotation optimization and the subsequent matrix orthonormalization. Because the matrix $\mathbf{H}$ is constructed from relative rotations computed after interpolation, the matrix $\mathbf{H}^T\mathbf{H}$ must be factorized for every frame. For the rotation optimization of 17k mesh, construction and factorization of $\mathbf{H}^T\mathbf{H}$, and back substitution take 0.21 sec, 0.25 sec, and 0.027 sec, respectively. The matrix orthonormalization of absolute rotations using SVD also takes a relatively long time, which is about 0.5 sec for a 17k mesh. However, the vertex optimization is done very efficiently because the construction and factorization of $\mathbf{L}$ is required once for all the frames, and we execute only back substitution during runtime. To summarize, without the multiresolution method, our method requires approximately 1 second to edit a 17k mesh.

Using the multiresolution method, we can edit a mesh in an interactive rate. Our method requires approximately 0.1 sec to edit a 17k mesh and 0.2 sec to edit a 140k mesh. This is a significant speedup over the original MeshIK that requires approximately 1 sec to solve a *single* Gauss-Newton iteration to edit an 80k mesh [2].

Limitations. Our method has limitations that need to be overcome. Although the use of the multiresolution method helps achieving interactive rates, fine details remain static. It is, therefore, difficult for our method to model complex deformation, for example, facial expressions generated by muscle contractions. Our method is probably suitable for large- and medium-scale deformation, and it is rather unfit for modeling small scale surface-detail deformations. Also, because we assign one interpolation weight for each example, our method do not accept the user to place many handles, for example, more than 10 or 20 handles. We believe that our global-to-local editing strategy based on

TABLE 1: Timing comparisons of each step with and without the multiresolution method (in seconds).

	Mesh size	No. Ex.	Interp. Rot Inv	Rotation optimization			Vertex optimization			Matrix ortho.	Coarse-to-Dense
				Const.	Factor	Solve	Const.	Factor	Solve		
w/o multires.	17k	10	0.12	0.21	0.25	0.027	[0.78]	[0.023]	0.003	0.50	—
With multires.	1k	10	0.01	0.01	0.01	0.001	[0.06]	[0.002]	0.001	0.03	0.008 (17k), 0.075 (140k)

From left to right: Mesh size, number of examples, interpolation of rotation-invariant encodings, rotation optimization (construction and factorization of $\mathbf{H}^T\mathbf{H}$, and back substitution), vertex optimization (construction and factorization of $\mathbf{L}$, and back substitution), matrix ortho-normalization using SVD, conversion of a coarse mesh to a dense mesh. Timings in brackets are done during the preprocessing stage.

translational/rotational controls works well for interactive posing of the model without using many handles, which can create a new shape in a wide range of poses. However, in the case where simultaneous manipulations of a large number of handles are required, for example, deforming the model using motion-capture data points, our method would fail to approximate deformations. This problem could be alleviated by using the weighted pose space deformation framework [5] to compute weights for each vertex instead of each example. Finally, our method lacks the extrapolation capability, which causes shear distortions when the pose is outside of the interpolation range. The ways to solve this problem may be to use a small weight for position constraints or to use examples with extreme poses.

8. Conclusion

Pose space surface manipulation is a novel example-based mesh editing technique that can deform the model naturally and that is able to adjust a pose locally. We provide both translational and rotational constraints to achieve direct manipulation of a surface to pose the model. Our method is reasonably efficient because, by inferring a pose from handles and by performing pose space interpolation, we are able to solve the problem with two linear systems, which avoids involved nonlinear optimization. With this two-step linear approach combined with the multiresolution deformation method, we achieve interactive rates without losing important deformation effects such as muscle bulging. The performance of our method would be further improved by a GPU implementation [11, 39]. It would be interesting to extend our method to edit other surface representations, such as multicomponent objects.

Acknowledgment

The authors would like to thank Brett Allen for the Arm and Shoulder datasets, Robert W. Sumner for the Elephant, Lion, Horse, and Cloth models, and Daniel Vlasic for the Performer model.

References

[1] J. P. Lewis, M. Cordner, and N. Fong, "Pose space deformation: a unified approach to shape interpolation and skeleton-driven deformation," in *Proceedings of the SIGGRAPH*, pp. 165–172, July 2000.

[2] R. W. Sumner, M. Zwicker, C. Gotsman, and J. Popovic, "Mesh-based inverse kinematics," in *Proceedings of the ACM SIGGRAPH*, pp. 488–495, August 2005.

[3] K. G. Der, R. W. Sumner, and J. Popovic, "Inverse kinematics for reduced deformable models," in *Proceedings of the ACM SIGGRAPH*, pp. 1174–1179, August 2006.

[4] P. G. Kry, D. L. James, and D. K. Pai, "Eigenskin: real time large deformation character skinning in hardware," in *Proceedings of the ASM SIGGRAPH Symposium on Computer Animation (SCA '02)*, pp. 153–159, July 2002.

[5] T. Kurihara and N. Miyata, "Modeling deformable human hands from medical images," in *Proceedings of the ACM SIGGRAPH Eurographics Symposium on Computer Animation (SCA '04)*, pp. 355–363, 2004.

[6] O. Weber, O. Sorkine, Y. Lipman, and C. Gotsman, "Context-aware skeletal shape deformation," *Computer Graphics Forum*, vol. 26, no. 3, pp. 265–274, 2007.

[7] R. Y. Wang, K. Pulli, and J. Popovic, "Real-time enveloping with rotational regression," *ACM Transactions on Graphics*, vol. 26, no. 3, Article ID 1276468, 2007.

[8] B. Allen, B. Curless, and Z. Popovic, "Articulated body deformation from range scan Data," *ACM Transactions on Graphics*, vol. 21, no. 3, pp. 612–619, 2002.

[9] D. Anguelov, P. Srinivasan, D. Koller, S. Thrun, J. Rodgers, and J. Davis, "Scape: shape completion and animation of people," *ACM Transactions on Graphics*, vol. 24, no. 3, 2005.

[10] N. Hasler, C. Stoll, M. Sunkel, B. Rosenhahn, and H. P. Seidel, "A statistical model of human pose and body shape," *Computer Graphics Forum*, vol. 28, no. 2, pp. 337–346, 2009.

[11] B. Bickel, M. Lang, M. Botsch, M. Otaduy, and M. Gross, "Pose-space animation and transfer of facial details," in *Proceedings of the ACM SIGGRAPH Eurographics Symposium on Computer Animation*, pp. 57–66, July 2008.

[12] Y. Lipman, O. Sorkine, D. Levin, and D. Cohen-Or, "Linear rotation-invariant coordinates for meshes," in *Proceedings of the ACM SIGGRAPH*, pp. 479–487, August 2005.

[13] O. Sorkine, D. Cohen-Or, Y. Lipman, M. Alexa, C. Rossl, and H. P. Seidel, "Laplacian surface editing," in *Proceedings of the 2nd Symposium on Geometry Processing (SGP '04)*, pp. 175–184, July 2004.

[14] Y. Yu, K. Zhou, D. Xu et al., "Mesh editing with poisson-based gradient field manipulation," *ACM Transactions on Graphics*, vol. 23, no. 3, pp. 644–651, 2004.

[15] M. Botsch and O. Sorkine, "On linear variational surface deformation methods," *IEEE Transactions on Visualization and Computer Graphics*, vol. 14, no. 1, pp. 213–230, 2008.

[16] R. Zayer, C. Rossl, Z. Karni, and H. P. Seidel, "Harmonic guidance for surface deformation," in *Proceedings of the Eurographics*, 2005.

[17] T. Popa, D. Julius, and A. Sheffer, "Material-aware mesh deformations," in *Proceedings of the IEEE International Conference on Shape Modeling and Applications (SMI '06)*, p. 22, June 2006.

[18] T. Igarashi, T. Moscovich, and J. F. Hughes, "As-rigid-as-possible shape manipulation," *ACM Transactions on Computer Graphics*, vol. 24, no. 3, 2005.

[19] S. Kircher and M. Garland, "Free-form motion processing," *ACM Transactions on Graphics*, vol. 27, no. 2, pp. 1–13, 2008.

[20] O. K. C. Au, C. L. Tai, L. Liu, and H. Fu, "Dual laplacian editing for meshes," *IEEE Transactions on Visualization and Computer Graphics*, vol. 12, no. 3, pp. 386–395, 2006.

[21] V. Kraevoy and A. Sheffer, "Mean-value geometry encoding," *International Journal of Shape Modeling*, vol. 12, no. 1, pp. 29–46, 2006.

[22] O. Sorkine and M. Alexa, "As-rigid-as-possible surface modeling," in *Proceedings of the EUROGRAPHICS/ACM SIGGRAPH Symposium on Geometry Processing (SGP '07)*, 2007.

[23] R. W. Sumner, J. Schmid, and M. Pauly, "Embedded deformation for shape manipulation," *ACM Transactions on Graphics*, vol. 26, no. 3, Article ID 1276478, 2007.

[24] M. Ben-Chen, O. Weber, and C. Gotsman, "Variational harmonic maps for space deformation," *ACM Transactions on Graphics*, vol. 28, no. 3, 2009.

[25] M. Kilian, N. J. Mitra, and H. Pottmann, "Geometric modeling in shape space," *Acm Transactions on Graphics*, vol. 26, no. 3, Article ID 1276457, 2007.

[26] O. K. C. Au, H. Fu, C. L. Tai, and D. Cohen-Or, "Handle-aware isolines for scalable shape editing," *Acm Transactions on Graphics*, vol. 26, no. 3, Article ID 1276481, 2007.

[27] M. Botsch, M. Pauly, M. Gross, and L. Kobbelt, "PriMo: coupled prisms for intuitive surface modeling," in *Proceedings of the Eurographics Symposium on Geometry Processing (SGP '06)*, pp. 11–20, 2006.

[28] J. Huang, X. Shi, X. Liu et al., "Subspace gradient domain mesh deformation," in *Proceedings of the ACM SIGGRAPH*, pp. 1126–1134, August 2006.

[29] X. Shi, K. Zhou, Y. Tong, M. Desbrun, H. Bao, and B. Guo, "Mesh puppetry: cascading optimization of mesh deformation with inverse kinematics," *ACM Transactions on Graphics*, vol. 26, no. 3, Article ID 1276479, 2007.

[30] R. W. Sumner and J. Popovic, "Deformation transfer for triangle meshes," in *Proceedings of ACM SIGGRAPH*, pp. 399–405, August 2004.

[31] M. Botsch, R. Sumner, M. Pauly, and M. Gross, "Deformation transfer for detail-preserving surface editing," in *Proceedings of the Vision, Modeling and Visualization*, pp. 357–364, 2006.

[32] I. Baran, D. Vlasic, E. Grinspun, and J. Popovic, "Semantic deformation transfer," *ACM Transactions on Graphics*, vol. 28, no. 3, 2009.

[33] K. Xu, H. Zhang, D. Cohen-Or, and Y. Xiong, "Dynamic harmonic fields for surface processing," *Computers and Graphics*, vol. 33, no. 3, pp. 391–398, 2009.

[34] U. Pinkall and K. Polthier, "Computing discrete minimal surfaces and their conjugates," *Experimental Mathematics*, vol. 2, no. 1, pp. 15–36, 1993.

[35] O. Sorkine, D. Cohen-Or, D. Irony, and S. Toledo, "Geometry-aware bases for shape approximation," *IEEE Transactions on Visualization and Computer Graphics*, vol. 11, no. 2, pp. 171–180, 2005.

[36] M. Garland and P. S. Heckbert, "Surface simplification using quadric error metrics," in *Proceedings of the SIGGRAPH Conference on Computer Graphics*, pp. 209–216, August 1997.

[37] A. Mohr and M. Gleicher, "Deformation sensitive decimation," Tech. Rep., 2003.

[38] Y. Chen, T. Davis, W. Harger, and S. Rajamanickam, "Algorithm 8xx: CHOLMOD, supernodal sparse cholesky factorizationand update/downdate," Tech. Rep. TR-2006-005, 2006.

[39] T. Rhee, J. P. Lewis, and U. Neumann, "Real-time weighted pose-space deformation on the gpu," in *Proceedings of the Eurographics*, 2006.

7

User Experiences While Playing Dance-Based Exergames and the Influence of Different Body Motion Sensing Technologies

Alasdair G. Thin, Craig Brown, and Paul Meenan

School of Life Sciences, Heriot-Watt University, Edinburgh EH14 4AS, UK

Correspondence should be addressed to Alasdair G. Thin; a.g.thin@hw.ac.uk

Academic Editor: Hanqiu Sun

Dance Dance Revolution is a pioneering exergame which has attracted considerable interest for its potential to promote regular exercise and its associated health benefits. The advent of a range of different consumer body motion tracking video game console peripherals raises the question whether their different technological affordances (i.e., variations in the type and number of body limbs that they can track) influence the user experience while playing dance-based exergames both in terms of the level of physical exertion and the nature of the play experience. To investigate these issues a group of subjects performed a total of six comparable dance routines selected from commercial dance-based exergames (two routines from each game) on three different consoles. The subjects' level of physical exertion was assessed by measuring oxygen consumption and heart rate. They also reported their perceived level of exertion, difficulty, and enjoyment ratings after completing each dance routine. No differences were found in the physiological measures of exertion between the peripherals/consoles. However, there were significant variations in the difficulty and enjoyment ratings between peripherals. The design implications of these results are discussed including the tension between helping to guide and coordinate player movement versus offering greater movement flexibility.

1. Introduction

Exercise involving dancing to music is a popular form of physical activity and from the arcade beginnings of Dance Dance Revolution (DDR), dance-based exergames (i.e., video games that use body movement to control them and require physical exertion to play them) have now become a popular mainstream activity [1]. Over the years a variety of different body-movement-based video game controllers have been developed to try to create more immersive video game play experiences. With the advent of many different types of low cost sensor devices, this trend is likely to continue. More recently, three different consumer body motion sensor peripherals for consumer video games consoles have come to the fore and attracted considerable interest (i.e., Nintendo Wiimote, Sony Playstation Move, and Microsoft Kinect) for their potential to open up new possibilities for body-movement-controlled video games. Given their growing popularity and broad age and demographic appeal, there is now significant interest in their potential to promote physical

activity and health [2–4] rather than just simply a novel form of game controller, and exergames have already been incorporated into physical education activities in schools [5, 6].

A low level of physical fitness is an important risk factor for premature mortality [7]. Despite the unequivocal health benefits of regular exercise, physical inactivity is a major health problem globally and has a wide range of health problems associated with it including high blood pressure, high cholesterol, type 2 diabetes, coronary heart disease, stroke, and some cancers [8]. In England, UK in 2008, health statistics indicate that 17% boys and 15% girls between the ages of 2 and 15 years were classified as being obese along with a quarter of men and women aged 16 and over [9]. The UK government's recommended amount of physical activity for children is at least 60 minutes of moderate intensity activity on every day of the week and for adults at least 30 minutes per day of moderate intensity exercise on five or more days of the week [10]. Recent data for England indicate that between the ages of 2 and 15 years, only a third of boys achieved this target for physical activity compared with a quarter of girls and only 39% men and 29% women reached the minimum recommended amount [9].

Given the meteoric rise of video games to become a very popular form of entertainment, they are not something that can easily be ignored. While *"all things in moderation"* is a good maxim to live by, it is more realistic and pragmatic to tap into the engaging nature of video games and steer players towards becoming healthier by replacing a proportion of their sedentary game play time with active games that require significant physical exertion [11]. It is perhaps unsurprising that making physical activity more enjoyable has been shown to increase participation [12].

DDR is based on a game controller which comprises a simple set of foot switches arranged in a 3 × 3 matrix on a pad that is approximately 0.8 m × 0.8 m in size. The game requires the player to step on the correct arrow on the dance pad in time with on-screen visual arrow cues, and points are awarded depending on how accurately the player times each step and for accumulating sequences of correct steps. Increasing the speed at which the arrows appear on the screen and the complexity of the arrow sequences makes the game harder and requires higher levels of motor skill and more rapid physical movement to perform. One of the first studies to assess the level of energy expenditure associated with playing DDR [13] (by measuring rates of oxygen consumption) reported levels of exertion that would meet the lower end of the intensity range of the American College of Sports Medicine's guidelines for aerobic exercise [14]. A further study of DDR, this time in children [15], had similar findings. When comparing experienced DDR players with beginners they found that the experienced players could play the game at a higher skill level and this led to greater levels of energy expenditure [16]. An international online survey of DDR players found that the main reasons people played the game was because it was fun, provided some form of exercise, and was something challenging to do [17]. Finally, it has recently been reported that a suitably modified form of DDR could be used by older adults (70+ years old) [18].

From a health perspective, the higher the level of physical exertion required to play an exergame, the greater the benefits that are likely to accrue. The arrival of dance-based exergames based on body motion sensing peripherals is therefore of significant interest in that they may have the potential to facilitate the desired higher levels of energy expenditure. However, because the various peripherals differ in the number of limbs that they track (and therefore the amount of active skeletal muscle mass), it is possible that they differ in their potential health benefits. The Wiimote (Nintendo) peripheral incorporates a triaxial accelerometer to detect motion and an optical sensor that enables the determination of where on the screen the controller is pointing to. The Playstation Move (Sony) peripheral incorporates both a tri-axial accelerometer and a tri-axial angular rate sensor and a magnetometer to correct for drift. A ball mounted on the end of the controller and illuminated from the inside by coloured LEDs is tracked by a camera mounted above the screen, and given that the size of the ball is known, it can be tracked in three dimensions. Finally, the Kinect (Microsoft)

peripheral is entirely camera-based and uses an infrared 3D depth scanning approach to motion tracking.

The first aim of this study was therefore to assess whether there were any influences of the different body motion tracking technologies on the levels of energy expenditure elicited while playing dance-based exergames as determined by direct measurement of oxygen consumption. The second aim was to assess if the technologies differed in the nature of the user experiences while playing the games in terms of perceived levels of physical exertion, game difficulty, and enjoyment ratings.

2. Methods

Subjects were recruited from within the student population at Heriot-Watt University. All participants gave written, informed consent and completed a health screening questionnaire. The study was subject to local ethics committee approval. Subjects' height and body mass were measured using a portable stadiometer (Holtain, Pembrokeshire, UK), and weighing scales (Seca 761, Birmingham, UK) respectively. In total, 11 subjects (9 male) were recruited and completed the study. Mean (±SD) age was 19.4 ± 1.5 years, height 1.76 ± 0.10 m, weight 74.6 ± 12.4 kg, and body mass index 24.0 ± 2.9 kg/m^2.

Three different consumer video games consoles (Nintendo Wii, Sony Playstation 3, and Microsoft Xbox 360) and, their separate associated body motion sensing technologies (as described in the Introduction) were used in the study. The exergames used in the study were Just Dance 2 (Ubisoft Entertainment), SingStar + Dance (Sony), and Dance Central (Harmonix) and for the Wii, Playstation 3, and Xbox 360 consoles, respectively. Six songs/dance routines (two from each game) were selected for use in study on the basis that the routines were all of similar tempo (beats per minute) and involved comparable amounts of arm and leg movements. The routines selected were as follows: Microsoft Kinect– *"Just Dance"* by *Lady Gaga* (Kinect1) and *"Drop It Like It's Hot"* by *Snoop Dogg* (Kinect2); Sony Playstation Move– *"U Can't Touch This"* by *MC Hammer* (Move1), and *"It's Like That"* by *Run-Dmc Vs. Jason Nevins* (Move2); Nintendo Wii– *"The Power"* by *Snap!* (Wii1) and *"Hey Ya!"* by *Outkast* (Wii2). Screen shots showing the game play screens from each of the three games are shown for illustration in Figure 1.

Physical exertion levels during the game play periods were assessed using a wearable, wireless telemetric recording system (Oxycon Mobile, VIASYS Healthcare, Hoechberg, Germany). Subjects wear a face mask and expired air flow is measured with a turbine impropeller and is simultaneously analysed for oxygen and carbon dioxide fractional concentrations. These measurements are then cross-product integrated on a breath-by-breath basis to determine the rates of oxygen consumption and carbon dioxide production. Before each testing session, the expired air flow sensor was calibrated using two separate flow rates according to the manufacturer's specifications and the gas analysers calibrated using a precision gas mixture. The gas analysis unit and the combined battery pack and radio transmitter unit are both held in place by a harness worn on the subject's back with

FIGURE 1: Game play screen shots for each body motion tracking peripheral. (a) Kinect (Dance Central), (b) Playstation Move (SingStar + Dance), and (c) Wiimote (Just Dance 2).

virtually no restriction on movement. Subjects also wore a heart rate monitor chest strap (Polar, Kempele, Finland) under their clothing, the signal from which is automatically picked up by the telemetric system. Physiological data were averaged over the duration of each game play period.

Immediately after completing each dance routine, participants completed three simple psychophysiological self-report measures. The first measure involved rating their perceived level of physical exertion using a numerical scale [19] (i.e., how hard a subject felt they were exercising). The second measure concerned how difficult subjects perceived each routine and used a visual analogue scale (VAS) comprising of a 100 mm line anchored with the labels "*Very Easy*" at one end and "*Very Difficult*" at the other with subjects asked to make a mark somewhere along the line [20]. The third and final self-report measure related to the level of enjoyment the subjects experienced also used a VAS; this time anchored by the labels "*Very Enjoyable*" and "*Very Boring.*"

The familiarisation session involved the subjects being introduced to the body motion sensing peripherals and the two selected dance routines on each of the three games consoles. Both the order of the consoles and the order in which each subject played each pair of routines were randomised. To help familiarise the subjects with the corresponding

sensations of physical exertion used in the self-report measure (as described above), immediately after the end of each routine the subjects were asked to rate their perceived level of exertion. After completing each pair routines on a given console, subjects had a short (five minutes) seated rest break to permit the equipment to be changed over to the next console.

In the measurement session, subjects were fitted with the telemetric physiological recording system (as described earlier) and wore it throughout the session. Subjects were seated, and baseline measurements taken for five minutes before the first game was played. All dance routines were played once except for the Xbox 360 games (Kinect1 & Kinect2) which were played twice because of their shorter duration in order for the game play time to be similar across all consoles. The order and timing of the routines were the same as for the familiarisation session and immediately after the end of each routine the subjects completed each of the self-report measures.

All data are presented as mean ± standard error of the mean (SEM). Data were compared using repeated measures analysis of variance except for each pair of game scores on the same technology platform which were compared using paired-sample t-tests. The association between game enjoyment and difficulty ratings was assessed using Pearson's product-moment correlation. The threshold for statistical significance was set at $P < 0.05$.

3. Results

The mean improvement in game scores between the familiarisation and testing sessions for each of the dance routines ranged from +13 to +35%. Comparing the game scores between routines using the same body motion sensing technology (and games console), the mean score for Kinect1 was significantly higher versus that for Kinect2 (+18%, $P < 0.05$) and the Move1 routine was also significantly higher than that for Move2 (+8%, $P < 0.05$). However, there was no significant difference between the mean scores for the two routines on the Wii console (Wii1 & Wii2).

Due to a loss of telemetric data capture with two of the subjects, complete sets of physiological data are only available for nine subjects. There were no differences in mean heart rate between any of the pairs of routines on the same console or between the different body motion sensing technologies (Figure 2). Similarly, there were no differences in the mean rates of oxygen consumption between routines or motion sensing technologies (Figure 3).

With regard to the psychophysiological self-report measures, there were also no differences in the mean ratings of perceived level of physical exertion between routines or motion sensing technologies (Figure 4). However, both Move1 and Move2 were reported by the subjects as being significantly more difficult than all the other routines on the other two consoles (Figure 5). Finally, comparison of the levels of perceived enjoyment of each of the routines indicated that the Kinect1 routine was rated significantly more enjoyable than Move1, Move2, and Wii2 routines (Figure 6) and the Kinect2 routine was rated significantly more enjoyable than the Move2 routine (Figure 6).

The results were also analysed according to the randomised order in which the subjects performed each of the routines and no evidence of any order effects was found (data not shown).

In order to investigate whether there was any association between perceived game difficulty and self-reported enjoyment ratings for each routine and body motion sensing technologies, the group means of each set of enjoyment rating scores were plotted against the corresponding group means of the difficulty ratings. The results of this analysis revealed a positive correlation between increasing perceived game difficulty and declining game enjoyment ratings (Figure 7).

4. Discussion

The main findings of this study were that while the three different consumer body motion sensors differ in the underlying technologies, and therefore the type and number of body limbs they are able to track the motion of, the separate dance-based exergames developed for each video game console all required comparable amounts of physical exertion (equivalent to moderate exercise) to play them. However, while the

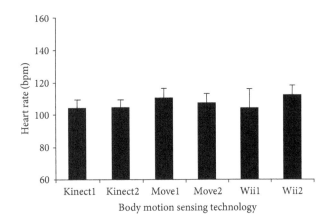

FIGURE 2: Heart rate (beats per minute) during each of the different dance routines using the various different body motion sensing technologies. Data are shown as mean ($n = 9$) and error bars indicate SEM.

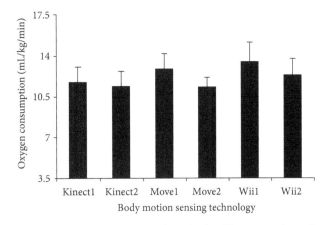

FIGURE 3: Oxygen consumption (standardised between subjects by expressing it in terms of mL per minute per kg body mass) during each of the different dance routines using the various different body motion sensing technologies. Data are shown as mean ($n = 9$) and error bars indicate SEM.

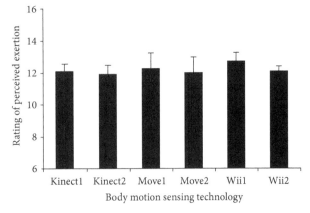

FIGURE 4: Rating of perceived exertion reported immediately after performing each of the different dance routines using the various different body motion sensing technologies. Data are shown as mean ($n = 11$) and error bars indicate SEM.

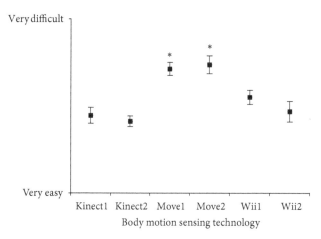

FIGURE 5: Rating of perceived game difficulty reported immediately after performing each of the different dance routines using the various different body motion sensing technologies. Data are shown as mean ($n = 11$) and error bars indicate SEM. *indicates significantly more difficult versus the other sensing technologies ($P < 0.05$).

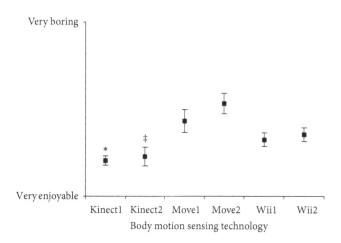

FIGURE 6: Rating of perceived game enjoyment reported immediately after performing each of the different dance routines using the various different body motion sensing technologies. Data are shown as mean ($n = 11$) and error bars indicate SEM. *indicates significantly more enjoyable versus Move1, Move2 and Wii2 ($P < 0.05$). ‡indicates significantly more enjoyable versus Move2 ($P < 0.05$).

perceived level of physical exertion that the subjects reported after completing each of the routines were comparable, the games were rated differently by the subjects in their levels of difficulty and this appeared to influence the level of enjoyment that they experienced.

Dance-based exergames normally comprise of a range of different songs and associated routines. The routines selected for use in the current study were selected on the basis that they all were at similar tempos and all involved comparable amounts of arm and leg movements. The results are somewhat surprising in that it was expected that routines using the Microsoft Kinect peripheral would elicit from the subjects more body movement during game play compared to the other two peripherals. This was because of its full body

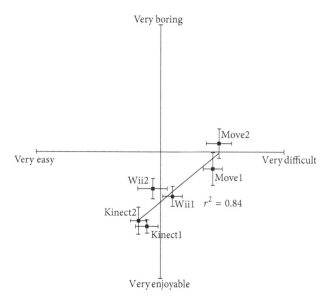

FIGURE 7: Group means ($n = 11$) for rating of game enjoyment plotted against rating of game difficulty for each separate dance routine and body motion sensing technology. Error bars indicate SEM. The data points were significantly correlated ($r^2 = 0.84$, $P < 0.05$).

motion tracking capability compared to the more limited tracking of only one arm by the other two peripherals. The absence of an observed difference in the measured rates of oxygen consumption between peripherals tends to suggest that the technological differences between the three body motion sensing peripherals do not matter in this regard. Furthermore, the measured rates of oxygen consumption in this study are comparable to previously published studies of dance-based exergames using original foot-switch game controllers [13, 15, 21].

It has previously been suggested that interactive forms of exercise may provide a degree of distraction from the sensations of exertional discomfort [22], which would be a significant benefit, particularly if the player is unaccustomed to exercising. It has already been shown [20] that a variety of different exergames can promote a flow state experience [23] that is in fact closer to sport than exercise because of the challenge-based nature of video game play. However, this issue has not been specifically investigated in relation to dance-based exergames. It is therefore of interest to consider whether the results of the present study show any evidence of distraction from the sensations of physical exertion. The numerical rating of perceived exertion scale has been designed and validated so that the values (reduced by a factor of 10) correspond reasonably closely to heart rate [19]. Thus, if dance-based exergames were also to provide a degree of distraction, then the mean ratings of perceived exertion values shown in Figure 4 would be expected to be lower, given the magnitude of the mean heart rates reported in Figure 2. Rather, the ratings of perceived exertion values are a little higher than might be expected for traditional forms of exercise at a comparable intensity. One possible explanation is that the significant involvement of the arms in the dance routines might have given the subjects the impression that the exercise was of a higher overall intensity than it actually was. Such a situation could arise since the arms have proportionally smaller skeletal muscle mass compared to the legs and therefore may be working at a higher metabolic rate. A further possible explanation for this observation is that the dance-based exergames require the player to focus specifically on rhythmically coordinating the movements of their limbs and this increased need for conscious proprioceptive awareness resulted in a greater instead of a lesser-perceived level of exertion.

Game developers are well versed in the need to pay careful attention to the balance of challenge versus player skill balance in order to present them with a meaningful challenge [24]. However, the results of the other self-report measures indicate that while the difficulty and enjoyment ratings of each pair of dance routine games on the same console were comparable, there were significant differences in the ratings between the various consoles (Figures 5 and 6). Furthermore, the correlation analysis presented in Figure 7 suggests that the games that were perceived to be easier were also the ones that the subjects reported as being more enjoyable and conversely higher levels of perceived difficulty were associated with reduced levels of enjoyment. There are several potential reasons that may account at least in part for these observed differences. The first is that there were significant differences between the games (and therefore peripherals) in the level of motor skill required to play them. The second is that the games differed in their thresholds of acceptability for timing accuracy of a player's movements. The third potential reason is that the body motion tracking peripherals differ in their underlying technologies and affordances and as a consequence vary in the type and number of limbs that they can track. The Kinect peripheral, by virtue of being able to track all four limbs, is best placed to potentially help guide and coordinate player movement. In contrast, the movement of a single arm detected by the Wiimote peripheral is only responsive to changes in relative rather than absolute position. As a consequence, the tracked arm is unlikely to need to follow such precise trajectories in space; moreover the player will also have considerable freedom of movement in their nontracked limbs. Finally, the Playstation Move peripheral by spatially tracking the absolute position of the motion of the player's arm requires greater spatial precision of movement, but the absence of any detection of lower limb movement means that it is less able to guide and coordinate player movement. Unfortunately it is not possible to make a clear distinction between these potential explanations outlined above. However, it does seem unlikely that any of the three games used in the current study would intentionally be designed to be significantly more difficult at the beginner level, given that they will have been subject to extensive play-testing. Instead, it seems more likely that the subjects found the games, that either more fully tracked and guided their movements, or permitted significant movement freedom, to be more enjoyable compared to the games that closely tracked a single limb (arm) but at the same time gave less overall feedback. This interplay between the degree of movement precision required and the nature and extent of the feedback given to a player is an important issue that needs to be

more fully investigated in order to help inform the design of future exergames.

In terms of the potential to promote health benefits, it is likely that most players who encounter dance-based exergames in social or physical education settings will do so at beginner or possibly intermediate skill levels and that considerable amounts of practice will be required to progress beyond these levels. Thus, from a health perspective, it would be highly desirable for dance-based exergames to be designed such that, even at beginner to intermediate skill levels, the games maximise the amount and intensity of body movement while at the same time providing an enjoyable and engaging game play experience. It is however recognised that this would not necessarily be an easy outcome to achieve. The most likely way in which this might be achieved would be to steer game progression towards increasing step rates coupled with less of an emphasis on increasing the complexity of moves (i.e., faster repetitive movement instead of greater complexity). It is probable that such an approach will also need some adjustment (reduction) in the temporal accuracy requirements for movements to be scored (at least at less advanced skill levels). Finally, the initial skill demands should be set at a very low level to make a game as widely accessible as possible and straightforward for players to follow, and the game should be carefully structured in a way that effectively facilitates player motor skill development and progression.

5. Conclusion

The results of this study suggest that while the three different body motion sensor peripherals differ in their underlying technologies and affordances, contrary to what was expected, they do not appear to differ in the amount of physical exertion they facilitate when used to incorporate body movement into dance-based exergames. However, based on the self-reports measures from the subjects, there appear to be differences in the game play experiences that they offer. While the reasons for this remain unclear and warrant further investigation, there is one particular issue that has been highlighted and is of major importance. Specifically, it is the relative influences on game play experience of whole body motion tracking that is able to more holistically guide and support player movement versus restricted limb motion tracking that is agnostic to the movement of nontracked limbs and therefore as a consequence offers players greater freedom of movement. Finally, the potential commercial and health benefits of widespread adoption and sustained use of dance-based exergames are significant. There is, therefore, also a need to investigate the factors that help to sustain long-term playing of dance-based exergames and how these might be optimised, if these benefits are to be realised.

References

[1] C. Sayre, "Video games that keep kids fit," *Time Magazine U.S*, vol. 170, no. 11, 2007.

[2] Investor EA Sports, "EA SPORTS Active Breaks a Sweat with Record-Setting Start," http://investor.ea.com/releasedetail.cfm?ReleaseID=387220.

[3] R. Maddison, L. Foley, C. Ni Mhurchu et al., "Effects of active video games on body composition: a randomized controlled trial," *American Journal of Clinical Nutrition*, vol. 94, no. 1, pp. 156–163, 2011.

[4] W. Peng, J.-H. Lin, and J. Crouse, "Is playing exergames really exercising? A meta-analysis of energy expenditure in active video games," *Cyberpsychology, Behavior, and Social Networking*, vol. 14, no. 11, pp. 681–688, 2011.

[5] L. Hansen and S. Sanders, "Interactive gaming: changing the face of fitness. Florida Alliance for Health, Physical Education," *Recreation, Dance & Sport Journal*, vol. 46, pp. 38–41, 2008.

[6] J. Mullins, "No limits; wave your arms, kick your feet and leap into the blue," *New Scientist*, vol. 190, pp. 38–41, 2006.

[7] S. N. Blair, J. B. Kampert, H. W. Kohl Jr. et al., "Influences of cardiorespiratory fitness and other precursors on cardiovascular disease and all-cause mortality in men and women," *Journal of the American Medical Association*, vol. 276, no. 3, pp. 205–210, 1996.

[8] M. V. Chakravarthy and F. W. Booth, "Eating, exercise, and "thrifty" genotypes: connecting the dots toward an evolutionary understanding of modern chronic diseases," *Journal of Applied Physiology*, vol. 96, no. 1, pp. 3–10, 2004.

[9] The NHS Information Centre Lifestyles Statistics, "Statistics on Obesity, Physical Activity and Diet," England, UK, 2010, http://www.ic.nhs.uk/statistics-and-data-collections/health-and-lifestyles/obesity/statistics-on-obesity-physical-activity-and-diet-diet-england

[10] Department of Health, "UK physical activity guidelines," http://www.dh.gov.uk/en/Publicationsandstatistics/Publications/PublicationsPolicyAndGuidance/DH_127931.

[11] R. Maddison, C. Ni Mhurchu, A. Jull, Y. Jiang, H. Prapavessis, and A. Rodgers, "Energy expended playing video console games: an opportunity to increase children's physical activity?" *Pediatric Exercise Science*, vol. 19, no. 3, pp. 334–343, 2007.

[12] R. K. Dishman, R. W. Motl, R. Saunders et al., "Enjoyment mediates effects of a school-based physical-activity intervention," *Medicine and Science in Sports and Exercise*, vol. 37, no. 3, pp. 478–487, 2005.

[13] B. Tan, A. R. Aziz, K. Chua, and K. C. Teh, "Aerobic demands of the dance simulation game," *International Journal of Sports Medicine*, vol. 23, no. 2, pp. 125–129, 2002.

[14] American College of Sports Medicine, *ACSM's Guidelines for Exercise Testing and Prescription*, Lippincott Williams & Wilkins, Philadelphia, Pa, USA, 2000.

[15] V. B. Unnithan, W. Houser, and B. Fernhall, "Evaluation of the energy cost of playing a dance simulation video game in overweight and non-overweight children and adolescents," *International Journal of Sports Medicine*, vol. 27, no. 10, pp. 804–809, 2006.

[16] K. Sell, T. Lillie, and J. Taylor, "Energy expenditure during physically interactive video game playing in male college students with different playing experience," *Journal of American College Health*, vol. 56, no. 5, pp. 505–511, 2008.

[17] J. Höysniemi, "International survey on the dance dance revolution game," *Computers in Entertainment*, vol. 4, no. 2, 2006.

[18] S. T. Smith, C. Sherrington, S. Studenski, D. Schoene, and S. R. Lord, "A novel Dance Dance Revolution (DDR) system for in-home training of stepping ability: basic parameters of system use by older adults," *British Journal of Sports Medicine*, vol. 45, no. 5, pp. 441–445, 2011.

[19] G. A. V. Borg, "Psychophysical bases of perceived exertion," *Medicine and Science in Sports and Exercise*, vol. 14, no. 5, pp. 377–381, 1982.

[20] A. G. Thin, L. Hansen, and D. McEachen, "Flow experience and mood states whilst playing body-movement controlled video games," *Games and Culture*, vol. 6, pp. 414–428, 2011.

[21] A. G. Thin and N. Poole, "Dance-based ExerGaming: user experience design implications for maximizing health benefits based on exercise intensity and perceived enjoyment," *Transactions on Edutainment*, vol. 4, pp. 189–199, 2010.

[22] T. G. Plante, A. Aldridge, R. Bogden, and C. Hanelin, "Might virtual reality promote the mood benefits of exercise?" *Computers in Human Behavior*, vol. 19, no. 4, pp. 495–509, 2003.

[23] M. Csikszentmihalyi, *Flow: The Psychology of Optimal Experience*, Harper & Row, New York, NY, USA, 1990.

[24] J. Chen, "Flow in games (and everything else)—a well-designed game transports its players to their personal Flow Zones, delivering genuine feelings of pleasure and happiness," *Communications of the ACM*, vol. 50, pp. 31–34, 2007.

8

Dynamic Difficulty Balancing for Cautious Players and Risk Takers

Guy Hawkins,[1] **Keith Nesbitt,**[2] **and Scott Brown**[1]

[1] *School of Psychology, Newcastle Cognition Laboratory, University of Newcastle, Callaghan, NSW 2308, Australia*
[2] *School of Design Communication and IT, University of Newcastle, Callaghan, NSW 2308, Australia*

Correspondence should be addressed to Keith Nesbitt, keith.nesbitt@newcastle.edu.au

Academic Editor: Daniel Thalmann

Dynamic balancing of game difficulty can help cater for different levels of ability in players. However, performance in some game tasks depends on not only the player's ability but also their desire to take risk. Taking or avoiding risk can offer players its own reward in a game situation. Furthermore, a game designer may want to adjust the mechanics differently for a risky, high ability player, as opposed to a risky, low ability player. In this work, we describe a novel modelling technique known as particle filtering which can be used to model various levels of player ability while also considering the player's risk profile. We demonstrate this technique by developing a game challenge where players are required to make a decision between a number of possible alternatives where only a single alternative is correct. Risky players respond faster but with more likelihood of failure. Cautious players wait longer for more evidence, increasing their likelihood of success, but at the expense of game time. By gathering empirical data for the player's response time and accuracy, we develop particle filter models. These models can then be used in real-time to categorise players into different ability and risk-taking levels.

1. Introduction

In designing a popular game, it would be beneficial to have a model of the ideal player. The designer could use this player profile to design just the right amount of difficulty and emotional impact into their game. No player would become bored with easy challenges or overburdened by difficult ones. All players could be fairly compensated for taking risks by a well-calculated reward structure. Everyone who played the game would receive the same optimal experience and level of entertainment. Unfortunately for the designer, it is unlikely that such an ideal player model exists.

To aid the design process, it is not unusual to categorise players into different groups. A typical division of such player types is the casual versus hard-core player, or the experienced versus inexperienced player. Such categories provide designers with general levels of player abilities allowing them to design corresponding levels of difficulty into the game mechanics.

The motivation for the designer is to balance game difficulty with player ability in such a way that the game is sufficiently challenging that it maintains interest and entertains across the broadest possible range of player abilities. This assumes that, to reward a player, their overall satisfaction is solely dependent on game difficulty and their ability to succeed in each challenge. However, there are other types of reward that can also be important for players. For example, how well the game allows the players to exercise their desired level of risk taking.

In this paper, we develop a novel model of the player using a technique known as particle filtering. Such a model can incorporate various levels of player ability while also considering the player's risk profile. Once developed, such a particle filter model is well suited to making dynamic adjustments in game difficulty. To develop the model, however, first requires the gathering of empirical data and fitting this data into an appropriate particle filter for the game scenario. This paper focuses on demonstrating the development of such a particle filter model and illustrating how it can be incorporated into the gameplay.

2. Utility and Risk

When considering player reward in terms of overall satisfaction, it is convenient to use terminology associated with economics, where overall satisfaction is described as "utility". The concept of utility can then be related to a person's preferred level of risk taking. For example, a typical division of management styles would be risk seeking, risk neutral, and risk averse [1]. Figure 1 relates these styles to utility, showing that a risk seeker is only satisfied when the payback is high, where conversely a risk averse individual is equally satisfied at low returns.

While risk taking profiles are more typically related to management styles or real-world activities such as gambling or stock market trading, they are also relevant to game designers. Risk taking profiles are particularly relevant for gameplay that involves making decisions based on incomplete information. In a game situation, where players must choose between alternatives, we could expect some players to take more risks than others. We might also expect that an individual's level of risk is associated with their level of enjoyment in the game. Risk seekers do not want to play it safe and cautious players do not want to risk it all.

How then can a designer deliver the best entertainment across the spectrum of risky and cautious players while also catering for different levels of ability in players? In this paper, we address this question by considering both the player's ability level and their risk-taking approach and describe how to dynamically recognise and adapt the gameplay based on these player attributes.

The dynamic modelling technique we use here is known as particle filtering [2]. Particle filters are simulation-based models that use sequential Monte Carlo methods. It is a novel approach in gaming terms and although it has been proposed as a way to incorporate intelligence into nonplayer characters [3] we are not aware of it being previously used for modelling players. Particle filters are promising models for describing cognition, and in particular decision making, as they involve updating beliefs about the state of the world as evidence accumulates over time.

Particle filters can readily model various levels of ability in human performance by just varying the number of particles in the filter. For example, a large number of particles can model statistically optimal behaviour, while a smaller number generates predictions similar to flawed, human-like behaviour.

Particle filters have been successfully used to account for behaviour in a number of psychological domains including language comprehension [4], categorisation [5], change detection [6], and determining reward rate payoffs [7].

Another useful feature of particle filters is that they can be updated in real time with a minimal computational overhead. This makes the algorithm ideal for dynamic balancing since the model can be included in the game mechanics without impacting on the speed of the game loop.

In the following section, we will briefly discuss dynamic balancing and then go on to describe a specific decision-making game challenge. We use this challenge to develop a casual game for gathering empirical data about player response time and accuracy in the challenge. The empirical data allows us, via the particle filter model, to generate estimates of both the player's ability and their risk profile. Finally, we illustrate how this model can be used to dynamically recognise and adapt the gameplay for a continuum of both novice to expert players, and risky to cautious players.

3. Balancing Difficulty

How should the designer adjust difficulty in a game challenge? Certainly, the difficulty of any game should normally increase as the game progresses, trying to match the player's increasing level of skill or in game powers. But where does the level of difficulty begin for each unique player? If the difficulty level starts too low, the player may become bored; if it starts too high, the player may become overwhelmed.

For the designer, the simplest approach is to allow players to choose their own difficulty level. Over time, many games in different genres have used this technique. The Atari 2600 console even provided a hardware switch to choose between two difficulty levels in games like Adventure [8] and Asteroids [9]. More recent games such as Quake [10], Halo [11], and Devil May Cry [12] provided more typical software-based difficulty levels that the player could select. Many other games provide adjustable difficulty settings allowing for easy, normal, hard, and extreme play. These difficulty levels are often given exotic names such as "piece of cake," "let's rock," "come get some," and "damn I'm good" as used in Duke Nukem [13].

The second approach to solving the difficulty level problem is to dynamically measure player performance during the game and adjust the difficulty based on how well the player is performing. This approach has also been utilised in a number of games. Some good examples are the third-person shooter, Max Payne [14], Far Cry [15], Left 4 Dead [16], and the Mario Kart [17] series of games. Indeed, the technique was commonly used in racing games and became known as "rubber-banding" as the mechanics of the game were adjusted to ensure the player was always held close to other cars, as if all the racers were held together by rubber bands [18].

A key feature of good dynamic balancing is transparency to the player. There is the danger that, when the mechanics are adjusted, the difficulty no longer matches the narrative. Left 4 Dead [16] attempts to overcome this problem by using their "AI Director" which dynamically adjusts the game's dramatics and pacing along with the difficulty. For example, spawning enemies are appropriately placed and numbered based on the player's current situation.

Dynamic balancing first requires identifying player ability followed by an appropriate adjustment of difficulty. Player ability can be measured by any number of parameters such as successful shots, life points, time to complete a task, or indeed any values used to calculate the game score. This

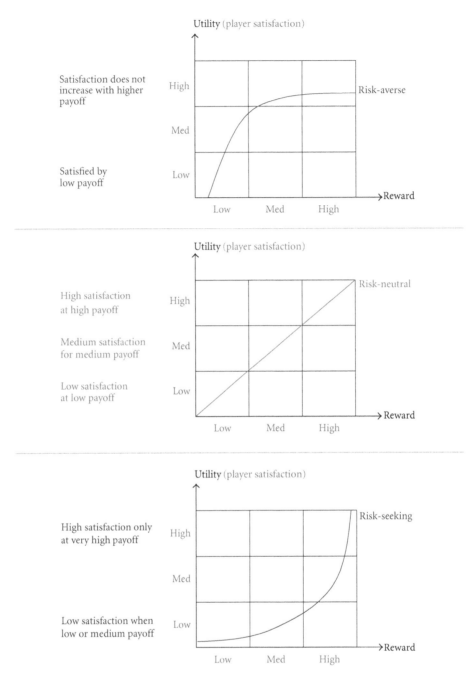

FIGURE 1: Three different risk profiles relating utility and reward. Note how risk seekers are only satisfied with large rewards accompanied by higher risks, while risk averse players prefer lower risk and reward decisions.

calculation has been called a "challenge function" [19] as it relates to how challenging the player is finding the game in its current state.

Depending on the game genre, typical adjustments to game mechanics either enhance player ability or adjust the ability of competing NPCs. Some examples include adjusting the speed, health, power, number, or spawn rate of enemies or the frequency or strength of player power ups. For example, in Max Payne the game dynamically adjusts the strength of enemies and can also provide different levels of aiming assistance for players. In the Mario Kart games, lower ranked players are more likely to receive items that improve their speed in future races.

Different approaches have been suggested for dynamic balancing. Hunicke and Chapman [20] and Hunicke [21] developed a first person shooter, called Hamlet, that automatically estimates the player's current requirement for core inventory items such as health, ammunition, shielding, and weapons.

Adjusting the intelligence of the NPCs is another approach that has been described. This can be achieved using sets of rules with a probability or weight attached to each rule and then dynamically adjusting the weight [22]. So, for a novice player, the NPC might be more likely to behave based on rules that are less effective and thus give the player a better chance. Other techniques based on reinforcement learning [23], and evolutionary algorithms [19], have also been used to adapt the intelligence of NPCs for the player's skill level.

The balancing approach by Yannakakis and Hallam [24] is more closely aligned with our own technique, as it uses experimental data from gameplay to develop a player model. Their models use different types of artificial neural networks that are trained through evolutionary techniques based on game features and player entertainment. Their aim is to predict the level of player satisfaction and adjust the game accordingly.

Our study also uses experimental data to develop player models but in the context of a decision-making challenge that we describe in the next section. To create our player models, we employ a novel technique called particle filtering which allows us to model both player risk taking as well as ability.

The idea of dynamic adjustment, however one implements it, rests on first measuring a player's ability, and then knowing how large an adjustment to make. Our model provides help on both these problems. It aids in measuring ability because it will not be "fooled" about a player's ability just because that player adopts an unusual level of risk or caution. Also, it helps in knowing how large the adjustments should be because it provides a predictive model of player behaviour.

4. A Simple Decision Challenge

In our study, we first developed a simple decision-making challenge where the difficulty became easier over time. The challenge requires a player to choose between possible alternatives where only one is correct. We describe the single correct alternative as the "target" and the other, incorrect possibilities as the "distracters." The difficulty of the challenge can be adjusted by two means: increasing the total number of distracters; or by increasing the similarity of the distracters to the target.

Players perform best when they choose the correct alternative as quickly as possible. However, the nature of the challenge is that the target becomes more evident as time passes. Because both response time and accuracy are important measures of success in the challenge, the player can be risky by responding earlier rather than later, but in doing this they run a greater chance of choosing the wrong alternative.

In our challenge, the possible alternatives consisted of 20 empty squares on a screen (Figure 2). As time passed, some of these squares gradually filled with dark blue dots. This was likened to raindrops filling a bucket and the player's task was to predict which bucket was filling the fastest. The filling process was based on a probability distribution. For example, time passed in discrete steps, and at each discrete time step, the distracter squares had a 40 percent chance of gathering a new fill event (a blue dot), while the target square had a 50 percent chance.

The player must choose the target square as quickly and accurately as possible. As time passes, the target square is more evident as we expect the actual distribution of raindrops to approach the probability settings. The closeness of the probability distributions, between distracters and target, affects the difficulty of the challenge and this is one of the parameters under the designer's control. The other parameter that can be controlled is the number of alternatives the player must choose from. In our challenge, we allowed for up to 20 alternatives.

As the display evolves over time, we expect the decision to become easier as the filling approaches the probability distribution. As Figure 2 shows, even with a 10 percent difference between the distracters and the target square, the task is not trivial. We expect risky players to make a decision quickly, based on little accumulated evidence. Because they respond quickly with insufficient information, we also expect them to make a number of incorrect choices. Note that players with high ability in this task may also respond quickly but would be more accurate. This demonstrates why response time alone is not sufficient to distinguish the risk profile of players and why we must also consider it in relation to their accuracy in the task.

5. Collecting Player Data

To allow us to develop our player model for the task, we first prototyped this simple challenge using Flash and Actionscript in a nongame context. It was deployed online and subsequently played by 31 first year psychology students from the University of Newcastle. Each player completed a total of 140 decision challenges from which we recorded response time and accuracy.

The number of active squares (K) displayed on any challenge was randomly chosen from $K \in \{2, 4, 6, 8, 10\}$, subject to the condition that each K appeared equally often for every player. The target square was randomly allocated to one of the active squares.

During each challenge, the display evolved in discrete steps of 15 events per second. We monitored this frame rate during the game and only used data from players whose computers met this frame rate. On each time step, each active square either accumulated a new dot or not. The distracters always filled with a probability of 40 percent while the target filled with a probability of 50 percent. This means that, on average, the target square accumulated 7.5 dots per second while each distracter square accumulated approximately 6.0 dots every second.

At the start of a challenge all squares began with a completely empty white background. Each time a new dot was accumulated a 2×2 pixel area within the square changed to a dark blue colour. The position of the new dot was chosen randomly from the remaining unfilled area of the square.

Players were instructed to identify the target as quickly as possible, but if they responded too early, they may incorrectly select a square that had, by chance, collected the most dots

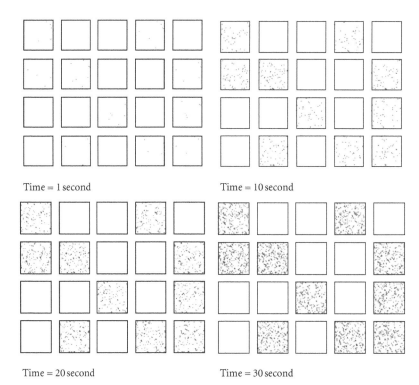

Time = 1 second   Time = 10 second

Time = 20 second   Time = 30 second

FIGURE 2: Four screen shots showing a decision challenge with ten alternatives at different time periods. As time progresses each of the active squares fill with dots based on independent probability distributions. In this case, the correct alternative is the square in the second column of the second row.

so far in the challenge. Participants were free to watch the display until they felt confident enough to make their decision. They recorded their choice by simply clicking on their chosen square.

After the participant chose a target square, a fast animation illustrated many more fill events very quickly. This rapid filling of the squares provided feedback to the player on whether they had selected the target square. If the player had correctly selected the target, a green outline was displayed around the chosen square. If the player's response was incorrect the chosen square's border was outlined in orange, and the true target square was outlined in green.

The mean performance of all players in terms of response time and accuracy is shown in Figure 3. Note how the average performance decreases with the number of alternatives but is higher than expected if players respond purely by guessing. This data is consistent with what we know about such challenges from Hick's Law [25, 26]. Hick's Law can be expressed in a number of ways, the most simple stating that mean response time (RT) and the logarithm of the number of choice alternatives (K) are linearly related: $RT = a + b \log(K)$. Hick's law generally provides good descriptions of data across many different types of decision-making tasks [27, 28].

6. The Game Scenario

We next transferred the simple decision challenge into a game scenario and made it available online. While the mechanics of the challenge remained the same, however, we provided a more elaborate backstory and integrated the challenge into a simple gameworld (Figure 4).

Players were introduced to a game titled "EMFants: Last Light." A mission brief informed participants they were commander of Dark-Stealth-6, a spaceship with time-hop propulsion, a "shadow-scope" to detect alien EMFants, and "blue-ray" armament. The goal of the game was identified as locating and destroying EMFants. Participants were provided with a backstory describing the electromagnetic-feeding (EMF) habits of the EMFant species. The EMFants escaped from a twin universe and have been detected in numerous galaxies. The player's goal was to destroy the EMFants before they rapidly spread to all known galaxies.

After the few introduction screens, players were informed of the layout of the game. The game mirrored a typical psychological experiment in structure, consisting of many trials within multiple blocks, although the trials in the game were described as "missions" that must be manually controlled (i.e., click a "next mission button"). At the start of each new block, players manually engaged Dark-Stealth-6's time-hop capabilities to navigate from one galaxy to another. This initiated a short animation representing the time hop.

Players were required to use their shadow-scope to detect the EMFant colonies. The shadow scope consisted of a number of squares that were being filled with dots (as in the original experiment). The EMFant colony growing at the fastest rate indicated the home of the EMFant queen (the target square). By clicking on the target, players

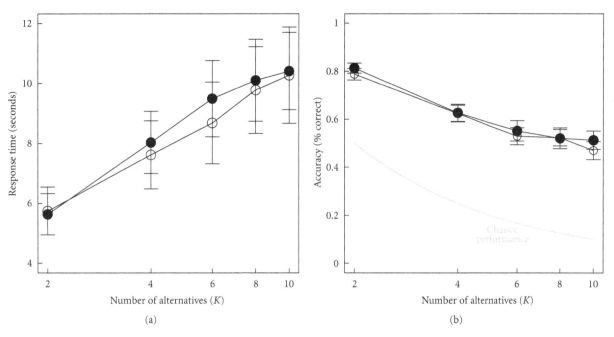

FIGURE 3: Mean response time (a) and decision accuracy (b) for the simple challenge and contextualised challenge (unfilled and filled circles, resp.).

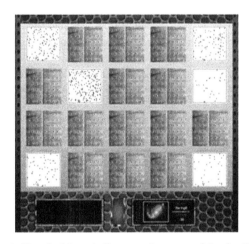

FIGURE 4: The decision challenge as it appeared in the EMFants game.

fired their blue-ray, described as an intense pulse of long-wavelength radiation, to destroy the EMFant colony. Players were informed that speed was essential to prevent EMFants spreading to other galaxies. Players were also instructed that accuracy was essential, since they only had one chance in each mission to fire the blue-ray, and if they did not destroy the colony of the queen, the EMFants would duplicate and spread to other galaxies.

Once each decision challenge began it proceeded in a statistically identical manner to the original simple experiment described previously. When a player selected a square the entire display quickly flashed blue as the blue-ray fired, followed by an outline of green (for a correct answer) or orange (for an incorrect answer) on the selected EMFant

colony. A correct answer was accompanied by a sound of a cheering crowd. An incorrect answer produced a disappointed "urrrgghh."

The EMFants game was completed online by 28 first year psychology students from the University of Newcastle. Each player completed 140 decision challenges, from which we recorded response time and decision accuracy. The parameters for the decision challenges were the same as the original challenge. Figure 3 demonstrates that player performance from the EMFants game is almost identical to the data from the simple version of the decision challenge. We, therefore, used the combined data from 59 players and over 8000 decision challenges to build our player model.

7. Modelling Players

Having collected adequate performance data, the next step of the process was to design an adaptive model of players that could both recognise the player's ability level and their risk-taking.

Assessing a player's risk level is not quite as straightforward as it sounds because of the interplay between risk taking and underlying ability. For example, a player who responds faster than average might be relatively risky, or they might instead have a very high ability level and are thus able to make fast responses without taking undue risks.

To disentangle risk level and ability, we apply a particle filter model to our empirical data to represent the player. Particle filtering is a recent development in cognitive theory [29] and provides a novel way of measuring a player's risk-taking profile and their underlying ability, without changes in one of these two constructs contaminating measurement of the other construct.

Particle filters are sequential Monte Carlo methods that approximate Bayesian posterior distributions. Particle filters allow estimated posterior distributions to be updated as new data arrive. These update algorithms do not require integration over the entire history of observed data (as in other integration methods, such as Markov Chain Monte Carlo). The calculations, therefore, remain psychologically plausible since they do not become increasingly taxing each time new data are observed.

A particle filter begins with a set of particles, each of which is treated as a sample from the posterior distribution of interest. For example, in our game challenge each particle represents a "guess" about which of the K choice alternatives is the correct target. On each frame of the game challenge, the particles are "evolved" to incorporate the new data that arrive regarding the fill rates of the squares. This evolution step usually involves resampling the particles according to their likelihood. Particles consistent with the new datum have a higher probability of being resampled. In contrast, unlikely particles are inconsistent with the observed datum and hence become rare over time.

We used the particle filter developed by Hawkins et al. [29] to model data from the game challenges. This particle filter model is illustrated conceptually in Figure 5. The particle filter model includes a mechanism to track the probability that each response option is the true target. This mechanism corresponds to the player's ability to differentiate the fill rates of each alternative and so detect evidence about which square is filling the fastest. A higher level of ability is represented by more particles. The particle filter also contains a decision mechanism to trigger a response based on the evidence probabilities. In terms of game players, the player's risk profile is captured in this response triggering mechanism. Higher risk players require less evidence than cautious players.

In the model, each particle holds a number from $1 - K$ corresponding to a belief about which square is the target. At the beginning of a decision, particles are randomly sampled from a uniform prior distribution. An illustrative set of $P = 10$ particles for a decision between $K = 4$ alternatives is shown in the top row of the right-hand side of Figure 5. In this example, three particles hypothesize that square 1 is the target (which it actually is), two particles that the target is 4 and so on.

On each frame of the game challenge, a fill event either occurred or did not occur in each square, and these are represented by the "evidence increments" in the shaded rectangle on the left of Figure 5. The uppermost row illustrates that on the first time step of the decision challenge a dot appeared in both of squares 3 and 4, but not in squares 1 or 2. The probability of this sequence of dots across the squares can easily be calculated under the hypothesis of each particle (assuming the true target and distracter fill rates are perfectly known). These probabilities are used to resample a new set of P particles for the next time step, with replacement. The outcome of this resampling is shown by the second row of particles.

After each time step of the decision challenge, the particle filter estimates the posterior probability that each square is

the target by calculating the proportion of particles representing that square, illustrated by the histograms on the far right side of Figure 5. These probability estimates represent the output of the evidence tracking mechanism. The number of particles in the filter controls the performance level, which is analogous to the player's ability. More particles make for better performance as this represents a larger sampling size and so a better approximation to the actual fill rates of the target and distracter squares.

The model predicts that a response is triggered whenever the largest posterior probability exceeds a criterion threshold (c). This criterion parameter determines the risk profile of the model, because a high probability threshold requires a lot of evidence to make a decision, so responses are slow but accurate (and vice versa for low probability thresholds). For example, in Figure 5, if the threshold was set at $c = 0.8$ the particle filter would have incorrectly responded (with square 4) after the fourth time step, since eight out of ten particles represented square 4 at that time.

For any particular ability level (i.e., number of particles, P) and risk profile (i.e., decision threshold, c), the particle filter model predicts a particular combination of accuracy and mean response time. By comparing these predictions to measurements from the game, we can abstract from raw data measurements (accuracy and response time) to the deeper psychological constructs of real interest: player ability and risk profile.

Figure 6 illustrates this process using data from our experiment. Each player's data are represented on the graph by a single plot point-determined by their mean accuracy (y-axis) and mean response time (x-axis). The grey lines on the graph show the particle filter's predictions for varying parameters. The close-to-straight lines show the predictions for a fixed level of risk (either a low, medium, or high value of the threshold parameter) and varying ability levels. The curved lines show the converse—different levels of risk for fixed ability. Comparing data against these predictions allows easy categorisation of player ability and risk. For example, data falling above the top curved line indicate very high ability, and data falling to the right of the right-most straight line indicate very cautious risk settings.

Figure 6 shows that the data from our experiments almost all fall nicely within the range of data patterns that the particle filter can predict, which suggests that the model provides a useful description of performance in this task. Note that the data from the two experiments (simple challenge and EMFants challenge) are represented separately in Figure 6 (unfilled and filled circles, resp.) but there appears to be little difference in terms of accuracy and mean response time.

8. Adjusting Game Difficulty

Having developed a particle filter model of the player, in this section, we demonstrate how to use the model to adjust the game mechanics appropriately.

Dynamic balancing first requires a player to be categorised in terms of their risk taking and ability. Our experimentally collected response data is used as the basis

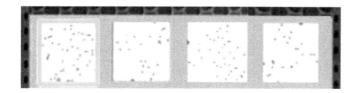

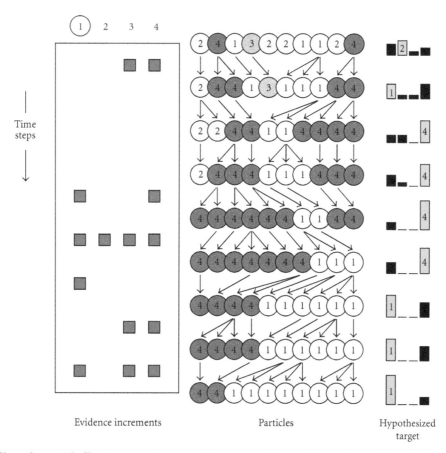

FIGURE 5: Example of how the particle filter incorporates new evidence on each frame (Figure adapted from Hawkins et al. [29]). Note how the player tracks evidence adjusting their belief at each time step. The number of particles in the model relate to the player's ability to do this tracking. Players will make a choice about the target when evidence exceeds some decision threshold. The amount of evidence required is related to the players risk profile.

of this grouping by considering the player's comparative response time and performance in the task. We can do this by calculating the player's mean accuracy and response time, either from an introductory level or continuously during the game by using a moving average.

The second aspect of dynamic balancing is the alteration of the mechanics to meet the designer's requirements for the game. We should note that having a mechanism for modelling the player in no way reduces the burden on the designer to develop appropriate adaptations to the gameplay. For means of example, we now provide description of one such adaptation that might be useful.

Consider a situation where the designer would like all players to meet an equivalent level of performance. For illustrative purposes, we defined the target performance level as the mean of response times and accuracy across all our experimental players, which was about 8 seconds and 60 percent accuracy. We then use the particle filter to make theoretical predictions of how we should change the probabilities for target and distracter buckets to try to achieve a set level of performance in two example players.

Previously, in Figure 1 we illustrated three basic types of risk taking and the associated player utility. In this work, we took two representative participants, one with high ability

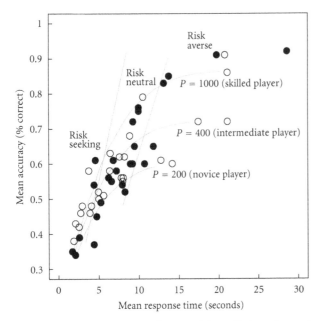

FIGURE 6: Data and particle filter model predictions from the experiment.

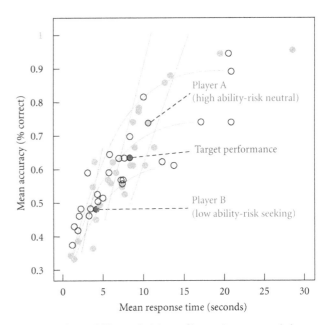

FIGURE 7: Player ability and risk profile can be measured dynamically to identify particle filter size (P) and decision threshold (c) parameters. These parameters can be used to adjust the degree of similarity between distracters and target and move different types of players to the same target performance.

who was risk neutral and one with low ability who was risk-seeking, marked in Figure 7 with the green and blue dots, respectively.

To approach the target performance level, we want the risk-seeking low ability player to increase mean task accuracy from their current score of about 0.48 to 0.6, and increase mean response time from about 4 seconds to 8 seconds. To increase response time, we need to reduce the fill probabilities (so squares fill more slowly), and to increase accuracy, we need to increase the difference between target and distracter fill probabilities (so the target "stands out" more than the distracters, and the participant makes fewer errors). For this participant's ability level and risk profile, the particle filter predicts that we should change the target fill rate from 50 percent to 18 percent, and distracter fill rates from 40 percent to 10 percent.

In contrast, for the risk neutral high-ability player to approach the target performance level, we want to decrease mean task accuracy from their current score of about 0.72 to 0.6, and decrease mean response time a little, towards 8 seconds. To maintain response time, we need to increase the overall fill probabilities a little (so squares fill a little more quickly), and to decrease accuracy, we need to decrease the difference between target and distracter fill probabilities (so the target is harder to differentiate from the distracters, and the participant makes more errors). For this participant, the particle filter predicts that we change the target fill rate from 50 to 80 percent, and distracter fill rates from 40 to 72 percent.

9. Discussion

Particle filters have considerable potential as models of cognition, and in particular decision making, as they involve updating beliefs about the state of the environment as evidence accumulates over time. By varying the number of particles in the filter the model can approximate a range in performance. For example, a large number of particles can model statistically optimal behaviour, while a smaller number generates predictions similar to flawed, human-like behaviour.

We investigated the use of particle filters for modelling players who undertake a decision-making challenge, where there are multiple alternatives and the player accumulates evidence over time. For such a task, it is desirable to understand players' risk versus caution profile, as well as their underlying ability level. Neither of these underlying psychological properties can be unambiguously inferred from raw observation of accuracy and response time.

Rather than developing ad hoc methods of combining the two measures into some composite, we have imported an appropriate decision theory from cognitive psychology that supports fast and efficient estimation of players' risk profile and ability. This approach does require some previous testing with players to gather empirical data. In this work, we illustrated this approach by gathering experimental data about player performance and using this to develop a model of player performance. Using this model, we demonstrated how difficulty level could be adapted during gameplay using the predictions of such a particle filter.

In this case, particle filters provided an efficient mechanism to develop such dynamic player models, providing parameters, P (the number of particles), and c (the decision threshold) that intuitively relate back to the underlying decision challenge. This intuitive relationship can be important for the designer, where a good understanding of the underlying mechanics can assist with other adaptations required in the gameplay. Making such online gameplay adaptations is an important step towards designing and developing games that ensure maximal reward for the widest possible range of player profiles.

References

[1] K. Schwalbe, *Information Technology Project Management*, Thomson Course Technology, Boston, Mass, USA, 4th edition, 2006.

[2] M. K. Pitt and N. Shephard, "Filtering via simulation: auxiliary particle filters," *Journal of the American Statistical Association*, vol. 94, no. 446, pp. 590–599, 1999.

[3] C. Bererton, "State estimation for game AI using particle filters," in *Proceedings of the 19th National Conference on Artificial Intelligence*, pp. 36–40, San Jose, Calif, USA, July 2004.

[4] R. Levy, F. Reali, and T. L. Griffiths, "Modeling the effects of memory on human online sentence processing with particle filters," in *Proceedings of the 22nd Annual Conference on Neural Information Processing Systems*, 2009.

[5] A. N. Sanborn, T. L. Griffiths, and D. J. Navarro, "A more rational model of categorization," in *Proceedings of the 28th Annual Conference of the Cognitive Science Society*, 2006.

[6] S. D. Brown and M. Steyvers, "Detecting and predicting changes," *Cognitive Psychology*, vol. 58, no. 1, pp. 49–67, 2009.

[7] S. K. M. Yi, M. Steyvers, and M. Lee, "Modeling human performance in restless bandits with particle filters," *Journal of Problem Solving*, vol. 2, pp. 81–101, 2009.

[8] Inc. Atari, "Adventure," [Atari 2600], USA: Inc. Atari, 1979.

[9] Inc. Atari, "Asteroids," [Atari 2600], USA: Inc. Atari, 1981.

[10] Id Software, "Quake," [PC], USA: GT Interactive, 1996.

[11] Bungie, "Halo," [Xbox], USA: Microsoft Game Studios, 2001.

[12] Capcom, "Devil May Cry," [PlayStation 2], USA: Capcom, 2001.

[13] Apogee Software, "Duke Nukem," [PC], USA: Apogee Software, 1991.

[14] Remedy Entertainment, "Max Payne," [Windows], USA: Gathering Of Developers, 2001.

[15] Crytek, "Far Cry," [Windows], France: Ubisoft, 2005.

[16] Valve Corporation, "Left 4 Dead," [Windows], USA: Valve Corporation, 2008.

[17] Nintendo, "Mario Kart," [Super Nintendo], Japan: Nintendo, 1992.

[18] O. Missura and T. Gärtner, "Player modeling for intelligent difficulty adjustment," *Lecture Notes in Computer Science*, vol. 5808, pp. 197–211, 2009.

[19] P. Demasi and A. Cruz, "Online coevolution for action games," in *Proceedings of the 3rd International Conference on Intelligent Games And Simulation (GAME-ON'2002)*, pp. 113–120, London, UK, 2002.

[20] R. Hunicke and V. Chapman, "AI for dynamic difficulty adjustment in games," in *Proceedings of the 19th National Conference on Artificial Intelligence*, pp. 91–96, San Jose, Calif, USA, July 2004.

[21] R. Hunicke, "The case for dynamic difficulty adjustment in games," in *Proceedings of the ACM SIGCHI International Conference on Advances in Computer Entertainment Technology (ACE '05)*, pp. 429–433, June 2005.

[22] P. Spronck, I. Sprinkhuizen-Kuyper, and E. Postma, "Difficulty scaling of game AI," in *Proceedings of the 5th International Conference on Intelligent Games and Simulation (GAME-ON'2004)*, p. 33, London, UK, 2004.

[23] G. Andrade, G. Ramalho, H. Santana, and V. Corruble, "Challenge-sensitive action selection: an application to game balancing," in *Proceedings of the IEEE/WIC/ACM International Conference on Intelligent Agent Technology*, pp. 194–200, Compiègne, France, September 2005.

[24] G. N. Yannakakis and J. Hallam, "Towards capturing and enhancing entertainment in computer games," in *Proceedings of the 4th Hellenic Conference on Artificial Intelligence*, pp. 432–442, Springer, Heraklion, Greece, 2006.

[25] W. E. Hick, "On the rate of gain of information," *Quarterly Journal of Experimental Psychology*, vol. 4, pp. 11–26, 1952.

[26] R. Hyman, "Stimulus information as a determinant of reaction time," *Journal of Experimental Psychology*, vol. 45, no. 3, pp. 188–196, 1953.

[27] W. H. Teichner and M. J. Krebs, "Laws of visual choice reaction time," *Psychological Review*, vol. 81, no. 1, pp. 75–98, 1974.

[28] A. T. Welford, *Reaction Times*, Academic Press, London, UK, 1980.

[29] G. Hawkins, S. D. Brown, M. Steyvers, and E.-J. Wagenmakers, "A particle filter account of multi-alternative decisions," in *Proceedings of the 43rd Annual Meeting of the Society for Mathematical Psychology*, 2010.

9

Analysis of Motivational Elements of Social Games: A Puzzle Match 3-Games Study Case

Marcel Toshio Omori and Alan Salvany Felinto

Computer Sciences Department, State University of Londrina, Londrina, PR 86051-980, Brazil

Correspondence should be addressed to Marcel Toshio Omori, marcelomori86@gmail.com

Academic Editor: Daniel Thalmann

The main motivational elements of the social network sites and the social network games will be shown according to studies already existent in the literature, highlighting the elements which motivate the players the most to play social *Match* 3-type games. Seven games have been analyzed: *Diamond Dash*, *Collapse! Blast*, *Mystic Ice Blast*, *Bricks Breaking*, *Plock*, *Gem Clix,* and *Blast!*. The results showed that asynchronous time, activities publishing, rewarding system, competition, and social status are the elements which motivate and stimulate the most the players to play.

1. Introduction

The social network sites show a great number of users [1], in particular Facebook which at the end of December 2011 owned more than 845 million active users per month [2]. At the same time, the social network games also prove a great popularity, an example is the game *FarmVille* present at the Facebook which in 2010 achieved a mark of 76 million active players per month [3]. Other more recent examples are *Angry Birds Friends* with 12 million active players per month and the most recent release of the game *FarmVille*, *FarmVille 2*, with more than 60 million active players per month [4].

Despite the success of these games, the social games have a lot of challenges to overcome, and one of them is attractiveness [5]. What are the elements which attract the players? Why do people play social games? There are a lot of studies at the literature about guides on good practice to develop interfaces, mechanics, gameplay, and ideal stories for the games [6], but for the social games which appeal more to the emotional side than to the actions themselves [3, 7], it is also necessary to identify the main personal, social, and psychological elements which motivate and stimulate the players to play. There are some studies about this emotional side such as the ones by Ines and Abdelkader [3], although the analysis is generally aimed at all kinds of games. At this study, we have focused on identifying the main motivational elements of the social *Match* 3-type games. One example of this type of game is *Diamond Dash* which has 19 million active players per month [4].

The goal of this kind of game is to destroy the greatest number of gems as possible within a determined period of time and obtain points. In order to destroy the gems, the player must find and click on the gems which have combinations of three or more gems of the same color. The mechanics of the game demand that the player should have a good visibility and mouse handling.

How come games which possess so simple arts, sounds, mechanics, and gameplay to the point of being developed in a short period of time of two months can attract millions of players? This study will not answer this question, but it will take the first step towards this discovery by means of the identification of the main motivational elements of the social *Match* 3-type games.

In order to identify the main motivational elements of this kind of game, we have chosen 7 games and requested a group of "gamers" of a university to evaluate them. There were 12 applicants altogether. The result of the evaluation will be shown at the following chapters.

The paper is divided into 7 sections. Section 2 brings some concepts about the social networking and its features, in particular Facebook. In Section 3, it will be shown the concepts about casual and social games, the difference between them, and their characteristics. Section 4 identifies the main motivational elements of the social network sites and the social network games according to studies already existent at the literature. In Section 5 it is explained the adopted analysis methodology. Section 6 shows the analysis results. Finally, In Section 7, it will be shown the discussions and the conclusions. Moreover we clarify the conflict of interests of this study by the end of the paper.

2. Social Network Sites

Social network sites (SNSs) are services based on the web which allow the person (1) to create a public or semipublic profile within a limited system, (2) to articulate a list of friends with whom he or she shares connections, and (3) to see and search through a list of connections which have the profiles created by other users of the system [8].

The social network sites are unique as they make it possible for the users to articulate and to make their social networks visible, and not for the fact that they allow to find friends and create new contacts [8]. At the majority of the SNSs, the individuals communicate mainly with people who are already part of their social network, that is, they are not necessarily looking for new friendships. The social network consists of visible profiles which show a list of friends who are also users of the system. The public viewing of these connections is the crucial component, inasmuch as it is through this list that the users are able to browse through the network [8].

2.1. Case Study: Facebook. Facebook is a social free network site, and its revenue is obtained by means of publicity, advertisement, and sponsors.

Facebook owns more than 800 million active users, and more than half of them access the website every day. On average, each user has 130 friends and spends 55 minutes a day at the website. Every 20 minutes, approximately 1.4 millions of invitations for events are sent, 1.8 millions of updates, status are done, 2.7 millions of messages are sent, 1 million of links are shared, more than 2.7 millions of uploads of pictures are accomplished, and 1.9 millions of friendship requests are accepted. Facebook is available in more than 70 different languages, and more than 200 million people a day access the website by using mobile gadgets [2]. Facebook is considered the greatest online SNS of the world [9].

The elements which facilitate the interaction include list of friends, *wall*, *pokes*, status, events, photos, videos, messages, chats, groups, and *like*. The list of friends is the Facebook's crucial element once the users can make it public and make it possible for others to browse the network through it. The *wall* is a term used for the Facebook tool which works as a notice board where the users post personal messages straight to another individual. Users can share photos, videos, and messages at the *wall* [10]. Besides, people can begin a greeting with others through the *pokes* service. Status is used to inform about the user's activities. The tool *events* allows to plan meeting or events and to

invite other people to participate. The photos and videos resources allow the user to upload albums, photos, videos, and comments. The communication with friends takes place through chatting and messages which can be private or public. People can create and/or affiliate in groups of interest by using the groups service. With the functionality *like*, the user can give a positive feedback about a determined content shared by their friends [2].

Due to the social and technological features, Facebook reached millions of users and became inserted at the people's day-by-day, becoming the center of attention of researchers in several aspects, such as the online and offline relationship functioning, at the technological features of the social communication networks and at the cultural differences when using this virtual environment [10].

2.2. Applications. Facebook's applications like the games are not part of the social network; they are external tools which can be added or installed at the user's profile. When the user starts to use some application, all of his or her friends will know about that, as the SNS informs all his or her friends about the fact. This is the first social interaction of the game [1].

Most of the Facebook's applications are not classified as a game, as they are relatively simpler than the other casual games, and they do not offer complex gameplay; generally, they are one- or two-click actions at the most. In order to accommodate all these applications which do not meet all the *gaming* requirements, the Facebook managers introduced a new category of games called *Just for Fun* [11].

Facebook's games appeal more to the emotional side (fun and humor) rather than to actions (gameplay). Instead of modeling and stylizing concrete actions for the game-play, which characterizes the games, Facebook's applications reduce these activities to a few clicks and focus on the interaction and expression features of the players [7].

3. Casual and Social Games

According to the International Game Developers Association [12], the casual games are applications addressed to con-sumers in general, that is, for those who are not *gamers*. This definition applies to the Facebook users, as most of them are not *hardcore* players [3]. In general, these kinds of games demonstrate simple gameplay; they are easy to play, consume little time from five to twenty minutes, and they focus on entertaining and casualness [12].

The social network games (SNGs), in turn, are applica-tions which use the SNS infrastructure and resources [13] and demonstrate asynchronous gameplay and mechanisms for multiple players [5]. At the traditional computer games, consoles, and cell phones, people play at the *singleplayer* or *multiplayer* modes against strangers. At the social games, the individuals play with friends and family members, which increases the attractiveness and entertainment of the game [1].

In comparison with the traditional games which have well-elaborated audio and graphics, the social games are relatively way simpler and demonstrate a lower development cost. According to D. H. Shin and Y. J. Shin [5], the development of conventional games might cost something around $2 million to $3 million, and the social games might cost something around $100.000 to $300.000 and generally consume less time to be developed; with several designers, the game release might last around 2 to 3 months. Another interesting fact is that the social games are most of times free of charge, which facilitates its distribution. Profit, at this case, is obtained through advertisement, marketing, virtual assets, and coins sales.

By analyzing some games, Rossi [1] classified the social games into two categories: *skill/knowledge* and *truly social*. At the former, the players carry out activities to get points which are exhibited publicly in rankings and/or social network site, which defies the players and creates competitions among them. At this case, the social status issue is the main characteristic of the game, as even if this does not offer entertainment, the users play in order to overtake their friends and to be the top at the ranking. Games such as *Crazy Planets, Minigolf Part, Geo Challenge, Word Challenge, Bowling Buddies,* and *Who Has The Biggest Brain?* are some examples of *skill/knowledge* games. Now, the *truly social* games show as main element the product management. The games *Restaurant City* and *Pet Society* are some examples of this category. At the former, the player is supposed to run the restaurant, and at the latter, he or she has to take care of his or her pet. In both cases, the social interaction occurs at the game itself, as the players must help each other in order to progress, the friends are not competitors, and the social networks are necessary strategical resources to play. So, the more friends the person has in his or her network, the more benefits he or she will obtain.

According to Sung et al. [14], the female audience is more active at the social games than men due to the fact that women feel more attracted for applications which offer more interaction and dialogues rather than actions.

4. What Are the Elements That Motivate the Users to Play?

Based on the studies existent at the literature, this topic will show the main characteristics and elements which motivate and stimulate the users to play SNGs.

4.1. Mechanics of the Social Network Games. According to Hamari and Järvinen [15], the mechanics of the game are a set of standard activities which are divided into two dimensions: the player dimension and the system dimension. The first one has the activities which the player can carry out in order to interact with the other players or with the game itself, and the second has the procedures which the system carries out according to the activities carried out by the player. Every mechanics of the game is directly related to the objectives of the game once the users carry out the activities in order to perform the objectives, and the system provides feedback related to the objectives. A practical example is present at the game *FarmVille* where the players harvest the fruits (player activity) and the system rewards him or her with coins of the game (system procedure).

At the SNGs, the social interaction tools provided by the SNSs are adapted at the mechanics of the game, that is, the mechanisms of relationship are inserted at the dimension of the game [15]. The game *FarmVille* shows these kinds of mechanisms, as the player has his or her personal objectives, to manage the farm, and he or she can interact with his or her friends through messages and by publishing the activities related to the game at his or her profile.

According to studies by Hamari and Järvinen [15], the mechanics of game which assure entertainment at the social games are the acquisition, retention, and monetization mechanics. The first mechanics is related to the items that the player can purchase during the game. Donating and receiving gifts and having friends as resources or helpers are some examples of acquisition. Now, the retention mechanics are related to the activities that the player perform in order to keep his or her items with himself or herself. An example is daily bonuses where the player obtains rewards for each day that he or she returns to play. Finally, the monetization mechanisms are the activities related to the purchasing of items or upgrades with real currency or the games currency. Some examples are the items which must be purchased so that the player can progress at the game or some upgrades which expire along the time and suggest that the player buy them again.

4.2. Time and Action Space. The social games show asynchronous gameplay, that is, the players do not need to be necessarily online at the same time to play [5]. Another time factor present so much at the *truly social* games is the presence of components which operate even at the absence of the player. For example, at the game *FarmVille*, the player can crop several fruits where each of them has a different time of ripening (some of them take hours and others take days) which after being planted, germinate and grow within a determined time even if the player is not present at the game. This tactics allows the player to adapt the game at the day-by-day, besides stimulating him or her to return to play, as if he or she does not return in time to harvest the fruits, these ones would rot and the player would not receive the rewards. It is realized that the time factor is an important characteristic at the social games as it allows the player to adapt the game according to his day-by-day [5]. Furthermore, Meurs [16] claims that this characteristic is ideal for the casual players who, on the contrary to the *hardcore* players, are not willing to spend a lot of time on games, which is characteristic of Facebook users [3].

Now, the action space of the social games is a personal environment and is not shared, as the presence of friends is symbolic and social interactions are fictitious [3]. The real interaction occurs through the SNS when the player performs any activity at the game and this is published for all of his or her friends. For example, at the game *FarmVille*, the player cannot interact with the friends' farms, but he or she can visit them, which creates an interaction feeling at the game, and it creates the real socialization through the social network site.

Benkler [17], Urista et al. [18], Joinson [19], and Lucas and Sherry [20] claim that the social interaction is one of the factors which motivate the users to make use of the SNSs.

4.3. Gratification.

Uses and Gratification (U&G) is a framework used to study how the media like the social media are used to satisfy the needs of different individuals with different objectives [21]. According to the analysis of Hou [22], gratification can be defined as the expectation of each individual related to media.

The gratifications of the social games according to Lucas and Sherry [20] are these six elements: competition, challenge, social interaction, fun, fantasy, and excitation. Among these, Sherry et al. [23] and Hamari and Järvinen [15] highlighted the competition as the most motivating element. Hou [22] pointed out the social interaction as a determining factor to encourage the players to play social games. Despite the fact that the fantasy has been cited as one of the motivations at the studies of Lucas and Sherry [20], Hou [22] showed at his studies that this element cannot bring positive results for the games, as many times, fantasy does not satisfy the expectations of the all the players.

According to Benkler [17], the social connectivity, psychological well-being, gratification, and material gaining are the main elements which motivate the users to use the SNSs. Urista at al. [18] claim that efficient communication through photos, music, videos, e-mails, and messages is the great gratification when using the social media. Still according to the author, efficient communications, curiosities about the others, popularity, and relationships are the main factors which motivate the users to use the social network sites. Joinson [19] also pointed out the social connectivity, identity sharing, contents, social investigation, and status updating as other motivation factors. Now, Kollock [24] pointed out the reciprocity, reputation, efficacy, fondness, and needs of group as some of the main elements which contribute and motivate the users to participate in online communities.

4.4. Murray's Psychological Needs at the Social Games.

According to Ines and Abdelkader [3], the success of the social games at Facebook is assured by the five Murray's psychological needs: material needs, power needs, affective needs, ambition needs, and information needs.

The material needs refer to the activities involving gaining, acquisition, retentions, construction, and organization [25]. The material gain cited by Benkler [17] as one of the motivations to use the SNS and the acquisition, retention, and monetization mechanics present at the games which according to Hamari and Järvinen [15] assure the entertainment can be inserted into this context. At the game, these needs can be satisfied through purchases and items gaining, coins, daily bonuses, among others. For example, at the game *Angry Birds Friends*, the player gains items for each day that he or she returns to play.

Concerning the power needs, these are related to the activities of humiliation, autonomy, aggression, respect, and dominance [25]. The motivational elements cited by other author, like reputation [24], competition [15, 20, 23, 24],

and social status [3] can be grouped at this necessity. One of the most common examples present at the games which meet these needs is the level mechanism. The player starts at level one, and gradually, along the progress or acquired experience at the game, his level will go up and consequently his or her social status. Hamari and Lehdonvirta [26] say at their studies that releasing new items for each level motivates the players to wish those products, which creates relation between the power needs and material needs.

The affective needs are related to the affiliation, group, rejection, care, and fragility activities [25]. People for being social creatures are constantly searching for other individuals to share interests, solve problems, meet, talk, ask for help, among others. All the related elements with these activities can be inserted into the context of affectivity. The main elements identified by Kollock [24] which contribute for the people to take part of online communities are reciprocity, fondness and group necessity as some examples. At the game *FarmVille*, for example, in order to increase his or her storage space, the player must ask for his or her friends' help to click on a link, and if he or she can have 10 clicks, the player obtains the extra space and his or her friends will get games coins for having helped.

Ambition needs are related to all the activities which generate accomplishment, exposure, and recognition [25], that is, they are activities which are related to personal satisfaction to reach or accomplish some objective. The challenge element identified at the studies by Lucas and Sherry [20] as a gratification element of the social games can be considered as part of this necessity. The presence of ranking at games like *Diamond Dash* satisfies these needs, as the player has the objective to overtake his or her friends and to be number one of the ranking and his or her score is shown to other players, which exposes his or her achievements and generates recognition.

Finally, the information need refers to the activities to obtain knowledge, educate, and keep updated [25]. All the elements and communication resources such as chatting, e-mail, list of friends which are using the same application, online and offline status, and registration of the last activities of friends can be inserted into this necessity. At the games, the information needs can be satisfied through tutorials and continuous feedback which teach the user to play and show what he or she is doing. Choi and Kim [27] also claim that tools of communication stimulate the players to continue playing.

4.5. Playfulness.

Like the other kinds of games, the success of the social games depends on game elements which retain the individual attention and involve him or her at the entertainment and satisfaction activity [3], which is denominated ludic, although its concept does not imply only the interests, abilities, challenges, or attention, as the playfulness is a state of mind and it mixes the cognitive spontaneity, social spontaneity, physical spontaneity, gladness manifestation, and sense of humor. This state of mind represents the willingness and is considered more important than entertainment itself, as first, it is the mind attitude which creates the preliminary to play and prepares the conditions for opportunities emerging and the actions to play and second, is just the external manifestation of this attitude [11]. The interesting part of this definitions is that it embodies not only the personal aspects but also the social ones, and both of them are main elements for the creation of playfulness which creates conditions and social situations so that the people express the personal meanings in a social structure [11]. Facebook is an example of that, as it uses the individual entertainment and the social tools, which makes that the users themselves create playfulness [3]. Curiously, the Facebook applications appeal more to the emotion and moods state than to actions themselves, which can be realized by the simple gameplay in the majority. One example is *Mafia Wars*, as to play it, the user only needs to click on a button to carry out a mission and acquire experience, and even with a very simple gameplay, the games has more than 27 million active players per month, which shows that there is something else besides its gameplay which stimulate the users to play [3]. Playfulness is present in all kinds of games regardless the platform [28].

4.6. Flow.

The "flow" concept was defined by the psychologist Csikszentmihalyi [29] as one focus state, pleasure, and entertainment; the person's attention is captured completely by something and the individual loses the notion of time and of everything around him or her and concentrates only at what is grabbing his or her attention. According to Schell [30], the game designers have as objective to create experiences interesting enough to attract the players' attention and to put them in "flow" state. To keep the players in this ideal state, it is necessary to have a balance between the abilities of the player and the challenges of the game, that is, the challenges must be proper for the current experience of the player, not very hard, not very easy, and the game must keep the balance between failure and success. Csikszentmihalyi [29] gives example of a student who is learning how to play tennis. At the beginning, the student will have no ability, and therefore the coach starts with basic and simple training sessions, which is still a challenge and fun for the student. As the student acquires new abilities, it is necessary that the coach shows new activities and new challenges, inasmuch as the basic tasks are already boring for the student. This concept comprises all kinds of activities, and thus it can be also applied at the SNGs.

4.7. Intrinsic and Extrinsic Motivations Theory.

According to studies by Chang and Chin [9], intrinsic motivation is characterized by performing of one task with no apparent effort an individual, as the activity itself is fun to be carried out, that is, the action itself is the reward for the individual. People will be more willing and will have more persistence in their intentions and behaviors when they are influenced by intrinsic motivations; so, entertainment is positively related to the motivation of playing.

Extrinsic motivation is defined as the performance of an activity in order to obtain a result or a reward [9]. Examples of extrinsic motivation are the *ease of use* and the *usefulness*.

Ease of use refers to the degree the person will not have difficulties when using an application or system. Now, the *usefulness* is defined as the degree of improvements and the performance of the task when using a specific tool. So, if a social game is useful and demonstrates to be easy when using it, the users will have good incentive to play [9].

4.8. Questions about Privacy and Security.

The questions about security and privacy at the social games, such as spam, accounts hijacking, and data and identity (ID) thefts are numerous and reduce the gameplay of the social games and consequently decrease the pleasure to play; however, the positive facts such as entertainment generally distinguish themselves against the negative aspects, that is, the players are influenced more by the positive factors than by the negative factors [5].

4.9. Virality.

Virality is a very important concept at the SNSs [15]. Helm [31] defines marketing viral, virality for marketing, as the following:

> *"Viral marketing can be understood as a communication and distribution concept that relies on customers to transmit digital products via electronic mail to other potential customers in their social sphere and to animate these contacts to also transmit the products."*

It is possible to realize that the developers use this practice to publish their games through the social network site. The publications are done through solicitations, invitations, events, and games activities which are sent for friends or are published at the user profile, where his or her friends can visualize them, to get interested and start to play. Wei et al. [32] points out this practice as a main element to the propagation of the games, as it reaches a great amount of users in a short period of time.

4.10. Kinds of Players.

The segmentation is a main concept present at the marketing literature, and its objective is to separate people into groups according to their characteristics. This practice is used by companies in order to direct its products for the proper clients. According to Hamari and Tuunanen [33], the marketing literature classifies the people into the following four main categories:

(1) geographic: classification of people according to address, city, state, country, among others. In the context of the games, the preference of the players can be influenced according the culture of his or her culture or continent [33];

(2) demographic: classifications done according to age, gender, education, social status, occupation, among others. For example, the average age of the students is 25 years old;

(3) psychographic: classification done according to attitudes, interests, or lifestyle of the person (e.g., extroverted people);

(4) behavioral: classification done according to the behavior of a person concerning the product (e.g., the player who plays every day during the work break).

Hamari and Tuunanen [33] claim in their studies that for the analysis for the kinds of players, the researchers do not show very interest in geographic and demographic segmentations.

Still according to Hamari and Tuunanen [33], Bartle is one of the authors with greater references for studies of player types. Through the behavioral analysis of the players at the games type MUD (Multi-User Dungeon), Bartle [34] defined two dimensions of kinds of players: *actions versus interaction* and *player-orientation versus world-orientation*, as it is shown in Figure 1. The kind of player is determined depending on the position in each of the axes (*actions versus interaction* and *player-orientation versus world-orientation*). The player will be the type *Killer* if he or she prefers *actions* and if he or she is *player-oriented*, and he or she will be *explorer* if he or she prefers *interaction* and if he or she is *world-oriented*.

Hamari and Tuunanen [33] claim that the kinds of Bartle players have a lot of criticism, and the most important one is that the behaviors of the players may vary during the time, which makes it impossible to determine in which category the player fits, although the player typology of Bartle is sufficiently useful to describe all kinds of possible players.

Yee [35], with the use of typology of players of Bartle, defined three factors which motivate the players to play online games: achievement, social aspects, and immersion. The factor achievement can be categorized at Murray's ambition needs.

4.11. Motivational Elements of the Social Games. Based on the studies demonstrated at the previous topics, we have identified the main motivational elements of the social games present at the literature, as Table 1 shows.

Some elements (subelements), due to the fact that they demonstrate the same principle, were grouped in wider elements (elements). For example, competition and social status were inserted at a more general context which is power needs.

The elements playfulness, intrinsic and extrinsic motivations, flow, and security were inserted at the context of the game elements as they are items which are related to the characteristics that the game itself demonstrate which attract the player attention. The playfulness refers to the satisfaction and entertainment that the game offers to the player. The intrinsic and extrinsic motivations are related to the usefulness of the game. Flow is used by the game designers to elaborate games with activities which grasp the player's attention. Security is related to the strategies and resources used at the game to offer greater safety to the user.

5. Methods

For the evaluation, it was chosen *Match 3*-type games as these ones demonstrate simpler gameplay and mechanics, which does not need very broad analysis related to the characteristics of the game itself, and like this, it allows to focus the research more on the personal, social, and

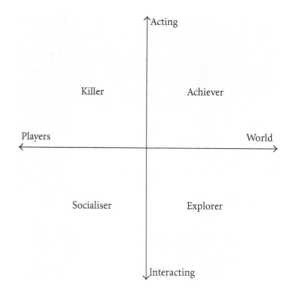

FIGURE 1: Bartle's player typology.

psychological aspects of the game which is the objective of this study. Another reason is that to analyze simpler games allows a faster and more precise analysis. All the 7 selected games are the same type (*Match 3*) and have similar gameplay and mechanics as it is shown in Figure 2. It was adopted this criterion as the results may vary for each type of game, for example, the preferences of the players may vary from a game to another, typology of Bartle players [34], and like this, a motivational element which is prominent for a game might not be for another one. The selected games for evaluation were *Diamond Dash, Collapse! Blast, Mystic Ice Blast, Bricks Breaking, Plock, Gem Clix,* and *Blast!*.

The participants are 12 "gamers" selected from a group of games of a university where 10 are males and 2 are females, 9 are computer science undergraduate students and 3 are music undergraduate students, and all of them are Brazilian. Each participant played all the games and evaluated the level of presence of each motivational element of each game with values between 1 and 5, where 1 meaning the lowest presence and 5 meaning the highest one. There is a definition of each value as follows:

(1) it does not have: the game did not show any characteristic of the motivational element;

(2) slightly visible: the game has the motivational element, but its presence at the game is minimum;

(3) visible: it is possible to notice the presence of the motivational element at the game;

(4) present: it is noticed easily the presence of the motivational element at the game;

(5) clearly present: the motivational element is present at the game in a clear and objective way.

TABLE 1: Main motivational elements of the social games.

Authors	Elements	Subelements	Examples
D. H. Shin and Y. J. Shin 2010; Meurs 2011 [5, 16]	Time	Asynchronous time	Single player
Ines and Abdelkader 2011; Benkler 2006; Urista et al. 2009; Joinson 2008; Lucas and Sherry 2004; Hou 2011; Wei et al. 2010 [3, 17–20, 22, 32]	Social interaction	Social fictitious presence	To help and to hire friends
		Publication of the activities	Wall post, send invitation for friends to play
Ines and Abdelkader 2011; Hamari and Järvinen 2011; Benkler 2006 [3, 15, 17]	Materialistic needs	Rewarding system	Daily bonuses
Ines and Abdelkader 2011; Kollock 1999; Lucas and Sherry 2004; Hamari and Järvinen 2011; Sherry et al. 2006; Hamari and Lehdonvirta 2010 [3, 15, 20, 23, 24, 26]	Power needs	Competition Social status	Ranking, weekly championships Level
Ines and Abdelkader 2011; Joinson 2008; Kollock 1999 [3, 19, 24]	Affective needs	Cooperation	To help friends
		Interest sharing	Gifts (to donate and to receive presents), group needs
Ines and Abdelkader 2011; Lucas and Sherry 2004 [3, 20]	Ambition needs	—	Objectives, challenges, achievements
Ines and Abdelkader 2011; Choi and Kim 2004 [3, 27]	Information needs	Cognitive spontaneity (learning)	Feedbacks, tutorials
Schell 2008; Rao 2008; Benkler 2006; Chang and Chin 2011; D. H. Shin and Y. J. Shin 2010; Csikszentmihalyi 1990 [5, 9, 11, 17, 29, 30]	Game elements	Playfulness Intrinsic and extrinsic motivations Flow Security	Arts, sound, gameplay, mechanics, story, fantasy, plot

TABLE 2: Level of presence of the motivational elements at the *Match* 3-type games.

Game	DiamonD dash	Collapse! Blast	Mystic Ice Blast	Bricks Breaking	Plock	Gem Clix	Blast!
Asynchronous time	4.5	4.3	4.2	4.1	4.1	4.8	4.6
Fictitious social presence	2.4	2.2	2.6	1.9	2.8	1.9	1.4
Activities publications	4.3	3.4	3.7	3.0	3.0	3.1	2.0
Rewarding system	4.7	3.9	3.6	1.6	2.4	2.4	1.3
Competition	4.3	3.5	3.0	2.3	3.3	3.0	1.4
Social status	4.5	3.6	3.8	2.4	3.3	3.0	1.5
Cooperation	3.0	2.5	3.3	1.6	2.0	1.2	1.0
Interests sharing	2.8	2.8	2.7	1.9	2.6	1.8	1.1
Ambition needs	2.8	2.9	2.8	1.9	2.3	2.2	1.7
Cognitive spontaneity	3.7	3.7	3.8	3.3	3.3	3.9	3.4
Game elements	3.5	2.8	4.0	1.8	3.5	4.1	2.6
Active users per month	16.400.000	1.600.000	980.000	350.000	50.000	10.000	100

In order to identify the elements which motivate the people the most to play *Match* 3-type games, we have verified the level of presence of each motivational element of each game, as well as the quantity of active players per month of each of them, and we have made a comparison among them. For example, if a determined element is strongly present in a game, but at the other its presence is low and the quantity of players of this game is meaningfully shorter than the first, then the element can be considered important, as its absence generated the drop at the quantity of active users of the game.

6. Results

Table 2 shows the presence of motivational level results of each game and the quantity of active players per month of each game. The levels of presence were calculated through the

FIGURE 2: Comparison of the games *Diamond Dash* and *Mystic Ice Blast*.

answers average of the participants, and the quantity of active players per month of each game was taken from AppData [4].

The element asynchronous time was strongly present in all the games, with level of presence higher than 4; hence, it is realized that the asynchronous gameplay is a very common practice at the *Match* 3-type games, which makes it necessary the presence of this element at the games.

The most highlighted elements were publications of the activities, rewarding system, competition, and social status, as the level of presence of these elements was higher than 4 only at the game *Diamond Dash* which is the game which has quantity of active players per month significantly higher than all the other games, a fact which proves the importance of the presence of these elements at the games. Furthermore, in all the other games, these four elements were the ones which were more present compared to all the other items, despite the level of presence being smaller than 4.

The social fictitious presence, despite of the games being immersed in a social network, is not a very present element in *Match* 3-type games. In all the games, its presence level was lower than 3. Other elements which are not also used so much at these kinds of games are the interest sharing and ambition needs, which also demonstrated levels of presence lower than 3 in all the games.

Cooperation is not also a very present element at the games; its level of presence was smaller than 4 in all of them, and therefore its presence was relatively higher at the three games with greater quantity of active players: *Diamond Dash*, *Collapse! Blast*, and *Mystic Ice Blast*, with level of presence next to 3, than all the others, having level of presence

smaller than 2. This proves that the cooperation may be a determining factor at the games.

The cognitive spontaneity level of presence was around 3.5 in all the games, a reasonable presence of the element which is enough for the fact that the games are in general simple and intuitive to learn and to play. It is then possible to say that it is not necessary to have detailed explanations on how to play these kinds of games.

Finally, the presence of the elements of game such as arts, sound, story, fantasy, and gameplay were strongly present at the games *Mystic Ice Blast* and *Gem Clix* with level of presence equal to 4. Nevertheless, the presence of these elements did not offer meaningful impacts at the attractiveness of the games, as games like *Collapse! Blast* demonstrated many more players than both games even with just 2.8 level of presence of these elements. Another example is the game *Bricks Breaking* which demonstrated more players than *Plock*, *Gem Clix*, and *Blast!*, even having less elaborated elements of the game than these three games.

7. Discussions and Conclusions

The results showed that the *Match* 3-type games have simple gameplay, and they do not show strong points at the fictitious socialization part, and their focus is on the competition and social status, a fact which classifies them at the category of *skill/knowledge* type of social game defined by Rossi [1], where the main objective is to compete with friends. In fact, the competition and the social status were the elements which were present the most in all the games, which favors the studies by Sherry et al. [23] and Hamari and Järvinen [15], who pointed out competition as the most motivating element of the game.

The importance of the publications of the activities may be related to the viral marketing, as the developers need to bring out their games so that they can reach a great quantity of users, and this publishing takes place when the players publish the activities of the games at the social network site, which generates other possible players and marketers of the game. This practice fits well into the definition of Helm [31] about viral marketing.

The game *Bricks Breaking* showed unexpected values, as the level of presence of the elements were lower than the games *Plock* and *Gem Clix* and even though it showed more active players than these two ones. This confirms that there are other factors which influence the games attractiveness, and we intend in further studies to identify these motivational elements.

This study showed that the main motivational elements of the *Match* 3-type social games are asynchronous time, publication of the activities, rewarding system, competition, social status, and cooperation. Among them, the publication of the activities, rewarding system, competition, and social status were the ones which demonstrated more influence at the quantity of active players. This can be realized at the game *Diamond Dash* which was the unique game which demonstrated high level of presence of these items, and it is the game with greater quantity of users. Furthermore, at the other games, these four items are the ones which are highlighted the most when compared to the other ones, which leads to the conclusion that the motivation of these games is mainly in these elements.

This paper may help the game designers to project their *Match* 3-type games with focus on the elements which motivate the most the users to play. We intend in further studies to apply the obtained results in this study in the development of a *Match* 3-type social game and verify the attractiveness of the game. Moreover, we also intend to identify the main motivational elements of other kinds of games.

Conflict of Interests

This study does not have any interest to advertise, to criticize, or to judge the games. The authors unique interest is the research, and all the citations related to the games were necessary due to the focus of the research.

References

[1] L. Rossi, "Playing your network: gaming in social network sites," in *Proceedings of DiGRA*, 2009.

[2] Facebook, http://newsroom.fb.com/.

[3] D. L. Ines and G. Abdelkader, "Facebook games: between social and personal aspects," *International Journal of Computer Information System and Industrial Management Applications*, vol. 3, pp. 713–723, 2011.

[4] AppData, http://www.appdata.com/.

[5] D. H. Shin and Y. J. Shin, "Why do people play social network games?" *Computers in Human Behavior*, vol. 27, no. 2, pp. 852–861, 2011.

[6] P. Sweetser and P. Wyeth, "Game flow: a model for evaluating player enjoyment in games," *ACM Computer in Entertainment*, vol. 3, no. 3, pp. 1–25, 2005.

[7] A. Järvinen, "Game design for social networks: interaction design for playful dispositions," in *Proceedings of the ACM SIGGRAPH Symposium on Video Games (Sandbox '09)*, pp. 95–102, ACM, August 2009.

[8] D. M. Boyd and N. B. Ellison, "Social network sites: definition, history, and scholarship," *Journal of Computer-Mediated Communication*, vol. 13, no. 1, pp. 210–230, 2007.

[9] C. Chang and Y. Chin, "Predicting the usage intention of social network games: an intrinsic-extrinsic motivation theory perspective," *International Journal of Online Marketing*, vol. 1, no. 3, pp. 29–37, 2011.

[10] V. Donmus, "The use of social networks in educational computer-game based foreign language learning," in *Proceedings of the 1st World Conference on Learning, Teaching and Administration (WCLTA '10)*, pp. 1497–1503, October 2010.

[11] V. Rao, "Facebook applications and playful mood: the construction of facebook as a 'third place'," in *Proceedings of the 12th International Conference on Entertainment and Media in the Ubiquitous Era*, pp. 8–12, fin, October 2008.

[12] International Game Developers Association, "Casual games 2008-2009 white paper," archives.igda.org/casual/IGDA_Casual_Games_White_Paper_2008.pdf.

[13] D. Y. Wohn, C. Lamp, and R. Wash, "The "S" in social network games: initiating, maintaining, and enhancing relationships," in *Proceedings of the 44th Hawwaii International Conference on System Sciences. IEEE Computer Society*, Washington, DC, USA, 2011.

[14] J. Sung, T. Bjornrud, Y. H. Lee, and D. Y. Wohn, "Social network games: exploring audience traits," in *Proceedings of the 28th Annual CHI Conference on Human Factors in Computing Systems (CHI '10)*, pp. 3649–3654, April 2010.

[15] J. Hamari and A. Järvinen, "Building customer relationship through game mechanics in social games," in *Business, Technological and Social Dimensions of Computer Games: Multidisciplinary Developments*, M. Cruz-Cunha, V. Carvalho, and P. Tavares, Eds., Hershey, 2011.

[16] R. V. Meurs, "And then you wait: the issue of dead time in social network games," in *Proceedings of DiGRA, Conference: Think Design Play*, January 2011.

[17] Y. Benkler, *The Wealth of Networks*, Yale University, 2006.

[18] M. A. Urista, Q. Dong, and K. D. Day, "Explaining why young adults use MySpace and Facebook through uses and gratification theory," *Human Communication*, vol. 12, no. 2, pp. 215–229, 2009.

[19] A. N. Joinson, "Looking at, looking up or keeping up with people?: motives and use of facebook," in *Proceedings of the Twenty-Sixth Annual SIGCHI Conference on Human Factors in Computing Systems (CHI '08)*, April 2008.

[20] K. Lucas and J. L. Sherry, "Sex differences in video game play: a communication-based explanation," *Communication Research*, vol. 31, no. 5, pp. 499–523, 2004.

[21] E. M. Perse and J. A. Courtright, "Normative images of communication media: mass and interpersonal channels in the new media environment," *Human Communication Research*, vol. 19, no. 4, pp. 485–503, 1993.

[22] J. Hou, "Uses and gratification of social games blending social networking and game play," *First Monday Peer-Reviewed Jornal on the Internet*, vol. 16, no. 7, 2011.

[23] J. L. Sherry, K. Lucas, B. S. Greenberg, and K. Lachlan, "Video game uses and gratifications as predictors of use and game preference," in *Playing Video Games: Motives, Responses, and Consequences*, P. Vorderer and J. Bryant, Eds., pp. 213–224, Mahwah, NJ, USA, 2006.

[24] P. Kollock, "The Economies of Online Cooperation: gifts, and public goods in cyberspace," in *Communities in Cyberspace*, M. A. Smith and P. Kollock, Eds., pp. 220–239, London, UK, 1999.

[25] H. A. Murray, *Explorations in Personality*, Oxford University, 1938.

[26] J. Hamari and V. Lehdonvirta, "Game design as marketing: how game mechanics create demand for virtual goods," *International Journal of Business Science and Applied Management*, vol. 5, no. 1, pp. 14–29, 2010.

[27] D. Choi and J. Kim, "Why people continue to play online games: in search of critical design factors to increase customer loyalty to online contents," *Cyberpsychology and Behavior*, vol. 7, no. 1, pp. 11–24, 2004.

[28] B. Kirman, "Emergence and playfulness in social games," in *Proceedings of the 14th International Academic Mindtrek Conference: Envisioning Future Media Environments*, pp. 71–77, ACM, October 2010.

[29] M. Csikszentmihalyi, *The Psychology of Optimal Experience*, HarperCollin e-Books, 1990.

[30] J. Schell, *The Art of Game Design*, Morgan Kaufmann, 2008.

[31] S. Helm, "Viral marketing—establishing customer relationships by 'Word of Mouse'," *Electronic Markets*, vol. 10, no. 3, pp. 158–161, 2000.

[32] X. Wei, J. Yang, and J. A. Adamic, "Diffusion dynamics of games on online social networks," in *Proceedings of the 3rd Conference on Online Social Networks (WOSN '10)*, 2010.

[33] J. Hamari and J. Tuunanen, "Meta-synthesis of player typologies," in *Proceedings of DiGRA Nordic Conference: Local and Global—Games in Culture and Society*, 2012.

[34] R. Bartle, "Hearts, clubs, diamonds, spades: players who suit muds," http://www.mud.co.uk/richard/hcds.htm.

[35] N. Yee, "Motivations of play in online games," *Journal of Cyber Psychology and Behavior*, vol. 9, no. 6, pp. 772–775, 2007.

10

More Than Flow: Revisiting the Theory of Four Channels of Flow

Ching-I Teng and Han-Chung Huang

Graduate Institute of Business and Management, Chang Gung University, Taoyuan 333, Taiwan

Correspondence should be addressed to Ching-I Teng, chingit@mail.cgu.edu.tw

Academic Editor: Daniel Thalmann

Flow (FCF) theory has received considerable attention in recent decades. In addition to flow, FCF theory proposed three influential factors, that is, boredom, frustration, and apathy. While these factors have received relatively less attention than flow, Internet applications have grown exponentially, warranting a closer reexamination of the applicability of the FCF theory. Thus, this study tested the theory that high/low levels of skill and challenge lead to four channels of flow. The study sample included 253 online gamers who provided valid responses to an online survey. Analytical results support the FCF theory, although a few exceptions were noted. First, skill was insignificantly related to apathy, possibly because low-skill users can realize significant achievements to compensate for their apathy. Moreover, in contrast with the FCF theory, challenge was positively related to boredom, revealing that gamers become bored with difficult yet repetitive challenges. Two important findings suggest new directions for FCF theory.

1. Introduction

The application of flow theory to multiple Internet contexts [1–4] reflects its prominent role in information systems research. In their pioneering work, Csikszentmihalyi [5] proposed the four channels of flow (FCF) theory, that is, flow, boredom, frustration, and apathy, and also posited that skill and challenge are major components in each of those channels.

Flow refers to the involvement of individuals in activities with full concentration and their subsequent enjoyment [6], whereas those individuals experience flow through high degree of skills to control challenges [1]. Such highly enjoyable experiences cause individuals to become more involved in related activities, allowing them to perceive enjoyment, control, and intrinsic enjoyment [2]. Therefore, high levels of skills and challenges create the perception of flow.

Boredom occurs when a person experiences monotony, insipidity, and a lack of stimuli [7]. Individuals may feel disinterested and lacking in concentration for an activity, resulting in unpleasant emotions [8]. Moreover, boredom creates a passive perception towards stimuli [9]. Enhanced skills likely shift individuals from involvement to boredom [8]. Therefore, highly skilled individuals are more likely to familiarize themselves with the stimuli related to an activity, subsequently giving rise to boredom.

Frustration refers to the inability of individuals to solve problems or satisfy demand involving discontent or insecure perceptions [7]. Although frustration may produce negative emotions under obstructions from individuals, circumstances, and things, Goodstein and Lanyon [10] suggested that frustration may motivate individuals to achieve certain goals. Therefore, frustration is occasionally regarded as essential to enhancing an overall experience [11].

Apathy refers to individual carelessness towards certain circumstances and an unwillingness to remain alert [7]. Apathy originates from obtaining a lower degree of achievement or having no interest in certain activities. Emotive feelings of unconcern and unwillingness lead to a failure to concentrate on certain activities. Therefore, individuals lacking sufficient capabilities cannot achieve success in activities, discouraging them from further interest or participation in related activities, and ultimately resulting in the feeling of apathy.

Dimensions of skill and challenge can determine the above four channels [5]. High skill and high challenge create flow; high skill and low challenge create boredom; low skill and high challenge create frustration; low skill and low challenge create apathy.

Of the four channels, flow has received the most attention in many disciplines [12–14], with notable examples found in studies on happiness [6], telepresence, time distortion [15], interactivity, involvement [16], and exploratory behavior [17], thus reflecting its widespread applicability.

However, boredom, frustration, and apathy have received lesser attention than flow, which represents a considerable research gap. The inability to thoroughly understand these factors makes it impossible for information system designers to assess how user skill and challenge profoundly impact their systems. Moreover, the exponential growth and acceleration of Internet applications warrants a closer examination of the FCF theory. Despite recent studies on boredom [8] and frustration [11], the FCF theory has not been studied from a structural perspective, that is, using structural equation modeling to examine the all model components simultaneously, thus reflecting another research gap.

Therefore, this study investigates whether skill and challenge create four channels, as posited by FCF theory. This study significantly contributes to current literature in three ways. First, the FCF theory posits that skill and challenge determine whether an individual experiences flow, frustration, boredom, and apathy [5,6]. While reexamining the four channels, this study explores how skill and challenge nurture those channels in online games.

Second, despite conjecturing that skill and challenge can predict flow, Skadberg and Kimmel [14] offered no supporting evidence, possibly owing to their lack of challenges requiring high skill levels. Given the ambiguous findings of their study, FCF theory warrants a closer examination in other information system contexts. Therefore, this study examines the role of FCF theory in online gaming, which involves difficult challenges and is also an important information medium.

Third, an exhaustive review by Hoffman and Novak [18] established the usefulness of flow in information systems research, revealing that the components of FCF theory are worthwhile research directions. Therefore, exactly how skill and challenge formulate the other three channels of boredom, frustration, and apathy must be examined. By addressing this theoretical gap, this study significantly contributes to future studies on flow and the other three novel and influential factors.

2. Theoretical Background

2.1. Flow. Flow refers to the highly enjoyable experience of intense concentration on a specific activity [6]. Individuals of any age, race, and culture can experience flow [6]. Although immersion is viewed as the prestate of flow due to the disorientation, flow shows a full commitment [19]. The degree of immersion is significantly affected by the results and significance of individual actions in a particular environment and the influence of those actions on the games [19]. Having received considerable theoretical and empirical attention, flow has been applied in many fields. According to previous studies, flow is essential to favorable user responses [2, 4], reflecting its relevance to information systems research. Notably, although having received considerable attention,

flow has seldom been examined with respect to the other three channels in the FCF theory, that is, boredom, frustration, and apathy.

Flow is also a notable function of the internal brain structure in humans. According to a previous study, both cognitive science and neuroscience are applicable in examining brain functions and analyzing the state of flow. The frontal lobe and medial temporal lobe structures containing higher cognitions developed with flexibility in cognition are associated with an explicit system [20]. However, such an implicit system also involves knowledge and skills acquired from basal ganglia, thereby achieving a high efficiency in processing information and making decisions. Based on the dilemma between flexibility and efficiency, the state of flow represents high skills that have been practiced for a considerable time in an implicit system without any interferences from an explicit one [20].

Although individuals may or may not remain pleased with a particular task, their emotional state can be monitored by psychological symptoms. The central nervous system and the peripheral nervous system, for example, blood pressure, respiration, and temperature, exhibit physiological signals, which are genuine and emotional processes that can be partially interpreted [7]. Since different levels of a challenge cause various emotional reactions, individuals tend to switch from active involvement to boredom when their skills are enhanced [8]. Conversely, when individuals can not further improve in terms of quality of skills, their emotional state may shift from active involvement to anxiety [8].

Antecedents of flow include a well-designed learner interface, positive user-computer interaction [21], playfulness, telepresence, control [22], skill, and challenge [14]. Of those antecedents, skill and challenge are the most widely discussed. Skill refers to the ability to resolve difficult problems [6] while challenge refers to a complex task requiring completion [1]. Highly skilled users faced with challenging problems are likely to experience flow [23], explaining why skill and challenge should be considered major antecedents of flow.

Despite the applicability of the flow construct in many activities [2–4], online games have received considerable attention [2, 4, 24]. For instance, flow experience extended when incorporating increased difficulty in games in terms of development of necessary metal states, thus providing a regular state of balance between increased challenges and skills [25]. Additionally, in comparison with playing online game via computer- and human-controlled opponents, that study also demonstrated that playing against competitors controlled by a real human creates more presence, flow, and enjoyment [25]. Moreover, skill and challenge are often discussed in terms of flow in online gaming [4], thus making online games highly appropriate for examining flow theories.

2.2. Flow Theories. Csikszentmihalyi [5] pioneered the theory of the three channels of flow, in which flow only appears after reaching a balanced state between skill and challenge. When individual skills fail to adequately respond, individuals experience anxiety; in contrast, when their skills exceed those required in specific challenges, individuals tend to search for more challenging activities [26]. In a flow experience, individuals experience control and intrinsic pleasures [2]. A previous study characterized the flow construct according to eight elements, that is a clear goal, feedback, challenges that match skills, concentration and focus, control, loss of consciousness, transformation of time, and a self-reinforcing activity [6].

Hoffman, Novak, and their colleagues [1, 17, 27] developed a conceptual model based on flow. Based on that model, three aspects were investigated. First, causes of flow for Internet users included both motivations, skills from the individual and vividness, and challenges from online activities. Second, the online experience made the individual more involved and focused, easily leading to flow. Third, the flow experience related to online activities triggered a positive attitude and thoughts for the individual, creating an impetus to increase learning ability. Additionally, the importance of variables changes over time. The skill levels may improve owing to the increased time spent on Internet sites. Conversely, challenge, telepresence, and the desire to explore online activities may diminish.

Several theoretical models or frameworks have been developed for flow. Agarwal and Karahanna [28] also proposed cognitive absorption in comparison with flow. Cognitive absorption refers to operating computer programs, and is considered as belonging to multidimensional perception constructs, including temporal dissociation, focused immersion, heightened enjoyment, control, and curiosity. Personal traits and cognitive absorption are also related. Both playfulness and personal innovativeness profoundly impact cognitive absorption. Additionally, technology use such as perceived usefulness and perceived ease of use may constitute major antecedents of cognitive absorption. Moreover, Richard and Chandra [16] investigated Web navigation behavior empirically, indicating that flow arises from enjoyment, time distortion, and telepresence is a highly effective means of elucidating the web navigation behavior of visitors. Such studies confirm that flow plays a major role in computer research.

The four channels of flow theory (the FCF theory) [5], that is, the leading theory on flow creation, posits that high/low skill levels and challenges create four channels: flow, boredom, frustration, and apathy. Of those, flow has received the most attention, likely owing to that flow triggers positive user responses. Flow is generally accompanied by enhanced happiness [6, 29], thus highly motivating users to engage in repetitive activities [30].

The FCF theory should be examined by evaluating flow and the other three factors at different skill and challenge levels, as posited by the FCF theory. Skill refers to the ability to engage in current activities [17]. Highly skilled individuals can overcome difficulties, subsequently creating intrinsic enjoyment. A high skill level may thus nurture flow. However, highly skilled individuals may consider themselves as experts, thus diminishing their interest and concentration level and increasing their feelings of boredom. Conversely, low-skilled individuals likely experience difficulties that prevent them from achieving their goals, subsequently increasing their feelings of frustration. Finally,

given their lack of skills to achieve goals, such individuals may become discouraged and withdraw from further activity. Restated, they become apathetic. Therefore, the FCF theory posits the following.

(H1a) Skill is positively related to flow.

(H1b) Skill is positively related to boredom.

(H1c) Skill is negatively related to frustration.

(H1d) Skill is negatively related to apathy.

Challenge refers to competition and obstacles encountered in activities [31]. Challenge may inspire individuals to win competitions and overcome obstacles, fostering a sense of achievement. However, too much challenge causes frustration while insufficient challenge leads to boredom [8]. Frustration occurs when individuals fail to progress further due to the inability to operate or perform well [11]. To do so, individuals must concentrate to fully realize their capabilities. Increased concentration is a major element of flow [6]. Thus, a high challenge is likely to create a flow experience. Challenges inspire individuals to win competitions and overcome obstacles, likely motivating them to seek new ways of winning, ultimately reducing their boredom. Conversely, challenges considered too difficult to overcome would prevent users from winning, ultimately increasing their frustration. Individuals may also be attracted to competitive challenges, which diminish feelings of apathy. Therefore, the FCF theory posits the following.

(H2a) Challenge is positively related to flow.

(H2b) Challenge is negatively related to boredom.

(H2c) Challenge is positively related to frustration.

(H2d) Challenge is negatively related to apathy.

The above eight hypotheses represent the foundation of the FCF theory [5] and were not initially developed in this study. This study reexamines the FCF theory owing to exponential growth and accelerated changes in Internet applications. Thus rather than proposing a new hypothesis, this study examines all eight hypotheses from the perspective of FCF theory. Figure 1 illustrates the research framework of this study.

3. Method

3.1. Sample and Data Collection. Testing the validity of the FCF theory requires a research context involving high/low user skills and challenges. Online game complexity may require collaborating in teams, solving problems, and exploring the game worlds. Online games can also be rather simple by only requiring minimum mental efforts. Online games thus involve high/low levels of challenges. Moreover, online gamers may range from novices to experts, creating high/low levels of skills. Thus, online games meet the criterion of this study to test the validity of the FCF theory. Moreover, online games have emerged as influential information systems. For instance, recent studies [32, 33] have established the relevance of online games in current research.

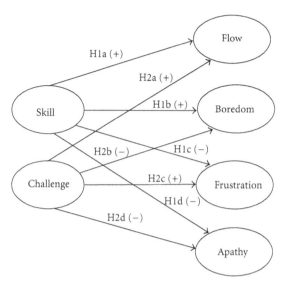

FIGURE 1: Theoretical framework.

To reduce the likelihood of a sampling bias owing to few sources of respondents, this study solicited respondents from more than twenty forums and electronic bulletins associated with online games. Data were collected using a web form. The web form cover pages stated that this study focused on gaming experiences. Respondents whom consented to participate were encouraged to enter a lottery in which 50 winners received a $US 16 gift certificate.

Participants were instructed to provide the name of their favorite games, their occupations, race, or other avatar identifiers. Among their favorite online games included World of Warcraft, Mabinogi, Lineage, and Crazyracing. Instructing respondents to rate their favorite games may reduce the likelihood of a memory bias, an approach which has been used in recent literature, for example, [32]. Such information was reviewed to verify the validity of the response, that is, whether respondent had online game playing experiences. When such information was determined to be meaningless or incorrect, the related response was considered invalid. Moreover, the internet protocol (IP) addresses and email addresses of the respondents were recorded and compared to eliminate respondents with multiple responses.

Of the 309 web forms submitted, 253 were valid, yielding an effective response ratio of 81.9%. Of the 253 respondents submitting valid forms, 63.9% were male; 46.2% were younger than 22 years old; 96.4% had attended colleges or universities (including graduate or above); 44.7% had a monthly disposable income exceeding $US 100. Hsu and Lu [34] observed that most online gamers had 1–3 years of experience playing online games. The respondents in this study had an average of 15.2 months experience playing online games, which corresponded to the findings of Hsu and Lu [34]. Over the past six months, the average time spent on the online game was 13.8 hours weekly.

In comparison with the study of Williams et al. [35], which surveyed players of *Everquest 2*, this study provided the following results of interest. Regarding the mean age of players, Williams et al. [35] indicated that the age of 31.6

years old matched the mean age of general US population (35.5 years old). Such findings contradicted the stereotype of young gamers. However, our findings somewhat differ from those of Williams et al. [35]. Most of our respondents ranged from 20 to 25 years old, reflecting that the local gamers are youth. Moreover, 80% of the respondents of Williams et al. [35] were male. Results of this study are consistent with those of previous studies in which 64% of the respondents were male. With respect to income and education distributions, *Everquest 2* players (as in [35]) came from more wealthy families than average ones. Conversely, respondents in this study had a low income since most of the adolescents had a lower than average income. In sum, characteristics of respondents in this study were largely young adults with low disposable incomes.

3.2. Measurement. Most measurement instruments came from previous studies. Items measuring skill, challenge, and flow were adapted from the scales of Novak et al. [17]. Pertinent literature lacks a consensus on how to measure flow [18]. Therefore, in this study, the scale of Novak et al. [17] was used, which was also used in an online gaming study of Hsu and Lu [2]. This study followed the study of Hsu and Lu [2] in explaining the flow concept to the participants prior to they providing responses to the study items regarding flow. The present study explained flow to the participants using two sentences: "Flow is the individual state of concentration in which time is perceived as still" and "Flow makes an individual experience intrinsic enjoyment." This approach of explaining flow and then directly measuring flow has been widely adopted in the literature [2, 17]. Moreover, participants in the present study did not raise any questions regarding the meaning of flow. Thus the measurement of flow in this study is adequate and understandable to participants. Items measuring boredom, frustration, and apathy originated from the scales of Kammann and Flett [36] and Kozma and Stones [37]. The measurement tools adopted Likert scales. All items involved a response option ranging from 1 (very disagreeable) to 5 (very agreeable), and were slightly modified to comply with the research context. All respondents were instructed to evaluate their favorite online games. Thus, "the game" in measurement items referred to the game favored by the individual respondent rather than to a single game specified for all respondents. Notably, rating favorite games may somewhat increase the scores of some constructs, but may not change the relations between constructs. Since hypotheses state relations between constructs, rating favorite games may not bring marked biases. Moreover, rating favorite games increases the number of games included in this study, subsequently enhancing the generality of the study findings. Such an approach has also been adopted previously [38].

This study performed a confirmatory factor analysis to directly assess measurement reliability and validity. Confirmatory factor analysis is extensively adopted to assessing the reliability and validity of psychological assessments [39, 40]. All measures had a Cronbach $\alpha > .7$, a composite reliability (CR) > .6, and an average variance extracted (AVE) >.5, which satisfied the reliability criteria of Bagozzi and Yi [41].

TABLE 1: Summary of confirmatory factor analysis.

	μ	SD	λ	α	CR	AVE
Skill				.87	.91	.72
I am extremely skilled at playing the game.	3.34	0.81	0.83			
I have rich knowledge regarding the game.	3.68	0.82	0.86			
Compared to most gamers, I am more familiar with the game.	3.20	0.95	0.91			
My skill in playing the game is superior to using other software.	3.31	0.92	0.78			
Challenge				.87	.90	.76
Playing the game challenges me to perform to the best of my ability.	2.93	0.98	0.90			
Playing the game challenges me.	3.35	0.97	0.78			
I find that playing the game stretches my capabilities to my limits.	2.80	1.00	0.93			
Flow				.87	.92	.85
I have experienced flow when playing the game.	3.00	1.15	0.85			
I frequently experience flow when playing the game.	2.51	0.98	0.99			
Boredom				.73	.98	.95
I feel much more skilled than other gamers when playing the game.	3.09	0.86	0.98			
Tasks in the game are very easy for me to complete.	3.11	0.85	0.66			
Frustration				.84	.90	.75
I find the game too frustrating.	2.33	0.81	0.71			
I find the game too complex.	2.30	0.83	0.88			
I find the game too difficult.	2.20	0.79	0.98			
Apathy				.96	.98	.91
I find the game boring.	2.20	0.86	0.95			
I find the game uninteresting.	2.18	0.86	0.98			
I find the game dull.	2.15	0.87	0.98			
I find the game unattractive.	2.05	0.83	0.90			

TABLE 2: Correlations between study constructs.

	1	2	3	4	5
(1) Skill	—				
(2) Challenge	.52**	—			
(3) Flow	.34**	.26**	—		
(4) Boredom	.69**	.40**	.30**	—	
(5) Frustration	−.12*	.15**	.07	−.17**	—
(6) Apathy	−.22**.	−.29**	−.18**	−.15**	.30**

Note: *$P < .05$, **$P < .01$.

All indicator loadings exceeded .5 and had t values > 2, which satisfied the convergent validity criterion of Anderson and Gerbing [42]. Moreover, the maximum squared correlation between constructs was below the minimum AVE, which satisfied the discriminant validity criterion specified by Fornell and Larcker [43]. Table 1 summarizes the confirmatory factor analysis results.

The theoretical model fits acceptably with the data (χ^2 = 532.39, RMSEA = .10, CFI = .89, IFI = .89, NFI = .88, SRMR = .06). Browne and Cudeck [44] recommended RMSEA, CFI, and IFI as the proper indices for evaluating the model fit. In this study, RMSEA equaled .10, approaching the criterion of Browne and Cudeck [45], since validity of the RMSEA index was doubted [46]. CFI approached .10, which is suggested by Bagozzi [47]. IFI also approached .10, as recommended by Bollen [48]. Moreover, SRMR was below .07, satisfying the criterion of Bagozzi [47].

Table 2 lists the correlations between the study constructs. Study constructs revealed moderate-to-low correlations, indicating the discriminant validity of the measures and minimal influence of common method variance (CMV). However, formal statistical testing may provide further evidence of the minimal influence of CMV. This study followed the suggestion of Podsakoff et al. [49] by using one construct CMV to explain the variance of all items. The model with CMV had a χ^2 value of 3867.70 with a degree of freedom of 135, subsequently creating the χ^2 value difference of 3335.31 (= 3867.70 − 532.39) and the degree of freedom difference of 11 (= 135 − 124). The χ^2 value difference (3335.3) exceeded the threshold value (19.68 = χ^2 (df = 11, α = .05)). Namely, the model *without* CMV significantly outperformed the model *with* CMV, supporting the negligible influence of CMV.

4. Results

Table 3 presents the demographic data for the study respondents. Also, the section of sample and data collection processes summarizes the demographics. To avoid redundancy, this section does not repeat the same information.

While performing a further analysis of the sample, this study portrayed the identification and appearance of online gaming players; whereas the number of male players was nearly twice that of female players and their educational background consisted mainly of university level (accounting

TABLE 3: Sample description.

Demographics	Classifications	Number	Percentage (%)
Gender	Male	162	64.0
	Female	91	36.0
Education	High school	9	3.6
	College or university	213	84.2
	Graduate or above	31	12.2
Monthly Disposable income	Under $100	140	55.3
	$101–$300	92	36.4
	$301 and above	21	8.3

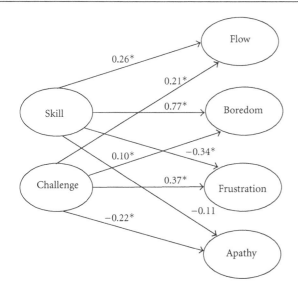

FIGURE 2: Results of Hypotheses Testing.

justified using structural equation modeling with direct paths from skill and challenge to each of the four channels.

4.1. Hypotheses Testing. The structural equation modeling method was adopted to examine whether skill and challenge determine the four channels of flow, as predicted by the FCF theory developed by Csikszentmihalyi [5].

Figure 2 summarizes the analytical results, which supported all propositions of the FCF theory with some interesting exceptions. First, skill was positively related to flow (path coefficient = .26, $P < .05$), which supported H1a. Skill was positively related to boredom (path coefficient = .77, $P < .05$), which supported H1b. Skill was negatively related to frustration (path coefficient = $-.34$, $P < .05$), which supported H1c. However, skill was insignificantly related to apathy (path coefficient = $-.11$, $P > .05$), which did not support H1d. This phenomenon may be owing to that low-skill users may still enjoy substantial achievements, which offset their feelings of apathy.

Moreover, challenge was positively related to flow (path coefficient = .21, $P < .05$), which supported H2a. Challenge was positively related to boredom (path coefficient = .10, $P < .05$), which was statistically significant (confidently nonrandom), yet was contrary to H2b. This unexpected finding may be owing to that difficult challenges may not always be novel ones. This finding can be explained by that either low or high challenges, gamers may become bored when similar patterns of challenge repeat frequently. For certain content of game design, repeatability of challenge may allow players to become accustomed to the game, possibly making it impossible for online gamers to satisfy anticipated results for both stimulating and innovative. Therefore, with a lack of stimuli contents, online gamers may perceive less fun but more boredom. Difficult yet repetitive challenges are not considered novel to users and tend to increase their feelings of boredom. This finding concerns how challenge and boredom are related rather than gamer preference. While positively related to frustration (path coefficient = .37, $P < .05$), which supported H2c, challenge was negatively related to apathy (path coefficient = $-.22$, $P < .05$), which supported H2d.

for 84.2% of gaming samples). Online game players are young adults who have few social experiences, a medium education level, and low disposable income. Restated, the time and the main purpose for the sample of the subjects to surf the Internet are to visit online gaming with high entertainment, followed by other secondary internet behaviors such as accessing email, using websites and learning online.

This study further elucidated the mechanism for formulating the four channels. Skill and challenge may either contribute individually to the formulation of the four channels or contribute interactively to their formulation, subsequently raising the issue of how skill and challenge affect the four channels. This study therefore performed an analysis of variance (ANOVA) to clarify the interacting effects of skill and challenge on the four channels. Median split method was also used to separate the sample into high-skill and low-skill groups and high-challenge and low-challenge ones. Skill (high versus low) and challenge (high versus low) were used as independent factors, while flow, boredom, frustration, and apathy were used as dependent factors.

Analytical results revealed no significant interaction between the effects of skill and challenge on the four channels ($F(1, 249) < 1.29$, $P > .26$). This phenomenon indicated that skill and challenge contributed to the four channels independently rather than interactively. The observation that skill and challenge impacted the four channels independently

5. Discussion

5.1. Major Findings and Theoretical Implications. This study has applied the four channels of flow (FCF) theory developed by Csikszentmihalyi [5] to online gaming. Although this study supports most of the propositions of FCF theory, some interesting exceptions are identified. As expected by the FCF theory, our results indicate that skill is positively related to flow and boredom, yet negatively related to frustration. Moreover, in-game challenge is positively related to flow and frustration, yet negatively related to apathy. Interestingly, challenge is positively (rather than negatively) related to boredom, which is inconsistent with FCF theory. This study also further elucidates the formulation of the four channels. Analysis results indicate that skill and challenge determine independently (rather than interactively) the four channels. Such a finding supports current literature that skill and challenge can predict flow.

The FCF theory posits that skill and challenge create the four channels of flow. However, except for flow, FCF research in recent decades has not elucidated these channels satisfactorily. This study therefore examines the formulation of the four channels of flow to test the validity of FCF theory. A significant and interesting exception is that challenge is positively related to boredom, thus warranting further study.

Results of this study are also compared with current flow literature. Hsu and Lu [2] applied the technology acceptance model (TAM) to explain acceptance of online games and the attitudes of online gamers. Hsu and Lu [2] found that the ease of using an online game can increase usefulness of it and create flow. Gamers who find a game too difficult to use may not perceive the usefulness of the game and may seldom experience flow. An online gamer may eventually stop playing a certain game. If challenges provide a reverse proxy for ease of use, the positive association between challenge and flow observed in this study is interesting, given the positive association between ease of use and flow reported by Hsu and Lu [2]. Further research is thus warranted to clarify how challenge, ease of use, and flow are related.

While identifying the features of social engagement among massive multiplayer online games (MMOs), Steinkuehler and Williams [50] established a theoretical framework on informal sociability. According to their results, online games resemble the "third places," which gamers use for participating in informal social activities. Such online participation becomes more feasible to accumulate social relations of gamers. That same study demonstrated that social aspect is a major determinant for online game use. In comparison, this study demonstrates that the flow aspect (intrinsic enjoyment with total concentration) is another major determinant for online game use. Restated, this study provides an alternative view on determinants of online game use, subsequently contributing to knowledge of gamer psychology in cyberspace.

Weibel et al. [51] found that emotional involvement and absorption constitute immersion. Moreover, openness, extraversion, and neuroticism predict immersion in a computer-mediated environment. The same investigator demonstrated the usefulness of gamer psychology in explaining gaming experiences. Results of this study correspond to those of Weibel et al. [51] by investigating gamer absorption (i.e., flow in the present study). However, our results differ from those of Weibel et al. [51] in introducing how gaming variables (i.e., gaming skill and challenge) can impact gamer-experienced absorption, thus enabling game designers or providers to help gamers experience flow and, ultimately, facilitate gamers feel immersed in one computer-mediated environment (i.e., online games in the present study).

5.2. Research Limitations and Future Research Directions. This study has tested the FCF theory in the context of online games. Although online games are a widely used information system, this represents a limitation of this study. Future studies may replicate the results of this study by applying FCF theory to other information systems in order to obtain further insight into the applicability of the FCF theory in other information systems.

Respondents filled out the questionnaire survey when they were available, increasing the accuracy of their memory retrieval. Previous studies have frequently adopted the approach of online survey without preceding gaming sessions [52], implying that memory bias may be acceptable in this case. However, such a design may fail to ensure that all respondents filled out the questionnaire survey immediately following their game play, thus representing another limitation of this study. We thus recommend that future studies devise an effective method to ensure that all respondents filled out the questionnaire survey immediately following their game play by using their computers at home, in a dormitory, or in an Internet café, where they are accustomed to play online games.

As flow increases the retention of online gamers, future studies may further clarify how customer loyalty and flow are related to computer user behavior. Further research should explore the potential applications of FCF theory in various disciplines such as social psychology, information management, and Internet marketing.

Hsu and Lu [2] suggested examining the role of personality in online gaming. Recent studies have demonstrated that personality traits are critical to achieve fulfillment and gaming behavior [53, 54]. Future studies may also further compare the likelihood of boredom, frustration, and apathy between online gamers with different personality traits.

Moreover, results of this study are consistent with four channels of flow theory developed by Csikszentmihalyi [5]. This study supports most propositions of the theory. However, two exceptions are observed: skill is insignificantly related to apathy; in addition, challenge is positively related to boredom. Future studies should address the same issue by using different measures for skill and challenge and by studying a multinational sample. Furthermore, future studies should address how boredom, frustration, and apathy influence user psychology and the behavior of information system users.

Exactly how gamers rate their favorite games is worth noting, which is done so in this study to increase the variation in terms of skill and challenge. If gamers rate games they dislike or do not like much, they probably have low levels of skill and challenge because they are not highly motivated to accumulate skills and try various challenges. Moreover, gamers likely quit playing games they dislike early on, thus reducing the validity owing to an increased memory bias. However, this issue is another limitation of this study. Future studies should include only gamers who simultaneously play multiple games, which may overcome this limitation at the cost of reduced sample representation.

A recent study [55] has examined whether specific personality traits are related to the individual tendency to experience flow. We recommend that future studies investigate the relations between the Big Five personality traits or other typologies of personality traits, as well as the individual tendency to experience flow. Hopefully, such a direction can bridge the gap between psychological and information science studies.

The present study measures flow using a "explain and then directly measure" approach is widely used by the literature [2, 12, 17, 55]. This approach has been adopted owing to its ability to directly measure the flow construct, rather than indirectly measure its correlates that may not equal the flow construct [17]. This approach regards flow as a unidimensional construct. However, some previous studies have regarded flow as a multidimensional constructs [16, 28]. Future studies regarding flow as a multidimensional constructs should use other scales.

The literature has examined the issue of the FCF theory [56]. However, the literature has problems of reliability and validity in measurement (e.g., Cronbach α < .7), casting doubts on the analytical results. Different from the literature, the present study has used the scale purification process to improve the measurement reliability and validity. That is, the analytical results of the present study are more dependable than those in the pertinent literature. Compared with the results in the literature [56], the present study is new in identifying the positive relation between challenge and boredom. The reason of the difference may be owing to the data reliability and validity prior to conducting analyses.

Acknowledgment

The authors thank National Science Council, Taiwan for financial support (NSC-96-2416-H-182-002-MY3).

References

[1] D. L. Hoffman and T. P. Novak, "Marketing in hypermedia computer-mediated environments: conceptual foundations," *Journal of Marketing*, vol. 60, no. 3, pp. 50–68, 1996.

[2] C. L. Hsu and H. P. Lu, "Why do people play on-line games? An extended TAM with social influences and flow experience," *Information and Management*, vol. 41, no. 7, pp. 853–868, 2004.

[3] C. Mathwick and E. Rigdon, "Play, flow, and the online search experience," *Journal of Consumer Research*, vol. 31, no. 2, pp. 324–332, 2004.

[4] C. I. Teng, L. S. Huang, S. P. Jeng, Y. J. Chou, and H. H. Hu, "Who are loyal customers in online games?" in *Proceedings of the International Consortium for Electronic Business*, pp. 312–313, ICEB Press, Waikoloa, Hawaii, USA, 2008.

[5] M. Csikszentmihalyi and I. S. Csikszentmihalyi, *Optimal Experience: Psychological Studies of Flow in Consciousness*, Cambridge University Press, Cambridge, UK, 1988.

[6] M. Csikszentmihalyi, "Happiness and creativity: going with flow," *The Futurist*, vol. 31, no. 5, pp. 8–12, 1997.

[7] Merriam-Webster Online Dictionary, "Frustration and apathy," January 2011, http://www.merriam-webster.com/.

[8] G. Chanel, C. Rebetez, M. Bétrancourt, and T. Pun, "Boredom, engagement and anxiety as indicators for adaptation to difficulty in games," in *Proceedings of the 12th International MindTrek Conference: Entertainment and Media in the Ubiquitous Era (MindTrek '08)*, pp. 13–17, ACM Press, October 2008.

[9] C. D. Fisherl, "Boredom at work: a neglected concept," *Human Relations*, vol. 46, no. 3, pp. 395–417, 1993.

[10] L. D. Goodstein and R. I. Lanyon, "The process of adjustment," in *Adjustment, Behavior, and Personality*, L. D. Goodstein and R. I. Lanyon, Eds., pp. 155–189, Addison Wesley, 1975.

[11] K. M. Gilleade and A. Dix, "Using frustration in the design of adaptive videogames," in *Proceedings of theACM SIGCHI International Conference on Advances in Computer Entertainment Technology (ACE '04)*, pp. 228–232, ACM Press, 2004.

[12] M. L. Korzaan, "Going with the flow: predicting online purchase intentions," *Journal of Computer Information Systems*, vol. 43, no. 4, pp. 25–31, 2003.

[13] M. J. Sánchez-Franco, "Exploring the influence of gender on the web usage via partial least squares," *Behaviour and Information Technology*, vol. 25, no. 1, pp. 19–36, 2006.

[14] Y. X. Skadberg and J. R. Kimmel, "Visitors' flow experience while browsing a Web site: its measurement, contributing factors and consequences," *Computers in Human Behavior*, vol. 20, no. 3, pp. 403–422, 2004.

[15] E. Bridges and R. Florsheim, "Hedonic and utilitarian shopping goals: the online experience," *Journal of Business Research*, vol. 61, no. 4, pp. 309–314, 2008.

[16] M. O. Richard and R. Chandra, "A model of consumer web navigational behavior: conceptual development and application," *Journal of Business Research*, vol. 58, no. 8, pp. 1019–1029, 2005.

[17] T. P. Novak, D. L. Hoffman, and Y. F. Yung, "Measuring the customer experience in online environments: a structural modeling approach," *Marketing Science*, vol. 19, no. 1, pp. 22–42, 2000.

[18] D. L. Hoffman and T. P. Novak, "Flow online: lessons learned and future prospects," *Journal of Interactive Marketing*, vol. 23, no. 1, pp. 23–34, 2009.

[19] L. E. Nacke and C. A. Lindley, "Affective ludology, flow and immersion in a first-person shooter: measurement of player experience," *Loading…The Journal of the Canadian Game Studies Association*, vol. 3, no. 5, 2009.

[20] A. Dietrich, "Neurocognitive mechanisms underlying the experience of flow," *Consciousness and Cognition*, vol. 13, no. 4, pp. 746–761, 2004.

[21] D. H. Choi, J. Kim, and S. H. Kim, "ERP training with a web-based electronic learning system: the flow theory perspective," *International Journal of Human Computer Studies*, vol. 65, no. 3, pp. 223–243, 2007.

[22] M. Zaman, M. Anandarajan, and Q. Dai, "Experiencing flow with instant messaging and its facilitating role on creative behaviors," *Computers in Human Behavior*, vol. 26, no. 5, pp. 1009–1018, 2010.

[23] C. Klimmt, A. Rizzo, P. Vorderer, J. Koch, and T. Fischer, "Experimental evidence for suspense as determinant of video game enjoyment," *Cyberpsychology and Behavior*, vol. 12, no. 1, pp. 29–31, 2009.

[24] D. Choi and J. Kim, "Why people continue to play online games: in search of critical design factors to increase customer loyalty to online contents," *Cyberpsychology and Behavior*, vol. 7, no. 1, pp. 11–24, 2004.

[25] R. Weber, R. Tamborini, A. Westcott-Baker, and B. Kantor, "Theorizing flow and media enjoyment as cognitive synchronization of attentional and reward networks," *Communication Theory*, vol. 19, no. 4, pp. 397–422, 2009.

[26] M. Csikszentmihalyi, *Beyond Boredom and Anxiety*, Jossey-Bass, San Francisco, Calif, USA, 1975.

[27] T. P. Novak, D. L. Huffman, and A. Duhachek, "The influence of goal-directed and experiential activities on online flow experiences," *Journal of Consumer Psychology*, vol. 13, no. 1-2, pp. 3–16, 2003.

[28] R. Agarwal and E. Karahanna, "Time flies when you're having fun: cognitive absorption and beliefs about information technology usage," *MIS Quarterly*, vol. 24, no. 4, pp. 665–694, 2000.

[29] H. Chen, R. T. Wigand, and M. S. Nilan, "Optimal experience of Web activities," *Computers in Human Behavior*, vol. 15, no. 5, pp. 585–608, 1999.

[30] J. Chung and F. B. Tan, "Antecedents of perceived playfulness: an exploratory study on user acceptance of general information-searching websites," *Information and Management*, vol. 41, no. 7, pp. 869–881, 2004.

[31] A. Rollings and E. Adams, *Andrew Rollings and Ernest Adams on Game Design*, New Riders, Indianapolis, Ind, USA, 2003.

[32] C. I. Teng, "Customization, immersion satisfaction, and online gamer loyalty," *Computers in Human Behavior*, vol. 26, no. 6, pp. 1547–1554, 2010.

[33] D. Weibel, B. Wissmath, S. Habegger, Y. Steiner, and R. Groner, "Playing online games against computer- vs. human-controlled opponents: effects on presence, flow, and enjoyment," *Computers in Human Behavior*, vol. 24, no. 5, pp. 2274–2291, 2008.

[34] C. L. Hsu and H. P. Lu, "Consumer behavior in online game communities: a motivational factor perspective," *Computers in Human Behavior*, vol. 23, no. 3, pp. 1642–1659, 2007.

[35] D. Williams, N. Yee, and S. E. Caplan, "Who plays, how much, and why? Debunking the stereotypical gamer profile," *Journal of Computer-Mediated Communication*, vol. 13, no. 4, pp. 993–1018, 2008.

[36] R. Kammann and R. Flett, "Affectometer 2: a scale to measure current level of general happiness," *Australian Journal of Psychology*, vol. 35, no. 2, pp. 259–265, 1983.

[37] A. Kozma and M. J. Stones, "The measurement of happiness: development of the Memorial University of Newfoundland Scale of Happiness (MUNSH)," *Journals of Gerontology*, vol. 35, no. 6, pp. 906–912, 1980.

[38] C. K. J. Wang, A. Khoo, W. C. Liu, and S. Divaharan, "Passion and intrinsic motivation in digital gaming," *Cyberpsychology and Behavior*, vol. 11, no. 1, pp. 39–45, 2008.

[39] C. I. Teng, S. S. Chang, and K. H. Hsu, "Emotional stability of nurses: impact on patient safety," *Journal of Advanced Nursing*, vol. 65, no. 10, pp. 2088–2096, 2009.

[40] C. I. Teng, Y. I. L. Shyu, W. K. Chiou, H. C. Fan, and S. M. Lam, "Interactive effects of nurse-experienced time pressure and burnout on patient safety: a cross-sectional survey," *International Journal of Nursing Studies*, vol. 47, no. 11, pp. 1442–1450, 2010.

[41] R. P. Bagozzi and Y. Yi, "On the evaluation of structural equation models," *Journal of the Academy of Marketing Science*, vol. 16, no. 1, pp. 74–94, 1988.

[42] J. C. Anderson and D. W. Gerbing, "Structural equation modeling in practice: a review and recommended two-step approach," *Psychological Bulletin*, vol. 103, no. 3, pp. 411–423, 1988.

[43] C. Fornell and D. F. Larcker, "Evaluating structural equation models with unobservable variables and measurement errors," *Journal of Marketing Research*, vol. 18, no. 1, pp. 39–50, 1981.

[44] M. W. Browne and R. Cudeck, "Single sample cross-validation indices for covariance structures," *Multivariate Behavioral Research*, vol. 24, no. 4, pp. 445–455, 1989.

[45] M. W. Browne and R. Cudeck, "Alternative ways of assessing model fit," in *Testing Structural Equation Models*, K. A. Bollen and J. S. Long, Eds., pp. 136–162, 1993.

[46] J. H. Steiger, "Point estimation, hypothesis testing, and interval estimation using the RMSEA: some comments and a reply to Hayduk and Glaser," *Structural Equation Modeling*, vol. 7, no. 2, pp. 149–162, 2000.

[47] R. P. Bagozzi, "Structural equation models are modelling tools with many ambiguities: comments acknowledging the need for caution and humility in their use," *Journal of Consumer Psychology*, vol. 20, no. 2, pp. 208–214, 2010.

[48] K. A. Bollen, *Structural Equations with Latent Variable*, John Wiley & Sons, New York, NY, USA, 1989.

[49] P. M. Podsakoff, S. B. MacKenzie, J. Y. Lee, and N. P. Podsakoff, "Common method biases in behavioral research: a critical review of the literature and recommended remedies," *Journal of Applied Psychology*, vol. 88, no. 5, pp. 879–903, 2003.

[50] C. A. Steinkuehler and D. Williams, "Where everybody knows your (screen) name: online games as 'third places'," *Journal of Computer-Mediated Communication*, vol. 11, no. 4, pp. 885–909, 2006.

[51] D. Weibel, B. Wissmath, and F. W. Mast, "Immersion in mediated environments: the role of personality traits," *Cyberpsychology, Behavior, and Social Networking*, vol. 13, no. 3, pp. 251–256, 2010.

[52] R. T. A. Wood, M. D. Griffiths, D. Chappell, and M. N. O. Davies, "The structural characteristics of video games: a psycho-structural analysis," *Cyberpsychology and Behavior*, vol. 7, no. 1, pp. 1–10, 2004.

[53] C. I. Teng, "Personality differences between online game players and nonplayers in a student sample," *Cyberpsychology and Behavior*, vol. 11, no. 2, pp. 232–234, 2008.

[54] C. I. Teng, "Online game player personality and real-life need fulfillment," *International Journal of Cyber Society and Education*, vol. 2, no. 2, pp. 39–50, 2009.

[55] C. I. Teng, "Who are likely to experience flow? Impact of temperament and character on flow," *Personality and Individual Differences*, vol. 50, no. 6, pp. 863–868, 2011.

[56] C. I. Teng and S. H. Lin, "Examination of four channels of flow," in *Proceedings of the 9th International Consortium for Electronic Business*, pp. 99–102, 2009.

11

Petri Net Model for Serious Games Based on Motivation Behavior Classification

Moh. Aries Syufagi,[1,2] Mochamad Hariadi,[3] and Mauridhi Hery Purnomo[3]

[1] *Multimedia Studies Program, Public Vocational High School 1, Jl. Tongkol No. 03, Jawa Timur, Bangil 67153, Indonesia*
[2] *Department of Information, STMIK Yadika, Jl. Bader No. 7, Kalirejo, Jawa Timur, Bangil 67153, Indonesia*
[3] *Electrical Department, Faculty of Industrial Technology, Institut Teknologi Sepuluh Nopember, Kampus ITS Keputih, Sukolilo, Jawa Timur, Surabaya 60111, Indonesia*

Correspondence should be addressed to Moh. Aries Syufagi; moh.aries.syufagi@gmail.com

Academic Editor: Hanqiu Sun

Petri nets are graphical and mathematical tool for modeling, analyzing, and designing discrete event applicable to many systems. They can be applied to game design too, especially to design serous game. This paper describes an alternative approach to the modeling of serious game systems and classification of motivation behavior with Petri nets. To assess the motivation level of player ability, this research aims at Motivation Behavior Game (MBG). MBG improves this motivation concept to monitor how players interact with the game. This modeling employs Learning Vector Quantization (LVQ) for optimizing the motivation behavior input classification of the player. MBG may provide information when a player needs help or when he wants a formidable challenge. The game will provide the appropriate tasks according to players' ability. MBG will help balance the emotions of players, so players do not get bored and frustrated. Players have a high interest to finish the game if the players are emotionally stable. Interest of the players strongly supports the procedural learning in a serious game.

1. Introduction

Nowadays, serious games and game technology are poised to transform the way of educating and training students at all levels. From the previous research about serious game, it is known that serious game supports the education process. Marsh et al. [1] and Clark [2] state that serious game is learning through games which contain pedagogical aspects and is a part of e-learning tools/media [3–5]. Clark [2], Arnseth [6], and Smith [7] further state that learning method using game is better than the conventional one, since animations of learning material in game activate students' long-term memories.

On the other hand, game learning has an inverse relationship with learning test in many instances. Clark [8] gives details; pedagogy in games is often based on unguided discovery such as; minimal guidance for high skill works, overwhelming discovery evidence without any assistance for beginners/novice learners [9, 10], discovery technique design, and some game cause memory overwork and decrease the learning process [11].

Overload will not occur if the level of players' motivation behavior is controlled. Inal and Cagiltay [12] explain the research of Csikszentmihalyi and emphasized the balance between an individual's skills and difficulties of tasks. He theorizes that the occurrence of flow experiences depends on this balance and that if the balance does not exist between the individual's skills and the task, flow experiences cannot occur. Heavier duty resulted in faster frustration; the challenges are too easy, getting bored quickly.

Proper classification of motivation behavior can be used to control the challenge of difficulty of the game. Providing an appropriate level of difficulty to the level of motivation behavior in a game scenario will balance the emotions of the players. The game cannot provide an appropriate difficulty level of task if the players' motivation behavior is unknown.

By contrast, Clark [8] in *Evaluating the Learning and Motivation Effects of Serious Games* explains that the tests of motivation are most often unreliable and invalid. Self-reported enjoyment does not aid learning, because there is an opportunity to manipulate data.

In this research, the proposal of the Motivation Behavior Game (MBG) is to eliminate the data manipulation of motivation tests in serious games. MBG is a model of indirect measurement of motivation levels. MBG is a players' motivation characteristics measurement by observing the players' motivation behavior; in this case, the players/respondents are students. The value of motivation behavior can be taken from the indicators that appear when a game takes place.

MBG is Pedagogic Player Character (PPC) based on artificial intelligent agent, and it can forecast the motivation character of players. Learning Vector Quantization (LVQ) method is used in MBG that functions to classify the players' motivation level. The teachers' data are neuron vector used in learning or supervising data in LVQ method. That will identify three multiobjective classifications in MBG, namely, mental effort, persistence, and active choice, taken from the players demonstration through the game.

Petri net is a tool used in the study of systems. Petri net theory allows a system to be modeled by a Petri net, a mathematical representation of the system [13]. Petri Net diagrams can become easier to read and to understand. It has a simple notation, being composed of only circles, bars, or boxes and at most three types of arcs, compared to UML's multiple diagram types using some of them for designing game systems. Text descriptions are usually very short, and not all transitions/places need names [14].

Analysis of the Petri net then can, hopefully, reveal important information about the structure and dynamic behavior of the modeled system. This information can then be used to evaluate the modeled system and to suggest improvements or changes [13]. The Petri nets' ability to model system with concurrent operations and conflicts is well documented. This can be of great help for game designers trying to model real-time action and strategy games [14].

2. Related Work

2.1. Motivation Measurement in Games. It is almost universally accepted that there is a positive correlation between motivation and learning. Instructional designers must pay more attention to motivational constructs when designing instruction and games. Bernard and Cannon [15] investigate the use of an emoticon based instrument, supporting the investigation with a study involving undergraduate students. At the end of each class period, the students were asked to indicate their level of motivation before and after the decision-making process, but before disclosure of results. Students used a 5-item, emoticon anchored scale ranging from highly unmotivated to highly motivated. This study has already noted the possibility of bias measurement resulting from administering questions relating to both motivations at the beginning and at the end of the class period. Another possibility is that the use of emoticons was too simplistic for the purpose.

Educational virtual games and simulations (EVGS) are also noted as agents that may enhance user motivation and satisfaction and subsequently engage learners in being innovative and the frequency they play. Higher levels of success in EVGS are measured by the intrinsic motivational factors created by the activity [16]. Konetes [16] analyzes the applications of learning simulations and games through the lens of the intrinsic and extrinsic motivational factors associated with different academic EVGS use. Learning to better control and apply these motivational concepts could enhance the value of educational simulations and magnify their impact and effectiveness.

Derbali and Frasson [17] investigated players' motivation during a serious game. The assessment of motivation was made using questionnaire (after Keller's ARCS model) and electroencephalography (EEG). Thirty-three subjects voluntarily took part in the test. Each subject was placed in front of two computers: one for playing and the other for answering the questionnaires. The result shows that the EEG wave's patterns are correlates with the increase of motivation during certain parts of a serious game play.

The motivation research in the game [15–17] is an extrinsic motivational. Thus, the motivation measurement process is still done separately of the game.

2.2. LVQ Method in Serious Game. Many studies use LVQ method for data classification in the game. Syufagi et al. [18] are designing the motivation measurement in game pedagogics. This research focuses on single objective motivation, that is, the classification level of mental effort only.

A Cognitive Skill Classification Based on Multiobjective Optimization Using Learning Vector Quantization for Serious Games [19] is LVQ research method in classification and optimization in multiobjective cognitive skill players.

Harini [20] studies Comprehensive Learning Achievement Affectivity using the LVQ method in serious game. This study aim at LVQ architecture to classify effective and ineffective use of time in serious games.

Abramson and Wechsler [21] show that the distributed representation found in Learning Vector Quantization (LVQ) enables the reinforcement in learning methods to cope with a large decision search space, defined in terms of equivalence classes of input patterns like those found in the game of Go. In particular, this paper describes S[arsa]LVQ.

2.3. Petri Net in Games. Araújo and Roque [14] describes an alternative; an approach to the modeling of game systems and game flow with Petri nets. They provide a case study to show that Petri nets can be used with advantages over other modeling languages.

Clempner [13] introduces a new modeling paradigm for the shortest path games representation with Petri nets. In this sense, he changes the traditional cost function by a trajectory-tracking function which is also an optimal cost-to-target function.

Brom et al. [22] present a technique for specifying plots of these scenarios, which underpins the story manager of Europe 2045. The technique is based on a modification of Petri nets. On a general level, this paper discusses the strengths and weaknesses of Petri nets implementation in virtual storytelling.

TABLE 1: Place on Motivation Behavior Game Model.

Place	Interpretation
P1	Problems arise in the game
P2	Identify players behavior
P3	Classification of Motivation Behavior Players
P4	Pattern of Motivation Behavior Players
P5	Motivation leveling algorithm
P6	Responds to the players level of motivation behavior as the reference to the selection of problem in game

TABLE 2: Some typical interpretations of transitions and places.

Input places	Transition	Output places
Input places	Transition	Output places
Preconditions	Event	Postconditions
Input data	Computation step	Output data
Input signals	Signal processor	Output signal
Resources needed	Task or job	Resources released
Conditions	Clause in logic	Conclusion(s)
Buffers	Processor	Buffers

TABLE 3: Formal definition of a Petri net.

A Petri net is a 5 tuple, $PN = (P, T, F, W, M_0)$ where

$P = \{p_1, p_2, \ldots, p_m\}$ is a finite set of places,

$T = \{t_1, t_2, \ldots, t_n\}$ is a finite set of transitions,

$F \subseteq (P \times T) \cup (T \times P)$ is a set of arcs (flow relation),

$W : F \rightarrow \{1, 2, 3, \ldots\}$ is weight function,

$M_0 : P \rightarrow \{0, 1, 2, 3, \ldots\}$ is the initial marking,

$P \cap T = \emptyset$ and $P \cup T \neq \emptyset$.

A Petri net structure $N = (P, T, F, W)$ without any specific initial marking is denoted by N.

A Petri net with the given initial marking is denoted by (N, M_0).

3. Design System and Method

The design system of MBG is illustrated in a model of Motivation Behavior Game with Petri net, and modeling functions use the LVQ method.

3.1. Petri Net. Petri nets were created by German mathematician Carl Adam Petri for the purpose of describing chemical processes [14]. They are graphical and mathematical tool for modeling [23], analyzing, and designing discrete event [14] applicable to many systems. Petri nets can be applied to other areas of game design, not just plot description or story managing [14].

Graphically, Petri nets are described as a diagram with circles (places), bar or squares (transitions), and arrows (arcs) connecting them [14]. To implement the Petri net interpretation needs to label the place and transition [24].

In [23], Murata shows some typical interpretations of transitions and their input and output places shown in Table 2, and the formal definition of a Petri net is given in Table 3.

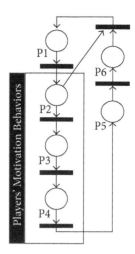

FIGURE 1: Model of Motivation Behavior Game with Petri net.

3.2. Model of Motivation Behavior Game with Petri Net. In addition to the development of motivation research in the game [15–17], there are also some researchers who use LVQ method for data classification in game [18–21]. MBG based on those two phenomena (motivation game and LVQ in game) are developed. Figure 1 shows the model of MBG with Petri net, whereas the interpretation of places on MBG model is shown in Table 1.

MBG is a game that measures the level of players' process-based motivation behavior; it gives more emphasis on the achievement level of interest, for example, calculating the number of leaving the problem, searching info, and using time to finish the job. The weakness of the measurement-based results is that it does not consider players' characteristics of the action in completing the mission in the game. Players' game characteristics are in the forms of motivation behavior in the process.

The result of the motivation behavior classification is used to level challenges of task in the game engine. The method of challenges leveling in game engine is using the algorithm which will adapt the motivation behavior classification. The accuracy of classification results will determine the accuracy of the game engine to provide the appropriate level of difficulty of the challenges in the task level generator. MBG supported achievement balance between an individual's motivation and difficulties of challenges. Moreover, it can prevent boredom and frustration.

The detail of MBG model with Petri net is shown in Figure 2, the interpretations detail of places on MBG model is shown in Table 4, and Table 5 shows the detail of transition.

For example A is Cognitive Steps containing all skill contest with tests forms or all competitions items in the game (P1 in Table 4). The number of skill contest (test)/competition (game) is $A = \{t, b, o, c, m, i\}$. $t, b, o, c, m,$ and i are players' parameter in playing the game. t is the number of how much time is used to finish the job (T208), b is the number of correct answers in the tests or the number of victory in the game (T207), o is the number of overlooking in tests or avoiding in games (T203), m is the number of mistakes in the tests or the number of loses in the game (T205), c is the number of

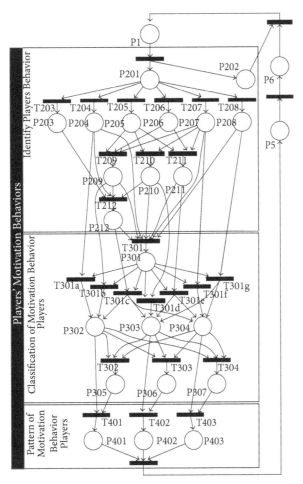

FIGURE 2: Details of Motivation Behavior Game Model.

TABLE 4: Details of place on Motivation Behavior Game Model.

Place	Interpretation
P1	Problems arise in the game
P201	Players resolve the problem
P202	Players avoid/leave the problem
P203	Number of how many times the players neglected the tests or avoided the games (o)
P204	Number of how many times the players search info (i)
P205	Number of wrong in tests or losses in games (m)
P206	Number of the players is uncertainty/to decline (escape) (c)
P207	Number of True in games or win in games (b)
P208	Number of how much the players use time to finish the job (t)
P209	Fixes the value of pick question/playing the game (q)
P210	Fixes the value of trying to answer/to finish (tr)
P211	Fixes the value of self-efficacy/Ability (e)
P212	Step report of player at some stage (st)
P301	Fixes the value of maximal (max)
P302	LVQ method to classify the players motivation behavior of active choice (ac) into; low active choice (ac_1), semi-active choice (ac_2), or high active choice (ac_3)
P303	LVQ method to classify the players motivation behavior of Persistence (ps) into low persistence (ps_1), semi-persistence (ps_2), or high persistence (ps_3)
P304	LVQ method to classify the players motivation behavior of mental effort (me) into low mental effort (me_1), semi-mental effort (me_2), or high mental effort (me_3)
P305	Value is one or zero
P306	Value is one or zero
P307	Value is one or zero
P401	Value is active choice (ac) or zero
P402	Value is persistence (ps) or zero
P403	Value is mental effort (me) or zero
P5	Motivation leveling algorithm
P6	Responds to the players level of motivation behavior as the reference to selection of problem in game

hesitation (canceled) in the tests or stepping back (escaping) from competition in the game (T206), and i is the number of how many times the players search info during the tests or to get help for the period of the game (T204).

tr = $\{b, m\}$ is the condition when players try to answer a number of tests or try to finish all competition of MBG modeling which is also the indication of players' correct item/victory and mistakes/loses (P210 and T210):

$$\text{tr} = \frac{b + m}{2}. \tag{1}$$

$e = \{0.5b, 0.3m, 0.2c\}$ is self-efficacy (P211 and T211) or ability, and also $q = \{b, m, c\}$ is the number of picking up questions from all of tests or playing all competition in the game (P209 and T209), that is, the content of players' characters in mistakes, correct items, and doubts in game:

$$e = 0.5b + 0.3m + 0.2c,$$
$$q = \frac{b + m + c}{3}. \tag{2}$$

st is step report of player at some stage in the game. $q \in$ st, tr $\in$ st, st = $\{\{b, m, c\}, \{b, m\}, o, i\}$ is the step of player playing the

game which contains picking up question, trying to answer, searching info, and overlooking in tests (P212 and T212):

$$\text{st} = \frac{o + i + q + \text{tr}}{4}. \tag{3}$$

Three domains of MBG are (i) mental effort, (ii) persistence, and (iii) active choice domain. $e \in$ me, st $\in$ me, me = $\{\{b, m, c\}, \{\{b, m, c\}, \{b, m\}, o, i\}, t, b\}$ is mental effort domain which contains self-efficacy, step, time, and correct items (P304 in Table 4). $e \in$ ps, st $\in$ ps, tr $\in$ ps, ps = $\{\{b, m, c\}, \{\{b, m, c\}, \{b, m\}, o, i\}, \{b, m\}, t\}$ is persistence

TABLE 5: Details of transition on Motivation Behavior Game Model.

Transition	Interpretation
T203	The result of the frequency of neglected in tests or avoided in games
T204	The result of how many times the players search info
T205	The result of wrong in tests or losses in games
T206	The result of the players is uncertainty (cancel)/to decline (escape)
T207	The result of true/win
T208	The count of how much the players use time to finish the job
T209	Average of loss (m), cancel (c), and victory (b) values
T210	Average of loss (m) and victory (b) values
T211	Sum of 30% loss (m), 20% cancel (c), and 50% victory (b) values
T212	Average of avoiding (o), searching info (i), picking question (q), and trying to answer (tr) values
T301	Obtain the highest value of the m, b, c, q, or tr (max. value)
T301a	Divide the i value by the max
T301b	Divide the q value by the max
T301c	Divide the st value by the max
T301d	Divide the tr value by the max
T301e	Divide the e value by the max
T301f	Divide the b value by the max
T301g	Divide the t value by the max
T302	Set one value if then value of high active choice (ac_3) in LVQ method is higher than value of high persistence (ps_3) or value of high mental effort (me_3), or else reset (zero value)
T303	Set one value if then value of high persistence (ps_3) in LVQ method is higher than value of active choice (ac_3) or value of high mental effort (me_3), or else reset (zero value)
T304	Set one value if then value of high mental effort (me_3) in LVQ method is higher than value of high persistence (ps_3) or value of active choice (ac_3), or else reset (zero value)
T401	To multiply
T402	To multiply
T403	To multiply

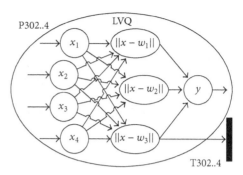

FIGURE 3: LVQ method in P302, P303, and P304 of Motivation Behavior Game Model.

high persistence, (vii) low persistence, (viii) semipersistence, and (ix) high persistence.

3.3. LVQ Method. Many methods can be used for classifying data. Learning Vector Quantization (LVQ) is the data classification method used in this research. LVQ is supervised Artificial Neural Network (ANN) using competitive learning method developed by Kohonen et al. [25], used in guided training from layers in ANN competition. Competitive layers will automatically learn to improve the classification of input vector performance periodically. When some input has very close distance vectors, those vectors will be grouped into the some class:

$$c = \arg\ \min \left\| x - w_j \right\|. \tag{4}$$

The algorithm of an LVQ includes learning and recalling processes. In the learning process, in order to achieve accurate classification, Euclidean distance (D_i) is utilized as a basic rule of competition [26]:

$$D_j = \left\| x - w_j \right\| = \sqrt{\sum_i \left(x_i - w_{ij} \right)^2}. \tag{5}$$

LVQ is used to classify data of input vector in MBG into three clusters. The input vector of LVQ is the weight of variables in MBG, namely, weight of trying to answer, picking up questions, competency, errors, and cancellation. The outcomes of LVQ are three clusters of motivation behavior data type, namely, mental effort (me), persistence (ps), and active choice (ac) motivation behavior with three levels of clusters each. Those levels are high, middle, and low levels:

$$\mathbf{x}_{1,\text{me}} \Longleftrightarrow t, \quad \mathbf{x}_{2,\text{me}} \Longleftrightarrow b, \quad \mathbf{x}_{3,\text{me}} \Longleftrightarrow e, \quad \mathbf{x}_{4,\text{me}} \Longleftrightarrow \text{st}, \tag{6}$$

$$\text{me}_j = \sqrt{\sum_i \left(\mathbf{x}_{i,\text{me}} - \mathbf{w}_{ij,\text{me}} \right)^2}, \tag{7}$$

$$C_{j,\text{me}} = \arg\ \min \left\| \mathbf{x}_{\text{me}} - \mathbf{w}_{j,\text{me}} \right\|,$$

me_j is the value of mental effort in MBG (P304 in Table 4), and $C_{j,\text{me}}$ is the classification of mental effort level. Three classes of mental effort are $j = \{1, 2, 3\}$, in which (i) the

domain which contains self efficacy, step, trying to answer, and time (P303 in Table 4), whereas, $q \in \text{ac}$, st $\in$ ac, ac = $\{\{b, m, c\}, \{b, m, c\}, \{b, m\}, o, i\}, i\}$ is an active choice domain which contains picking up question, step, and searching info (P302 in Table 4). To classify this domain, LVQ method is used (shown in Figure 3).

$L = (s, j)$ is MBG representative (P305, P306, and P307 in Table 4), s is the notation of three domains in MBG, and j is three levels in every domain. L has nine probability outcomes; those are (i) low mental effort, (ii) semimental effort, (iii) high mental effort, (iv) low persistence, (v) semipersistence, (vi) value of j is equal to one at j, me for low condition of mental effort representation index, (ii) semimental effort index will be presented with j having value of two at j, me, and (iii) three is the value of j at j, me for index of high mental effort conditions. The variables t, b, e, and st for mental effort have weight ($\mathbf{w}$). The weight of me in j class is $\mathbf{w}_{j,\text{me}}$.

ps_j is the value of persistence variable in MBG (P303 in Table 4), $C_{j,\text{ps}}$ is the classification of persistence level. Three persistence classes are $j = \{1, 2, 3\}$ in which (i) j value which is one at j, ps is used as a representation index for low persistence, (ii) j which is two at j, ps is the index for semipersistence, and (iii) j which is three at j, ps is the index for high persistence. The weight of ps in j class is $\mathbf{w}_{j,\text{ps}}$:

$$\mathbf{x}_{1,\text{ps}} \Longleftrightarrow t, \quad \mathbf{x}_{3,\text{ps}} \Longleftrightarrow e, \quad \mathbf{x}_{4,\text{ps}} \Longleftrightarrow \text{st}, \quad \mathbf{x}_{5,\text{ps}} \Longleftrightarrow \text{tr}, \tag{8}$$

$$\text{ps}_j = \sqrt{\sum_i \left(\mathbf{x}_{i,\text{ps}} - \mathbf{w}_{ij,\text{ps}}\right)^2}, \tag{9}$$

$$C_{j,\text{ps}} = \arg \min \left\| \mathbf{x}_{\text{ps}} - \mathbf{w}_{j,\text{ps}} \right\|,$$

ac_j is the value active choice variable in MBG (P302 in Table 4) in which $C_{j,\text{ac}}$ is the classification of active choice level. Three active choice classes are $j = \{1, 2, 3\}$ where (i) j which is one at j, ac variable means the index for low active choice, (ii) j which is two at j, ac is the index for semiactive choice, and (iii) j which is three at j, ac is index for high active choice. The weight of ac in j class is $w_{j,\text{ac}}$:

$$\mathbf{x}_{4,\text{ac}} \Longleftrightarrow \text{st}, \quad \mathbf{x}_{6,\text{ac}} \Longleftrightarrow q, \quad \mathbf{x}_{7,\text{ac}} \Longleftrightarrow i, \tag{10}$$

$$\text{ac}_j = \sqrt{\sum_i \left(\mathbf{x}_{i,\text{ac}} - \mathbf{w}_{ij,\text{ac}}\right)^2}, \tag{11}$$

$$C_{j,\text{ac}} = \arg \min \left\| \mathbf{x}_{\text{ac}} - \mathbf{w}_{j,\text{ac}} \right\|.$$

Some researchers use the optimum method based on LVQ [12, 23]. L is the classification of MB optimum conditions. L is defined at three probability optimum conditions, namely, (i) mental effort, (ii) persistence, and (iii) active choice. MB is the classification of MBG outcome that can be defined at nine probability optimum conditions, namely, (i) high mental effort, (ii) semimental effort, (iii) low mental effort, (iv) high persistence, (v) semipersistence, (vi) low persistence, (vii) high active choice, (viii) semiactive choice, and (ix) low active choice:

$$L = \arg \min \left\| \{\text{me}_3, \text{ps}_3, \text{ac}_3\} \right\|,$$

$$\text{MB} = \begin{cases} C_{j,\text{me}}, & \text{if } L = \text{me}_3 \\ C_{j,\text{ps}}, & \text{if } L = \text{ps}_3 \\ C_{j,\text{ac}}, & \text{if } L = \text{ac}_3. \end{cases} \tag{12}$$

L is considered as mental effort if high mental effort (me_3) value is smaller than high persistence (ps_3) and smaller than high active choice (ac_3) too (T304 in Table 5). Then MB is low mental effort if $C_{j,\text{me}}$ value is close to low mental effort value. MB is semimental effort if $C_{j,\text{me}}$ value is close to semimental

effort value, and then, MB is high mental effort if $C_{j,\text{me}}$ value is close to high mental effort value.

The description of L is persistence; that is when the value of high persistence (ps_3) is smaller than high mental effort (me_3) and smaller than high active choice (ac_3) too (T303 in Table 5). MB is low persistence if $C_{j,\text{ps}}$ value is close to low persistence value, MB is semipersistence if $C_{j,\text{ps}}$ value is close to semipersistence value, and MB is high persistence if $C_{j,\text{ps}}$ value is close to high persistence value.

L is active choice outcome probabilities which is obtained if the value of high active choice (ac_3) is smaller than high mental effort (me_3) and smaller than persistence (ps_3) too (T302 in Table 5). Then, MB is low active choice if $C_{j,\text{ac}}$ value is close to low active choice value, MB is semiactive choice if $C_{j,\text{ac}}$ value is close to semiactive choice value, and MB is high active choice if $C_{j,\text{ac}}$ value is close to high active choice value.

4. Experiment

We conducted a survey to twenty teachers to obtain three characteristics of motivation behavior. The reason of choosing teachers as the respondents is to get the ideal motivation behavior characteristics based on the assumption that teachers are the best motivation behavior evaluator. Furthermore, the fact that teachers have the qualification as pedagogic assessors which is shown by their diplomas, certificates, and teaching experience is also taken into consideration. Therefore, teachers are reliable in determining the parameters of motivation behavior indicators for their pupils.

The population is senior high school teachers that consist of two groups, twelve respondents are math and science teachers, and eight respondents are social teachers.

Teachers will give weight of the variable reference that can influence the value of type (L) and class (C) of motivation behavior. Variable reference from teachers includes using time (t), correct/victory (b), self-efficacy (e), step report (st), trying to answers (tr), picking questions (q), and searching info (i).

Parameters of motivation behavior characteristic value can be used as a motivation behavior reference. The reference of motivation behavior is the value of ideal motivation behaviors. Values of the parameters in the motivation behavior reference data are obtained from the classification of the teachers' survey data. Data of motivation behavior characteristic from teachers will be applied on learning rate of the LVQ motivation behavior pattern.

Populations of motivation behavior classification in this research are 33 pupils, including 18 males and 15 females. The respondents are students in a senior high school who are 16 to 19 years old. They are used to test the MBG system based on LVQ that will classify the student's motivation.

Values of t, b, o, c, m, and i are taken when students play the game. The variables of t, b, o, c, m, and i are players' characteristic of motivation behavior. These variables are the input of MBG.

To ensure that MBG is really measuring behavioral motivations of individual player's character, the measurements are repeated. To determine the consistency of the level of

TABLE 6: Weight of motivation behavior reference.

Using time (t)	Correct/victory (b)	Self-efficacy (e)	Step report (st)	Try to answers (tr)	Pick questions (q)	Search info (i)	Class (C)	Motivation behavior type (L)
0.860	0.159	0.150	0.369	—	—	—	Low	
0.141	0.869	0.820	0.900	—	—	—	Semi	Mental effort (me)
0.120	0.830	0.849	0.141	—	—	—	High	
0.100	—	0.860	0.498	0.900	—	—	Low	
0.810	—	0.100	0.900	0.129	—	—	Semi	Persistence (ps)
0.900	—	0.130	0.100	0.100	—	—	High	
—	—	—	0.120	—	0.498	0.498	Low	
—	—	—	0.820	—	0.100	0.139	Semi	Active choice (ac)
—	—	—	0.873	—	0.879	0.869	High	

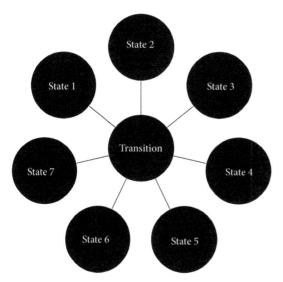

FIGURE 4: Scenario of Motivation Behavior Game Model.

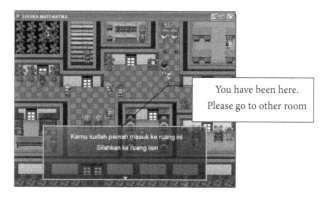

FIGURE 5: Screen shoot of transition place.

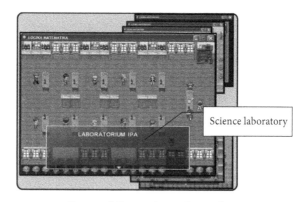

FIGURE 6: Screen shoot of state place.

motivation for the players repeated measurements up to 7 times with 7 different states, players must complete different task types at each state. In this game, the level of difficulty and the environment are made in the same conditions.

Scenario game at MBG is shown in Figure 4. Players must complete the tasks within each state. After completing the task the player will return to later transition into another state. Game is complete if the player has completed the task of all existing states.

From Scenario of Motivation Behavior Game in Figure 4, screen shoot transition place at MBG is shown in Figure 5. Players must be go in this place to choice the state. Players who had entered into a certain space (state) cannot do it again. Player is directed to take the new state.

Screen shoot one of state place at MBG is shown in Figure 6. Of the transition location, players will be entered into one of the existing state spaces (one of seven states). Players must complete the tasks in each state. Players cannot leave the room before completing the task, at least 75% of all available tasks. This is done for players to master learning.

5. Result

5.1. Value of Motivation Behaviors. MBG is embedded in sensitivity of teachers in the game. It is because MBG data training is taken from the teachers. The data observation from the teacher is ideal data that can be used as training data in LVQ method. LVQ training outcome is used as weight value reference of motivation behavior classification. Table 6 is the result of LVQ training (from data teachers) which includes weight of using time (t), weight of correct/victory (b), weight of self-efficacy (e), weight of step report (st), weight of trying

TABLE 7: Results of experiments in State 7.

ID respondent	Mental effort class (C_1)	Persistence class (C_2)	Active choice class (C_3)	Motivation behavior type (L)	Motivation behavior classification (MB)	Percentage from all respondents
1	Semi	Low	High	Active choice	High active choice	
2	Semi	Low	High	Active choice	High active choice	
3	Semi	Low	High	Active choice	High active choice	
4	Semi	Low	High	Active choice	High active choice	
6	Semi	Low	High	Active choice	High active choice	
9	Semi	Low	High	Active choice	High active choice	
12	Semi	Low	High	Active choice	High active choice	
13	Semi	Low	High	Active choice	High active choice	
15	Semi	Low	High	Active choice	High active choice	58%
16	Semi	Low	High	Active choice	High active choice	
17	Semi	Low	High	Active choice	High active choice	
19	Semi	Low	High	Active choice	High active choice	
20	Semi	Low	High	Active choice	High active choice	
22	Semi	Low	High	Active choice	High active choice	
24	Semi	Low	High	Active choice	High active choice	
25	Semi	Low	High	Active choice	High active choice	
27	Semi	Low	High	Active choice	High active choice	
31	Semi	Low	High	Active choice	high active choice	
32	Semi	Low	High	Active choice	High active choice	
21	Low	Low	Semi	Active choice	Semi active choice	
28	Semi	Low	Semi	Active choice	Semi active choice	12%
29	Low	Semi	Semi	Active choice	Semi active choice	
30	Semi	Low	Semi	Active choice	Semi active choice	
5	Semi	Low	Semi	Mental effort	Semi mental effort	
7	Semi	Low	Semi	Mental effort	Semi mental effort	
8	Semi	Low	Semi	Mental effort	Semi mental effort	
10	Semi	Low	Semi	Mental effort	Semi mental effort	24%
11	Semi	Low	Semi	Mental effort	Semi mental effort	
14	Semi	Low	Semi	Mental effort	Semi mental effort	
18	Semi	Low	Semi	Mental effort	Semi mental effort	
26	Semi	Low	Semi	Mental effort	Semi mental effort	
23	Low	Semi	Semi	Persistence	Semi persistence	6%
33	Low	Semi	Semi	Persistence	Semi persistence	

to answers (tr), weight of picking questions (q), and weight of searching info (i). The value of Table 6 is a reference weight value of motivation behavior in the MBG. The table value shows the character of motivation behavior reference which is in accordance with the players' character.

5.2. Motivation Behavior Classification. From (7), (9), (11), and (12), it can be stated that this research is a method implementation in game to know the three motivation behaviors from 33 players (students) and three motivation levels in each motivation behavior.

Table 7 shows the result of experiment in State 7. Fifty-eight percent players have high active choice motivation

behavior. Twelve percent have semiactive choice motivation behavior; twenty-four percent have semimental effort, while six percent have semipersistence motivation behavior.

Table 8 shows the number of players at each state (State 1 to State 7) which is classified into six motivation behaviors, namely, high mental effort, semimental effort, low mental effort, high persistence, semipersistence, low persistence, high active choice, semiactive choice, and low active choice. In the mental effort classification, players tend to be dominantly at the semimental effort. Players on the persistence motivation behavior are dominant on low persistence, whereas high active choice for players tends to have active choice motivation type.

TABLE 8: The number of players based on motivation behavior at each state.

Motivation behavior		State						
		1	2	3	4	5	6	7
Mental effort	Low	0	0	1	4	1	3	4
	Semi	29	32	29	28	32	30	29
	High	4	1	3	1	0	0	0
Persistence	Low	29	31	28	22	31	25	30
	Semi	4	2	5	9	2	8	3
	High	0	0	0	2	0	0	0
Active choice	Low	6	17	17	0	0	0	0
	Semi	3	0	2	18	15	19	14
	High	24	16	14	15	18	14	19

6. Discussion

Some advantages of MBG compared to previous studies on measuring motivation is it does not require additional instruments besides the game being played like in the methods applied by Derbali and Frasson [17]. It is due to the fact that MBG is assessments embedded in immersive games to reveal the behavior of player's motivation. MBG as an indirect measurement of motivation levels avoids bias measurement due to a self-reported enjoyment done by Bernard and Cannon [15] in their research. This indirect measurement of players' motivation characteristics is done by observing the players' motivation behavior. MBG is model assessments of intrinsic and extrinsic motivation as described by Konetes [16].

6.1. Analysis of Motivation Behavior Characteristic. The characteristic of motivation behavior is divided into three objective groups, namely, mental effort, persistence, and active choice motivation behavior. Mental effort motivation behavior is the first objective motivation performance of the players during the process of completing a game mission; the players with mental effort motivation have the characteristics as follows: being always confident with high level of efficiency to using time, never making mistakes, having a high competence (high self-efficacy), and being effective to finish the tasks thoroughly.

Persistence motivation behavior is the second objective motivation performance at the time of completing the mission of the game. Persistence has objective characteristics including; tendency to low self-efficacy, low efficiency in using time, few trials to answer, and finish the tasks thoroughly.

Active choice is the third objective performance of the players' motivation during serious games. The characteristic of active choice including tendency to search information, always respond to get the questions, and low efficiency in solving the problem thoroughly.

6.2. Motivation Behavior Game Multiple Objective. The result of experiment is shown in Table 7. MBG is identified from the motivation behavior of 33 respondents.

MBG represents the three motivation behavior references; those are mental effort, persistence, and active choice motivation behavior references. This is the MBG multiobjective. Player's performance will be strong in one motivation behavior reference and weak in the other. The first objective is mental effort (C1), the second objective is persistence (C2), and the third objective is active choice (C3). Table 7 shows, how the 33 respondents are having the nature of multi objective of each type of motivation behavior.

6.3. Validation of Measurement. Figure 7 shows two examples of the level of player's consistency; Figure 7(a) is the consistent result of the player's motivation level; while Figure 7(b) is the opposite, the results of player's motivation level are not consistent.

Level of motivation shown by notation of numbers: level 1 is the low motivation, level 2 is the middle motivation (semi), and level 3 is the high motivation. The consistency is measured by the changes of players motivation level at each game stage (stage 1 to stage 7). The lower deviation of motivation level among stages is the higher the validity of the measurements is; otherwise the higher deviation of motivation level among stages, the lower the validity of the measurement. Figure 7(a) is an example of the level of minimum deviation (0%), which is a characteristic of a valid measurement, because the measurement of the level of motivation of a player generates a consistent value on the same level although for different tasks. And Figure 7(b) is an example of the level of maximum deviation (100%); this is a characteristic of an invalid measurement, because the measurement of the level of motivation of a player generates inconsistent values on the same level on each task. Deviation of player motivation level is determined by using (13)

$$D_p = \sum_s \left(x_s - \overline{x}_{sp} \right)^2. \tag{13}$$

The measurements results of the player's mental effort level are shown in Figure 8. The activity of each player in resolving the seven states is depicted on horizontal lines, the level of players motivation represented by line position at level 1, 2, and 3. Level 1 is the lowest level of low mental effort, level 2 is middle level called semimental effort, and level 3 is the highest level of motivation called high mental effort. Figure 8 shows the tendency of players' dominant motivation consistency at the semimental effort.

The measurement results of persistence levels shown in Figure 9: level 1 is the lowest level called low persistence, level 2 is middle level called semipersistence, and level 3 is the highest level called high persistence. Figure 9 shows the tendency of players' dominant motivation consistency on the level of low persistence.

The measurement results of active choice levels shown in Figure 10: level 1 is the lowest level called low active choice, level 2 is middle level called semiactive choice, and level 3 is the highest level called high active choice. Figure 10 shows the tendency of few players' dominant motivation consistency on the level of high active choice.

Table 9 shows the percentage of the number of players based on the deviation levels of motivation. Deviation level

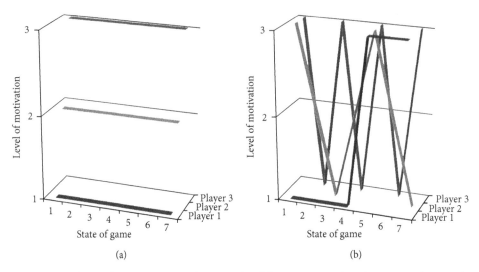

(a)   (b)

FIGURE 7: The consistency level of player's motivation (a): the example of deviation rate of 0% (minimum deviation); as the characteristic measurement results are valid, the players are consistent with the level of motivation (b): the example of deviation rate of 100% (maximum deviation); as the characteristic measurement results are invalid, the players are not consistent with the level of motivation.

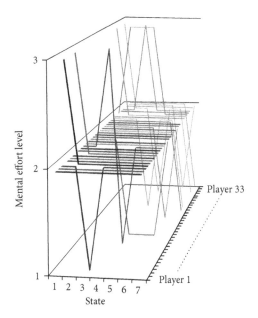

FIGURE 8: Level of players' mental effort in State 1 to State 7.

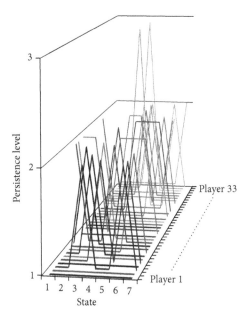

FIGURE 9: Level of players' persistence in State 1 to State 7.

column is the division of the three levels of motivation deviation on each task, namely, none (0%), ≤25%, and ≤50% deviation. The percentage shown in Table 9 is the percentage of the number of players from the entire cast (33 students). As described in Figure 1, the measurement is considered invalid if the measurement repeated times will produce the same value (none deviation). By contrast, measurements are declared invalid if the measurement done several times produces a very high deviation (maximum deviation). These deviation values are expressed in percentage 0% (none deviation) up to 100% (maximum deviation).

Table 9 shows the number of players is consistent in the motivation level, which is characterized by low values of the deviation rate, so that measurements of motivation by

TABLE 9: The number of players based on deviation level.

Motivation behavior	Deviation level	Number of players	Percentage of all players
Mental effort	None	19	58%
	≤25%	31	94%
	≤50%	33	100%
Persistence	none	13	39%
	≤25%	31	94%
	≤50%	32	97%
Active choice	None	8	24%
	≤25%	19	58%
	≤50%	27	82%

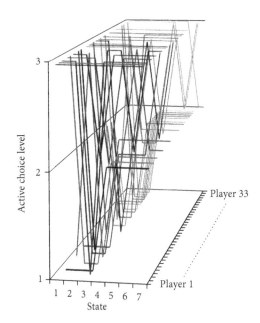

FIGURE 10: Level of players' active choice in State 1 to State 7.

MBG can be said to be valid. More than 50% of players have a deviation of less than or equal to 25%. Even for mental effort and persistence over 90% of players have a motivation deviation of less than or equal to 25%.

7. Conclusion

In MBG modeling research, the model of MBG with Petri net and function of motivation behavior identification can be gotten. LVQ method is used to classify player's characteristic in playing games.

In MBG classification research, the game can identify the players' motivation behavior. Players can be classified into three motivation behavior clusters namely, (i) mental effort, (ii) persistence, and (iii) active choice; the percentage of each classification is 24% semimental effort, 6% semipersistence, 58% high active choice, and 12% semiactive choice.

In a further research, it is hoped that MBG can provide feedback to determine the level or be used as a guide in game. Individual behavior can influence the scenario changes in game. MBG can be fun and vary based on the personality challenges in serious games.

To wrap up, it can be concluded that the MBG is embedded assessments of motivation behavior with the sensitivity of teachers in the serious game. MBG disposed has strong multiobjective character of motivation behavior classification. Thus, there is a need of the optimum method based on LVQ. Indirectly, MBG always observes the fluctuation in the interest of the players. MBG informs an accurate level of motivation behavior; it strongly supports the completeness learning in serious game.

References

[1] T. Marsh, W. L. Wong, E. Carriazo et al., "User experiences and lessons learned from developing and implementing an immersive game for the science classroom," in *Proceedings of HCI International 2005*, Las Vegas, Nev, USA, July 2005.

[2] D. Clark, "Game and e-learning," Sunderland: caspian learning, April 2009, http://www.caspianlearning.co.uk.

[3] H. Ndahi, "The use of innovative methods to deliver technology education laboratory courses via distance learning: a strategy to increase enrollment," *Journal of Technology Education*, vol. 17, no. 2, pp. 33–42, 2006.

[4] A. Hayashi, C. C. Chen, and H. Terase, "Aligning IT skills training with online asynchronous learning multimedia technologies," *Information Systems Education Journal*, vol. 3, no. 26, pp. 3–10, 2005.

[5] N. P. Ololube, "Appraising the relationship between ICT usage and integration and the standard of teacher education programs in a developing economy," *International Journal of Education and Development Using Information and Communication Technology*, vol. 2, no. 3, pp. 70–85, 2006.

[6] H. C. Arnseth, "Learning to play or playing to learn—a critical account of the models of communication informing educational research on computer gameplay," *The International Journal of Computer Game Research*, vol. 6, no. 1, 2006.

[7] J. H. Smith, "The games economists play—implications of economic game theory for the study of computer games," *The International Journal of Computer Game Research*, vol. 6, no. 1, 2006.

[8] R. E. Clark, "Evaluating the learning and motivation effects of serious games," Rosier school of Education Center for Creative Technologies, Augustus 2010, http://projects.ict.usc.edu/itgs/talks/ Clark_Serious Games Evaluation.ppt.

[9] R. E. Mayer, "Should there be a three-strikes rule against pure discovery learning? the case for guided methods of instruction," *American Psychologist*, vol. 59, no. 1, pp. 14–19, 2004.

[10] P. A. Kirschner, J. Sweller, and R. E. Clark, "Why minimal guidance during instruction does not work: an analysis of the failure of constructivist, discovery, problem-based, experiential, and inquiry-based teaching," *Educational Psychologist*, vol. 41, no. 2, pp. 75–86, 2006.

[11] R. E. Clark and S. Choi, "Five design principles for experiments on the effects of animated pedagogical agents," *Journal of Educational Computing Research*, vol. 32, no. 3, pp. 209–225, 2005.

[12] Y. Inal and K. Cagiltay, "Flow experiences of children in an interactive social game environment," *British Journal of Educational Technology*, vol. 38, no. 3, pp. 455–464, 2007.

[13] J. Clempner, "Modeling shortest path games with Petri nets: a Lyapunov based theory," *International Journal of Applied Mathematics and Computer Science*, vol. 16, no. 3, pp. 387–397, 2006.

[14] M. Araújo and L. Roque, "Modeling games with petri nets," Digital Games Research Association (DiGRA) 2009, http://www.digra.org/dl/db/09287.37256.pdf.

[15] R. R. S. Bernard and H. M. Cannon, "Exploring motivation: using emoticons to map student motivation in a business game exercise," *Developments in Business Simulation and Experiential Learning*, vol. 38, pp. 229–240, 2011.

[16] G. D. Konetes, "The function of intrinsic and extrinsic motivation in educational virtual games and simulations," *Journal of Emerging Technologies in Web Intelligence*, vol. 2, no. 1, pp. 23–26, 2010.

[17] L. Derbali and C. Frasson, "Players' motivation and EEG waves patterns in a serious game environment," *Intelligent Tutoring Systems*, vol. 6095, no. 2, pp. 297–299, 2010.

[18] M. A. Syufagi, M. Hariadi, and M. H. Purnomo, "Model of mental effort assessment in pedagogic games based On LVQ method," in *Proceedings of SESINDO2008 Conference*, pp. 556–564, ITS, Surabaya, Indonesia, December 2008.

[19] M. A. Syufagi, M. Hariadi, and M. H. Purnomo, "A cognitive skill classification based on multi objective optimization using learning vector quantization for serious games," *ITB Journal of Information and Communication Technology*, vol. 5, no. 3, pp. 189–206, 2011.

[20] S. M. Harini, *Classification of comprehensive learning achievement effectivity in senior high school students based on mathematical logic game using LVQ Method [M.S. thesis of Electrical Engineering]*, Institut Teknologi Sepuluh Nopember (ITS), Surabaya, Indonesia, 2009.

[21] M. Abramson and H. Wechsler, "A distributed reinforcement learning approach to pattern inference in go," CiteSeerx, 2011, http://citeseerx.ist.psu.edu/viewdoc/summary?doi=10.1.1.9.7035.

[22] C. Brom, V. Šisler, and T. Holan, "Story manager in 'Europe 2045' uses petri nets," in *Proceedings of the International Conference on Virtual Storytelling (ICVS '07)*, vol. 4871 of *Lecture Notes in Computer Science*, pp. 38–50, Strasbourg, France, 2007.

[23] T. Murata, "Petri nets: properties, analysis and applications," *Proceedings of the IEEE*, vol. 77, no. 4, pp. 541–580, 1989.

[24] D. L. Rahakbauw and Subiono, "An implementation of petri net Hybrid synthesis in manufacture system," 2011, http://digilib.its.ac.id/public/ITS-Master-13439-Paper.pdf.

[25] T. Kohonen, J. Hynninen, J. Kangas, J. Laaksonen, and K. Torkkola, "LVQ_PAK—the learning vector quantization program package version 3.1," Rakentajanaukio 2 C, SF-02150 Espoo Finland, 1995.

[26] C.-R. Che, L.-T. Tsai, and C.-C. Yang, "A neural network approach for random samples to stratified psychometrical population," in *Proceedings of the WSEAS International Conference on Sociology, Psychology, Philosophy*, pp. 51–54, Penang, Malaysia, March 2010.

12

A Framework for Adaptive Game Presenters with Emotions and Social Comments

Effie Karouzaki[1] and Anthony Savidis[1,2]

[1] Human-Computer Interaction Laboratory, Institute of Computer Science, Foundation for Research and Technology Hellas, N. Plastira 100, Vassilika Vouton, 70013 Heraklion, Crete, Greece
[2] Department of Computer Science, University of Crete, Knossou Avenue, 71409 Heraklion, Crete, Greece

Correspondence should be addressed to Effie Karouzaki, karuzaki@ics.forth.gr

Academic Editor: Alexander Pasko

More and more games today try to adjust their gameplay to fit individual players; however, little work has been carried out in the same direction towards game presenter characters. Game commentary should take into account players' personalities along with game progress in order to achieve social player-adapted comment delivery that boosts the overall gameplay, engages the players, and stimulates the audience. In our work, we discuss a framework for implementing artificial game presenter characters that are based on game actions and players' social profiles in order to deliver knowledgeable, socially oriented comments. Moreover, the presented framework supports emotional facial expressions for the presenters, allowing them to convey their emotions and thus be more expressive than the majority of the commentary systems today. We prove our concept by developing a presenter character for multiplayer tabletop board games which we further put under usability evaluation with 9 players. The results showed that game sessions with presenter characters are preferred over the plain version of the game and that the majority of the players enjoy personalized social-oriented comments expressed via multimedia and emotions.

1. Introduction

Our work on game presenter characters has been motivated by the popularity of television game shows and the lack of an analogy in the domain of computer-based entertainment. A significant amount of games played on TV shows are computer-based tabletop ones (Wheel of Fortune, Power of Ten, Who Wants to Be a Millionaire, etc.) with an overall setup emphasizing and amplifying social interaction. Game show presenters are identified as one of the 7 key attributes of appreciation of TV game shows [1]. From a social perspective, they are responsible for keeping the game socially engaging and stimulating. More specifically, presenters provoke social interaction in order to keep the players and the audience constantly motivated and alerted about the game progress. For this purpose, they rely on individual player profiles, current challenge, previous performance, and statistics to provide feedback commonly involving humor, reward, sympathy, surprise, disappointment, enthusiasm, agony, and anticipation.

Nowadays, more and more games incorporate artificial commentator systems (Pro Evolution Soccer Series [2], Buzz! [3], etc.). Such systems are based on game events and use prerecorded voices of actors, game commentators, and TV-show presenters in order to feel more realistic to players. Some of these games ask for player names, in order to use them when addressing to each player. This is a very simple yet extremely clever technique to personalize the presenter's comments and make players get more into their game role, thus achieving a better gaming experience. RoboCup commentary systems [4, 5] receive game events as input and output text and voice that comment on these events. The *Byrne* commentary system [6] also utilizes a visual representation of the presenter's face which incorporates emotion expressions. All such game commentators exhibit the same, predefined behavior for all players, taking into account only their game progress. They will make the same comments regardless if their players are young or old, businessmen or unemployed, or single or married. In other words, they do not use adaptive social feedback to make game comments. However, a significant amount of work has been done on adaptive social feedback in the field of educational games. As teaching and learning are both social activities, game agents need to be informed about players' social characteristics and use them to control the gameplay and come up with stimulating and engaging comments that will motivate the students to play and learn. The fact that agents with adaptive social feedback can be used to boost the overall gaming experience and improve the learning process is widely accepted, and a lot of scientific work has been done towards this direction [7–11].

Although playing multiplayer games is also considered a highly social activity (such as learning and teaching), little work exists that combines the adaptive social feedback with game presenter characters in this field. We believe that social feedback, used in educational games in order to boost learning, can also be used by game presenter characters in order to better motivate the players and stimulate the audience. Towards this direction, we present a framework for building artificial game presenter characters with emotions, capable of delivering knowledgeable social comments, adapted to individual profiles and game progress for tabletop multiplayer computer games. Our framework utilizes input such as game events and player profiles (containing information about player's name, occupation, age, social status, etc.) and keeps track of incoming information about game progress to *decide and deliver player-adapted and context-sensitive social feedback*.

In particular, comparing to existing methods, we propose a game presenter character with adaptive emotions through multiple emotion states, each state adapted and related to the performance, progress, and profile of each individual player. During game play, and for the current player, the character performs transitions of the corresponding emotion state, while making such emotions visible to the audience through animated facial expressions and eventually deciding player-adapted social comments. This way, the presenter is able to adopt a social behavior that enhances the overall gaming experience. As a case study, we discuss the implementation and evaluation of such a presenter character following our framework for tabletop computer games.

Our framework reveals the first-class components inherent in building presenter characters, with clear separation of concerns across the various components. The latter enables independent development of components and supports better software organization, while it facilitates extensibility and maintainability. Overall, the framework prescribes responsibilities and interoperation among components in a way that can be used to realize different presenter behaviors for various game categories.

In order to prove our concept, we have implemented a game presenter character for *2D board games*, called Amby, based on the proposed framework (a two-minute video of our character in action is available at http://www.ics.forth .gr/hci/files/plang/AmbyVideo.avi). Amby receives raw game events as input and processes them for producing valuable game comments and computing self-emotions. These comments are further adapted to each player separately, based on their social profiles and their in-game progress. Our character also incorporates a range of emotions and communicates them to the audience via animated facial expressions. Amby adjusts his emotional state for each player separately, based on their social profile and their game progress.

Amby's setup was designed to resemble TV-show game setups as illustrated on Figure 1. He is displayed on a separate screen close to the game board and communicates with the game via network messages. He is capable of delivering comments by utilizing a wide range of multimedia, namely, text, images, animations, sound effects, background music, and speech. Amby is also capable of displaying facial expressions to convey emotions.

Our focus was to prove that a game presenter character following the proposed framework is able to make knowledgeable, personalized comments and that his/her presence enhances gaming experience and contributes to player satisfaction. Moreover, the produced system is easily extended and adjusted to fit different games' categories. Our evaluation proves that players favored Amby's presence in the game and found his behavior interesting and engaging. The choices made for each one of the framework components when implementing this case study are detailed within the respective sections. The user evaluation of our work is analyzed in Section 4.

2. Related Work

More and more games today try to incorporate adaptation mechanisms that adjust game parameters to fit individual gameplay. Nowadays, a technique named dynamic game difficulty balancing (DGD) is used, in which the game monitors player performance in order to adjust its difficulty accordingly. For example, Hunicke and Chapman's game [12] controls the game environment settings in order to make challenges easier or harder, while Resident Evil 5 [13] employed a system called the "Difficulty Scale" that grades the players' performance and uses it to adapt the enemy difficulty level. Finally, Mario Kart series [14, 15] features distributing bonus items that help an individual driver get ahead of their opponents based on a driver's position. Other games allow for static personalization through preferences. This method allows players to adjust game attributes themselves before play, in order to fit their preferences. Finally, there is an increasing trend towards using genetic algorithms and machine-learning techniques in order to learn from player's gameplay and adjust the nonplayer characters to become more and more challenging. For example, Demasi and Cruz [16] built intelligent agents employing genetic algorithm techniques to keep alive agents that best fit the user level. All these games monitor player activity and make decisions about adjusting game properties (level difficulty, enemy strategy, etc.). Our work also monitors game activity in order to collect information about each player's progress and the overall game state. However, we focus on game

FIGURE 1: Setup of the Amby presenter character for a tabletop game, resembling TV-show games.

presenter characters; so in our case, the data collected through game monitoring is used for adapting the comments made by the presenter. We also use players' profiles in order to personalize comments and provide adaptive social feedback. The latter is widely used in pedagogical agents with great success [7–11]. Such agents are intended to boost learning experience and are incorporated into educational games. They are aware of the player profile and they adjust their behavior (in the form of feedback) in order to keep them interested and motivated. For example, Conati and Manske [17] discuss how to improve the feedback provided to players, while [18] adds socially oriented conversational abilities to an existing "teachable agent" in order to enhance student's experience within the game. In our work, we use adaptive social feedback for building game presenters for any game, without focusing on learning. Educational game presenters may use individual player information in order to react differently for each one of them and for making knowledgeable comments that fit their profile. Our character differs in the means that we use multiple versions of state parameters per player profile and that we allow adaptation rules to be based on comparisons with other players. For example, comments can be made about which player is doing better in game, which has the highest score, and so forth. Finally, the use of emotions is gaining ground in games. Complicated mechanisms for capturing and interpreting user emotions are incorporated in games that further adapt their gameplay according to these emotions. For example, an abstract cognitive architectural model is proposed in Imbert and de Antonio [19] aiming to support emotions and social behavior, although emotion-driven reasoning is not an explicit component. In affective games, researchers try to find ways of inducing, processing, and utilizing players' emotions in order to take them into account when designing their games. Player's emotions can be utilized to dynamically adapt the gameplay in order to keep players challenged and motivated. Gilleade and Dix used frustration in the design of adaptive videogames [20], while Sykes and Brown try to induce player's emotions through the gamepad [21] in order to control difficulty level in a game. Finally, The Affective Mirror (AM) [22] is an affective multimodal interface that adapts itself to the user's perceived affective state. In our work, we utilize emotion states for the presenter, in order to enhance the social feedback provided. We do not use any mechanism of capturing actual player emotions and we do not make any assumptions about them either. Our target is to build presenter characters that can dynamically build emotions for players based on their profiles and their game progress. The adoption of affective computing features on top of the current implementation may further enrich the personality of our presenter; however, such extra effort was beyond the scope of the discussed work.

Game presenter characters are not new in the bibliography. There are several commentator systems able to present sport or TV-show-like games. These systems try to resemble human behavior. In sport games, these systems work pretty well, as the real TV commentators take into account only game events and are not interested in viewers' personalities or emotions. For example, successful sport commentary systems are incorporated in commercial games like Pro Evolution Soccer [2]. Also, a lot of work has been done for artificial commentators in RoboCup games (see [4, 5]). Closer to our work is the "Byrne" system [6], in which a digital character provides automatic soccer commentary and supports facial expressions and verbal narrative *adapted to the current game state by processing annotated game events.* Byrne's automatic narration relies on the notion of observers, being special objects which make abstract conclusions about the game, while they may also post remarks. Some technical issues regarding Byrne are as follows: (i) emotion generation does not consult the previous emotion states (has no emotional memory); (ii) the type of remarks by observers cannot be globally tuned (cannot adapt to a particular audience); (iii) it has no adaptive behavior (cannot comment on the social profile of a particular soccer player). Byrne is targeted for RoboCup commendation so it takes into account

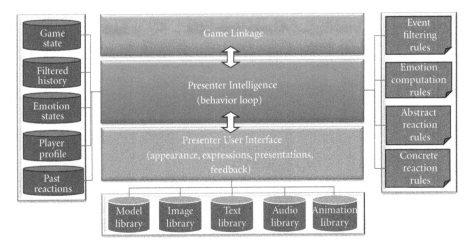

FIGURE 2: The high-level architecture of the framework.

only player progress. The proposed framework, however, supports the construction of presenter characters that make social comments, in the means that (i) comments that are not game specific and (ii) they can be personalized through player's profiles and action history. For example, comments such as "well done John" and "Suddenly you're doing a lot better that your opponents" can be characterized as social because they are personalized and can be made in any game, in opposed to "great tackling" and "nice uppercut" that can be made only in specific kind of games and do not contain any personalized information. In our framework, the progress of several players can be also compared and used inside the comment lines (e.g., "You have more points than Maria").

Finally, game presenters are also incorporated into TV-inspired video games. These presenters are based only in events received from the respective game and have no adaptation towards the players' social profiles. Quiz-like games such as Buzz! [3] but also video-game versions of many TV shows (Who Wants to Be a Millionaire, Wheel of Fortune, Deal, etc.) incorporate 3D presenters with complicated graphics, expressions, and body postures who, although being able to comment on game progress, are completely ignorant of player's emotions and social profiles. As a result, they make the same comments over and over again, regardless if they address to kids, adults, males, or females. Our work discusses game presenters that are aware of the players, their profiles, and their progress in order to make comments. They also utilize emotion states and facial expressions in order to be more expressive. We present an integrated extensible and adaptable framework for building such characters for any multiplayer game, and we discuss our experience from implementing such a game presenter for multiplayer board games (case study).

3. Framework

This section presents the necessary information that will guide other researchers for enhancing their games through artificial presenter characters that incorporate emotions and

are able to make player-adapted, knowledgeable comments. Firstly, we will present the software architecture of the framework (Section 3.1), and then we will detail each of its components in separated sections. In Section 3.2, we will present the component linking the game and the presenter character (Game Linkage), and in Section 3.3, we will analyze the behavioral loop of our character focusing on the enhanced sense-think-act loop and detailing each state separately. Finally, in Section 3.4, we will present the user interface component of the proposed architecture.

3.1. Software Architecture. The system's software architecture, which is visualized under Figure 2, was designed to provide a flexible yet powerful model for building artificial game presenters. Components with different functional roles in the system are clearly separated, providing the flexibility to developers to choose among different implementations for each component. Appropriate communication protocols (APIs) are further defined in order for the different architecture components to cooperate.

The overall architecture is divided into three major components: *Game Linkage, Presenter Intelligence,* and *Presenter User Interface. Game Linkage* component is the one connecting the game with the presenter character, so it has to provide a communication protocol by which the two components will exchange information. The *Presenter Intelligence* is the framework's larger component. It encapsulates an improvement of the traditional sense-think-act loop for game characters by introducing *reflect* and *adapt* as two extra processing stages to support affective processing and adaptive reactions, respectively. Such extra stages are inherent in the role of our character as a game presenter and are likely unnecessary for typical nonplayer characters of traditional games. The Presenter Intelligence needs to consult the game state, the player's progress, the player's profile, the filtered history, and their own past emotions and reactions in order to make decisions about which game events to comment and the way in which these comments are to be delivered (facial expressions, animations, images, text, speech, audio, or music). This information is presented on the left part of Figure 2, while the AI rules which describe the decision-making process are displayed on the right part of the same figure. Finally, the *Presenter User Interface* component is displayed at the bottom part of Figure 2. This component practically undertakes the look and feel of the presenter, being also responsible for providing all the functionality necessary for delivering the multimedia-enhanced comments and the character's emotions. A communication protocol is necessary here to describe this functionality.

3.2. Game Linkage. The Game Linkage component provides all the necessary functionality for the game presenter to communicate with the host game. For this purpose, a communication protocol must be agreed between them, describing the specific messages and the content that the two parts will exchange. The majority of these events depend on the game genre; however, they should include every game specific aspect that the presenter would be interested to, such as game state information and specific player actions. Table 1 summarizes the most common events needed for multiplayer tabletop board games. In Section 5, more examples of such communication protocols are given that would suit other game genres as trivia and race games.

Both the presenter and the game side must implement such a communication protocol in order to cooperate. Whenever a player performs an action in the game, or the game state changes for some reason, the presenter must receive the corresponding event and pass it to the Presenter Intelligence component in order to be capable of making valuable comments.

3.3. Presenter Intelligence. In order for game presenters to support social comments, we propose a behavioral model that builds on the traditional sense-think-act loop for game characters. More specifically, we argue for two extra processing states: *reflect*, that computes the presenter's new emotional state, and *adapt*, that takes into account the players' social profile along with their overall game progress in order to decide the exact comment or reaction for them. Overall, the behavioral loop breakdown is as follows.

(a) *Sense*: in this state, the presenter character receives several stimuli from its environment. Input signals can also be enriched with extra semantic content via filtering rules. For example, a dice roll can be characterized as low or high depending on the number and sides of the dices rolled.

(b) *Reflect*: the presenter updates its current emotional state. The presenter "recalls" its emotions for the player in turn and decides a new emotional state depending on the previous one and the received game events.

(c) *Think*: this state utilizes the results from the sense and the *reflect* states in order to decide an abstract reaction suitable for the current game situation. For example, the presenter may decide to comment on a

player's repeated failures to open a door in the game. The exact reaction will be decided in the adapt state.

(d) *Adapt*: in this state, the presenter takes into account the player's profile in order to infer the most suitable way to convey the comment decided. For example, repeated failures to open a door may result in a humorous comment and a cartoonish animation if the player is younger than 10 years old or in a criticizing comment if the player is adult. This state also decides the multimedia combinations to use for delivering these comments.

(e) *React*: finally the chosen reactions are to be realized through the character's visualization components. Several multimedia such as images, videos, sound effects, music, animations, text bubbles, speech synthesis, and facial expressions (emotions) must be synchronized in order to convey the decided comments and emotions to the players and audience. Essentially, this state produces the output of the presenter character, which will be given to the *User Interface* component for rendering.

The output of each state is available to all subsequent states. The complete behavioral loop along with a visual explanation of each state is illustrated under Figure 3. All states are detailed in their respective sections further in this paper.

As we stated before, the presenter needs to process input events and player profile information in order to come up with emotion reactions and player-adapted social comments. In order to make decisions, the character needs some written AI logic, in the form of rules. This is called *Rule System* and comprises the backbone of the character's AI. In order to build a rule system, programmers are free to choose among several programming languages. Typical general-purpose rule-based systems like Prolog and scripting languages such as Python and Lua are among the most popular choices. Other options include standard programming languages like C# or Java, ad-hoc rule languages like XML and customized rule languages such as DMSL (Source code publicly available from: http://www.ics.forth.gr/hci/files/plang/DMSL.ZIP). The latter was introduced by Savidis et al. [23] and was our choice for our case study for several reasons. DMSL is a small-scale easy-to-use domain specific language with flexible syntax. It supports an external profile as a dynamic record, where user profiles can be encompassed and application oriented data can be introduced. Moreover, the specification of independent decision rules can be made by defining uniquely named decision blocks; this makes the language verifiable relying on predicate calculus.

We strongly argue for separating the character's AI rules from the rest of the system. By doing so, one can gain better control over the character's logic, and programmers are able to experiment with the behavior rules without interfering with the rest of the system. The presenter can easily be programmed to adopt different personalities depending on the current set of rules that they follow. For example, a set of rules can correspond to decisions that a kind-hearted

TABLE 1: The most common messages of the communication protocol (API) for tabletop board games.

Message ID	Message content	Explanation
Start game	Number of players	New game session begins
End game	—	Current game session ends
Set initial score	Player Id, score	Defines the score with which a player starts. It may not be the same for all players since some games may adopt player characters with different abilities and starting values
Set initial lives	Player Id, total lives	Defines which the initial player life is. It may not be the same for all players since some games may adopt player characters with different abilities and starting values
Score change	Player Id, score variation	Triggered when a player's score points changes
Lives change	Player Id, lives variation	Triggered when a player's life changes
Extra turns	Player Id, turns variation	Notifies the presenter whenever a player loses or gains one or more turns
Turn begins	Player Id, turn number	Notifies the presenter about the current player (whose turn begins now)
Turn end	Player Id, turn number	Notifies the presenter that a player have just finished their turn
Possible paths	Player Id, number of possible paths	Triggered when a player needs to make a choice among several possible paths to proceed
Door pass Door fail	Player Id, door Id	Triggered when a player tries to pass through a game door
Cross-point pass	Player Id, cross-point Id	Triggered when player crosses a certain point of the game path (defined by the game developer)
Pause/resume	Is paused	The game is paused/resumed
Play multimedia	Player Id, media type, media URL	The game specifically asks the presenter to reproduce a multimedia file

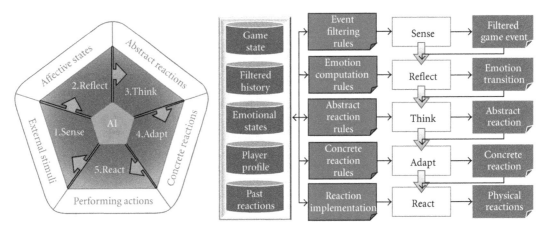

FIGURE 3: The proposed behavior loop for game presenter characters. Although not shown for clarity reasons, the output of each state is available to subsequent states if needed.

presenter would make, while another set of rules can describe decisions for an evil presenter that enjoys player failures. If the AI is decoupled from the rest of the code, then the programmers are able to switch presenter behaviors just by switching the AI rule set. In our case study, we utilized external files containing DMSL rules in order to define the character's personality. By altering the rule files (written in readable text form), or by switching them with others, we could experiment with our character's behavior.

3.3.1. Sense

(a) Event Interception and Filtering. Monitoring of game and player activities is technically analogous to interaction monitoring, the latter constituting an essential component of adaptive interfaces. It conceptually maps to the *sense* stage of the behavior loop, realizing the basic perception capabilities of the presenter. Practically, by the means *sense*, we describe all kinds of input that a presenter character can get. This input comes from the Game Linkage component. Some of these inputs must be further tagged with extra semantic information in order to be processed correctly. Input events that contain numeric values, for example, should be characterized based on the value's scale. A game presenter cannot say whether 10 score points from a bonus is considered good or poor, because it depends on maximum score points that one can get from bonuses and how often the bonuses contain such score points. Similarly for a racing

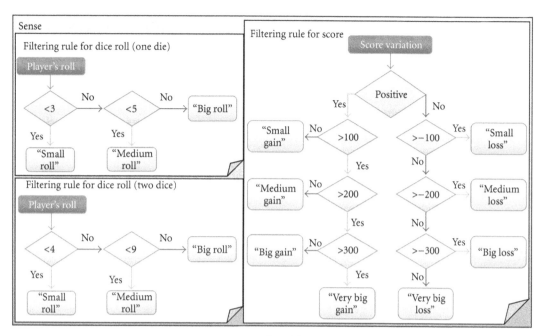

FIGURE 4: Examples of filtering rules.

game, filtering rules can contain game-specific information such as a car's maximum speed in order for the presenter to determine if the player is going fast enough or not. More examples about the usage of filtering rules in other game concepts are given in Section 5.

In this sense, extra logic is required to "filter" such values and practically map their absolute value to a value range or an abstract value characterization ("big score gain," "medium roll," "few path choices," and so on). This can be achieved by the use of external filtering rules, which provide this extra context to the presenter. In our case study, we received raw events from the game and we used filtering rules to add semantic context to the ones that did not make sense without it. In Figure 4, some examples of filtering rules are depicted.

Filtering rules are also useful when we need to adapt the presenter's behavior to fit another game of the same genre. Instead of altering numeric values across all AI rules, one can just alter the filter rule that controls that value. For example, consider a presenter character for arcade games. Many of them have very similar game mechanics but differ when it comes to score and life points. In that case, the same presenter character would need only to change the filtering rules for score and life points instead of searching through the AI rules for finding hard-coded values and changing the character's logic there.

(b) Game History Bookkeeping. In order to make knowledgeable comments about each player progress in game, the events received in the *sense* state should be kept in memory for further processing and statistic analysis. This procedure helps the character "remember" the game progress for each player separately and be aware of their habits, their choices, and their game history in general. This kind of data is useful

for game commentators—actually the event bookkeeping and the assumptions that can be made out of data analysis can make the difference between a mere announcer of the game events and a game commentator. In our case study, previous actions in the game can trigger comments such as "now that you obtained the key, you should be able to unlock the door that you couldn't pass earlier" or "you keep losing score for three rounds in a row." Such comments could help the players through the game and keep them constantly engaged and active. Furthermore, they can stimulate the game audience, as they can hear and see a game presentation close enough to human presentation, that is, containing interesting knowledgeable comments instead of mere event announcements.

3.3.2. Reflect (Emotion State Transitions). The reflect state in the character's behavior cycle is where the presenter's emotions are decided. The presenter keeps a self-emotion state for each player, which is decided based on player actions. For example, the presenter remembers that they were happy about player 1, disappointed for player 2, and so forth. Whenever a player's turn comes, the presenter recalls their emotion state for this player and uses it in order to decide new emotion states. These states' outcome can be further used for comment decision-making in the subsequent states.

The reflection mechanism helps for better gaming immersion and enhanced gaming experience and is very successful in TV-show games where human presenters tend to convey their own emotions to the public. Notice that as players take turns, the presenter may rapidly switch moods as it returns to its previous emotional state with each player. We used this cyclothymic behavior as a mechanism to provoke humor in the game. Our hypothesis was confirmed during the evaluation session, where the majority of the players

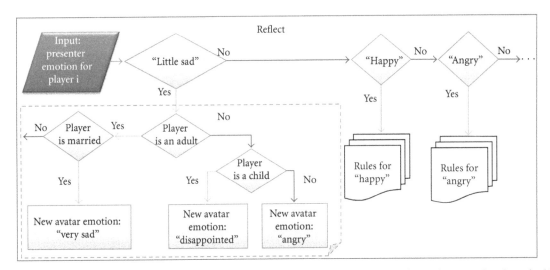

FIGURE 5: Emotion rules for "Big Score Loss." The presenter was previously in a "Sad" emotional state because the player had lost a lot of scores. As player lost score again in this round, the presenter computes a new emotional state.

FIGURE 6: The affective state space of our character as an adaptation to the Circumplex model.

actually found this behavior pleasant and funny. However, if such a behavior is not desired, developers can use the presenter's emotion for player i-1 (who have just finished their turn) as an extra input to the reflect state and use decision rules to provoke smoother emotion transitions for their character. We did not use any such mechanism.

In our proposed framework, we emulate the reflection mechanism by inserting the reflect state inside the presenter's behavior loop. As we mentioned above, the presenter keeps an emotion state for each player. Each time an input event comes for a player (via the sense state), the presenter character should compute his/her new emotional state based on his/her previous state and the input event. Such computation is made via reflection rules described by the rule system. An example of *reflect* rules is displayed in Figure 5.

Game designers can base their presenter character's emotion transitions on any cognitive model in order for their character to be believable. Reflection rules can be defined for

the presenter emotions based on this model. For each player, the presenter keeps an action history thus being aware of player progress and recent actions. Based on this progress, the presenter can have expectations regarding the player and make appropriate emotion transitions according to the current game event following the cognitive model. It should be recalled that game events are semantically rich, carrying information on everything that happens regarding the game progress, not merely restricted to device input. In our case study, we based Amby's emotional transitions on a simplified version of the Circumplex model [24], illustrated under Figure 6. Comparing to the original Circumplex model, our version does not contain aspects that we consider meaningless in an entertainment context such as (i) *fear* and *disgust* emotions; (ii) distinction among *activation* and *deactivation* since we consider no tangible trophy affecting player lives after the game; (iii) intermediate states for *sadness* like *guilt* or *depression*. Transitions are allowed only between

FIGURE 7: Amby's facial expressions that reflect *his emotions for the players*.

neighbour emotions. Any transition is allowed to and from the "Calm" state.

We argue that the presenter should incorporate a wide range of emotions with intensity values (e.g., one can be a little or very angry). The more emotion states a presenter supports the more realistic would the presenter's behavior be. In our case study, we utilized 7 basic emotions, being "Happiness," "Sadness," "Enthusiasm," "Reassurance," "Anger," "Disappointment," and "Calmness." Amby, however, was capable of making three more expressions, "negative surprise," "Discouragement," and "Encouragement" which we used as transitions between the basic ones. Amby's facial expressions that reflect the basic emotions and the transition expressions are displayed in Figure 7. The majority of our evaluators found Amby to be expressive enough and the range of emotions to be sufficient.

3.3.3. Think (Deciding Abstract Comments).

The *think* state follows the *sense* and the *react* state in the behavior loop as displayed in Figure 3. The *sense* state receives external input events from the host game and filters them to induce extra semantic information via filtering rules. Next, the react state computes the new emotional states for the presenter. Taking into account all this information, the *think* state is now in charge of deciding the character's actions. In this state, only abstract reactions are decided (next state, i.e., adapt, will undertake the refinement of those abstract reactions into specific commands). Together, *think* and *adapt* states of the behavior loop form the character's AI. The utilization of the rule system is necessary for both states in order to make decisions.

To give an example of the think process, let us say that we play a game and come to a point where the player had lost a lot of score points in the previous two rounds. At the current round they gain—let us say—a third of their score back. The *think* state must decide if a comment should be made about

this. The flowchart diagram of the logic rules that will guide the presenter through this decision is given in Figure 8. The output of that state is the decision to "comment on regaining part of score." We will later see in the adapt state (in Figure 9) how such decisions can result into more personalized and adapted comments for each player.

3.3.4. Adapt (Adapting Social Comments).

Imagine that you play a board game and a friend of yours sits next to you and comments on your progress. Your friend is aware of your profile, your social status, your name, your age and they can think of excellent comments that a virtual game presenter would never made. We propose the same idea for all kinds of game presenters. Based on our evaluation study, we argue that being aware of the player profile results into more engaging comments for both payers and audience. A presenter should react differently if they address players with different social profiles. For example, if the presenter decides to show an image in order to encourage the player, a cartoon-like image will be chosen for a child while a more serious one will be chosen for an adult. Additionally, for adults, the game presenter can make use of players' social status, occupation, hobbies, and so forth to comment on their in-game decisions. For example, in a quiz game, the presenter can excuse a player for not knowing the answer because *"it is outside of their job field,"* while if it is a child, the presenter will be able to make a comment about *"not learning stuff like that at school."* In the proposed framework, every player has a profile containing key aspects of their social status along with their name and their age. The profile is loaded at startup, and remains in memory during the game so that the presenter character would be able to consult it at any time.

Taking into account the abstract reaction that was decided in *think* state, the *adapt* state consults the player profile in order to decide more concrete reactions for the presenter. The adaptation process takes place with the use

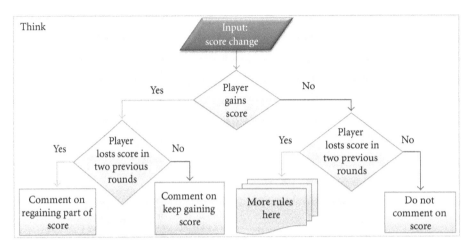

FIGURE 8: Example of a decision rule diagram used in the *think* state. The output decision suggests that a comment action should be made about "regaining part of score." The latter will be fed to the adaptation rules for further processing.

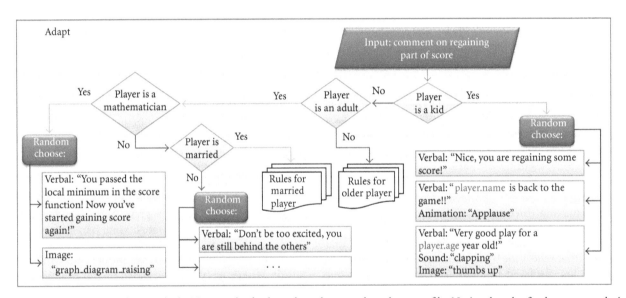

FIGURE 9: How a presenter character's decision can be further adapted to match a player profile. Notice that the final comment choice is made among reaction combos. In verbal comments, the "player.name" and "player.age" will be replaced with the corresponding attributes from player profile.

of the rule system. In the general case, adaptation rules may radically differ from the AI logic, so they can be described in another language (using another rule system) or provided by a separated component. In every case, the adaptation system should provide rules for adjusting each of the abstract decisions induced from the *think* state in order to be able to produce concrete presenter reactions. Presenter reactions may contain several multimedia, which can be either combined or used separately. The adaptation logic provider can define combinations of multimedia that match together and can be played concurrently to deliver the desired presenter behavior. For example, a closing door animation can be combined with a creaking sound effect, and an encouraging text comment may be accompanied by a cheering sound and an image depicting a gold medal. A multimedia file may be contained in a lot of combos,

and combos themselves can contain random choices (any appraisal comment can be combined with any cheering or clapping sound).

By organizing the presenter's reaction in this way, we can ensure that their behavior will be coherent no matter how many multimedia are chosen to be displayed concurrently. Regarding the presenter's behavior, an extra mechanism is needed to ensure that the character will not repeat their comments too often. We can achieve this by remembering the presenter's past reactions and excluding them from the reaction pool. Only when all possible reaction combos are used, the presenter is able to choose one of them again. This way, and provided that a wide set of reaction combos are available, the presenter character will seldom repeat his/her comments. A simple example of the adaptation logic is given in Figure 9. The *think* state has decided to deliver a comment

TABLE 2: A generic communication protocol between the user interface and the Presenter Intelligence components.

Message ID	Message content	Explanation
Load animations	URL	Load animations from a given path
Load audio	URL	Load audio files (sound effects and music) from a given path
Load images	URL	Load images from a given path
Set emotion expression	Expression Id	Instructs the presenter character to perform the respective facial expression for transitioning to the given emotion
Show comment	Text, position, font, size, color	Instructs the presenter to draw a text comment to screen. Arguments font, font size and color are optional
Show image	URL, position, size	The presenter is ordered to display an image on screen
Play audio	URL, volume, repetitions	The presenter is ordered to play an audio file
Notify audio finished	Audio notification Id	When the audio finishes, the presenter need to notify the intelligence framework through an appropriate notification id
Play video	URL, volume, position, size	The presenter is ordered to play a video on the screen
Notify video finished	Video notification Id	When the video finishes, the presenter needs to notify the intelligence framework via calling this given function
Play animation	Animation Id, animator	User interface framework needs to provide a way of displaying animations
Notify animation finished	Animation notification Id	When the audio stops, the presenter needs to notify the intelligence framework via calling this given function
Say comment	Comment text	Uses speech synthesis
Set background image	URL	Allows setting the background of the presenter character
Set presenter size	Size, position	The presenter character may need to change size in order to emphasize on something or in order to make room for other displaying objects (like images, videos, and animations)
Set presenter position	Position	The presenter may need to move around the screen

about a player regaining some of their score. The player's age is used for picking a set of proper reaction combos. Then a reaction combo is picked randomly from the set. Notice that the reaction sets do not contain past reactions.

In our case study, we incorporated player profiles containing information about their names and their ages. The players' profiles can be modified dynamically during gameplay, incorporating values that hold information about their game progress (for convenience, every player-related attributes that are considered useful to the presenter can be stored directly into the player's profile). The result was two-fold: the players were addressed by name, and our character could adjust his output comments to fit their age range. Evaluation results showed that all players were happy to hear their names from Amby's mouth, and most of them noticed the different treatments among the different ages. Additionally, diversifying the output comments helped the presenter to avoid repeating himself, adding plurality to his expressions, and thus keeping the players and the audience stimulated. The player's profiles helped in the presenter's emotional computation too, since he was programmed to be more soft-hearted towards younger players and more austere to others.

3.3.5. React (Delivering Comments and Expressions). The final state in the behavior loop of our framework is *react.* This state's target is simple: bring the comment decisions made at the previous states to life. In order to do that, the framework needs to utilize the Presenter User Interface component which is capable of displaying the desired multimedia. Additionally, the same component will take over the looks of the presenter character and perform their facial expressions in order to convey their emotions. In the react state, the presenter character receives the decisions taken from the *reflect* and *adapt* states (character's emotions and comments resp.). These decisions must be mapped to specific messages to send to the *Presenter User Interface Component* such as "Show Image," "Play Audio," or "Set Emotion Expression." This functionality is provided by the Presenter User Interface component through a specified API (an example of such an API is displayed in Table 2).

The *react* state has also the role of action coordinator. As each presenter's comment may contain concurrent animations, sounds, images, text, and so forth, these must be well organized and synchronized perfectly in order to provide a smooth output. The presenter's facial expression should be also tuned and timed, and smooth transitions between any two emotions must be programmed. The latter is necessary, because the presenter changes emotions and facial expressions frequently, and more often than not a new emotion is completely different from the previous one. For example, at the beginning of each player's round the presenter recalls the previous emotion for the player, which can contradict the current emotion. In our case study, we used intermediate state as medians whenever such transitions should happen. Timing has the first role when it comes to playing other multimedia too. Some of the issues that need

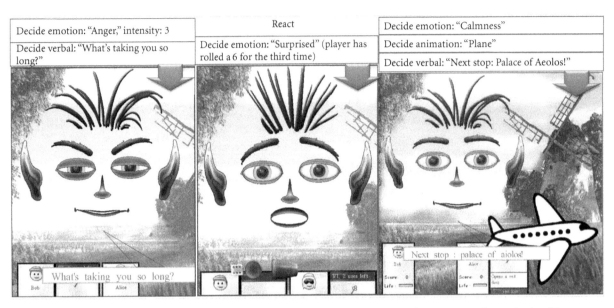

Decide emotion: "Anger," intensity: 3	React	Decide emotion: "Calmness"
Decide verbal: "What's taking you so long?"	Decide emotion: "Surprised" (player has rolled a 6 for the third time)	Decide animation: "Plane"
		Decide verbal: "Next stop: Palace of Aeolos!"

FIGURE 10: Examples of Amby reactions. At the top part, we display the decisions that correspond to each visual image.

to be addressed in this state are the following.

(i) Sound effects must accompany animations when decided together.

(ii) Images and text should be displayed for a while and then disappear.

(iii) Animation films and images should not hide the verbal comments.

(iv) If the character utilizes a speech synthesis tool.

(a) One verbal comment must wait for the previous one to stop first (otherwise multiple voice comments will sound concurrently).

(b) Lip synchronization must be scheduled carefully in order to feel natural.

(v) The presenter's face should never freeze. Emotions must come and go, and blinking must be scheduled frequently.

(vi) Facial expressions must change smoothly from one to another.

In Figure 10, we display three screenshots of our presenter character (Amby) to show how facial expressions, comments, and images can be combined towards a smooth result. A video of Amby is also available online (a two-minute video of our character in action is available at http://www.ics.forth.gr/hci/files/plang/AmbyVideo.avi).

3.4. Presenter User Interface. In order to visualize the presenter character, a user interface component is required. Such a component must provide all the necessary functionality for handling the multimedia libraries and displaying the presenter character along with the multimedia-enhanced comments on a screen. Programmers are able to choose among several options depending on each presenter's needs (GUI libraries, game engines, standard programming languages such as Java, C#, and so on). The user interface component undertakes the management of the media libraries, that is, the 2D or 3D models, still images, animations, audio files, and videos. In order for the user interface and the Presenter Intelligence components to communicate, it is necessary to establish a protocol offering the required functionality. In Table 2, an example of such a protocol is presented.

In our case study, we adopted an in-house game engine for 2D games in order to build our character's user interface. The adoption of a cartoon-like appearance for our character was mainly due to practical reasons, since our primary objective has been to develop a game presenter with emotions as an adaptive system, rather than to experiment with animated facial expressions. In this context, we designed an anthropomorphic character, with emphasis on outlines of facial characteristics rather than on visual details. This way, we had the flexibility of easily deriving expressions by transforming only key features such as the eyes, eyebrows, and mouth. Finally, all character activities, including facial expressions, social feedback, and the maintenance of game statistics, are handled through generic components manipulating external media files such as images, audio, or animation definitions. This way, not only distinct actions were handled by merely mapping to corresponding media files but also the presenter's reactions became easily extensible.

4. Evaluation

4.1. Process. The evaluation process has been coordinated by usability experts and involved 9 users aged between 8 and 35. The users have been invited to evaluate the game presenter character of a tabletop game, with particular emphasis put in collecting feedback on whether the overall game experience is improved compared to the game alone. The evaluation of the game per se was not part of the process since we needed to focus only on the evaluation of the game presenter. The procedure is described below.

All users were put together in one group, and the evaluators explained the game mechanics to them. Participants were then free to play the game for 15 minutes without Amby's presence and then play another 15 minutes with Amby (no player or player activities have been simulated). In both sessions, the participants were asked to think aloud in order for the coordinators to take notes. After the gaming sessions, they were asked to complete a questionary about their experience. The questions used the *Likert scaling technique* [25] to measure user's satisfaction about Amby. Some of the investigated topics were which version of gameplay do players preferred, whether Amby made the game more engaging for the players and the audience, whether he was expressive enough (sufficient number of emotions), and whether he was annoying or not. A couple of questions were used to evaluate Amby's adapted comments per se; however, it was made clear to the participants that comment lines were written by game authors based on their personal gaming experience and they were in no way representative for all players (e.g., game authors think that a comment such as "come on, it's not the end of the world" would be encouraging for a child and can be chosen by a presenter being in a encouraging state when addressing to a child). For commercial games, however, a presenter's comment lines should be written by psychologists and game experts in order to represent his/her emotions and be adapted to players' profiles. Nevertheless, they turned out to be fairly good. Finally, the participants were asked to enumerate a few things they liked and/or disliked about the game presenter character. Their comments along with their answers to the questioner were collected and analyzed. The most important findings are listed below.

4.2. Results. As we stated before, all the answers given from the participants were collected and analyzed by the usability experts. In Figure 11, some of the most important questions are presented, along with the participants answers to them. As the questions used the Likert scale, each participant ranked a given statement from 1 to 5, 1 representing the "total disagree" and 5 representing the "total agree" to it. For each question, the weighted average value of all answers is presented (blue bars).

Additionally, user comments about what they liked and/or disliked about our game presenter character were summarized. We present the evaluation results below.

Things that players liked about Amby were as follows:

(i) cartoonish appearance (younger players mostly),

(ii) expressive animations,

(iii) use of several multimedia for commenting the game,

(iv) most of the comments were unique,

(v) content-aware comments,

(vi) personalized comments.

Things that players did not like about Amby were as follows:

(i) cartoonish appearance (adult players mostly),

(ii) cannot adjust the volume level,

(iii) Amby's complains about not playing quick enough (part of Amby's logic decided to make a comment like *"What's taking you so long?"* each time a player was idle for a long time),

(iv) Computer-generated voice. Proposed prerecorded audio files,

(v) some comments were not as good as hoped.

The evaluation showed that although Amby was a case study implementing only part of the proposed framework, his presence clearly enhanced the gaming experience. Amby's appearance issues can be resolved by better graphics and/or by utilizing another UI component, volume level is just a matter of configuration, and time to wait until making a comment for idle players as well as the comments made are changed easily via altering the AI logic, which is decoupled from the rest of Amby's structure. Finally, the synthetic voice always lacks proper fluctuation, tone, and emotion in comparison to human voice. However, recorded voices can be incorporated very easily as well. Each recorded phrase would be an audio file with a unique id, and the rules inside the *adapt* state would make sure that verbal comments (as texts) and corresponding audio files are decided together (as combos).

5. Discussion

Although most of our examples refer to tabletop board games, the framework can be utilized for building presenters for almost any multiplayer game. The key lies in the fact that the Presenter Intelligence is based merely on game events and player profiles and is decoupled from the rest of the game code. The game designers should supply the presenter with game events (Game Linkage) and write logic rules based on these events. For example, if we needed to build a presenter for a quiz game, the communication protocol between the game and the presenter would include events regarding the questions, the help available, timing issues, player progress, and so forth. Table 3 summarizes an example of the most common events for this kind of games. The Presenter Intelligence component should utilize logic rules that rely on these game events along with player profile to make knowledgeable comments, such as "For a lawyer, you answer physics questions pretty fast," "your kid would know how to answer that," and "although you are the youngest player, you've reached the bonus first!" and so on.

For a nonturn-taking game, whenever the presenter receives an *important* game event for a player, the respective player profile is directly supplied to the rule system. Unimportant events are either filtered by higher-level rules or are ignored. Such a game example might be a racing game, where all players play concurrently, that is, there is clearly no turn-taking discipline. In this case, the game would

Important evaluation answers (1/2)

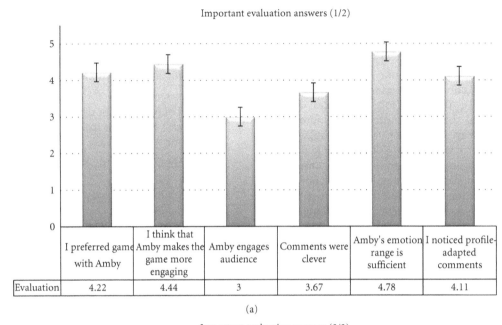

	I preferred game with Amby	I think that Amby makes the game more engaging	Amby engages audience	Comments were clever	Amby's emotion range is sufficient	I noticed profile-adapted comments
Evaluation	4.22	4.44	3	3.67	4.78	4.11

(a)

Important evaluation answers (2/2)

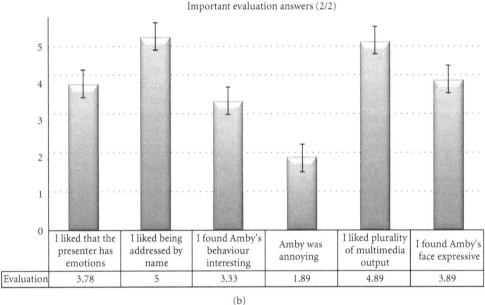

	I liked that the presenter has emotions	I liked being addressed by name	I found Amby's behaviour interesting	Amby was annoying	I liked plurality of multimedia output	I found Amby's face expressive
Evaluation	3.78	5	3.33	1.89	4.89	3.89

(b)

FIGURE 11: Evaluation diagrams for the most important questions about Amby. For the evaluation we used the Likert scale. The diagrams illustrate the weighted average values (their numeric form can be seen below each question) given by 9 evaluators. The black lines represent the standard error.

post events to the presenter in real time, reflecting actual player actions or related progress. An indicative list of such events is shown in Table 4. Then, an appropriate set of rules should be encompassed in the intelligence component of the framework to decide comments with a social style suited to this particular genre.

Game presenters should be directly aware of the game they present, so, inevitably many of the events in the Game Linkage are specific to a particular game. But also, the majority of such events can be reused across games of similar genre or common game mechanics. Most of the reflection and intelligence rules would also apply to a wide range of

similar games or games with similar mechanics. For example, rules that refer to dice should be common to any game that adopts the dice mechanism. Filtering rules (detailed in Section 3.3.1(a)) can be used to fine-tune details such as the number of dice used in each game. The user interface component doesn't need to change.

In order to introduce alternative presenter characters for the same game, one should have two or more different rule sets describing the presenter actions in each case. For example, if a game has a good presenter and game authors wish to experiment with an evil one, they would have to make a rule set that describes this behavior and

TABLE 3: The most common messages of the communication protocol (API) for Trivia games.

Message ID	Message content	Explanation
Start game	Number of players	New game session begins
End game	—	Current game session ends
Turn begins	Player Id, turn number	Notifies the presenter about the current player (whose turn begins now)
Turn ends	Player Id, turn number, answered correctly, time up	Notifies the presenter that a player have just finished their turn. Also informs the presenter why the turn ended (player gave an answer or time was up)
Question	For player Id, category, type, Is checkpoint, time to answer	Notifies the presenter that a question for player X has been asked. The Category of the question (e.g., history) and the question type (e.g., multiple choices) must be known, along with how much time has the player to answer
Player pressed buzzer	Player Id, time	Notifies the presenter whenever a player presses their buzzer. The presenter can compare the time from such events and comment on player reflexes
Player asks help	Player Id, help type, helps left	Notifies the presenter that a player has asked for help
Player reached checkpoint	Player Id, check point Id	Notifies the presenter that a player has reached a checkpoint in the game
Score (Money) changed	Player Id, amount	Notifies the presenter whenever a player gains or losses score (or money)
Pause/Resume	Is paused	The game is paused/resumed

TABLE 4: A sample of common messages of the communication protocol (API) for race games.

Message ID	Message content	Explanation
Start race	Number of players	New game session begins
End race	List of players and positions	Current game session ends. The list of players is used to denote their order (who came first, whether a player was close enough to finish, whether they are left behind)
Route selected	Route, miles, difficulty, day/night, forward/backward, location	Notifies the presenter about the selected route.
Overtake	Player 1, player 2, time	Notifies the presenter whether a player is now ahead of another.
Gained bonus	Player, bonus	Notifies the presenter each time a player gets a bonus
Turbo boost	Player, amount	Notifies the presenter if a player uses turbo
Pit stop	Player, elapsed time	Notifies for a player pit stop and the elapsed time
Checkpoint	Player, checkpoint, time	Notifies whenever a player reaches a checkpoint
Pause/Resume	Is paused	The game is paused/resumed

chooses the appropriate comments. The latter may be a time-consuming process, since the respective rule set may be quite big and complicated in order to take into account as many aspects of player profiles and game progress as possible. However, once the rules are there, switching behaviors at startup is only a matter of loading the respective rule set. The proposed framework does not support switching behaviors during gameplay. Images, animations, and sound effects can also be changed by selecting the respective resource paths without affecting other implementation aspects of the presenter. In this case, the Game Linkage and the user interface components do not require modifications since all changes are local to the Presenter Intelligence component, while the communication semantics are not affected.

Finally, for adopting an alternative appearance for the presenter, one needs to replace only the user interface component. Both Game Linkage and the Presenter Intelligence component are not affected. For example, game developers wish to upgrade from 2D to 3D, they need to implement the visualization and animations using an appropriate 3D graphics library.

The proposed architectural framework is modular and flexible to be applied for building game presenters across various game categories. Apparently, game presenters need to convey game-related comments. Following our framework, the adjustments required to support games of similar genres are practically of a small scale.

6. Additional Features

In this section, we will discuss our experience about the presenter character we implemented, along with some extra features we added. As mentioned before, our game presenter character, named Amby, is designed to comment on multiplayer turn-taking tabletop board games. We used a board game named "The four elements" developed by an in-house game engine. The game features multiple players, each of them having score points, a life-bar (0–100), and

FIGURE 12: An example of player's state and inventory as shown on Amby's screen. Both players have their inventories open. The blue shadow behind Bob's head indicates that it is his turn to play.

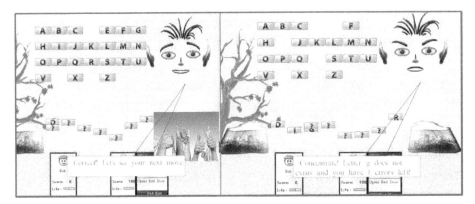

FIGURE 13: Screenshots from the Hangman minigame.

an inventory able to hold items. Throughout the gameplay, the player can pick up, drop, use, and lose inventory items. Some of these items are used to unlock doors inside the game; others can be used to transfer to specific locations, others to give life, and so forth. Each inventory item has a name, a description, an icon, and usage times (e.g., a life potion may have up to two usages). Without Amby's presence, the players with their lives and inventory are all displayed on the game terrain via soft dialogues [26]. As our game presenter character was designed to function on a separate screen from the game, we decided that he should undertake the display of the player icons, their score, their life, and their inventory in order to free some space on the board-game screen. Players should be able to interact with their inventory with game controls, and Amby should display the inventory for them. Amby was also responsible of displaying the dice (again without Amby it would be displayed on the game terrain as well). In Figure 12, an example of player state and inventory as shown on Amby's screen is displayed. Specified containers display the player's avatar (or photograph or icon), their name, their score points, and a life-bar showing their life points left.

The blue shadow behind the player icon indicates whose turn it is (in Figure 12 its Bob's turn). We also display player inventories next to player containers. Due to space limits, Amby displays only one item at a time. From top to bottom, we display item's placed within the inventory list (1/1 means this is the first object in the list containing 1 item), how many usages are left for this object, it's icon, a two-row text description, and its name. All inventory-control events are received from the game via the "*Game Linkage*" component.

The same applies for inventory commands. When a player needs to see their inventory, he or she uses the dialogs provided by the game in order to control what they see on Amby's screen.

Another additional feature we implemented for Amby is a set of minigames offered by Amby to the host game. The latter is unaware of their implementation details and their gameplay but is capable of requesting them and utilizing their outcome when players finish their play. More specifically, we have implemented two minigames, Hangman and a card-draw. The game may have in-game obstacles that introduce challenges for players in order to proceed. Such a challenge may require a player to succeed in a mini game. In this case, the game will ask Amby to start a minigame session providing some extra information such as the difficulty level. Amby consults the player profile (through think/adapt processes) and decides the specific game parameters for the mini game. To give an example, let us say that the game requests Amby to start a *difficult Hangman* minigame for a player. Amby consults the player profile to decide the word, as a difficult word for a child may be easy for an adult. Then the game session starts. As all input events must come from the game (so that the player doesn't change controls), Amby requests letters from the game. As the player provides these letters, the game sends them to Amby, and he decides if the letter belongs to the word or not and proceeds accordingly. Of course, Amby remains active and keeps commenting on player' progress within the mini game. When the minigame finishes, Amby informs the game about the outcome (win or lose, time elapsed, incorrect letters given, etc.) and continues commenting on the main game. Figure 13 contains two

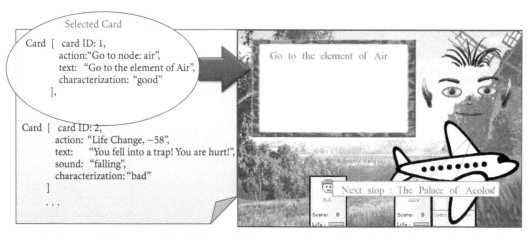

FIGURE 14: An example of the card-draw game. On the left, we display part of the configuration file that contains all cards. In this example, the random choice yields the first card.

screenshots of our implementation of the Hangman mini game.

The second mini game that we supported was a card-draw. Essentially the game asks Amby to draw a card, display it to the player, and send the card action to the game. The cards are described into configuration files, and Amby makes a random choice among them. Each card describes the action that will be sent back to the game, a text containing the legend of the card and a characterization. The last field is necessary because Amby doesn't have AI rules for deciding specific reactions for each card. Instead, generic rules are provided for commenting on card categories—for example, "if the card's action is a *Go to*" then decide to show an airplane or a boat animation" and "if the card's characterization is good, then set Amby emotion to Happy."

An example of a configuration file for the cards along with Amby's reaction when drawing it is displayed in Figure 14. When the game is over, that is, when the card is drawn and displayed, Amby informs the game about the result, that is, the card's action. The game then executes this action and the gameplay continues. In our example, Amby sends to the game the action "Go to node: air."

7. Summary and Conclusions

In this paper, we have presented a framework for building artificial game presenter characters with emotions, capable of delivering knowledgeable social comments, adapted to individual profiles and game progress. The framework has three major components being Game Linkage, Presenter Intelligence, and Presenter User Interface, each of them having a distinct role. Game Linkage provides the presenter with events containing player actions and game state, being practically everything that a game presenter might be interested in. The Presenter Intelligence computes the character's actions and emotions following an enhanced version of the classical sense-think-act loop, being sense, reflect, think, adapt, and react. States reflect, think, adapt, and react utilize the corresponding sets of logic rules,

describing the character's actions and emotion transitions based on player's profiles, their in-game action history, and the overall game progress. Finally, the Presenter User Interface component utilizes some graphic library to synchronize and deliver the decided actions. The latter includes facial animations for delivering presenter's emotions and a wide range of multimedia for commenting purposes, being sound effects, music, images, videos, animations, text, and speech synthesis. Following our framework, we built a presenter character for a multiplayer tabletop board game and put it under evaluation with 9 users.

In this sense, our work demonstrates the feasibility of a generic framework for game presenters with adaptive social comments. The emphasis on the architectural split between the game input linkage, core character intelligence, and the user interface allows for the framework applicability to different kinds of games. The presented framework also enables researchers to experiment with alternative presenter behaviors, and adopting more advanced character visualization since modifications in the Presenter Intelligence component does not affect Game Linkage and user interface. Additionally, the evaluation process has concluded that the game presenter improves the overall game experience and amplifies the social interaction within multiplayer game sessions. The combination of humor together with social comments relying on personalization through player profiles and gaming history played a key role in this context. Another important element improving game experience is how comments are delivered, involving several multimedia resources such as text, images, video, animations, sound effects, music, and facial expressions. The latter is used to convey presenter emotions to players and improve the overall social interaction. In this work, we did not focus on computing the actual emotions of players, something strongly related to the affective computing field and usually deploying computer vision. We followed an alternative path of making an artificial presenter dynamically building emotions for players based on their profiles and the way they act and perform in the game. The adoption of affective computing features on top of the current implementation may further enrich the personality of our presenter; however, such extra effort was beyond the scope of the discussed work.

We believe that our framework can be a guide for game developers towards creating presenter characters for their games, encompassing emotions and adaptive social feedback. Moreover, we hope to inspire researchers to experiment with alternative presenter behaviors and appearances in several kinds of games.

Disclosure

This paper has not been published elsewhere (except in the form of an abstract or as part of a published lecture, review, or thesis) and is not currently under consideration by another journal published by Hindawi or any other publisher.

References

[1] B. Gunter, "Understanding the appeal of TV game shows," *Zeitschrift Für Medienpsychologie*, vol. 7, no. 2, pp. 87–106, 1995, PhycINFO.

[2] Pro Evolution Soccer Series, http://en.wikipedia.org/wiki/Pro_Evolution_Soccer_(series).

[3] Buzz! Game series, http://www.buzzthegame.com/en-gb/.

[4] D. Voelz, E. Andrè, G. Herzog, and T. Rist, "Rocco: a RoboCup soccer commentator system," in *Proceedings of the ROBOCUP-98: ROBOT Soccer World Cup II*, vol. 1604/1999 of *Lecture Notes in Computer Science*, no. 50-60, 1999.

[5] E. Andrè, K. Binsted, K. Tanaka-Ishii, S. Luke, G. Herzog, and T. Rist, "Three RoboCup simulation league commentator systems," *AI Magazine*, vol. 21, no. 1, pp. 57–65, 2000.

[6] K. Binsted and S. Luke, "Character design for soccer commentary," in *RoboCup-98: Robot Soccer World Cup II*, M. Asada and H. Kitano, Eds., vol. 1604 of *Springer Lecture Notes in Computer Science*, pp. 22–33, 2008.

[7] C. Conati and M. Manske, "Evaluating adaptive feedback in an educational computer game," in *Intelligent Virtual Agents*, vol. 5773/2009 of *Lecture Notes in Computer Science*, pp. 146–158, 2009.

[8] C. Conati and M. Klawe, "Socially intelligent agents in educational games," in *Socially Intelligent Agents—Creating Relationships with Computers and Robots*, K. Dautenhahn et al., Ed., Kluwer Academic Publishers, Dordrecht, The Netherlands, 2002.

[9] C. Conati and X. Zhao, "Building and evaluating an intelligent pedagogical agent to improve the effectiveness of an educational game," in *Proceedings of the International Conference on Intelligent User Interfaces (IUI '04)*, pp. 6–13, Island of Madeira, Portugal, January 2004.

[10] P. H. Tan, S. W. Ling, and X. Y. Ting, "Adaptive Digital Game-Based Learning Framework," in *Proceesings of 2nd International Conference on Digital Interactive Media and Entertainment and Arts (DIMEA '07)*, pp. 142–146, Perth, Western Australia, 2007.

[11] S. M. Fisch, "Making educational computer games 'educational'," in *Proceedings of the Interaction Design and Children (IDC '05)*, pp. 56–61, June 2005.

[12] R. Hunicke and V. Chapman, "AI for dynamic difficulty adjustment in games," in *Proceedings of the 19th National Conference on Artificial Intelligence*, pp. 91–96, usa, July 2004.

[13] Resident Evil 5 Official Strategy Guide, "Prima Publishing," 2009.

[14] Mario Kart series, http://en.wikipedia.org/wiki/Mario_Kart.

[15] Dynamic Game Difficulty Managing, http://en.wikipedia.org/wiki/Dynamic_game_difficulty_balancing#cite_ref-0.

[16] P. Demasi and A. Cruz, "Online coevolution for action games," in *Proceedings of the 3rd International Conference on Intelligent Games and Simulation*, pp. 113–120, London, UK, 2002.

[17] C. Conati and M. Manske, "Adaptive feedback in an educational game for number factorization," *Frontiers in Artificial Intelligence and Applications*, vol. 200, no. 1, pp. 581–583, 2009.

[18] A. Gulz, M. Haake, and A. Silvervarg, "Extending a teachable agent with a social conversation module effects on student experiences and learning," in *Proceedings of The 15th International Conference on Artificial Intelligence in Education*, vol. 6738/2011 of *Lecture Notes in Computer Science*, pp. 106–114, Auckland, New Zealand, 2011.

[19] R. Imbert and A. de Antonio, "An emotional architecture for virtual characters," in *Proceedings of the International Conference on Virtual Storytelling (ICVS '05)*, Springer Lecture Notes in Computer Science, no. 3805, pp. 63–72, 2005.

[20] K. M. Gilleade and A. Dix, "Using frustration in the design of adaptive videogames," in *Proceedings of the ACM SIGCHI International Conference on Advances in Computer Entertainment Technology (ACE '04)*, pp. 228–232, Singapore, 2004.

[21] J. Sykes S, "Affective gaming: measuring emotion through the gamepad," in *Proceedings of the Extended Abstracts on Human Factors in Computing Systems (CHI EA '03 CHI '03)*, 2003.

[22] S. Shahid, E. Krahmer, M. Swerts, W. A. Melder, and M. A. Neerincx, "You make me happy: using an adaptive affective interface to investigate the effect of social presence on positive emotion induction," in *Proceedings of the 3rd International Conference on Affective Computing and Intelligent Interaction and Workshops (ACII '09)*, pp. 1–6, Amsterdam, The Netherlands, September 2009.

[23] A. Savidis, M. Antona, and C. Stephanidis, "A decision-making specification language for verifiable user-interface adaptation logic," *International Journal of Software Engineering and Knowledge Engineering*, vol. 15, no. 6, pp. 1063–1094, 2005.

[24] J. Russell and G. Lemay, "Emotion concepts," in *Handbook of Emotion*, M. Lewis and M. Haviland-Jones, Eds., Guilford Press, New York, NY, USA, 2000.

[25] R. Likert, "A technique for the measurement of attitudes," *Archives of Psychology*, vol. 22, no. 140, pp. 1–55, 1932.

[26] A. Savidis and Y. Lilis, "Player-defined configurable soft dialogues: an extensible input system for tabletop games," in *Proceedings of the 5th ACM International Conference on Interactive Tabletops and Surfaces (ITS '10)*, pp. 287–288, November 2010.

13

Building Community and Collaboration Applications for MMOGs

George Adam, Christos Bouras, Vaggelis Kapoulas, and Andreas Papazois

Computer Technology Institute & Press "Diophantus" and Computer Engineering & Informatics Department, University of Patras, N. Kazantzaki, Panepistimioupoli, 26504 Rion, Greece

Correspondence should be addressed to Christos Bouras, bouras@cti.gr

Academic Editor: Mark Green

Supporting collaborative activities among the online players are one of the major challenges in the area of Massively Multiplayer Online Games (MMOG), since they increase the richness of gaming experience and create more engaged communities. To this direction, our study has focused on the provision of services supporting and enhancing the players' in-game community and collaboration activities. We have designed and implemented innovative tools exploiting a game adaptation technology, namely, the In-game Graphical Insertion Technology (IGIT), which permits the addition of web-based applications without any need from the game developers to modify the game at all, nor from the game players to change their game installation. The developed tools follow a design adapted to the MMOG players' needs and are based on the latest advances on Web 2.0 technology. Their provision is performed through the core element of our system, which is the so-called Community Network Game (CNG) Server. One of the important features provided by the implemented system's underlying framework is the utilization of enhanced Peer-to-Peer (P2P) technology for the distribution of user-generated live video streams. In this paper, we focus on the architecture of the CNG Server as well as on the design and implementation of the online community and collaboration tools.

1. Introduction

One of the most interesting potentials that Massively Multiplayer Online Games (MMOGs) developers and operator have is that they can offer to the online players the possibility to interact with a large number of other players as well as to collaborate and compete in a large variety of gaming situations. The majority of these activities are made in the context of online communities that can be built around the game and where players of MMOGs tend to join to connect with people with common interests and passions and to share their in-game experience [1]. The Community Network Game (CNG) [2] is an EU-funded research and innovation project that researches and develops in-game activities using the In-game Graphical Insertion Technology (IGIT) and that proposes an architecture that combines efficiently the client-server infrastructure for the MMOG activities with a Peer-to-Peer (P2P) overlay for the delivery of user-generated live video.

IGIT is an innovative technology that permits replacing game's objects and inserting User-Generated Content (UGC) within the game in real time. Using IGIT, the in-game avatars can be customized with players' images, external 3D objects can be inserted within the game screen, and other types of windows, for example, external applications, can be inserted as a new layer on top of the game screen. It is important that IGIT's features are offered without the need for the game developers to change the game's code in the MMOG client or server [1]. This MMOG "independence" is achieved through a game adaptation process and an integrated browser's rendering engine, which permits that the same technology implementation can be used in the same way on multiple games, and thus making CNG a generic application able to address directly multiple MMOGs and MMOG operators.

In this paper, we describe the high-level design and the system architecture components developed within CNG system for the support of community and collaboration applications. Furthermore, we provide a detailed design of the system's architectural elements starting with details about the CNG Server's components and continuing with the Web 2.0 applications. The most important aspects of system's design and implementation are described. the used interfaces and protocols, as well as the system modules and the internal design specification. We focus on the features that distinguish CNG collaboration tools from a typical social networking website and we highlight any design issues that can potentially contribute in future standardization processes for WWW and open social networking.

The remainder of the paper is structured as follows. Section 2 reviews existing systems in the area and compares similar systems' achievements with those of CNG. Section 3 provides an overview of the CNG system's architecture and focuses on the supported community and collaboration tools. The design of the CNG Server architecture with regards to the online community and collaboration tools is presented in Section 4. The first results on our collaborating experience within CNG environment are presented in Section 5. In Section 6 we conclude, and, finally, in Section 7 we present our expectations as well as the planned next steps of this work.

2. Similar Systems and CNG Progress

Currently, many MMOG creators tend to build online communities around their games and to allow their players creating their own content and sharing it. In order to have a common look-and-feel around multiple games, a new trend towards the game adaptation frameworks and Online Meta-Gaming Networks (OMGNs) was arisen. There are several game adaptation and OMGN products that have been created so far, like Steam [3] and XFire [4], with the XFire being the most notable one among them, as mentioned in several studies including [5, 6]. XFire achieves game adaptation and provides a set of tools that appear in an overlay on top of the game screen. XFire is a free product and does not need any modification of the game code. Some of the most important features that XFire supports are the following:

(i) text and voice chat,

(ii) screenshot and video sharing,

(iii) live video streaming,

(iv) interconnection with external Instant Messaging (IM) networks.

(v) web browsing.

All of the above features can be launched within the game screen, eliminating the disruption of the player's in-game experience since quitting of the game application is not needed.

Using IGIT, CNG is able to introduce innovative community and collaboration activities between gamers. MMOG serving systems can provide only limited and low-volume out-of-game services via their central servers. By the reduction of the processing and network load, the new game features and applications offered by CNG are able to overcome the limits that the majority of the current MMOG providers face. CNG community and collaboration applications appear within the game environment and can be accessed and manipulated by the players without the need to interrupt their gaming experience. These services are offered by the CNG Server (or multiple CNG Servers) which is the core of the CNG system architecture. One of the

most important services offered by CNG is the streaming of user-generated live video among the online players using P2P technology. In the context of this service, CNG has researched and developed an innovative architecture that permits sharing of live video streams between multiple players via P2P without interrupting the MMOG data flow [8]. This P2P technology includes techniques for the creation of a dynamically optimized scalable network for the distribution of live video streamed from one player to another or from one to many players. The generated live stream traffic constitutes a major challenge given that it creates flows within a network already used by the MMOG data flows. To this direction, the project has researched and developed new techniques for P2P live video streaming that respect the MMOG client-server traffic (i.e., show "MMOG-friendliness"). The corresponding P2P tracker constitutes part of the CNG Server and has persistent communication with the CNG Client applications (peers) being responsible for the coordination and organization of the peers in order to assure an efficient and "MMOG-friendly" P2P live video communication. It should be noted that the implementation of online community and collaboration applications is based on Web 2.0 technology which is widely used for social and UGC-sharing activities. Further enhancements have been added to support the in-game activities as well as to make use of the features offered by the IGIT technology.

Table 1 lists the CNG key features and shows whether they are offered by the current game adaptation products or not. The most significant in-game adaptation frameworks have been considered in this comparison, namely, XSteam [3], XFire [4], PLAYXPERT [9], Overwolf [10], and Raptr [11]. It is obvious that XFire is the most notable among the similar systems. The progress of CNG beyond the current similar systems can be summarized in the following directions:

(i) innovative network technologies for live video sharing over a P2P overlay network,

(ii) game-oriented social networking, collaboration and video-editing tools,

(iii) innovative web technologies appropriate for the in-game rendering of the online community and collaboration tools,

(iv) advanced game adaptation technologies for 2D texture replacement and 3D object insertion at game-spots indicated by the user.

It should be noted that all of the above technologies have been developed in an MMOG "independent" and "friendly" manner.

3. The CNG System

In this section we provide a high-level overview of the CNG system's architecture and present the online community and collaboration tools designed to support MMOG communities.

TABLE 1: CNG features support by the most significant similar systems (source: [7]).

Feature	XFire	PLAYXPERT	Steam	Overwolf	Raptr
Texture replacement					
In-game overlay	✓	✓	✓	✓	✓
Video capture	✓	✓		✓	
Video edit					
Video upload	✓			✓	
Live video	✓				
Instant messaging	✓	✓	✓	✓	✓
Audio chat	✓		✓		✓
File sharing					
Online blogging					
SDK free	✓	✓		✓	✓

3.1. Overview of CNG Architecture. Figure 1 provides an overview of the CNG system's architecture. The CNG system consists of two basic elements, namely, the CNG Client and the CNG Server. The CNG Client has been designed as a framework that runs together with the game itself on the user's machine. On the other hand, the CNG Server consists of a set of components providing the various services for community and collaboration activities as well as for live video sharing. Figure 1 also depicts the MMOG Server entities as well as the network flows related to the CNG and MMOG services provision. It is obvious that the generic MMOG architecture is not modified since the game content is still transferred through the MMOG Server(s).

The CNG Client is an application that integrates the game application and provides the framework enabling the user to access the MMOG as well as the CNG toolbox. This framework is able to embrace any online game application simply by a configuration process that can be executed easily by an inexperienced user. The CNG Client includes all the software that is necessary for the game adaptation, that is, the IGIT libraries, as well as the P2P module.

The CNG Client's P2P module is responsible for the live video sharing over P2P among the peers. It has a dual role based on whether it is located in a source or sink peer. In a source peer it is responsible for the captured video adaptation and streaming to the appropriate sink peers. Within a sink peer the P2P module is responsible for receiving the video streams, retransmitting them to other peers when necessary, as well as for the adaptation of the received video data in order to play back the video initially captured in the source peer. In order to achieve the above procedure in an efficient manner, the P2P module interacts with the P2P tracker in order for the P2P tracker to build and manipulate the P2P overlays. The P2P module also includes mechanisms that add reliability and improve the performance of the P2P system. These mechanisms include schemes for congestion control, forward error detection, and correction of packet losses. The P2P module has also been designed to create a UDP traffic that is "friendly" to the game's TCP traffic. "MMOG friendliness" has been implemented in the sense that the CNG P2P module is able to adapt the use of network resources by identifying

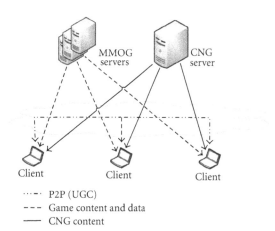

FIGURE 1: The CNG network architecture (source [1]).

the available network capacity and thus respecting the game traffic flows [8].

Within the CNG Client framework, the various CNG tools are offered to the players through the CNG toolbox. The CNG toolbox is the web application that is initially rendered within the game screen through the IGIT technology. It provides access to the various Web 2.0 tools for social networking, collaboration, video editing, and video sharing over P2P, which are all developed within CNG project. CNG toolbox also provides access to other services like access to external IM applications and web search engines. The IGIT module provides controls for the look-and-feel of all the out-of-game CNG tools on the game screen including their size, position, and transparency. A JavaScript API has been implemented within the IGIT module to provide the necessary IGIT functionality to the Web 2.0 tools [1].

The CNG Server is the core of the CNG system and has a twofold role within it. First, it provides the CNG online community and collaboration web services to the connected CNG Clients, and, second, it monitors the P2P communication as a P2P tracker. As a web server, CNG Server provides all the CNG community and collaboration services, the video and graphics tools that are provided in the CNG set of tools. As a fully integrated and standalone system, web server also hosts additional applications like media services, administration UIs, and applications for the interaction with external social web services like Facebook, Twitter, and YouTube. It should be noted that the CNG Server architectural design permits that all the above services can be hosted on the same or multiple machines. As a P2P tracker, CNG Server is responsible to interact with the various P2P modules within the CNG Clients, to organize of the P2P overlays for achieving an efficient live video diffusion. Finally, the P2P tracker hosts all the common information entities that are to be accessed by the peers [12].

3.2. Social Networking and Online Collaboration. CNG Server hosts various community tools that offer online collaboration services to users. The tools are accessible to the users through the GNG Toolbox. Since they are web based, the CNG Client retrieves all the necessary information from the CNG Server in order to provide these applications to the user.

The community tools are based on the Web 2.0 technology and are following the science-driven and interoperable design. The users are able to interact, communicate, and collaborate with each other in a social networking platform. In this architecture, the users are considered to be both consumers and producers of the generated content. As long as the CNG Server acts as a social networking system, it considers four different types of user-to-user relationship:

(1) idol,

(2) fan,

(3) friend,

(4) friend of a friend.

Assuming that player A adds player B to his (A's) friend list means that player A is now a fan of player B and player B is an idol of player A. If player B also adds player A to his (B's) friend list then player A will be friend of player B and player B will be friend of player A. Finally, if player C is a friend of player B, he has just become a friend of a friend of player A. The friend list can be organized by creating various groups of friends.

Community tools provide a wide variety of interactive applications. The members are able to interact and communicate to each other using many available tools, from simple private messaging to live video streaming. The tools are intended to be accessible within the game environment. Taking this into account, they are having minimal style.

The design of the web tools can support and present many forms of user-generated content. Firstly, the Wall application is a community tool in which the users can publish posts in a common thread. The users can view posts made by other users and can interact by replying or republish them to his Facebook and Twitter accounts.

The user can create his personal blog, create custom polls, or upload files. These features are widely used in social networks and are considered to be very essential tools for the members of gaming communities. The proposed design follows the principle that the user-generated content should be exposed only to authorized groups. When uploading a

file, creating a poll, and so forth, the user specifies the access restrictions, thus the content may be publicly available or only available to a group of friends.

Voice chat applications are very popular to gamers as long as they support voice conversations besides text-based chat. CNG Server includes a voice chat tool that can be used for real-time communication among the connected members. Every user can create his own chat room providing information about who are authorized to join it.

IM belongs to the real-time text-based communication systems, between users that use any supported devices. As the majority of The Internet users are using IM services, the need of interconnection with such external services arises. Following the users' needs, CNG Server integrates browser-based IM systems that support multiple networks, like Windows Live Messenger [13] and gTalk [14].

4. Design and Architecture

In this section we present the architectural components developed within CNG to provide the online community and collaboration tools, namely, the user interface, the web server, the database, and the chat application. We describe the chat application separately since a large part of its functionality has been implemented to run within the CNG Client and because it is the sole system's module that interacts with the media services of the CNG Server. Figure 2 illustrates an overview of the system design for the provision of the community and collaboration services.

Before presenting the architectural components in more detail we summarize the user needs that led to the CNG system and the design presented in this paper.

4.1. User Needs for Community Activities within MMOGs. The CNG project has conducted a user needs' analysis and an initial research on stakeholders' requirements. The results are available in [15] and are outlined in [16]. This research identifies why players communicate with others, what they share and how, as well as what they find frustrating about using current community related tools. Some of the main points found in this work are summarized below.

(i) The interviewees were frustrated by the use existing community tools, because of reduced immersion, communication difficulties and privacy issues, and poor usability of tools.

(ii) Some of the interviewees have used or were aware of similar systems, low awareness and poor ease of use being the hurdles to adoption.

(iii) Many reported that if the process of using such tools was made easier, they would be more likely to try it.

(iv) The key social/community functions that were particularly popular include video sharing, chat services and in-game web browsing.

(v) The results support the development of a range of social/community function, in game, without the need to minimize the game screen.

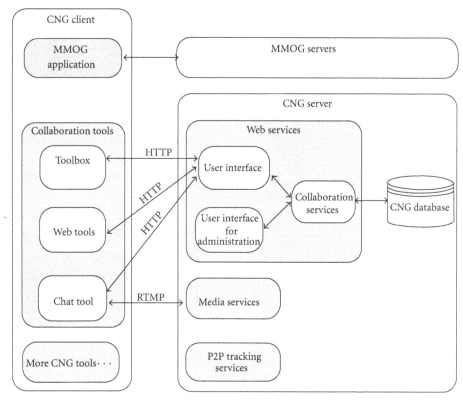

FIGURE 2: System architecture for the provision of community and collaboration services.

These findings formed the basis for the selection of the CNG tools to support social and community activities from within multiplayer games and the design of the CNG system, detailed in the following sections.

4.2. User Interface. As discussed previously, IGIT technology permits the in-game rendering of web content and thus the CNG online community and collaboration tools are implemented as web pages that are rendered inside the game window and corresponding to various independent widgets that are offered to the players. The graphical design for these widgets follows a simple and clear approach, so as not to dominate over the game scene itself onto the screen and therefore without affecting or distracting the user's in-game experience. Figure 3 depicts some examples of these widgets.

The CNG tools have customizable layout by making use of advanced web technologies. This is to accommodate both the various users' preferences and styles, as well as the different positioning options in the different games since the CNG collaboration tools should not overlap the game's on screen tools and options. The customization options can also be used to offer different layouts for different scenes of the game and/or different views.

Using IGIT, the CNG tools behave as floating windows within the game and thus achieve to appear as part of the game. The importance of this functionality is that it enhances the game experience without any need for the players quitting the game and breaking their in-game experience. It should be noted that positioning the CNG collaboration

FIGURE 3: Examples of CNG community and collaboration tools' widgets.

tools outside the game window, for example, next to right side of the game window, has also been considered but gamers seem to prefer the tools rendered on top of the game window. IGIT permits that the tools' containers can be highly customizable in terms of size, position, and transparency. Two different positioning, transparency setting, and sizing options are depicted in the two screenshots of Figures 4 and 5 where RedBedlam's MMORPG, the so-called "The Missing Ink" [17], is being used within CNG framework. The first screenshot shows the layout of the blogging widget when the user has expanded the widget's height and therefore a vertical alignment of the panes in the widget is more suitable in terms of usability and visibility. The second one shows the "Wall" widget layout in case the user has expanded the widget's width and therefore a horizontal alignment of the panes in the widget is more suitable.

Finally, an important challenge during the design of the CNG User Interface is the support of multiple game resolutions and screen sizes. To this direction, the CNG online community and collaboration tools have been designed in a manner that is independent of the game resolution selected by the user. This adaptation to the game screen configuration is not limited to the size of the CNG tools' windows but also considers their web content. At the initiation of the session, the game screen configuration is read through the IGIT JavaScript library and communicated to the CNG Server. Based on this input, CNG Server generates dynamically the appropriate dimensions of the CNG windows as well as consistent Cascading Style Sheet (CSS) files for the various elements (including Flash objects) consisting the web content, thus, achieving a consistent layout of the CNG tools' windows.

4.3. Web Server. The web server is the CNG Server's component responsible for the provision of the online community and collaboration services. The web server consists of two components: the UI component, which is the part of the web server that constitutes the presentation-tier, and the backend component, which is the part of the web server that constitutes the business logic-tier. The web server is based on the the Elgg social networking engine [18].

4.3.1. UI Component. The UI Component is the interface of the overall web server towards the web browser instances in the CNG Client side. At this point it should be noted that the client side of the CNG system is executed within a container that is able to display web content on top of the game, using web browser instances. The UI component provides the client side with the CNG user interface and the Web 2.0 online collaboration tools as web content, that is, HTML, JavaScript, and Flash objects. The web browser instances in the CNG Client side can communicate directly with the UI component in order to be provided with these services. With this arrangement it is possible to update and extend the CNG user interface and the CNG Web 2.0 online collaboration tools without changing the CNG Client.

An additional service offered by the UI Component is the provision of the web-based interface that is necessary for the administration of the web server. This interface is available to the users that have privileges as administrators on the CNG system.

4.3.2. Backend Component. The backend component is in the core of the overall web server and it is the mid-tier between

FIGURE 4: RedBedlam's "The Missing Ink" game with integrated CNG collaboration tools, where widget panes are in vertical alignment.

FIGURE 5: The same game with integrated CNG collaboration tools, where widget panes are in horizontal alignment.

the other parts of the system, that is, the UI Component and the Database. The purpose of the backend component is to provide all the functionality that is related to the Web 2.0 community and collaboration applications that the CNG system offers and integrates with the games played. This functionality includes also the management of these web applications, as well as the management of the involved entities, for example, users, access groups, and so forth.

In addition the backend component also offers authentication and authorization services, to the rest of the system that might require it. Although the authorization and authentication is designed as part of the backend component, since the user accounts and the access rights are a key part of the social applications, the pertinent functionality is provided also using a simple and clear interface that other servers and/or modules can use. The backend component stands between all other components and the database, hiding the database schema and database implementation details, from the rest of the system.

4.3.3. External Social Networks. CNG Server has the capability to interact with other existing external social networks. The system's design includes interconnection with Facebook [19] and Twitter [20] and single sign-on functionality. The user has to follow an one-time setup phase in which he enters his Facebook and Twitter credentials and an access token is generated. In this setup phase, the user has to authorize the corresponding CNG application to grant write permissions in his account. The credentials are used only to acquire a permanent token and are not stored in CNG Server.

After this initialization step, the messages that are posted using the community tools can be posted to his Twitter and Facebook walls. This procedure is done at server side, without prompting the user to provide his credentials for logging in to his social networks accounts. The design of the interconnection with the above networks can be considered secure, as long as no credentials are stored in the CNG Server but only the access tokens. These tokens are valid only for usage by the declared network address of CNG Server.

4.4. Chat Application. Chat application can be considered as a real-time communication channel which enables two or more online users to chat using text and voice. It can provide both private and group chat using chat rooms that the users can create. In group chat, all the users on the chat room must be connected to the CNG Server but in the case of private messaging, the messages sent to offline users will be delivered as soon as the users log back in. A notification for new messages is presented to the user when there are any new unread messages and the chat window is enabled but not visible.

We have chosen Adobe Flash [21] technology for the implementation of the CNG web-based chat application. This choice was done by observing a lot of benefits in comparison with other solutions like Java and HTML. The most important are the simplicity of the implementation that Flash offers and the client side compatibility. Flash is a multimedia platform that is used for graphic animations and is able to provide interactivity to web pages. Some of its features include the support of bidirectional multimedia streaming and capturing the users' input devices, including microphone and camera. The Adobe Flash Player is a very popular multimedia and application player supporting Shockwave-Flash (SWF) files. It is integrated as a plugin at most web browsers and is available on many platforms. Its efficiency relies on the fact that it uses vector graphics to minimize file size and create files that save bandwidth and loading time. Finally, the selection of HTML5 was discouraged in the current implementation while it is a new technology that supports audio (and video) playback but not capturing and therefore it cannot adequately cover the CNG chat application functionality.

Chat application was designed to be simple and easy to use in order to not require a lot of resources and degrade the gaming experience. An overview of the intefaces between the involved system modules is depicted in Figure 6. Like every CNG web tool it is applied as a module in CNG Server and it is located at server side. This architecture enables the maintenance of this tool independently from the system. A replacement of this tool with a tool that relies on different technology is also possible without introducing any overhead to CNG Client software.

A media server is used as an application server for the chat services. Flash is accompanied by open-source solutions like the Red5 Media Server [22], which is used for the support of the media streaming functionality. Red5 is an open-source RTMP server written in Java that can be used for text, audio, and video chat applications. It supports audio/video streaming (FLV and MP3), client stream recording (FLV only),

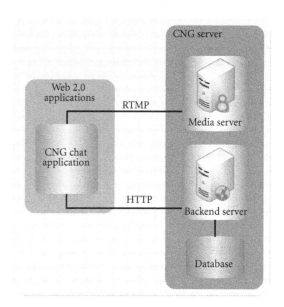

FIGURE 6: Overview of the interfaces for CNG chat application.

and live stream publishing. This server handles the CNG chat application requests by implementing the Real-Time Messaging Protocol (RTMP) protocol for all multimedia transmissions of the chat application.

The Flash objects that are provided by the CNG Server are intended to provide web-based text and voice communication in an asynchronous mode in order to implement an interactive web application. The chat application maintains a permanent connection between the user and the media server as long as the user is connected. Thus, the user can retrieve data asynchronously without interfering with the display and behavior of the existing page.

The CNG chat application acts both as transmitter and as receiver at client side. As a transmitter, it is able to capture voice and text messages and transmits them to the media server, while as a receiver it can receive voice streams and messages and reproduce them in the client side. The backend component's role is to be responsible for room management and also for access management in cooperation with the media server. Users have to select from the list of the users joined in the room, which voice streams they wish to receive. They can also send text messages to public (in-room) chat or to individual (private) user. The communication within the chat service is not direct between two users, but the messages and streams are transferred through the media server. Figure 7 presents the operation of the CNG chat application with respect to its interaction with the CNG Server in the form of a sequence diagram.

4.5. Database. The database is part of the CNG Server and constitutes the data-tier of the CNG Server's 3-tier architecture. The main part of the data stored in the database are the data for the CNG community and collaboration tools. As mentioned before, the web server and the CNG tools are based on the Elgg social networking engine [18], and therefore the CNG database follows the schema required by Elgg.

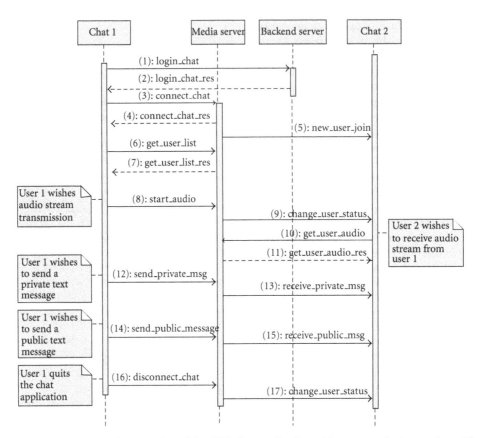

FIGURE 7: Sequence diagram presenting the operation of the CNG chat application with respect to its interaction with the CNG Server.

In order to be extensible, this schema models the entities and the entity relationships in general and allows specific entities and relationships that are inherited from the general entities and relationships. The schema for the "Entities" and the "Entities_Relationships" tables is shown in Figure 8. The main entities used are the User_Entities, The Group_Entities, and the Object_Entities. The "User_Entities" table and the "Object_Entities" table model the CNG system users and the user groups defined in the CNG system, respectively. The "Object_Entities" table models the social network objects like the video streams, the blog posts, the uploaded files, and the bookmarks. Figure 9 shows the part of the schema for these main entities.

Further to these entity types, the nature of an entity can be further specified through the definition of subtypes. For example, an entry in the Entities that is also related to an entry in the "Object_Entities" table and is related with the subtype entry "chatRoom" is interpreted as an entry for a chat-room object. Similar approach is followed for all the other community and collaboration objects. The subtypes are mainly used for the objects entities, for example, wall posts or video streams, but can also be used for all the other types of entities. The subtypes are modeled by the "Entity_Subtypes" table, which is related with the "Entities" table, as shown in Figure 10.

Moreover, additional information can be added to entities in two ways. The first way is the addition of metadata, which is information that can be added to an entity to describe it more precisely. For example, tags, an ISBN number, or a file would fall under metadata. The second way is the addition of annotations, which are generally information added by third parties. For example, comments and ratings are both annotations. Metadata and annotations are modeled by the "Metadata" and "Annotations" with an additional "Metastring" table to store the actual stings of extra information, which is linked to the entities through the "Metadata" and "Annotations" tables, as shown in Figure 11.

Finally for granular access control every entity, annotation, and piece of metadata is related to an entry in the "Access_Groups" table that models the access rights and is related through the "Access_Group_Memberships" table to the "Entities" table, thus signifying which entities, for example, users, have access to the entity at hand, for example, a live video stream. The relevant part of the schema is shown in Figure 12.

This flexible design of the database schema provides extensibility to the system, in terms of the possibility for having additional social objects, additional relationships between the objects, additional information to existing objects, and so forth.

4.6. Administrative and Monitoring Tools. As the CNG Server provides online tools to many users at the same time, it is important to monitor the system's performance and also the online tools usage using administrative and monitoring tools. The users are free to interact with the online community using the CNG tools and it is always possible to generate

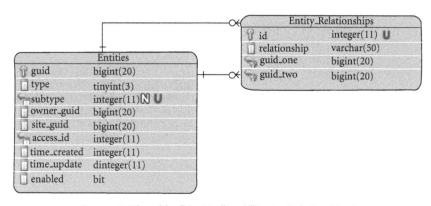

FIGURE 8: The tables "Entities" and "Entity_Relationships."

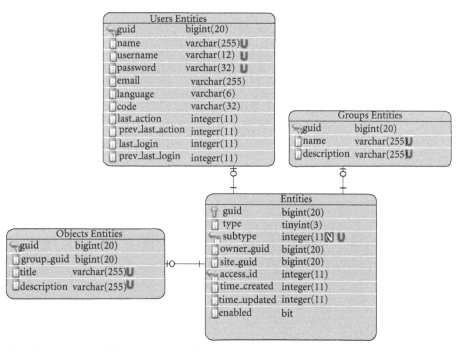

FIGURE 9: The tables "Users_Entities," "Groups_Entities," and "Object_Entities" as well as their relationship with the "Entities."

inappropriate content. In these cases, the administrative tools are used in order to supervise the CNG community network and avoid the distribution of content that violates the terms of service. The users can report any content that they feel that breaches standards on social, religious, cultural, or other grounds. Then, the administrators are finally able to moderate and review any reported user or content.

Administrative tools include an interface for the administrators of the CNG system to manage the CNG system using network administration tools and a control panel for users' accounts administration. The administrative procedures provide statistics like the number of registered users, groups, existing polls, issued blog posts, wall posts, uploaded files, shared streams, and information about currently online users. The administration panel provides full access to users of the system. It supports operations for adding, removing, activating, and deactivating a user and also resetting passwords and promoting users as system administrators.

A common usage of the users' administration tool is when a user generates some appropriate content and should be banned from the administrator.

CNG Server can be configured by setting its basic properties like the URL of the website for the provision of the Web 2.0 collaboration tools, along with its name and description. The administrator can also set the sites email address, the sites default language, and whether secure access through HTTPS is used or not. Apart from global configuration settings, the administrator can activate or deactivate any tools and also configure their parameters. The CNG community network is designed to be modular and can be considered as a compilation of different online tools. That means that the community network can be totally changed by enabling or disabling some tools. With this functionality the collaboration tools could be easily extended and maintained without affecting the whole system. Furthermore, as the administrator is able to configure the tools' parameters it

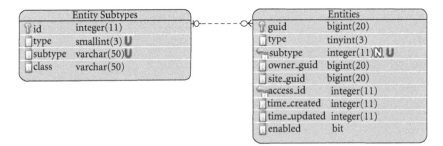

FIGURE 10: The "Entity_Subtypes" table.

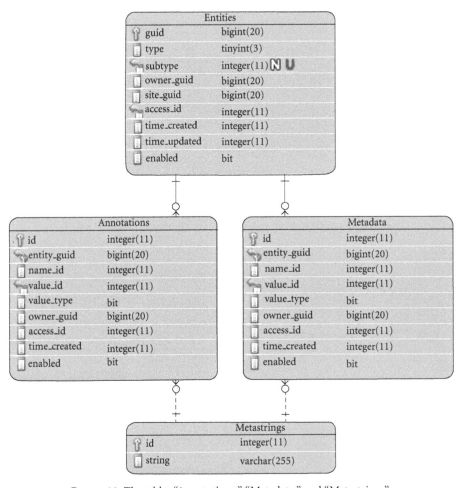

FIGURE 11: The tables "Annotations," "Metadata," and "Metastrings".

means that the configuration of each tool may be changed online at anytime by the administrators without interrupting the other tools.

The monitoring tools log the users' activity within the CNG tools and intend to provide information on the users' behavior in the form of detailed logs as well as through visual aggregated statistics. The implementation of the tools has been based on the Elgg [18] framework's infrastructure. These tools are used in combination with the other online verification tools in order to provide a complete view of the systems behavior. CNG Server provides a system diagnostics tool that generates a text file with all the configuration

information of the system. This information includes all the paths to the files installed in the web server and all the installed collaboration and community tools and any necessary related details. Moreover, the diagnostics tool provides information on the global parameters of the system, such as the Server's environment, IP, URL, and connected database.

Apart from generic diagnostic tools, CNG Server includes monitoring tools that are related to specific collaboration tools. The tool for live video streaming is considered as one of the most important and most frequently used tool of CNG system. The monitoring of live video streams

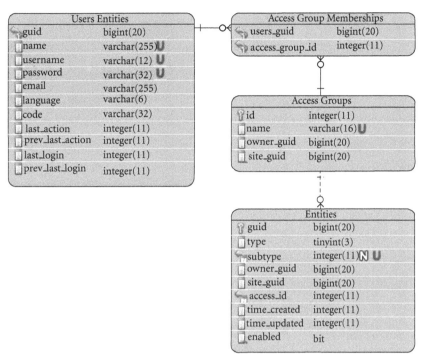

FIGURE 12: The "Access_Groups" and "Access_Group_Membership" tables for the application of access controls to entities.

requires a dedicated monitoring tool that will be able to provide detailed information. The implementation of this monitoring tool is illustrated in Figure 13.

The monitoring tools intend to analyze the traffic of the CNG tools usage at the highest possible level. The main functionality relies on collecting real data and analyzing them in order to extract knowledge about the usage of CNG community and collaboration tools. It is obvious that the usage of packet capturing (sniffing) software, for example, Wireshark, is discouraged in this case, since the desired information exists at the application layer. On the other hand, the existing common web analytics tools (like Google Analytics [23]) could be used for monitoring the CNG system usage but in a generalized way. They are not able to depict the CNG tools usage because they have no information about CNG tools or users. Thus, the existing common web analytics are not suitable for such in-depth analysis. The implemented web-monitoring tools provide this type of CNG tools analysis and of course can be used for extracting generalized results for the system usage.

These web-monitoring tools are integrated to the CNG Server and are fully accessible from the administration panel of the CNG Server (of course for the CNG Server's super-users). They exploit the existing technology for the Web 2.0 tools. The logged information is stored in the MySQL database of the system and the results can be viewed from the existing CNG web interface. Moreover, the "Google Chart Tools" [24], which is a state-of-art web-technology for data visualization, is used for rendering charts at client side using JavaScript.

The logging is executed at every user HTTP request towards the CNG Server. The system parses the requested

FIGURE 13: Live video streams' monitoring on the web server.

URL and then finds the referring tool. Furthermore, it utilizes the same URL and the HTTP request method (GET or POST) in order to identify the action of the user within the CNG tool. The results of the web-monitoring process can lead to a variety of conclusions. The collected information reflects the activity of the user on the CNG tools. The results can be organized in various ways based on the choices of the system's verification engineer or administrator. A filtering procedure that organizes the results (a) per user, (b) per tool, and (c) per action has been implemented for this purpose. This filtering procedure is depicted at the following flowchart.

The results are real time presented to the administrator and they are available at three formats: tables, pie charts, and raw logs. Each table shows the results in two columns. The first column refers to the object that is monitored and the second column refers to the hits. At pie chart, the objects are coloured and labelled. This representation is used for visualizing the table content, thus the administrator is able to quickly identify which objects are popular.

Logs

Ip	date	tool	action	url	method
150.140.8.30	2011-10-11 11:28:08	gameboard	view own	ouranos.ceid.upatras.gr/cng/cngrepo/elgg/pg/gameboard/owner/adam	GET
150.140.8.30	2011-10-11 11:25:40	gameboard	view own	ouranos.ceid.upatras.gr/cng/cngrepo/elgg/pg/gameboard/owner/adam	GET
91.217.154.194	2011-10-06 13:08:28	voicechat	authenticate	ouranos.ceid.upatras.gr/cng/cngrepo/elgg/mod/cngvoicechat/authenticate.php	POST
91.217.154.194	2011-10-06 13:08:24	voicechat	chatroom	ouranos.ceid.upatras.gr/cng/cngrepo/elgg/pg/voicechat/brest-room	GET
91.217.154.194	2011-10-06 13:05:05	voicechat	authenticate	ouranos.ceid.upatras.gr/cng/cngrepo/elgg/mod/cngvoicechat/authenticate.php	POST
91.217.154.194	2011-10-06 13:05:03	voicechat	chatroom	ouranos.ceid.upatras.gr/cng/cngrepo/elgg/pg/voicechat/brest-room	GET
91.217.154.194	2011-10-06 13:01:33	voicechat	authenticate	ouranos.ceid.upatras.gr/cng/cngrepo/elgg/mod/cngvoicechat/authenticate.php	POST
91.217.154.194	2011-10-06 13:01:30	voicechat	chatroom	ouranos.ceid.upatras.gr/cng/cngrepo/elgg/pg/voicechat/brest-room	GET
91.217.154.194	2011-10-06 12:58:20	voicechat	authenticate	ouranos.ceid.upatras.gr/cng/cngrepo/elgg/mod/cngvoicechat/authenticate.php	POST
91.217.154.194	2011-10-06 12:58:13	voicechat	chatroom	ouranos.ceid.upatras.gr/cng/cngrepo/elgg/pg/voicechat/brest-room	GET
91.217.154.194	2011-10-06 12:57:56	voicechat	authenticate	ouranos.ceid.upatras.gr/cng/cngrepo/elgg/mod/cngvoicechat/authenticate.php	POST
91.217.154.194	2011-10-06 12:57:52	voicechat	chatroom	ouranos.ceid.upatras.gr/cng/cngrepo/elgg/pg/voicechat/brest-room	GET
91.217.154.194	2011-10-06 12:57:46	voicechat	myrooms	ouranos.ceid.upatras.gr/cng/cngrepo/elgg/mod/cngvoicechat/myrooms.php	GET
91.217.154.194	2011-10-06 12:57:46	voicechat	create	ouranos.ceid.upatras.gr/cng/cngrepo/elgg/action/cngvoicechat/create?__elgg_ts=1317895045&__elgg_token=4bd5c90fa2aca447ecb0b81d0efa0624	POST
91.217.154.194	2011-10-06 12:57:25	voicechat	create	ouranos.ceid.upatras.gr/cng/cngrepo/elgg/mod/cngvoicechat/create.php	GET
91.217.154.194	2011-10-06 12:57:19	voicechat	myrooms	ouranos.ceid.upatras.gr/cng/cngrepo/elgg/mod/cngvoicechat/myrooms.php	GET
91.217.154.194	2011-10-06 12:57:06	people	adam	ouranos.ceid.upatras.gr/cng/cngrepo/elgg/pg/friends/adam	GET

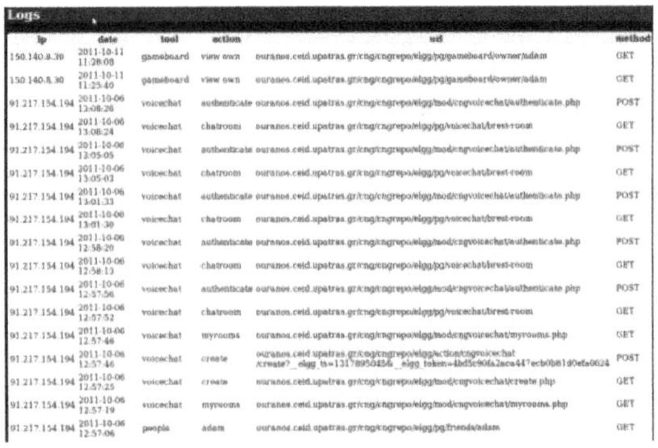

FIGURE 14: Raw logs for a specific user's activity.

Raw logs are presented in a table with the columns: IP, Date, Tool, Action, URL, Method. The rows represent the users' interaction on the CNG tools. This output format can be used for in-depth monitoring of activity within a specific tool or of a specific user. Next, Figure 14 displays the logs of a specific user.

When a tool filtering is applied, then an action analysis for the selected tool is presented. The verification engineer/administrator can observe which tools are popular and which actions are popular for a specific tool. For example, Figure 15 shows the action monitoring for the "Blog" tool. Finally, it is worth mentioning that special care has been given in order for all the above tools to be automatically extended in case additional tools/user activities are added in the CNG Server.

5. Internal Testing

The prototype of the CNG system including the CNG Server and the collaboration tools implemented, based on the presented design, has undergone a testing phase, called internal testing or closed alpha testing. During this phase the CNG system was used together with the TMI on game, by a small number of users, that are members of the CNG consortium and students. Although the purpose of the internal testing was to verify the correct operation of the CNG system and identify problems and bugs to be fixed, this testing gave some initial insights into the usability of the system and its expected acceptance.

The testers found that the CNG system did not affect the game's responsiveness and that the CNG tools work well. The testers appreciated the ability to change the size of the CNG widgets and rearrange them, as to minimize interference with the in-game experience. They also appreciated the ability to change the opacity of the CNG widgets and render them at a configurable level of transparency.

However, it should be mentioned that this internal testing procedure was not meant as a large-scale verification, and the tester demographics may not be representative of the target group's (the players of online games) demographics. Therefore a more complete picture on how the users experience CNG will be available after the completion of the large scale CNG verification.

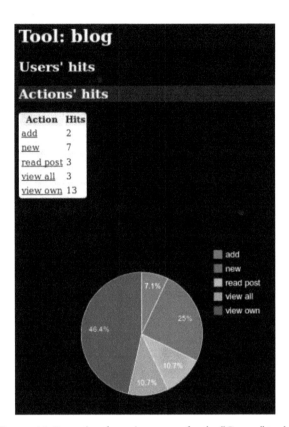

FIGURE 15: Reporting the actions usage for the "Groups" tool.

6. Conclusions

In this paper, we presented the system developed in the context of the CNG project in order to provide online community and collaboration services to MMOG players. After a brief introduction of the CNG system and its key features, which are, namely, the IGIT technology and the live video streaming over P2P, we described the CNG system's high-level architectural design. Then we focused on the system's design and implementation for the provision the online community and collaboration tools. We presented a detailed description of the CNG system's core element, that is, the CNG Server as well as the relevant aspects of the CNG Client. Our analysis included details on the user and administration interfaces, the element's structure, and the functionality for both the CNG Server and Client. All the relevant architectural components were described including the web server, the CNG database, as well as the client-side Web 2.0 components with respect mainly to the CNG chat. It should be noted that, during the presentation of the above aspects, we highlighted all the innovative design and implementation features that distinguish CNG collaboration tools from a typical social networking website.

7. Future Work

The next step of this work is the evaluation of the design and the CNG system, during the CNG verification phase. Tests will be conducted, with the engagement of online players, for an extended period of time (approximately 2 months). During this process, online users will be led to use the TMI online game both without and with the CNG system. The assessment of the CNG system will be performed through the collection of feedback from the users through online questionnaires and with the aid of the implemented verification and monitoring tools.

As the design of the CNG system is based on real user needs and is influenced by the user preferences, it is expected that the verification phase will confirm the system's usability, and the players' intention to use it in order to enhance their in-game experience. It is also expected that the verification process will produce several comments for enhancing and fine-tuning the CNG system, making it more appealing to the users.

In addition, since the CNG collaboration tools extensively use and integrate open or de facto WWW standards, several possible contributions to the standardization processes have been identified so far. The first possible contribution could be to the specification of the CSS. CNG system has been designed to support multiple MMOG resolutions and the collaboration tools have to be rendered consistently in all resolutions, therefore it is required to render the content in a resolution-independent manner. Anther possible contribution of CNG to WWW standards could be a set of specifications for audio and video capturing and visual effects support within HTML. Finally, a new set of social relations, typically used within games, as well as support for user-generated multimedia content over online communities, can be contributed to open social networking standards.

Acknowledgments

The authors wish to thank Kerry Fraser-Robinson from RedBedlam for his ideas on the in-game social terminology, Jonathan Freeman and Eva Ferrari from i2 media research for their recommendations on the users' needs, as well as all the partners belonging to the CNG project consortium for their collaboration. The research leading to these results has received funding from the European Commission's Seventh Framework Programme (FP7, 2007–2013) under the grant agreement no. ICT-248175 (CNG project).

References

[1] S. Ahmad, C. Bouras, R. Hamzaoui et al., "The community network game project: enriching online gamers experience with user generated content," in *Proceedings of the 2nd International Conference Creative Content Technologies (CONTENT '10)*, Lisbon, Portugal, 2010.

[2] CNG project—the community network game, 2011, http://www.cng-project.eu/.

[3] Steam, the ultimate online game platform, http://store.steampowered.com/.

[4] Xfire gaming simplified, http://www.xfire.com/.

[5] S. Bergsträber, T. Hildebrandt, C. Rensing, and R. Steinmetz, "Virtual context based services for multiplayer online games to facilitate community participation," *Multimedia Tools and Applications*, vol. 45, p. 347, 2009.

[6] S. Shen and A. Iosup, "The xfire online meta-gaming network: observation and highlevel analysis," in *Proceedings of the International Symposium on Audio-Visual Environments and Games (HAVE '11)*, Qinhuangdao, China, 2011.

[7] The CNG Consortium, "D2.10: soa and guideline for technology, ugc, and collaboration tools," Tech. Rep., CNG Project, 2011, http://www.cng-project.eu/?page_id=59.

[8] S. Ahmad, C. Bouras, R. Hamzaoui et al., "The community network game project: enhancing collaborative activities in online games," in *Networked & Electronic Media Summit (NEM Summit '10)*, Barcelona, Spain, 2010.

[9] Playexpert, home of kochava, gamerdna, and trueoverlay technology, http://www.playxpert.com/.

[10] Overwolf adds facebook, skype, video recording, messenger and much more to you favorite games!, http://www.overwolf.com/.

[11] Raptr: What are you playing?, http://raptr.com/.

[12] The CNG Consortium, "D3.1: system architecture and detailed design of games adaptation, 3d and ugc," Tech. Rep., CNG Project, 2011.

[13] Windows live messenger im service, http://messenger.live.com/.

[14] Google talk, http://www.google.com/talk/start.html.

[15] The CNG Consortium, "D2.1: users and uses of games and community activities," Tech. Rep., CNG Project, 2010.

[16] E. Ferrari, J. Lessiter, and J. Freeman, "Users and uses of multiplayer games and community activities," in *Proceedings of the Networked & Electronic Media Summit (NEM Summit '11)*, Torino, Italy, 2011.

[17] The missing ink, http://www.missing-ink.com/.

[18] Elgg—open source social networking engine, http://elgg.org/.

[19] Facebook social networking service, http://www.facebook.com/.

[20] Twitter social networking service,http://www.twitter.com/.

[21] "Adobe ash multimedia platform software," http://blogs.adobe.com/flashplatform/.

[22] Red5 media server, http://www.red5.org/.

[23] Google analytics, http://www.google.com/analytics/.

[24] Google chart tools, http://code.google.com/apis/chart.

14

Modeling a Virtual World for the Educational Game Calangos

Angelo C. Loula,[1] Leandro N. de Castro,[2] Antônio L. Apolinário Jr.,[3] Pedro L. B. da Rocha,[4] Maria da Conceição L. Carneiro,[5] Vanessa Perpétua G. S. Reis,[5] Ricardo F. Machado,[6] Claudia Sepulveda,[7] and Charbel N. El-Hani[8]

[1] *Intelligent and Cognitive Systems Lab, State University of Feira de Santana, 44036-900 Feira de Santana, BA, Brazil*

[2] *Natural Computing Laboratory, Mackenzie Presbyterian University, 01302-090 São Paulo, SP, Brazil*

[3] *Computer Science Department, Federal University of Bahia, 40170-290 Salvador, BA, Brazil*

[4] *Laboratory of Terrestrial Vertebrates, Institute of Biology, Federal University of Bahia, 40170-290 Salvador, BA, Brazil*

[5] *Institute of Education Gastão Guimarães, 44026010 Feira de Santana, BA, Brazil*

[6] *Graduate Studies Program in History, Philosophy and Science Teaching,*
 Federal University of Bahia and State University of Feira de Santana, 44036-900 Feira de Santana, BA, Brazil

[7] *Department of Education, State University of Feira de Santana, 44036-900 Feira de Santana, BA, Brazil*

[8] *Institute of Biology, Federal University of Bahia, 40170-290 Salvador, BA, Brazil*

Correspondence should be addressed to Angelo C. Loula; angelocl@uefs.br

Academic Editor: Mark Green

Ecology plays a central role in biology and deserves special attention in scientific education. Nonetheless, the teaching and learning of ecology face a number of difficulties. In order to tackle these difficulties, electronic games have recently been used to mediate ecology learning. This paper presents an electronic game that fulfills these gaps in order to make the students' work with ecological concepts more concrete, active, and systematic. The paper presents the computational model of the ecological system included in the game, based on a real ecological case, a sand dune ecosystem located in the semiarid Caatinga biome, namely, the sand dunes of the middle São Francisco River, in the state of Bahia, Brazil. It includes various ecological relationships between endemic lizards and the physical environment, preys, predators, cospecifics, and plants. The engine of the game simulates the physical conditions of the ecosystem (dune topography and climate conditions with their circadian and circannual cycles), its biota (plant species and animal species), and ecological relationships (predator-prey encounters, cospecific relationships). We also present results from one classroom study of a teaching sequence structured around Calangos, which showed positive outcomes regarding high school students' understanding of thermal regulation in ectothermic animals.

1. Introduction

Ecology deserves special attention in biological education because its object of study, namely, the spatial and temporal patterns of distribution and abundance of organisms, as well as their causes and consequences [1, 2] plays a central role in biology. Moreover, ecological knowledge gains additional importance in the current context of environmental crisis.

Despite its relevance, ecology teaching and learning face a number of difficulties. Key ecological concepts, such as ecological succession, food chains, and cycling of matter, are widely recognized as difficult to learn [1, 3, 4]. Accordingly,

there is evidence that the students' knowledge on various aspects of ecology is insufficient [5].

To overcome these difficulties, electronic games have recently been used to support ecology learning, but the available ones usually lack educational goals, are not related to real situations, and do not incorporate tools specifically designed to enhance scientific abilities. The game presented here fulfills these gaps as a resource aimed at promoting learning about ecology by making ecological concepts more concrete to the students and, also, engaging them with conceptual learning in ecology in a more active manner. The game, called Calangos (a popular name for lizards in Northeast Brazil) is based on a real ecological case situated in the dunes of the middle São Francisco River, in the state of Bahia, Brazil, investigated by Brazilian researchers (e.g. [6, 7]). The game (freely available at http://calangos.sourceforge.net/) is intended to provide the students with an environment that allows an adequate understanding of ecological processes. The objective of this paper is to present the model of the simulated ecological system, based on the real ecological case, included in the game and present results from one classroom study of a teaching sequence structured around Calangos. Particularly, the paper addresses the modeled dune environment and the ecological processes involving three lizard species that inhabit this environment.

The computational models developed include graphical models for reproducing the visual aspect of real elements of the sand dunes as game elements, mathematical models to define functions for game variables, and behavior models to describe actions and activities of nonplayable characters based on the behavior of real animals. All of these computational models operate during game play to generate a complex simulation of elements and relationships. Such simulation engine underlying the game corresponds to a flexible set of game rules and provides multiple possible trajectories for an open game play to achieve the proposed goal, a feature that differentiates serious games from mere edutainment games [8]. Serious games combine the analytical and questioning nature of scientific endeavors with the intuitive freedom and rewards of imaginative and artistic acts. In brief, serious games offer a way of exploring serious intellectual and social problems [9, 10].

The paper is organized as follows. The following section presents related work on educational games about ecology. Next, it described the real ecological case in which the game and its ecological model were based. Finally, the Calangos game is described, focusing on the ecological model developed, leading to the final remarks.

2. Related Work

The use of games to support educational activities has been studied for a long time [11]. In the case of electronic games, however, it was only recently that teachers started to use them in schools as a tool to help the teaching and learning process. Among the electronic games available to use in educational settings, a number of them are biology/ecology-inspired games that might, at least potentially, help ecology teaching and learning. This section discusses the main features of some of these games.

CellCraft (http://www.carolina.com/category/teacher+resources/interactive+science+games+and+simulations/cell-craft.do) is a simple online game that takes students inside a cell where they can learn about how a cell works and which challenges it faces to survive in a hostile environment. The game encourages students to balance resources and grow a robust cell to fight off coldness, starvation, and viruses. It follows a linear path: the students are guided to go through fixed steps and perform specific tasks to move to the next step. The strategy is easy to program and control. This approach guarantees that the students have access to all the information they need to learn a specific topic. Nevertheless, this kind of guided path eliminates the freedom of choice that a real game should provide to the player, forcing the students to follow a standard pattern for acquiring knowledge.

Web Earth Online (http://www.webearthonline.com/) is a multiplayer web-based 2D game where each player can choose to play as a mammal, reptile, or bird. The game simulates a very detailed ecosystem, but it is not clear if it is based on real data. Variables like temperature, weather, rainfall pattern, and direction of air flow are used to control the simulation process. There are many kinds of interaction in the game, such as those between the player and the agents (e.g., predators, preys) and between the player and elements of the ecosystem (e.g., trees, rivers). As a strategy game, the choice of which kind of interaction the player will use is the main challenge of the game. So, for different problems, the player may choose different strategies, and different players may choose different strategies to achieve the same solution. This could be used as a learning tool, but the game did not take advantage of this feature in this way. In fact, there is no explicit educational goal to achieve. The player could play forever or, at least, until it reaches the point where there is no other player to interact with (something common in multiplayer games). Another fact that corroborates the lack of interest about the learning process is the time needed to develop the character. The player must play the game for days to make his/her character grow and evolve. This long period of play does not help the player to perceive the relations between his/her strategy and the ecological concepts involved. It is difficult to evaluate if the model used for the simulations is trustworthy or precise, because there is no indication that the simulation is based on a real ecosystem.

Spore (http://www.spore.com/) is a multigenre single-player God game that allows the player to develop a virtual species. The species starts as a microscopic organism and can evolve into a complex animal. Once the player reaches this stage, he/she can start to guide groups of individuals to develop social relations. In the advanced stages, the user faces the challenge of leading the species to dominate its planet and then finally to its ascension into space, where it interacts with alien species across the galaxy. So, during the evolution of the game, the player experiences different perspectives from different evolutionary stages of a species. Although this game is motivated by many biological concepts like evolution, ecosystems, mutation, and so forth, there is no real model governing these processes. Moreover, there are features that may directly promote the development of misconceptions, such as the fact that the player can obtain new body parts by examining bone piles or skeleton parts found in the landscape, or by defeating some creatures. Thus, from an educational point of view, it is difficult for the player to build any valid correlation between how life evolves during the game and how a real life form could evolve on earth or any other planet. Despite its success as an entertainment game, Spore seems to bring limited educational contributions.

By analyzing the games from a historical point of view, it is possible to see a change between games developed in the 1990's and games developed in the 2000's. Older games, like

SimAnt (http://www.mobygames.com/game/simant-the-electronic-ant-colony), SimEarth (http://www.mobygames.com/game/simearth-the-living-planet), Lion (http://www.mobygames.com/game/lion), Empire of Ants (http://www.mobygames.com/game/empire-of-the-ants), and SimPark (http://www.mobygames.com/game/simpark), are simulation-based games that try to model, in a precise way, the relations between its elements and players. Some of them (e.g., Lion and SimEarth) have an explicit concern with educational issues. Others (e.g., SimAnt and SimPark) do not have this kind of feature but are based on biological information, which can provide the player with important feedback about what is going on in the environment. However, many newer games are usually based on web technology and poorly developed. They usually borrow strategies from traditional games, like quiz, puzzles, and memory games, changing only the theme, inserting biological or ecological content, or simply using pictures of animals or plants.

In this context, Calangos was developed with a major concern to reproduce a real environment, ruled by a model that is highly precise to give the player a feeling as close as possible to the lizard in its own habitat. At the same time, the game is expected to be able to reinforce the playful atmosphere of a good game, improving the interest of the player to discover which strategy can leave his/her character to achieve the game's goal: grow and reproduce. Finally, the game allows the player to access dispersion graphs that relate variables that describe the past performance of the lizard, allowing him/her to analyze the results of the strategies that he/she adopted in the past, so that he/she can adjust future strategies. Calangos explicitly incorporates tools specifically designed to enhance a key scientific ability, namely, that of interpreting graphs. To the extent of our knowledge, Calangos is the only educational game focused on biology/ecology that has a climate model based on real data and linked to models of the ecological relations between individual organisms and the environment, also based on real data, which, moreover, includes tools for the development of scientific abilities.

3. The Real Ecological Case

The ecological case modeled in Calangos is situated in the sand dunes of the middle São Francisco River (Figure 1), in the state of Bahia, Brazil. This ecosystem hosts an endemic and diversified flora and fauna and has been studied by Brazilian researchers for some decades now [6, 7]. Thus, the game not only brings a Brazilian ecosystem to the students' attention, but also the contributions of the Brazilian scientific community to the understanding of this ecosystem.

To succeed in the game, the student must develop an efficient strategy for the day-to-day activity of a lizard (choosing between individuals from three different endemic species, *Tropidurus psammonastes*, *Cnemidophorus* sp. nov., and *Eurolophosaurus divaricatus*). The lizard must be able to choose microhabitats that provide suitable conditions of temperature and humidity and, thus, be capable of behaviorally regulating its temperature. It should also be able to avoid predators and find food to survive and grow, and, after

FIGURE 1: Picture from the sand dunes of the middle São Francisco River.

reaching adulthood, to find a sexual partner and reproduce, after fighting other males, if necessary.

The game simulates the dune environment by taking into account its real features, most of which have been specifically investigated on site. The dunes present a periodic topography, with summits, slopes, and valleys. The topography is associated with changes in the plant communities, as different plant species show different affinities for those positions. The topography, in turn, influences the distribution of resources (thermal environment, food) that are used by the animals (arthropods and vertebrates). Different plant species present different abundances in the dunes and provide different resources to the animals, including food. Animal species exhibit specific patterns of aggregation and use the available resources differently. Some are preys and predators of other animal species, and those eaten by the lizards have species-specific nutritional properties. Other species do not have trophic relationships with the lizards but may influence the resources available to them, as well as other kinds of interactions of the lizards with their environment. This is the case, for instance, of a local rodent (*Trinomys yonenagae*) that digs galleries in the sand that can be used as refuges by the lizards.

Daily changes in the position of the sun lead to changes in the temperature of the air and sand and in the air humidity. Seasonal changes in the climate influences the day temperature and humidity, as well as the primary productivity of plants and, therefore, the availability of food resources to animals.

The relevance of building the game inspired in this real case is twofold: (a) it allows the development of a quite realistic and nature-inspired model, given the availability of field information; and (b) it brings to the focus a relevant Brazilian ecosystem from the Caatinga Biome, which is probably one of the poorest known by most of the students in Brazil. Moreover, if the game is used by international students, this is quite an interesting example of a semiarid, savannah-like ecosystem with several endemic species, which is even more poorly known by foreign students.

4. The Computer Game *Calangos*

Calangos is a simulation and action game with 3D visualization in the first and third person. In the currently available game level, the player controls a lizard from one of the three medium-sized endemic species of the sand dunes ecosystem (*Tropidurus psammonastes*, *Cnemidophorus* sp. nov., and *Eurolophosaurus divaricatus*).

It is an electronic educational game that works as a tool to support ecology teaching and learning (and also evolution in Level 4) at the secondary school level. Therefore, it is not a tool for direct exposure of contents to be learned by the student player. Rather, learning is to take place as a consequence of the player's experience in trying to deal with problem situations. While trying to be successful in facing the challenges of the simulated environment, the player has to develop a strategy to control its character and must take into account the game dynamics and rules, and, consequently, the simulated ecological processes. To develop this strategy, the student player has to access dispersion graphs showing relations between variables chosen by him/her from a menu of variables, evaluate what has happened in his/her previous strategy, and modify it aiming at improving the outcomes.

Four game levels are planned for Calangos. At the first level, the student player chooses among the three species of lizards mentioned above and acts as the main character, with the objective of successfully surviving, developing, and reproducing. Level two adds a lizard editor, in which the player can select different morphological, physiological, and behavioral characteristics to build a new lizard to play, with the same objectives of Level 1. The characteristics included in the lizard editor and their variants are also based on biological studies about real lizards. In Level 3, the player goes from a single individual to a population of lizards still in ecological time, with the objective of establishing a dynamical equilibrium for this population. Level 4 is the last level, which changes from the ecological time to the evolutionary time, with the player not only facing population challenges but also having to deal with the evolution of the lizards through many generations. The first level is already developed and Level 2 is currently being implemented; the two last levels are being designed and prototyped. In this paper, the goal is to describe the artificial ecological system modeled on the grounds of the real ecological case described before. This simulated ecology was developed for the first level of the game but also provides a basis for the subsequent levels, being adjusted and expanded for specific requirements. At this first level, the player begins as a lizard early in its life, situated in the dunes terrain, in which there are relevant elements from the ecosystem of the São Francisco River dunes that can be involved in ecological relations with the player-controlled lizard. As a tool to support ecology teaching and learning, the game demands that the student make use of concepts related to different ecological relationships in order to overcome the challenges faced by the lizard to survive, develop, and reproduce successfully. The next sections describe the ecological modeling of the game.

4.1. Modeling Ecology. As the player controls a lizard, the relevant ecological relationships modeled for the game were prey-lizard, predator-lizard, vegetation-lizard, lizard-lizard, and lizard-physical environment (Figure 2). Among the elements involved in ecological relationships, there are various species of plants, typical preys of lizards, various species of lizard predators, and also animals not involved in the food chains in which the lizards are engaged. Other cospecific lizards are also present in the environment, engaging in ecological relationships (e.g., competition for territory, preys, and breeding). Besides, there are abiotic elements that are part of the ecosystem, such as the climate and terrain.

Each element and each relationship were initially described by the biologists that are part of the project team by means of texts and pictures based on the published literature and accumulated knowledge [6, 7]. The terrain, animals, and vegetation were visually modeled in three dimensions, so as to reproduce their actual visual aspect. More importantly, computational models were proposed to describe all the relevant elements and relations and establish the game simulation dynamics.

The simulation models underlying the game define an open-ended environment with multiple outcomes and game experiences and, thus, give rise to a game with a complex and flexible set of rules. In the game, simulation represents consequences to causes in an open manner, without using fixed game rules that heavily constrain player actions [3]. The player is free to move the lizard around the environment, establishing ecological relationships with any of the elements modeled. Each player experiences a different game trajectory every time the game is played. The game strategy is the behavior defined by the player when controlling the lizard at every instant of game play, carrying out the challenge of conducting the lizard to survive, develop, and reproduce.

Game simulation dynamics can be evaluated by the player through dispersion graphs made available within the game, which can show relations between variables chosen by the player. The player can make use of such graphs for decision making, by correlating the different simulation variables along time. The better the player understands the constraints and rules underlying simulation, the better he/she understands the relevant ecological relations and the more successful tends to be his/her game strategy.

It is important to note that the developed computational models had particular requirements, as they should be part of a computer game. The proposed models had to be executed in real time in a 3D rendering game engine and, thus, the algorithms involved could not be computationally expensive. Moreover, the goal was not to build predictive, or even fully descriptive, models of the real case. Instead, the proposed models had to describe the real case only partially, in what was necessary for the game requirements, while keeping enough plausibility and adequacy to be used as a learning tool for ecological relationships, providing valid learning experiences for the players. To put it differently, it was not the aim to accurately represent all variables from the real case, but, instead, to meet the requirement that the players' perception of the elements and their relationships should

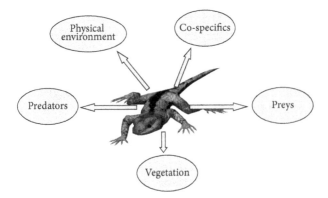

FIGURE 2: Ecological relationships modeled in the game.

be realistic enough for him/her, providing an immersive experience with fidelity to the reality representation. Despite this, it was not arbitrary implementation of the real case, but an approximation of the dynamical ecological model of the real case, considering the demands imposed by the fact that it is a game.

4.1.1. Physical Environment.

The terrain and the climate were selected as physical elements to be modeled, since they are very important for the game dynamics. The artificial terrain corresponded to dunes with height and length in accordance with the sand dunes of the middle São Francisco River in the Ibiraba village (Municipality of Barra, Bahia, Brazil). Terrain limits were the river itself, a village and fences, also following information from the real region.

To model climate, the relevant variables were temperature, air humidity, and rainfall. More specifically, several variables composed the temperature: air temperature, soil temperature, and temperature in burrows made by the endemic rodent Trinomys yonenagae, which are also used by the lizards.

These climate variables affect, directly or indirectly, internal variables of the lizard. They had to model climate dynamics and, therefore, had to vary temporally along the days and months, following seasonal changes. Besides, these variables should also vary spatially, establishing microclimates corresponding to shadows from the vegetation and rodent burrows.

To establish a time flow, a virtual clock was created, parameterized by the computer real clock. Since it is a game and human interaction with the simulation is involved, time flow could not be too slow or too fast, since this could compromise playability. The default time rate is 1 virtual day every 3 minutes and 1 virtual month every 3 days, but the time rate can be configured by the player. This way the student player can experience the day-night cycle and seasons within a single class time. Moreover, a day and night cycle is also visually simulated by varying light conditions in the game and also sun and moon movements in the sky.

The spatial climate variations correspond to microclimates with more amenable or stable climate conditions. These shelters are shadows produced by solar irradiation blockage

by the vegetation and also the gallery systems dug by T. yonenagae. These microclimates are crucial for ectothermic animals, such as the lizards.

Physical Environment: Temperature and Humidity. The first variable modeled was the air temperature and its temporal variation. Analysis of temperature variations in twenty-four hours cycles from data obtained by the Brazilian National Meteorological Institute (INMET) showed a pattern of daily variations following sunrise and sunset (Figure 3). A similar daily pattern, but in opposing phase, can be observed in the case of air humidity: the higher the temperature, the lower the humidity. In rainy days, air humidity is always high and stable.

This daily pattern of air temperature variation was empirically approximated by a time function with a curve equation for day time and a line equation for night time. This daily temperature function was parameterized by the daily highest and lowest temperatures. To determine the highest and lowest temperatures for each day in the game, historical mean values of highest and lowest temperatures for each month during various years were obtained from INMET (Table 1). The mean and standard deviation values were calculated for each month, estimating normal distribution random variables for the highest and lowest temperatures.

To establish the daily temperature variation for each new day simulated in the game, values are drawn from random variables for the highest and lowest temperatures for a given month, parameterizing the temperature function. The following function was proposed and used to model air temperature:

$$T_{air}(t)$$

$$= \begin{cases} \dfrac{T_{max} - T_{nextmin}}{18} \cdot (t - 6) + T_{nextmin}, \\ \qquad\qquad\qquad 0 \leq t \leq 5 \\[2ex] T_{min} + (T_{max} - T_{min}) \cdot \sin\left((t-6)\dfrac{\pi}{16}\right), \\ \qquad\qquad\qquad 5 < t \leq 14 \\[2ex] \dfrac{T_{max} + T_{nextmin}}{2} + \dfrac{T_{max} - T_{nextmin}}{2}\cos\left((t-14)\dfrac{\pi}{14}\right), \\ \qquad\qquad\qquad 14 < t < 22 \\[2ex] \dfrac{T_{max} - T_{nextmin}}{18}(t-30) + T_{nextmin}, \\ \qquad\qquad\qquad 22 \leq t \leq 24, \end{cases}$$

$$(1)$$

where t is the time in hours (0–24 hour), T_{max} is the maximum temperature for the current day, T_{min} is the minimum temperature for the current day, and $T_{nextmin}$ is the minimum temperature for the following day.

More important to the game than the air temperature is the soil temperature, since lizards are in close contact with the sand. To estimate the relationship between air temperature

TABLE 1: Monthly mean temperatures measured in a meteorological station at Barra, Bahia, from 1978 to 2008. Data obtained from INMET (http://www.inmet.gov.br/).

Month	Maximum temperature	Minimum temperature
January	$32.6 \pm 2.6°C$	$21.0 \pm 1.7°C$
February	$32.8 \pm 2.5°C$	$21.4 \pm 1.6°C$
March	$32.3 \pm 2.4°C$	$21.0 \pm 1.6°C$
April	$32.7 \pm 2.0°C$	$20.5 \pm 1.7°C$
May	$32.5 \pm 1.9°C$	$19.1 \pm 2.2°C$
June	$31.9 \pm 1.5°C$	$17.2 \pm 2.0°C$
July	$32.1 \pm 1.3°C$	$16.6 \pm 2.0°C$
August	$33.1 \pm 1.6°C$	$17.5 \pm 2.4°C$
September	$34.5 \pm 1.7°C$	$19.9 \pm 2.1°C$
October	$35.3 \pm 2.1°C$	$22.0 \pm 1.8°C$
November	$33.8 \pm 3.0°C$	$21.7 \pm 1.7°C$
December	$32.9 \pm 2.8°C$	$21.3 \pm 1.5°C$

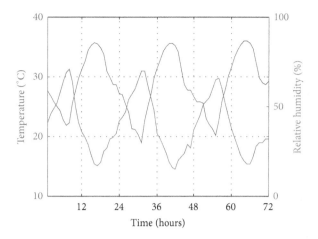

FIGURE 3: Temperature and air humidity measured in a meteorological station at Barra, Bahia, municipality in which the dunes region is located, for a period of 3 days in September 2008. Data obtained from INMET (http://www.inmet.gov.br).

and soil temperature, we relied on measurements made by biologists of the project team. It was verified that soil temperature is higher than air temperature, showing an approximately quadratic relation to the latter and, also, that there is a temporal latency between them, probably due to thermal inertia. Soil temperature was modeled as a quadratic function of the air temperature with a delay of one hour and higher amplitude. The following function was used to model soil temperature:

$$T_{air}(t) - 0.0425 \cdot (T_{air}(t))^2 + 3.9, \qquad (2)$$

where the constants were empirically determined to approximately fit the data.

Temperature in microclimates (climate spatial variations) was also modeled after air temperature. According to the measurements made by the biologists of the project team, temperature inside burrows also had a delay compared to air temperature, but its amplitude variation was much smaller than the latter. Temperature in the shadow was modeled as being more moderate than the air temperature during sunlight hours, with a reduction of up to 5%. Soil temperature in the shadow was up to 10% lower than soil temperature in sand in open sun.

In addition to temperature, air relative humidity is also an important variable. The air humidity function was modeled as a time function similar to temperature, but in opposing phase. The mean value and amplitude variation of humidity in days without rain were determined from daily temperature values, in a relation estimated by real data. For rainy days, humidity is kept saturated at 100%. The following function was used to model air humidity:

$$H(t) = \begin{cases} -3.9 \cdot T_{air}(t) + 158, & \text{if not raining} \\ 100, & \text{if raining,} \end{cases} \qquad (3)$$

where the constants were empirically determined to approximately fit the data.

To determine when rain would occur, it was first assumed that if rain occurred, it would last for the whole day. To determine in which days in a month it would rain, historical rain data from INMET were analyzed, establishing mean values and standard deviations for each month and, thus, a random variable with normal distribution for the monthly amount of precipitated rain. Finally, to determine if it would rain in a certain day in the game, it was assumed that the month with the highest rain level was a month in which it rained every day. During simulation, after drawing a value for rain level in a given month from the respective random variable, this value is divided by the highest rain level to determine an estimated number of rainy days. The estimated number of rainy days divided by the number of days in a month gives a probability of rain in each day in that month.

Figure 4 illustrates the simulated air temperature and humidity in the game. It shows a roughly similar pattern to the real data exhibited in Figure 3. Figure 5 shows the different temperature variables modeled in the game.

4.1.2. Fauna. The ecological relationships of lizards, predators, and preys and also the relationships between the lizard controlled by the player and its cospecifics are elements of the fauna that need to be modeled. Preys and predators present in the game were defined by the biologists in the team, in accordance with the actual animals found in the real ecological case and in studies on the diet of the lizards. These animals were graphically modeled, reproducing their visual aspect and enforcing immersion, and behaviorally modeled, representing actions and activities that are relevant to the ecological relationships.

Predators include the terrestrial, diurnal bird seriema (*Cariama cristata*), a nocturnal owl, the diurnal hawk southern Caracara (*Caracara plancus*), the nocturnal snake jararaca (*Bothrops neuwiedi*), a diurnal Colubridae snake, the

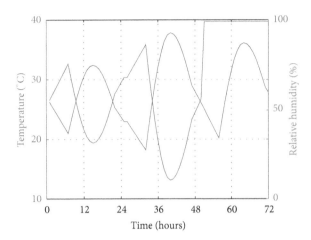

FIGURE 4: Simulated air temperature and humidity for three days, with rain in the third day, for the month of September.

hoary fox (*Lycalopex vetulus*), the wildcat, and the large-sized lizard tegu (*Tupinambis merianae*). All of them have a visual three-dimensional model and exhibit a simple behavior of wandering around the terrain. If a predator approaches a lizard (either the player's or others), it starts chasing the lizard until it gets close enough to attack it (Figure 6). The lizard can only hide from predators if it enters into burrows or if it is close to plants. Every time the player's lizard is attacked, it loses energy. A full predation is not possible upon a single predator attack to preserve game playability.

Ants, termites, maggots, grasshoppers, beetles, and spiders are the preys present in the game, all with a three-dimensional visual representation. We defined three types of behavior for the preys in order to approximate general differences found in the actual behavior of these animals and to add complexity to the building of survival strategies by the students. Beetles, grasshoppers, and maggots keep wandering in the environment, at different velocities. Spiders stay around a plant, moving occasionally. Ants and termites wander in groups around plants. Each prey type appears in different numbers in the environment, depending on whether it is night time or day time.

To eat the preys, the lizard has to get close to them (Figure 7). Each prey type corresponds to a different nutrition level (energy and hydration provided to the lizard) in order to allow the player to experience the dietary diversity observed in the real lizards. These nutrition levels were set based on current biological information in a way that adds plausibility to the model.

There are also interactions between the player's lizard and other cospecific lizards. Male and female cospecific lizards exhibit different behaviors that were inspired by current scientific knowledge on lizard patterns of action during social encounters.

The player always controls a male lizard and every time it gets closer to another male there can be a dispute for territory or for female choice (Figure 8). The dispute starts with head-bobbing, when a lizard nods to indicate that it is ready to fight, trying to make the other individual flee. In the game,

a lizard may flee from the player's lizard with a probability proportional to their size difference but only if the player's lizard executes bobbing. Without bobbing, the other male will always start a fight with the player's character. The fight involves getting close to the other lizard and biting it, taking energy away, proportionally to the difference in size. If the other male reaches a low energy level, it flees and gives up the dispute.

The female lizard interacts with the male lizards only for mating and reproducing. The final objective of the lizard is to live and reproduce as much as possible. The female will only reproduce with a male lizard if it is the only one around her. If two males are near a female, one of them has to flee before the female agrees to mate. As explained above, this may involve fights between the lizards. Once reproduction occurs, the female cannot reproduce again for a whole day. Every time the player's lizard reproduces, its score (which is an egg count) is increased by one. Since the player's lizard begins as an infant, only after twelve months it reaches sexual maturity and is able to reproduce. Before that, the player has to develop and survive.

4.1.3. Flora. The flora present in the game is composed of fifteen different species of plants, all graphically modeled, also to enforce immersion. These plants have a characteristic distribution in the real sand dunes: some of them are found in the summit of the dunes, some in the slope, and others only in the valley. The same distribution is also present in the game simulated environment.

In the real dunes, plants are also part of the food chain of the lizards: some of them produce flowers and some produce both flowers and fruits which can be eaten by the lizards, therefore contributing to the lizard's energy and hydration (Figure 9). Moreover, the production of flowers and fruits by the plants follows seasonal variations. All these aspects were simulated by the game and, therefore, the player can notice the influence of seasonal changes in the lizard's diet.

Besides being a food source, plants are also sources of amenable microclimates. Shadows are placed only around plants (Figure 9), which are also hiding spots for the lizards to avoid predators.

4.1.4. Player's Lizard. The player's lizard is the main character and source for the experience of ecological relationships. Therefore, it is the most complex element in the game, since every ecological interaction comprises features to be developed in this character.

There are many variables and processes related to the player's lizard that were planned to incorporate relevant biological concepts to the game (Figure 10; see Table 2 for variables). The most relevant variables are energy, hydration, and internal temperature.

Energy is a value between 0% and 100% that represents the energy stored by the lizard. Energy lowers every second due to energy expenditure, which involves basal energy expenditure necessary to keep the lizard alive and energy for movement. Basal energy expenditure can vary depending on the internal temperature: temperatures above the ideal range

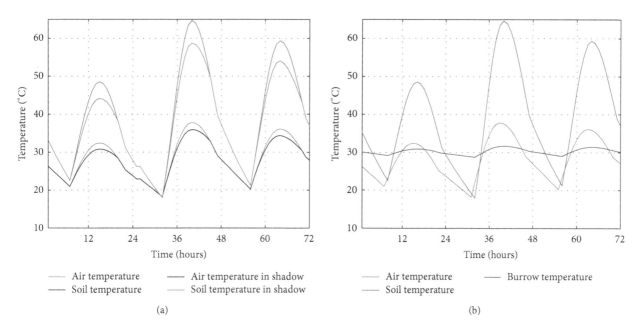

FIGURE 5: Simulated temperatures for three days in different conditions.

FIGURE 6: A predator (seriema) attacking the lizard.

FIGURE 8: Male and female lizards close to the player's lizard.

FIGURE 7: Lizard approaching a prey (spider).

FIGURE 9: Lizard and plants in the dunes. Note the shadows under the plants and the white flower on the floor in front of the lizard.

TABLE 2: Player's lizard main variables.

Variable	Range/unit
Energy	0% to 100%
Hydration	0% to 100%
Internal temperature	0°C to 50°C
Age	0 to 36 months
Energy expenditure	0% to 100% per time unit
Size	0% to 100%

raise the basal energy expenditure, whilst temperatures below that lower the expenditure but make the lizard lethargic. Energy for movement depends on the lizard speed: running speed has higher energy expenditure, walking speed has a lower expenditure, and standing still has no expenditure besides the basal one. Energy rises when the lizard eats preys, flowers, or fruits, with each of them contributing to a different amount of energy and hydration.

The current energy for the player's lizard is defined according to the following equations:

$$\text{Energy}(t) = \text{Energy}(t-1)$$
$$-\text{TotalEnergyCost}(t) + \text{FoodEnergy}(t),$$

$$\text{TotalEnergyCost}(t)$$
$$= \text{BasalEnergyCost}(t) \cdot \text{TemperatureCost}(t)$$
$$\cdot \text{MovementCost}(t),$$

$$\text{BasalEnergyCost}(t) = \text{INITENCONS} \cdot \text{SIZEFACTOR},$$

$$\text{TemperatureCost}(t)$$

$$= \begin{cases} \dfrac{1}{(1 + \text{TCOST}_{\text{low}} \cdot (\text{IT}_{\text{low}} - \text{InternalTemp}(t)))}, \\ \qquad \text{InternalTemp}(t) < \text{IT}_{\text{low}}, \\ 1, \\ \qquad \text{IT}_{\text{low}} \leq \text{InternalTemp}(t) \leq \text{IT}_{\text{high}}, \\ 1 + \text{TCOST}_{\text{high}} \cdot (\text{InternalTemp}(t) - \text{IT}_{\text{high}}), \\ \qquad \text{InternalTemp}(t) > \text{IT}_{\text{high}}, \end{cases}$$

$$\text{MovementCost}(t) = \begin{cases} \text{COSTRUN}, & \text{runnning} \\ \text{COSTWALK}, & \text{walking} \\ 1, & \text{stopped}, \end{cases}$$

(4)

where FoodEnergy is how much energy was gained by eating; INITENCONS is a constant that represents how much time it takes for all initial energy (50%) to be consumed; SIZEFACTOR is a constant proportional to the relative size of the lizard; the bigger the lizard the higher the basal energy expenditure; TCOST is a constant that represents how much total energy expenditure is reduced ($\text{TCOST}_{\text{low}}$) or increased ($\text{TCOST}_{\text{high}}$) when internal temperature is

below the minimum ideal temperature (IT_{low}) or above the maximum ideal temperature (IT_{high}); COSTRUN and COSTWALK are constants that represent how much the total energy expenditure is increased when the lizard is running or walking.

Hydration is also a value between 0% and 100%. It rises when the lizard feeds and lowers gradually along time when air humidity is lower than a threshold of 40%.

The internal temperature is a crucial variable for the lizard, since it is an ectothermic animal that cannot rely on internal metabolism to regulate temperature and, thus, must regulate temperature behaviorally, moving to cooler or warmer places when it needs to diminish or increase its temperature, respectively. The player should try to maintain the lizard's temperature at an ideal range, close to 38°C, a value also inspired by the real species. If the lizards' temperature is out of the ideal range, the basal energy expenditure is altered as explained before. When the internal temperature rises above a maximum temperature value, the lizard dies. If the internal temperature is lower than the ideal range, the lizard does not die but suffers a speed reduction and starts having a growing chance of failing to execute actions such as eating (biting food) or fighting other male lizards.

Internal temperature varies according to the soil temperature, but not instantly, as the lizard has a certain thermal inertia to thermal equilibrium

$$\text{InternalTemp}(t) = \text{InternalTemp}(t-1) + \text{TEMPEQ}$$
$$\cdot (\text{SoilTemp}(t) - \text{InternalTemp}(t-1)),$$

(5)

where t is time in hours, InterTemp is the lizard's internal temperature, SoilTemp is the soil temperature, and TEMPEQ is a constant defining how fast internal temperature converges to soil temperature. At the beginning of the game, the thermal inertia is low, with a high value to TEMPEQ, but TEMPEQ lowers as the lizard's size increases.

The lizard's size increases according to its age. At the end of every month, the mean energy value determines how much the lizard's size increases. If the monthly mean energy was 100%, then the lizard grows at a maximum rate at the end of that month. If the mean energy value is lower than 100%, then the lizard's size increases at a proportionally lower rate. As a lizard grows, its walking and running speed increases, but so does the movement and basal energy expenditures. Therefore, a larger lizard can chase preys faster and also flee faster from predators, but it has to eat more to keep its energy level.

5. Simulating the Ecological Relationships

The computational models described above amount to a representation of the ecological case upon which the game is based. During game play, all these models are effectively operated, providing a simulated environment where the lizard controlled by the player is situated. To increase awareness and understanding of the different ecological processes and relationships, information about the environment and the lizard, besides being simulated, needs to be observed by the player.

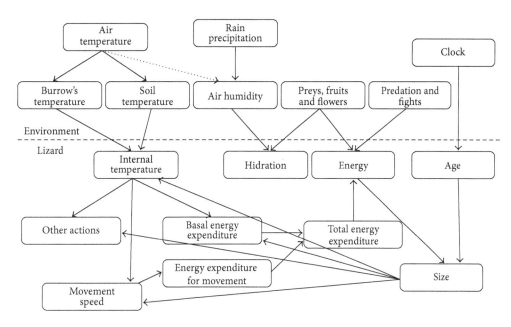

FIGURE 10: Diagram of the most relevant variables for the player's lizard and for the environment, showing also the relations among them.

Therefore, the user interface has to visually present relevant aspects of the various elements. The visualization of elements such as the terrain, fauna, and flora is straightforward, since such elements were graphically modeled and positioned, so the user sees them from a first-person or third-person perspective. Variables, such as soil temperature, internal temperature, and energy, however, have to be exhibited by means of other graphical user interface components.

While playing the game, the student player has instant information regarding the lizard and the environment, such as time, energy level, hydration, internal temperature, air temperature, air humidity, age, sexual maturity, and number of successful reproductions. Moreover, the player can also have access to time graphs for the past 24 hours of many variables, including internal temperature, hydration, air temperature, soil temperature, humidity, energy, and energy expenditure, by means of an interface that allows him/her to select which variables he/she want to plot in two-dimensional dispersion graphs (Figure 11).

To illustrate results obtained by the simulation models during game play, Figure 12 shows a sample of 24-hour graphs of some variables. This sample simulation was done playing the game for one simulated day that lasted 3 minutes in real time. The 24-hour period started at sunrise. The lizard went out in the sun, looking for preys and eating them. As night started, the lizard was attacked by a predator.

As can be noted by the graphs, climate variables are not continuously updated during simulation, but only hourly. This was done because climate variables do not change rapidly and also because it was a way of reducing computational cost.

At sunrise, air and soil temperatures were low and thus the player's lizard had its internal temperature decreased (Figure 12(a)). As the environmental temperature raised and the lizard was under the sun, the lizard's internal temperature

stopped dropping and began to increase. The time where the highest internal temperature was observed did not match the time showing the highest air temperature, as the lizard is more affected by the soil temperature, which has a delay in relation to the air temperature. Besides, the lizards' internal temperature also had a short delay compared to the soil temperature, due to thermal inertia.

While the air temperature increased, the air humidity decreased but never reached a level below 40% (Figure 12(b)). Therefore, the lizard's hydration never decreased in this 24-hour period. But it increased every time the lizard ate a prey and so did its energy value. Every increase in energy and hydration was due to the lizard's feeding.

Energy expenditure varies a lot during this simulation (Figure 12(c)). Every sudden increase with subsequent decrease in energy expenditure was due to the lizard's movements, as running increases energy consumption. Energy expenditure also varied due to changes in basal energy expenditure as the lizard's internal temperature varied. The higher the internal temperature, the higher the basal energy expenditure. At hour 18, energy level dropped considerably. This happened because the player's lizard was attacked repeatedly by a predator while standing still. Every attack promoted an energy level decrease. Afterward, the lizard fled running from predator and got near a tree to hide from it. The lizard stayed in this position as the 24-hour period ended.

Energy, temperatures, humidity, and hydration are variables that can have their instant value and time variation observed by the player inside the game. The sample play described here illustrates how the ecological dynamics inside the game can be evaluated by the player to better understand game play and therefore determine a better game strategy.

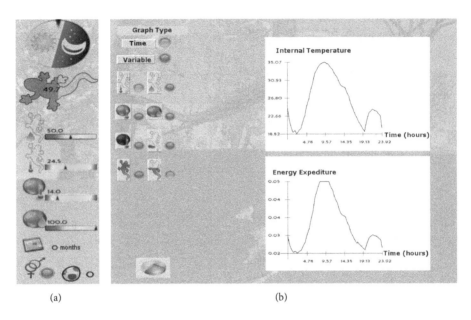

(a)   (b)

FIGURE 11: During game execution, the player has access to instant values of various simulated variables (a) and also to changes along time of these variables by means of a graph generator interface (b).

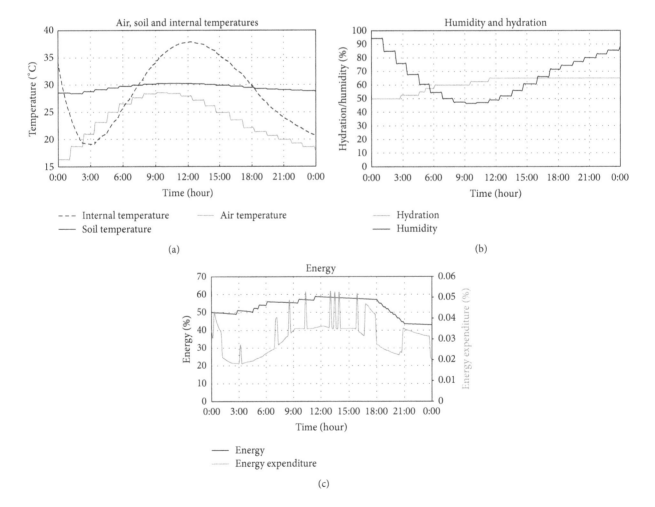

(a)   (b)

(c)

FIGURE 12: Graphs for a 24 h period of game simulation showing temporal variation in (a) temperatures, (b) hydration/humidity, and (c) energy.

6. Using Calangos in the Science Classroom

In order to investigate the educational potential of the game Calangos, we used it in the science classroom as part of a teaching sequence for ecology teaching at the high school level, in a public school in Feira de Santana, Bahia, Brazil. Given the educational goals of the teaching, we focused on its contribution to teaching and learning about ecological niche, one of the key subject matters in ecology, which can be addressed through the game.

In many textbooks, the ecological niche is treated as an organism's "profession" in the ecological systems, in connection with Whittaker and colleagues' proposal of distinguishing between niche and habitat [12]. Nevertheless, as discussed by Sepulveda and El-Hani, this conception of niche is inadequate to build an understanding that can help teaching and learning about evolution and, for that matter, also ecology, since it does not stress the role of limiting factors and competition in either the structuring of ecological systems or the evolutionary process [13]. Other conceptions about niche are more appropriate for these educational goals, such as Hutchinson's conception of the niche as a n-dimensional hypervolume delimited by the environmental conditions and resources defining the requirements of a species to survive and exhibit its mode of living [14].

We developed the teaching sequence structured around Calangos. In this study, we were guided by the hypothesis that Calangos could help in promoting the construction of an understanding of this conception of ecological niche, more specifically, based on the analysis of thermal regulation as one of the challenges for lizard survival implemented in the game. The teaching sequence include six steps: (1) presentation of the game and its playing dynamics, (2) use of the game by students pairs, (3) proposal of hypotheses for the survival difficulties faced by the lizards (in the game) by means of discursive interactions between students and teacher, (4) discussion of the challenge of thermal regulation in the game, (5) orientation for the students to consider the behavior of the variables found at the side bar and the graphs made available by the game (since they typically pay scant attention to them while playing), and (6) an explicit approach of the Hutchinsonian niche by the teacher, applied to the context of thermal regulation and using students' experience with the game.

The teaching sequence was implemented in three high school first year classes in two 100-minutes sessions, involving 45 students ranging from 15 to 16 years. Both sessions were fully videotaped, comprising 10 recording hours. In the video-taped classes, we selected episodes in which discursive interactions between students and between them and the teacher allowed us to evaluate the students' behavioral engagement in the activities [15] and the meaning making process about the ecological niche in the context of thermal regulation [16]. Moreover, we applied a questionnaire in a pretest-posttest design in order to evaluate the game role in promoting conceptual learning. The questionnaire comprises three task situations evaluating students' understanding about (1) the relation between environmental temperature variation and body temperature variation in ectothermic animals, (2) the behavioral strategies used by these animals for regulating body temperature, and (3) the concept of ecological niche. For evaluating (1), a graph was presented, showing the increase of environmental temperature and the increase of the lizard internal body temperature along time, followed by one question concerning what information the students were able to extract from the graph, and another question requiring that they explain why frequent temperature variations in a semiarid environment challenged lizard survival. For (2), a picture showing lizard behavioral changes in different periods of the day was provided, and then the students were asked to explain why the lizard remained below a rock at noon, how the shown behavioral changes were related to the relation between environmental and body temperature previously analyzed, and what those behavioral changes revealed with regard to the lizard survival strategies. For (3), the questionnaire provided a scenario describing the sand dunes of the middle São Francisco River, which provided the real case for developing Calangos, and the students were prompted to write a text describing the challenges faced by the lizards to survive and reproduce in that environment. To write the text, they were asked to use the following terms: ecological niche, environmental temperature, soil temperature, lizard internal temperature, hypothermia, hyperthermia, survival, predator, and reproduction. We obtained questionnaires for 18 students in both pretest and posttest. We discuss below some results for providing a glimpse of the results obtained with Calangos use in the science classroom. Finally, to evaluate students' experience while playing Calangos, we asked them to answer the following simple question: "what did you think of the game Calangos?"

In the classroom, discursive interactions during which the biological phenomena simulated in Calangos were discussed, we could observe that the students were capable of articulating their experiences while playing the game with the challenges for the survival of an ectothermic animal. The following excerpt provides an example:

> Teacher. What else happened in the game?
>
> Students. We died.
>
> Teacher. Why?
>
> Student 1. Due to high temperature.
>
> Student 2. Due to malnutrition and low temperature.
>
> Teacher. How do you solve this problem, death by high temperature?
>
> Student 3. Isn't just stay in the shadow?
>
> Student 4. But then the lizard dies from the cold.
>
> Student 3. That's true.
>
> Student 5. Then, he should go to the shadow and to the sun to even the body temperature. Not to even… to adjust.
>
> Student 6. To balance the temperature.
>
> Teacher. Kind of adjusting. Why does this happen with lizards? Why do lizards have "cold blood"? What would "cold blood" mean?

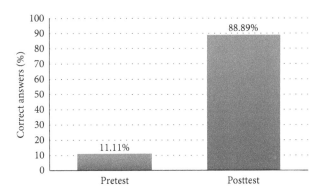

FIGURE 13: Percentage of correct answers to the question about the behavioral strategies used by lizards for regulating body temperature.

Student 5. It depends on the sun to keep...

Teacher. It depends on the environment to regulate internal temperature. They are ectothermic animals.

This finding agrees with the questionnaire data, in which most students (12 out of 18) showed in their answers that they understood how the body temperature of ectothermic animals varies with the environmental temperature. One student, for instance, wrote in the pretest that temperature variation common in semiarid environments are a challenge for the life of a lizard that needs to maintain a stable body temperature. In the posttest, the same student showed a deeper understanding of the phenomenon at stake, writing that the animal needs to control its internal temperature and, thus, should use behavioral strategies to regulate body temperature, exposing itself to the sun or moving to shadowed microenvironments depending on how the body temperature varies with the environmental temperature. With the experience of playing and discussing about Calangos in the classroom, this student's understanding shifted from a superficial view on lizard body temperature control to a deeper view including important aspects related to behavioral strategies for temperature regulation.

When the students were asked in the questionnaire to explain why a lizard remained below a rock at noon, their answers in the pretest did not relate the fact that lizard stayed below the rock to body temperature regulation (Figure 13). As an example, we can mention the following answer: "he is resting, because the sun is too hot and he goes below the rock to rest". In the posttest, in turn, most of them explained that behavior as a strategy used by the animal to keep its body temperature within an adequate range (Figure 13). This student's answer provides an example: "environmental temperature is too high at this time and then it protects itself in the shadow, so that its body temperature is not raised, and, thus, it avoids death."

Concerning the concept of ecological niche, the learning outcomes were much more limited. In the pretest no student used the term "ecological niche" in their texts. In the posttest, only four students used the term "ecological niche" in their texts, suggesting that most of them did not master its meaning after the intervention. This interpretation is reinforced by

answers like the following: "the lizard living in this environment (sand dunes) depends on the soil temperature and the ecological niche to survive." These limited outcomes are likely to be related to the rather abstract nature of the Hutchinsonian niche, showing that it will be necessary in future applications of the teaching sequence using Calangos to expand on the its discussion in the classroom, paying also more attention to the shifting from the more concrete situations experienced by the students in the game and the more abstract reasoning involving in treating the niche as a n-dimensional hypervolume.

Other students' answers showed promising outcomes for this shift to a more abstract understanding of the niche, since they identified environmental factors affecting the lizard chances of survival and reproduction, which amount to an important step towards formulating the Hutchinsonian interpretation of the niche. In the pretest, 11 students mentioned some biotic and/or abiotic variable influencing the survival and reproduction chances. In the posttest, this was observed in 17 out of the 18 students. Here is an example: "there are several challenges that the lizard should face, such as escaping predators, feeding, and finding water. But the worst problem is how to keep the temperature and this demands survival strategies, such as staying in the shadow" (posttest).

Besides supporting conceptual learning, the game Calangos motivated the behavioral engagement of the students in interpreting and discussing the biological phenomena simulated in the game, as we could observe in the classroom discursive interactions. This was also shown independently in the questionnaire answers. All 18 students regarded the game as interesting, fun, and educationally important. A student, for instance, described her experience with the game as follows: "very nice and interesting, because we end up getting involved in the game. I felt as I was myself there".

7. Conclusion

Electronic games can be a relevant resource for ecology teaching and learning. Calangos is a game that can aid in this task by providing a simulated scenario based on a real ecological case. The simulated ecosystem developed for the game includes a variety of ecological relationships related to a lizard controlled by the student player. The computational models developed, which were discussed in this paper, define a complex network of interrelated elements. To achieve survival and reproductive success, the player must define his/her strategy, facing challenges such as that of deciding when and what to hunt and eat, while paying close attention to the behavioral regulation of the lizard's temperature. To better define a game strategy, the player must understand, however, the game mechanics and this entails that he/she must comprehend the ecological dynamics. In this way, ecological contents can be learned in an active and consistent manner.

An important asset for the development of the simulated ecosystem for the game was the presence of a multidisciplinary team of biological, science education, and computer science researchers. During the whole development process, software requirements were defined and reviewed to better cope with both biological plausibility and educational objectives. We already investigated the game potential for promoting ecology learning and supporting ecology teaching in the classroom, as discussed above, producing evidence for its contributions for teaching and learning about key ecological matters, such as thermal regulation through behavior in ectothermic animals. We found some limits, however, in promoting learning of more abstract concepts, such as the Hutchinsonian niche, through a teaching sequence structure around the game. The next step in the project is to assess and validate the game as a learning tool in a broader set of high school classrooms, using a new version of the teaching sequence addressing the limits observed in this previous study.

Conflict of Interests

The authors declare that there is no conflict of interests regarding the publication of this paper.

Acknowledgments

The authors would like to acknowledge Marta Vargens, Yupanqui Julho Muñoz, Emerson Silva de Oliveira, Thiago do Carmo Lima, Jairo Henrique dos Santos Calmon, Carlos Bezerra, Paulo César de Alencar Gonçalves Filho, Fladmy Alves de Souza, Jônatas dos Santos Correia, Leonardo Lima and Eduardo de Oliveira, who have participated in the research project, and also the support of FINEP, CNPq, Fapesp, Fapesb, and UEFS. CNPq granted PLBR and CNEL a research fellowship during the development of this work. They are also thankful to the students involved in the high school classroom study reported here.

References

[1] E. Sander, P. Jelemenská, and U. Kattmann, "Towards a better understanding of ecology," *Journal of Biological Education*, vol. 40, no. 3, pp. 119–123, 2006.

[2] S. M. Scheiner and M. R. Willig, "A general theory of ecology," *Theoretical Ecology*, vol. 1, no. 1, pp. 21–28, 2008.

[3] T. R. Cottrell, "Capturing difficult botanical concepts with a net of previous knowledge," *The American Biology Teacher*, vol. 66, no. 6, pp. 441–445, 2004.

[4] J. D. Proctor and B. M. H. Larson, "Ecology, complexity, and metaphor," *BioScience*, vol. 55, no. 12, pp. 1065–1068, 2005.

[5] B. H. Munson, "Ecological misconceptions," *Journal of Environmental Education*, vol. 25, no. 4, pp. 30–34, 1994.

[6] P. L. B. Rocha, L. P. Queiroz, and J. R. Pirani, "Plant species and habitat structure in a sand dune field in the brazilian Caatinga: a homogeneous habitat harbouring an endemic biota," *Revista Brasileira de Botânica*, vol. 27, no. 4, pp. 739–755, 2004.

[7] P. L. B. Rocha and M. T. Rodrigues, "Electivities and resource use by an assemblage of lizards endemic to the dunes of the São Francisco River, northeastern Brazil," *Papéis Avulsos de Zoologia*, vol. 45, pp. 261–284, 2005.

[8] D. Charsky, "From edutainment to serious games: a change in the use of game characteristics," *Games and Culture*, vol. 5, no. 2, pp. 177–198, 2010.

[9] C. C. Abt, *Serious Games*, University Press of America, Lanham, Md, USA, 1987.

[10] D. R. Michael and S. L. Chen, *Serious Games: Games that Educate, Train, and Inform*, Thomson Course Technology, Boston, Mass, USA, 2005.

[11] D. Fundenberg and D. K. Levine, *The Theory of Learning in Games*, MIT Press, Cambridge, Mass, USA, 1998.

[12] J. H. Whittaker, S. A. Levin, and R. B. Root, "Niche, habitat and ecotope," *American Naturalist*, vol. 107, no. 955, pp. 321–338, 1973.

[13] C. A. S. Sepulveda and C. N. El-Hani, "Adaptacionismo versus exaptacionismo: o que este debate tem a dizer ao ensino de evolução?" *Ciência & Ambiente*, vol. 36, pp. 93–124, 2008.

[14] G. E. Hutchinson, "Concluding remarks," *Cold Spring Harbor Symposium on Quantitative Biology*, vol. 22, pp. 415–427, 1957.

[15] J. A. Fredricks, P. C. Blumenfeld, and A. H. Paris, "School engagement: potential of the concept, state of the evidence," *Review of Educational Research*, vol. 74, no. 1, pp. 59–109, 2004.

[16] E. F. Mortimer and P. H. Scott, *Meaning Making in Secondary Science Classrooms*, Open University Press, Maidenhead, UK, 2003.

15

Analytical Ballistic Trajectories with Approximately Linear Drag

Giliam J. P. de Carpentier

Linnaeusstraat 32 bis, 3553 CE Utrecht, The Netherlands

Correspondence should be addressed to Giliam J. P. de Carpentier; giliam@decarpentier.nl

Academic Editor: Jue Wang

This paper introduces a practical analytical approximation of projectile trajectories in 2D and 3D roughly based on a linear drag model and explores a variety of different planning algorithms for these trajectories. Although the trajectories are only approximate, they still capture many of the characteristics of a real projectile in free fall under the influence of an invariant wind, gravitational pull, and terminal velocity, while the required math for these trajectories and planners is still simple enough to efficiently run on almost all modern hardware devices. Together, these properties make the proposed approach particularly useful for real-time applications where accuracy and performance need to be carefully balanced, such as in computer games.

1. Introduction

A ballistic trajectory is the path of an object that is dropped, thrown, served, launched, or shot but has no active propulsion during its actual flight. Consequently, the trajectory is fully determined by a given initial velocity and the effects of gravity and air resistance. Mortars, bullets, particles, and jumping computer game characters (between key presses) are all examples of ballistics, while actively controlled aircraft and rocket-propelled grenades are not.

Describing the exact motion of an object in free fall is a classic problem that can become quite complex when including effects like drag, turbulence, height-dependent medium pressure, position-dependent gravity, buoyancy, lift, and rotation. For this research paper, the problem will be approached on a relatively pragmatic level, as it will be based on a reasonably simple drag model that does not consider the dynamics of projectile rotation and assumes that wind, gravity, and terminal velocity all remain fixed over the whole trajectory. As a result, some accuracy will be sacrificed for the sake of computational efficiency and flexibility in practical use, while still maintaining much of the essence of the ballistic motion through a resistive medium. Although such a choice does not make much sense for most scientific and military applications, it does make sense for computer games,

where performance is typically more important than physical correctness.

Currently, computer games hardly ever use trajectories influenced by air resistance when complex planning is required. That might partially be because implementing a computer player that is capable of quickly calculating the ideal angle to fire a mortar with a fixed initial speed to hit a given target, for example, is harder when having to take into account drag and wind conditions. In fact, the added complexity and computational intensity that would be required for working with many of the current drag models might simply not be justifiable.

This paper introduces a trajectory model that is designed to fit in the gap where working with accurate models would be too complex and working with simple dragless parabola-shaped trajectories would be insufficient. The proposed model's use and practicality will be demonstrated by covering a number of its properties and showing how these trajectories can be planned in a variety of ways.

In Section 2, previous work is shortly considered. In Section 3, the new model will be introduced and qualitatively compared to other models. In Section 4, the first planner is covered. Other planners use a different space as explained in Section 5 and will be covered in Section 6. This is followed by a discussion of Future Work in Section 7, the Conclusion in

```
double GetTimeToTargetRWithMinimalInitialSpeed(double k, double vInfinity,
                                               double rX, double rY) {
    //1. Start by getting coefficients for the function f(t) = a4*t∧4 + a3*t∧3
    //+ a1*t + a0 which is 0 at the sought time-to-target t. Solving f(t) = 0
    //for t > 0 is equivalent to solving e(u) = f(1/u)*u∧4 = a0*u∧4 + a1*u∧3 +
    //a3*u + a4 = 0 for u where u = 1/t, but the latter is more well-behaved,
    //being a strictly concave function for u > 0 for any set of valid inputs,
    //so solve e(u)=0 for u instead by converging from an upper bound towards
    double kVInfinity = k * vInfinity, rr = rX * rX + rY * rY; //the root and
    double a0 = -rr, a1 = a0 * k, a3 = k * kVInfinity * rY; //return 1/u.
    double a4 = kVInfinity * kVInfinity;
    double maxInvRelError = 1.0E6; //Use an achievable inverse error bound.
    double de, e, uDelta = 0;
    //2. Set u to an upper bound by solving e(u) with a3 = a1 = 0, clamped by
    //the result of a Newton method's iteration at u = 0 if positive.
    double u = std::sqrt(kVInfinity / std::sqrt(rr));
    if (rY < 0) u = std::min(u, -vInfinity / rY);
    //3. Let u monotonically converge to e(u)'s positive root using a modified
    //Newton's method that speeds up convergence for double roots, but is likely
    //to overshoot eventually. Here, "e"= e(u) and "de"=de(u)/du.
    for (int it = 0; it < 10; ++it, uDelta = e / de, u -= 1.9 * uDelta) {
        de = a0 * u; e = de + a1; de = de + e; e = e * u;
        de = de * u + e; e = e * u + a3; de = de * u + e; e = e * u + a4;
        if (!(e < 0 && de < 0)) break; //Overshot the root.
    }
    u += 0.9 * uDelta; //Trace back to the unmodified Newton method's output.
    //4. Continue to converge monotonically from the overestimated u to e(u)'s
    //only positive root using Newton's method.
    for (int it = 0; uDelta * maxInvRelError > u && it < 10; ++it) {
        de = a0 * u; e = de + a1; de = de + e; e = e * u;
        de = de * u + e; e = e * u + a3; de = de * u + e; e = e * u + a4;
        uDelta = e / de; u -= uDelta;
    }
    //5. Return the solved time t to hit [rX, rY], or 0 if no solution exists.
    return u > 0 ?1/u: 0;
}
```

ALGORITHM 1: Specialized C++ Quartic Solver.

Section 8, and the References. The included Algorithms 1 and 2 contain C++ functions that efficiently solve the two most complex planning problems.

2. Previous Work

The motion of ballistic projectiles has been covered in many physics papers and textbooks, and all of these use their own set of assumptions to create an approximate model of the forces acting on a projectile. Although some ballistics research focuses on effects like shape and orientation [1], spin [2], or (sub)orbital flight [3], most works on ballistic trajectories assume a fixed gravitational pull and use a simplified drag model. These drag models typically ignore all effects of in-flight rotation and are only dependent on the local velocity relative to the medium and on a given fixed terminal velocity or drag coefficient.

The used drag model influences both realism and computational complexity. For example, when no drag force is applied, the trajectory will always be a parabola, which is easy to work with and plan for. If the drag force is chosen to be linear in velocity, an explicit function describing the trajectory can be found by solving a set of linear differential equations [4]. This transcendental function is already computationally harder to calculate and even harder to plan with (i.e., solve for) [5]. To approximate reality even better, the drag force can be made quadratic in the object's velocity relative to the medium. But as no exact analytic solution for the resulting trajectory exists, calculating a trajectory requires either crude approximation or numerical integration, and planning a trajectory requires reiteration [6–8].

The research in this paper is based on a novel approximation of the trajectory function that follows from the linear drag model, sacrificing some of its moderate accuracy for a further increase in both efficiency and flexibility.

3. The Approximated Trajectory

3.1. Ballistic Parameters. Before presenting the proposed trajectory function and its properties, the necessary ballistic

```cpp
double GetTimeToTargetRGivenInitialSpeedS(double k, double vInfinity, double rX,
                                          double rY, double s, bool highArc) {
  //1. Start by getting coefficients for the function f(t) = a4*t^4 + a3*t^3
  //+ a2*t^2 + a1*t + a0 which is 0 at the sought time-to-target t. Solving
  //f(t) = 0 for t > 0 is equivalent to solving e(u) = f(1/u)*u^3 = a0*u^3 +
  //a1*u^2 + a2*u + a3 + a4/u for u where u = 1/t, but the latter is more
  //well-behaved, being a strictly convex function for u > 0 for any set of
  //inputs iff a solution exists, so solve for e(u) = 0 instead by converging
  //from a high or low bound towards the closest root and return 1/u.
  double kRX = k * rX, kRY = k * rY, kRXSq = kRX * kRX, sS = s * s;
  double twoKVInfinityRY = vInfinity * (kRY + kRY), kVInfinity = k * vInfinity;
  double a0 = rX * rX + rY * rY, a1 = (k + k) * a0;
  double a2 = kRXSq + kRY * kRY + twoKVInfinityRY - sS;
  double a3 = twoKVInfinityRY * k, a4 = kVInfinity * kVInfinity;
  double maxInvRelError = 1.0E6; //Use an achievable inverse error bound.
  double maxV0YSq = sS - kRXSq;//maxV0YSq is the max squared "V0.y" that leaves
  double e, de, u, uDelta = 0; //enough "V0.x"to reach rX horizontally.
  //2. Set u to a lower/upper bound for the high/low arc, respectively.
  if (highArc) {// Get smallest u vertically moving rY at max possible +v0.y.
     double minusB = std::sqrt(maxV0YSq) - kRY;
     double determ = minusB * minusB - (twoKVInfinityRY + twoKVInfinityRY);
     u = (kVInfinity + kVInfinity) / (minusB + std::sqrt(determ));
     maxInvRelError = -maxInvRelError; // Convergence over negative slopes.
  }else if (rY < 0) {// Get largest u vertically moving rY at most neg. v0.y.
     double minusB = -std::sqrt(maxV0YSq) - kRY;
     double determ = minusB * minusB - (twoKVInfinityRY + twoKVInfinityRY);
     u = (minusB - std::sqrt(determ)) / (rY + rY);
     //Clamp the above bound by the largest u that reaches rX horizontally.
     u = std::min(s / rX - k, u);
  }else u = s / std::sqrt(a0) - k; // Get the (largest) u hitting rX
  //horizontally a.s.a.p. while launching in the direction of [rX,rY].
  //3. Let u monotonically converge to e(u)'s closest root using a modified
  //Newton's method, almost scaling the delta as if the solution is a double
  int it = 0; //root. Note that "e" = e(u) * u^2 and "de" = de(u)/du * u^2.
  for (; it < 12; ++it, uDelta = e / de, u -= 1.9 * uDelta) {
     de = a0 * u; e = de + a1; de = de + e; e = e * u + a2; de = de * u + e;
     e = e * u + a3; e = (e * u + a4) * u; de = de * u * u - a4;
     if (!(u > 0 && de * maxInvRelError > 0 && e > 0)) break; //Overshot.
  }
  u += 0.9 * uDelta; //Trace back to unmodified Newton method's output.
  //4. Continue to converge monotonically to e(u)'s closest root using
  //Newton's method from the last known conservative estimate on the convex
  //function. (Note that in practice, u will have converged enough in <12
  for (; u > 0 && it < 12; ++it) {  //iterations iff a solution does exists.)
     de = a0 * u; e = de + a1; de = de + e; e = e * u + a2; de = de * u + e;
     e = e * u + a3; e = (e * u + a4) * u; de = de * u * u - a4;
     uDelta = e / de; u -= uDelta;
     if (!(de * maxInvRelError > 0)) break; //Wrong side of the convex "dip".
     if (uDelta * maxInvRelError < u && u > 0) return 1 / u; //5a. Found it!
  }
  //5b. If no solution was found, return 0. This only happens if s (minus
  //a small epsilon) is too small to have a solution, the target is at the
  return 0; //origin, or the parameters are so extreme they cause overflows.
}
```

ALGORITHM 2: Specialized C++ Quartic Solver.

parameters will be defined here first. Starting with a general note, vector variables in this paper are always distinguished from scalar variables by the $\rightarrow$ symbol above their names. Also, the length of any vector $\vec{a}$ is denoted as $\|\vec{a}\|$, which is equal to $\sqrt{\vec{a} \cdot \vec{a}}$, where $\cdot$ is the dot product.

A ballistic object is assumed to be launched from the initial position $\vec{p}_0$ with the initial velocity $\vec{v}_0$ at time $t = 0$. Furthermore, the object will be travelling through a medium (e.g., the air) which itself travels at the fixed (wind) velocity $\vec{v}_{medium}$. It is also pulled by gravity at the fixed gravitational acceleration g, which is roughly $9.81\,\mathrm{m/s^2}$ for "earthly" applications. The amount of drag k while moving through the medium is defined as follows.

$$k = \frac{1}{2} \frac{g}{\|\vec{v}_{terminal}\|}. \qquad (1)$$

Here, $\vec{v}_{terminal}$ is the invariant terminal velocity relative to $\vec{v}_{medium}$ that is reached eventually as the forces of gravity and air resistance finally cancel each other out. On earth, that is equivalent to saying that $\vec{v}_{terminal}$ is the fixed velocity that is approached when the object is dropped from an enormous height on a windless day. Lastly, the absolute terminal velocity $\vec{v}_\infty$, being the absolute velocity approached when time t goes to ∞, is therefore

$$\vec{v}_\infty = \vec{v}_{terminal} + \vec{v}_{medium}. \qquad (2)$$

Together, $\vec{p}_0$, $\vec{v}_0$, $\vec{v}_\infty$, and k uniquely define a trajectory in the proposed model. To give a real-world example of the parameters defined above, suppose a tennis ball with a terminal velocity of $30\,\mathrm{m/s}$ is served at $50\,\mathrm{m/s}$ at a $30°$ angle from the $381\,\mathrm{m}$ high roof of the Empire State building into a $10\,\mathrm{m/s}$ horizontal wind in 2D. Then, $\vec{p}_0 = [0, 381]$, $\vec{v}_0 = [50\cos(30°), 50\sin(30°)] \approx [43.30, 25]$, $k = 0.1635$, and $\vec{v}_\infty = [-10, -30]$. The trajectory resulting from these values is shown in Figure 1.

3.2. Deriving the Trajectory Function. In terms of the parameters defined above, the differential equation for the exact linear drag model has the following analytic solution:

$$\vec{p}_{linear}(t) = \frac{1}{2k} (\vec{v}_0 - \vec{v}_\infty)\left(1 - e^{-2kt}\right) + \vec{v}_\infty t + \vec{p}_0. \qquad (3)$$

This function calculates the 2D or 3D position $\vec{p}_{linear}$ on a trajectory at time t where $t \geq 0$. The above function is far from new and will not be explained here in detail, as it has already been covered in many textbooks [4], occasionally even targeting game developers in particular [9] (albeit with slightly different notation and parameter definitions).

The function above will not be used directly in this paper. Instead, it will be approximated by substituting its exponential function e^x with the first degree rational function $(2 + x)/(2 - x)$ shown in Figure 2. One of the reasons for selecting this approximation over all possible other approximations to e^x is that it has a value, first derivative and second derivative that match those of e^x at $x = 0$. This means that it approximates e^x near $x = 0$ well and therefore will guarantee a good approximation of $\vec{p}_{linear}(t)$ near $t = 0$. Furthermore,

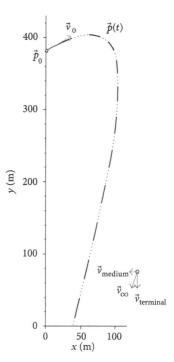

FIGURE 1: Serving a tennis ball from the Empire State Building upwind.

the first derivative of $(2 + x)/(2 - x)$ monotonically decreases from 1 to 0 as x tends from 0 to $-\infty$, similar to the first derivative of e^x itself. When used to approximate e^x in $\vec{p}_{linear}(t)$, this property will cause the initial velocity to monotonically converge to the terminal velocity over time. Note that no polynomial approximation of e^x has this specific property, and of all possible rational functions that do possess the above properties, the proposed approximation is the simplest and thus the most efficient. Lastly, its inverse is also a first degree rational function, resulting in relatively simple algebraic solutions for all (otherwise algebraic) equations that use it to approximate e^x.

When the exponential function in $\vec{p}_{linear}(t)$ is substituted by the rational approximation, the following function is the result

$$\vec{p}(t) = \frac{(\vec{v}_0 + kt\vec{v}_\infty)\,t}{1 + kt} + \vec{p}_0. \qquad (4)$$

Because of the aforementioned properties, $\vec{p}(t)$ will not only be more efficient to compute on modern computers, but it will also still share many of its characteristics with $\vec{p}_{linear}(t)$ and allow trajectory planning to be done with relative ease. The remainder of this paper mainly revolves around exploring these and other properties of $\vec{p}(t)$ together with their implications.

3.3. A Qualitative Comparison. As $\vec{p}(t)$ is only an approximation, it will differ from the linear drag model's trajectory function it is based on, as well as from the results of other models. For comparison purposes, the trajectories that follow from launching three different sport balls using four different

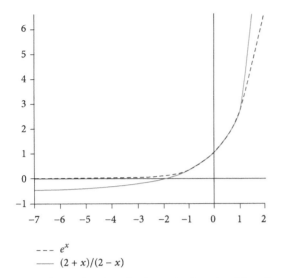

$$--- \quad e^x$$
$$\underline{\qquad} \quad (2 + x)/(2 - x)$$

FIGURE 2: Approximating e^x using a simple rational function.

models are plotted side by side in Figure 3. All balls are launched at an 45° angle at 50 m/s on a windless earthly day ($g = 9.81 \text{ m/s}^2$). The different drag models are calibrated to respect the respective ball's terminal velocities (except for the dragless model, which always has an infinite terminal velocity).

Each of the alternating thick and thin segments in the trajectories shown in Figure 3 (and in all other trajectory plots in this paper, for that matter) represents a projectile's movement over a period of exactly one second, making it possible to not only compare the shapes of the trajectories but also their local speeds. The results from the novel $\vec{p}(t)$ function are plotted in black, the results from the linear drag model $\vec{p}_{\text{linear}}(t)$ are plotted in blue, and the results of the physically (most) correct quadratic drag model simulation $\vec{p}_{\text{quadratic}}(t)$ are plotted in green. Lastly, the red parabola $\vec{p}_{\text{dragless}}(t)$ represents the trajectory of each of the three balls in a perfect vacuum (in other words, when there is no drag and $\vec{v}_\infty$'s length goes to infinity).

When comparing the trajectories for $\vec{p}(t)$ to the results of the two more accurate drag models, they are certainly different but they still reasonably mimic these in look, feel, and properties. Consequently, the proposed model is physically at least quite plausible and is probably accurate enough for most computer game purposes. Furthermore, in some cases, $\vec{p}(t)$ is actually closer to $\vec{p}_{\text{quadratic}}(t)$ than $\vec{p}_{\text{linear}}(t)$, making it in these cases arguably even physically more accurate than the model it is approximating to. Lastly, the trajectories for all three drag models perfectly approach $\vec{p}_{\text{dragless}}(t)$ when $\vec{v}_\infty$'s length goes to infinity.

3.4. Exploring Some of p(t)'s Properties. The function $\vec{p}(t)$ given by (4) can be factored, solved, and parameterized in many different ways. For example, basic algebra allows it to be written as $\vec{p}(t) = a\vec{v}_0 + \vec{b}$ as well, where $a = t/(1 + kt)$ and $\vec{b} = \vec{v}_\infty(t - a) + \vec{p}_0$. Note that in this form, the initial velocity is separated from all other factors, and it becomes immediately

clear that $\vec{p}(t)$ is a linear function in terms of $\vec{v}_0$. This implies that when launching multiple objects at some $t = 0$ with all properties equal except for the initial velocity, each of these objects has the same value for a and for $\vec{b}$. This feature may be exploited in particle explosion systems on modern GPUs, for example, requiring only one evaluation of a and $\vec{b}$ per frame per explosion (layer) on the CPU and one MAD (multiply-and-add) GPU instruction per particle per frame to calculate each particle's position.

The linearity of $\vec{p}(t)$ in terms of the initial velocity $\vec{v}_0$ can also be used for many other purposes. For example, in Figure 4, $\vec{p}(t)$ is used to calculate the green and blue positions for two different "extreme" initial velocities, which are interpreted as the top-left and bottom-right positions of a textured rectangle or *quad*. Note that the (signed) size of the quad is thus simply $\vec{p}_{\text{green}}(t) - \vec{p}_{\text{blue}}(t) = (a\vec{v}_{0,\text{green}} + \vec{b}) - (a\vec{v}_{0,\text{blue}} + \vec{b}) = a(\vec{v}_{0,\text{green}} - \vec{v}_{0,\text{blue}})$. Furthermore, all the bilinearly interpolated texels within this quad, including the red one, will move over $\vec{p}(t)$ trajectories themselves as well by virtue of the linearity in terms of the initial velocities. In other words, each texel will follow a $\vec{p}(t)$ trajectory with some initial velocity that is interpolated bilinearly between the different extreme initial velocities, as if the individual texels themselves are under direct control of a physics simulation. Consequently, it should be physically plausible to use the above to scale sprites and billboards of, for example, simple smoke (for which $\vec{v}_\infty$ would typically be upwards to simulate positive buoyancy), explosion debris, and fireworks.

Many other useful properties can easily be derived from $\vec{p}(t)$ as well. For example, the velocity $\vec{v}(t)$ of $\vec{p}(t)$ is

$$\vec{v}(t) = \frac{\partial \vec{p}(t)}{\partial t} = \frac{\vec{v}_0 + kt(2 + kt)\vec{v}_\infty}{(1 + kt)^2}. \tag{5}$$

The nonnegative time $t_{\text{top},\vec{n}}$ at which the trajectory hits its maximum in the direction of a given unit-length vector $\vec{n}$ can be found by solving $\vec{v}(t) \cdot \vec{n} = 0$ for t assuming that the direction to find the maximum in is pointing away from $\vec{v}_\infty$ (i.e., $\vec{v}_\infty \cdot \vec{n} < 0$). If that assumption is false, then the top will be at time $t = 0$. The solution to both cases is summarized by the following formula:

$$t_{\text{top},\vec{n}} = \frac{\sqrt{1 - \min(0, (\vec{v}_0 \cdot \vec{n})/(\vec{v}_\infty \cdot \vec{n}))} - 1}{k}. \tag{6}$$

This $t_{\text{top},\vec{n}}$ may be used with (4) to get the trajectory's maximum position in the $\vec{n}$ direction. Note that when $\vec{n}$ is axis-aligned, the dot products in (6) can be optimized away. For example, when $\vec{n}$ is equal to the $+y$ axis, then $t_{\text{top},\vec{n}}$ becomes

$$t_{\text{top},y} = \frac{\sqrt{1 - \min(0, \vec{v}_{0,y}/\vec{v}_{\infty,y})} - 1}{k}. \tag{7}$$

See Figure 5 for an example of $\vec{v}(t)$ and $\vec{p}(t_{\text{top},y})$.

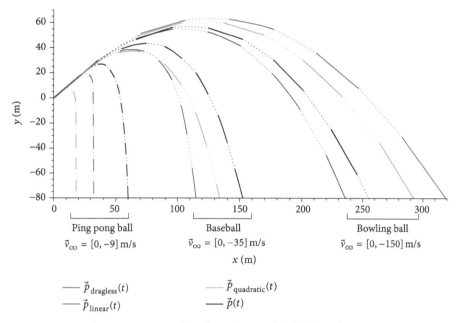

FIGURE 3: The trajectories resulting from four models for three different ball types.

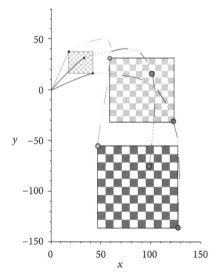

FIGURE 4: The trajectory of a textured quad.

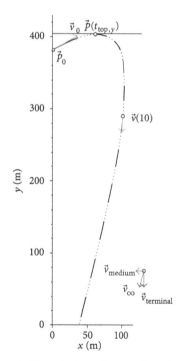

FIGURE 5: The velocity and y-top of a trajectory.

4. Planning in World Space: Hitting a Target at a Given Time

When a projectile needs to hit some given target position, $\vec{p}(t)$ can be used to solve or "plan" the initial velocity that leads to precisely hitting this target at some given future point in time. To be more specific, when trying to hit some position $\vec{r}$ at the given time t_r, the solution is found by solving $\vec{p}(t_r) = \vec{r}$ for $\vec{v}_0$, which results in the following formula:

$$\vec{v}_0 = k\left(\vec{r} - \vec{p}_0 - \vec{v}_\infty t_r\right) + \frac{\vec{r} - \vec{p}_0}{t_r}. \qquad (8)$$

In Figure 6, this formula is used to plan the trajectories to six different target $\vec{r}$ positions, all taking exactly ten seconds to reach their target. In other words, $t_r = 10$, which results in having exactly five thick and five thin segments per trajectory in this figure.

One interesting property of this function is that the x and y components (or the x, y, and z components in the 3D case) of $\vec{v}_0$ are completely independent from each other. As a direct consequence, similar projectiles that target the

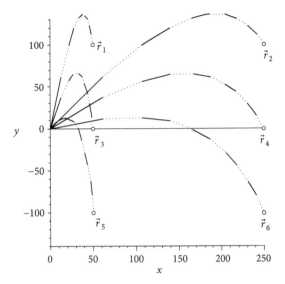

FIGURE 6: Planning to hit all six different target positions in exactly ten seconds.

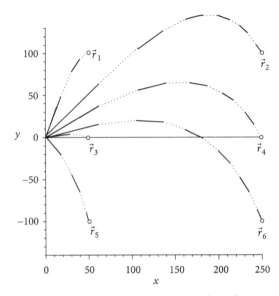

FIGURE 7: Planning trajectories to six targets, taking the exact same time as travelling with 25 m/s over the straight line from initial to target position.

same horizontal distance but a different height will always move at the same horizontal speed over the whole trajectory and vice versa. Also, trajectories for targets at equal height but different horizontal distances will all have the same top height, as can be observed in Figure 6 as well.

Note that the given time parameter t_r could be any positive value, including the one that is dependent on another function of $\vec{r}$. One simple example of such a function is $t_r = \|\vec{r} - \vec{p}_0\|/v_{\text{straight}}$, where v_{straight} is a given average speed over the straight line from $\vec{p}_0$ to $\vec{r}$. In Figure 7, this is illustrated using $v_{\text{straight}} = 25$ m/s.

A function for t_r could be made arbitrarily complex. The time planners that will be explored in Section 6 are examples of moderately complex functions, solving different additional constraints for t_r given $\vec{r}$. But even more complex planners would be necessary if t_r and $\vec{r}$ were to be dependent on each other. This can happen, for example, when a moving target needs to be hit while planning to launch at a fixed speed, making t_r influence the prediction of the future target position $\vec{r}$, which influences t_r again. These relationships are not explored in detail in this paper, but it is worth mentioning that some of these problems may be solved iteratively by starting with a rough estimate for t_r and then letting it converge to the right solution by repeatedly going from t_r to $\vec{r}$ and from $\vec{r}$ to an improved t_r. These iterations could possibly even be spread over multiple frames to amortize costs, for example, improving accuracy with each new frame.

5. The Principal Frame of Reference and Its Properties

Most planners for $\vec{p}(t)$ are still to be presented. However, as these planners depend on a special frame of reference to keep the required planner math as simple as possible, this frame of reference will be covered here first.

Inspecting $\vec{p}(t)$ reveals that the function always outputs $\vec{p}_0$ plus a linear combination (i.e., a weighted sum) of $\vec{v}_0$ and $\vec{v}_\infty$. Geometrically, this implies that all trajectories, even with wind coming from any 3D direction, are guaranteed to lie on a plane spanned by $\vec{v}_0$ and $\vec{v}_\infty$ which passes through $\vec{p}_0$. Consequently, $\vec{p}(t)$ may be rewritten as

$$\vec{p}(t) = x(t)\,\vec{X} + y(t)\,\vec{Y} + \vec{p}_0, \qquad (9)$$

where $\vec{X}$ and $\vec{Y}$, respectively, describe an orthonormal tangent and bitangent direction in *world space* of the plane over which the projectile moves. Within this plane's 2D frame of reference, the vector $[x(t), y(t)]$ describes the movement on the trajectory over time relative to $\vec{p}_0$ and in terms of this alternative x axis (i.e., the tangent) and y axis (i.e., the bitangent).

Put into terms perhaps more familiar to computer graphics and game developers, the 2D function $[x(t), y(t)]$ is like a procedural UV coordinate that defines a projectile's location on an unwrapped plane which maps UV $[0, 0]$ to $\vec{p}_0$ and has an orthonormal tangent vector $\vec{X}$ and bitangent vector $\vec{Y}$. All this is shown in Figure 8, where the trajectory $\vec{p}(t)$ is visualized as the intersection between the described plane (on which is thus lies) and another curved surface.

Although there is an infinite amount of ways to define the $\vec{X}$ and $\vec{Y}$ vectors, the following definitions are used in this paper for their particularly useful properties:

$$\vec{X} = \frac{\vec{d} - (\vec{d} \cdot \vec{Y})\,\vec{Y}}{\left\|\vec{d} - (\vec{d} \cdot \vec{Y})\,\vec{Y}\right\|},$$

$$\vec{Y} = \frac{-\vec{v}_\infty}{v_\infty}. \qquad (10)$$

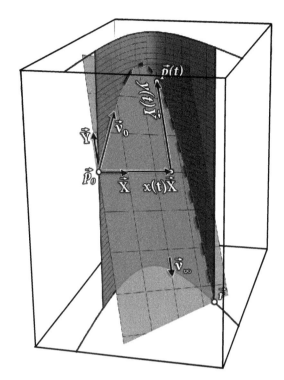

FIGURE 8: A 3D trajectory with wind at an angle, and its decomposition on the principal plane (in blue).

Here, v_∞ is used as a shorthand for $\|\vec{v}_\infty\|$. And $\vec{d} = \vec{v}_0$ if $\vec{v}_0$ is already known. In the case that $\vec{v}_0$ is not (yet) known, any position relative to $\vec{p}_0$ known to be lying on the trajectory may be used for $\vec{d}$ instead. For example, use $\vec{d} = \vec{r} - \vec{p}_0$ when targeting the position $\vec{r}$. Note that in the case that $\vec{v}_\infty$ and $\vec{d}$ are collinear, the trajectory can be described by movement solely in the $\vec{Y}$ direction. To still get a valid 2D basis in that case, an arbitrary vector that is noncollinear should be used for $\vec{d}$ instead.

The frame of reference defined by $\vec{p}_0$, $\vec{X}$, and $\vec{Y}$ is what will be called the trajectory's *principal space*. It is called that because this space allows the math describing the trajectory to be decomposed into a particularly compact and well-behaved form. In particular, wind and gravity do not affect movement over the principal $\vec{X}$ axis at all, but solely over the principal $\vec{Y}$ axis. This allows the function $x(t)$ in (9) to be simplified as will be shown and put to good use soon.

The second useful property of this principal space is that it guarantees that $v_x \geq 0$. That is, all initial and in-flight velocities expressed in principal space are guaranteed to have nonnegative values on the x axis, causing ballistic objects to never move to or be on the negative x side of this space, even though they obviously can still move in any direction in world space. Similarly, targets are never on the negative x side in principal space either. The advantage of this property is that it once again will allow for further simplifications in some of the planner math that is still to be discussed.

The third useful property of this particular space is that it is easy to convert from world space to principal space and

back as $\vec{X}$ and $\vec{Y}$ are orthonormal. Converting from any world space position $\vec{p}$ to the position $[x, y]$ in principal space and vice versa can simply be done using (11) and (12), respectively as follows:

$$[x, y] = \left[(\vec{p} - \vec{p}_0) \cdot \vec{X}, (\vec{p} - \vec{p}_0) \cdot \vec{Y} \right], \tag{11}$$

$$\vec{p} = x\vec{X} + y\vec{Y} + \vec{p}_0. \tag{12}$$

Similarly, it is possible to efficiently convert from any world space velocity $\vec{v}$ to the principal velocity $[v_x, v_y]$ and back using (13) and (14), respectively as follows:

$$\left[v_x, v_y\right] = \left[\vec{v} \cdot \vec{X}, \vec{v} \cdot \vec{Y} \right], \tag{13}$$

$$\vec{v} = v_x\vec{X} + v_y\vec{Y}. \tag{14}$$

Starting a new notational convention here for clarity, vector names (i.e., variables decorated with a $\rightarrow$ symbol) are only used for variables in world space, while variables in principal space never use this decoration and always represent individual scalar quantities. So, for example, $\vec{v}_x$ is the x component of the vector representing the world space velocity $\vec{v}$, while v_x is a scalar representing a velocity in the x direction in principal space.

Now that the frame of reference itself has been covered, it is possible to define the two scalar functions that make up the principal space trajectory function $[x(t), y(t)]$:

$$x(t) = \frac{v_{0,x}t}{1 + kt}, \tag{15}$$

$$y(t) = \frac{\left(v_{0,y} - ktv_\infty\right)t}{1 + kt}. \tag{16}$$

These functions are derived by transforming $\vec{p}(t)$ into this space using (11). Note that gravity and wind do indeed not affect movement over the x direction in this space. And $[x(0), y(0)]$ is equal to $[0, 0]$, which means that trajectories in principal space always start at the origin (while starting at $\vec{p}_0$ in world space).

The simpler formula for $x(t)$ makes it possible to uniquely invert the function to get the time t at which the x component of a certain position will be reached given the horizontal initial velocity. The solution is as follows:

$$t = \frac{x}{v_{0,x} - kx}. \tag{17}$$

Here, $0 \leq x \leq v_{0,x}/k$, as that is the valid range of $x(t)$ for $t \geq 0$ as defined by (15). By plugging (17) into (16), the following explicit y-for-x relationship is found:

$$y(x) = \frac{\left(kv_\infty x/\left(kx - v_{0,x}\right) + v_{0,y}\right)x}{v_{0,x}}. \tag{18}$$

This function always has exactly one y value for each valid x value, which would not necessarily be true for an explicit trajectory function in any other space. This property is demonstrated in Figure 9, showing a trajectory that is equivalent to the trajectory shown in Figure 1 but which is now plotted using $y(x)$ in principal space, perfectly overlaying the original trajectory when mapped back into world space.

For completeness, the principal space counterparts of the world space properties described by (5), (6), and (7) are given here as well. Consider

$$v_x(t) = \frac{v_{0,x}}{(1+kt)^2},$$

$$v_y(t) = \frac{v_{0,y} - kt(2+kt)v_\infty}{(1+kt)^2},$$

$t_{\text{top},\vec{n}}$

$$= \frac{\sqrt{1 + \max\left(0, [v_{0,x}, v_{0,y}] \cdot [n_x, n_y] / (v_\infty n_y)\right)} - 1}{k}$$

$$t_{\text{top},y} = \frac{\sqrt{1 + \max\left(0, v_{0,y}/v_{\infty,y}\right)} - 1}{k}.$$

(19)

Lastly, the local slope in principal space in terms of time (i.e., $v_y(t)/v_x(t)$) and in terms of x (i.e., $\partial y(x)/\partial x$) is as follows:

$$\frac{v_y(t)}{v_x(t)} = \frac{v_{0,y} - kt(2+kt)v_\infty}{v_{0,x}},$$

$$\frac{\partial y(x)}{\partial x} = \frac{v_{0,y} + v_\infty}{v_{0,x}} - \frac{v_{0,x}v_\infty}{(kx - v_{0,x})^2}.$$

(20)

6. Planning in Principal Space

As the planners in this section all depend on the properties of trajectories in principal space, the most relevant properties are briefly repeated here. Per definition, any ballistic object in principal space is launched from the origin, any target has a nonnegative x component, and the combined effect of gravity and wind results in a v_∞ value that is exactly in the $-y$ direction. As the planners will expect their parameters to be specified in principal space, the parameters of any world space problem need to be converted to this space before they can be used. To recap the necessary steps (assuming the problem involves hitting some target position $\vec{r}$), start by defining the actual principal space's $\vec{X}$ and $\vec{Y}$ axes using (10) with $\vec{d} = \vec{r} - \vec{p}_0$. Next, convert $\vec{r}$ (or any other requested position) to principal space using (11) to get $[r_x, r_y]$.

All planners covered here will return the exact time t_r at which the target $[r_x, r_y]$ must be hit to meet the planner's given constraints. To get the actual initial velocity in principal space that leads to hitting $[r_x, r_y]$ at this t_r, both $p_x(t_r) = r_x$

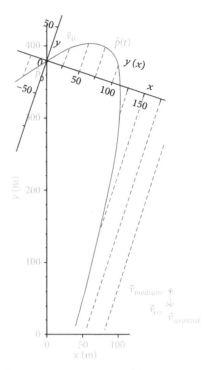

FIGURE 9: The same Empire State Building trajectory example as from Figure 1 but seen from the principal frame of reference.

and $p_y(t_r) = r_y$ need to be solved for $[v_{0,x}, v_{0,y}]$, which can be done using the following two formulas:

$$v_{0,x} = r_x\left(k + \frac{1}{t_r}\right),$$

(21)

$$v_{0,y} = r_y\left(k + \frac{1}{t_r}\right) + kv_\infty t_r.$$

(22)

To get the initial velocity in world space from these, it is possible to convert $[v_{0,x}, v_{0,y}]$ to $\vec{v}_0$ using (14). But $\vec{v}_0$ may also be directly calculated from t_r and $\vec{r}$ through (8). Now that it is clear how to make use of principal space planners in general, the actual planners are presented.

6.1. Hitting the Target Given Another Position to Pass Through. A trajectory can be planned to pass through both position $[q_x, q_y]$ and through target $[r_x, r_y]$ by solving $y(q_x) = q_y$ and $y(r_x) = r_y$ for $v_{0,x}$, and using (17) on r_x and $v_{0,x}$ to get t_r. This specific form of planning may be useful to shoot through a hole or exactly over an object at $[q_x, q_y]$ to hit $[r_x, r_y]$, example. The solution to at what time the position $[r_x, r_y]$ needs to be hit is as follows:

$$t_r = s + \sqrt{s\left(s + \frac{2r_x}{k(r_x - q_x)}\right)},$$

(23)

where $s = (r_x q_y - r_y q_x)/2v_\infty q_x$. Note that the line from the origin to the target position with the smallest x must be at least as steep as the line from the origin to the position with

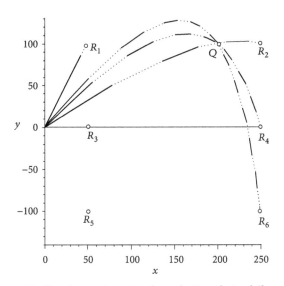

FIGURE 10: Planning trajectories through Q and six different R targets.

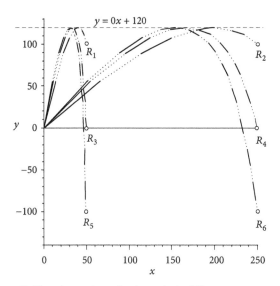

FIGURE 11: Planning trajectories through six different targets, touching a line at each top.

the largest x for a valid trajectory (and thus a real solution) to exist. That is, $q_y/q_x \geq r_y/r_x$ if $q_x < r_x$, and $r_y/r_x \geq q_y/q_x$ if $q_x > r_x$. In Figure 10, two of the six targets do not meet this requirement, explaining why there are only four trajectories there.

6.2. Hitting the Target While Touching a Line. When looking for the time t_r at which a trajectory passes through $[r_x, r_y]$ and touches the line $y = ax + b$ in principal space, $\partial y(x)/\partial x = a$ has to be solved for x first, which can then be used to solve $y(x) = ax + b$ for $v_{0,x}$. Both $v_{0,x}$ and r_x can then be used again with (17) to get t_r. The solution may be written as follows.

$$t_r = \frac{s + \sqrt{s^2 + kv_\infty \left(ar_x - r_y\right)}}{kv_\infty}, \tag{24}$$

where $s = \sqrt{bkv_\infty} + (1/2)k(ar_x - r_y + b)$. Note that a real solution can only exist when $b \geq 0$ and $ar_x + b \geq r_y$. That is, the line must always pass through or be above the initial and the target position.

In the example presented in Figure 11, the line to be touched is chosen to be horizontal, leading to a specification of the trajectories' vertical tops in principal space. But it is also possible to find the t_r that leads to hitting a top defined in another space. For example, to let a trajectory's top touch the world-space plane with normal $\vec{n}$ and through point $\vec{q}$, $y = ax + b$ becomes the line in principal space that describes the intersection between this plane and the trajectory's principal plane. In that case, $a = -(\vec{X} \cdot \vec{n})/(\vec{Y} \cdot \vec{n})$ and $b = ((\vec{q} - \vec{p}_0) \cdot \vec{n})/(\vec{Y} \cdot \vec{n})$. As always, when $\vec{n}$ is axis-aligned, the dot products can be optimized away. For example, when only interested in trajectories exactly hitting a world space height h at their tops (in the $+y$ direction), this simplifies to $a = -\vec{X}_y/\vec{Y}_y$ and $b = (h - \vec{p}_{0,y})/\vec{Y}_y$.

The principal space slope a can also be calculated from the slope w of a world-space elevation angle θ_{world} (i.e.,

$w = \tan(\theta_{\text{world}}))$ by using the conversion formula $a = (\text{sign}(\vec{Y}_y)w\sqrt{s(\vec{X}_y^2 + \vec{Y}_y^2) - w^2} - s\vec{X}_y\vec{Y}_y)/(s\vec{Y}_y^2 - w^2)$, where $s = 1 + w^2$ and $\text{sign}(x) = [x \geq 0] - [x < 0]$. This a is only valid if an equivalent elevation with a positive x component in principal space exists, which is the case if $s(\vec{X}_y^2 + \vec{Y}_y^2) - w^2 \geq 0$ and $[1, w] \cdot [\sqrt{1 - \vec{X}_y^2}, \vec{X}_y] > 0$. This world-space elevation conversion may be particularly useful when used together with the next two principal-space planners.

6.3. Hitting the Target Given the Initial Slope. This subsection is about finding the time t_r at which a projectile will hit position $[r_x, r_y]$ while being launched at slope a. Planning this way may be useful when there is control over the projectile's initial speed but not over its direction (e.g., for some weapon mounted on a fixed rig).

This problem is actually simply a special case of the previous planner, where $b = 0$, meaning that the problem is equivalent to finding the trajectory that touches the line $y = ax$. After substituting b in (24) and applying some basic algebra, the solution may be written more compactly as follows:

$$t_r = \frac{s + \sqrt{s(s + 2v_\infty)}}{kv_\infty}, \tag{25}$$

where $s = (1/2)k(ar_x - r_y)$. Obviously, the slope a has to be steeper than the line from the origin to the target position (i.e., $a > r_y/r_x$) for a solution to exist, which is the case for all but one target position in Figure 12.

6.4. Hitting the Target Given the Target Slope. Similarly, it is possible to hit $[r_x, r_y]$ given the exact slope a at the target position. This type of planning allows for exact control over the angle at which a target is hit. Again, this can be seen as a special case of the planner from Section 6.2, using $r_y - ar_x$ as the value for b. When substituted and simplified, this results in the following more direct formula:

$$t_r = \sqrt{\frac{r_y - ar_x}{kv_\infty}}. \tag{26}$$

For this particular planner, the slope a needs to be less than the slope of the line from the origin to the target position (i.e., $a < r_y/r_x$). Consequently, only five of the six targets have a valid trajectory in Figure 13.

6.5. Hitting the Target Given the Arc Height or "Curviness".

The time t_r can also be calculated for a target position $[r_x, r_y]$ and an "arc height" b. Here, b is defined as the maximum difference in the y direction between the trajectory and the straight line from origin to target. Equivalently, b may be interpreted as the height in principal space of the smallest parallelogram containing the whole trajectory, as shown in Figure 14. This problem is another special case of the "line touching" problem and can be solved by substituting r_y/r_x for a in (24). After applying some basic algebra, the resulting formula may be written as follows:

$$t_r = \frac{b}{v_\infty} + 2\sqrt{\frac{b}{kv_\infty}}. \tag{27}$$

This function is particularly intuitive to plan with when

$$b = h\sqrt{r_x^2 + r_y^2}, \tag{28}$$

where h defines the "curviness" of the trajectory. For example, $h = 0.01$ always leads to a low arc for any target position, while $h = 0.5$ always leads to a fairly high arc.

6.6. Hitting the Target with (Almost) Minimal Effort.

A trajectory can also be planned to hit a target at $[r_x, r_y]$ with the smallest initial speed (and thus the least amount of energy) possible. Planning a trajectory this way requires finding the positive time-to-target t_r which solves $\partial(v_{0,x}^2 + v_{0,y}^2)/\partial t_r = 0$, where $v_{0,x}$ and $v_{0,y}$ are defined by (21) and (22), respectively. This equation can be expanded into the following form:

$$\left(k^2 v_\infty^2\right)t_r^4 + \left(k^2 v_\infty r_y\right)t_r^3 - k\left(r_x^2 + r_y^2\right)t_r - \left(r_x^2 + r_y^2\right) = 0. \tag{29}$$

Like all quartic equations, solving this in a closed form is possible but difficult to do robustly [10]. In practice, quartic equations are typically solved for any or all of their roots by generic iterative root solvers [11]. But by exploiting domain-specific knowledge, it is also possible to implement a specialized iterative solver for (29) that is guaranteed to efficiently converge to the right root directly. One possible implementation is presented as a C++ function called *GetTimeToTargetRWithMinimalInitialSpeed()* in Algorithm 1. There, the equation is first transformed into an equivalent but more well-behaved strictly convex quartic function for which a conservative initial guess for t (or rather, u) is calculated,

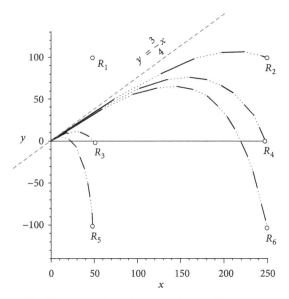

FIGURE 12: Planning trajectories through six different targets, all starting with the slope 3/4.

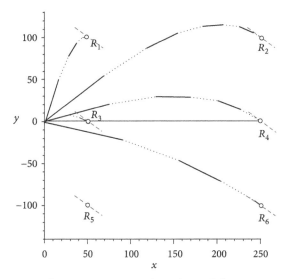

FIGURE 13: Planning trajectories through six different targets, all ending at the slope −3/4.

which is then refined using multiple (but typically less than a total of six) modified or normal conservative Newton's method iterations. This implementation has been carefully crafted with both robustness and efficiency in mind. As with any implementation, numeric precision can become an issue when using extreme values, but results for practical ranges are typically within a few *float* epsilons of the exact value. See the comments in the implementation itself for more details.

Alternatively, when only a rough approximation of the minimal effort solution is needed, the simpler "curviness" planner from (27) and (28) could be used with $h = 1/4$. This approximation is fairly accurate for larger values of v_∞, as it actually converges perfectly to the exact solution when v_∞ goes to infinity. But for high friction scenarios, the difference

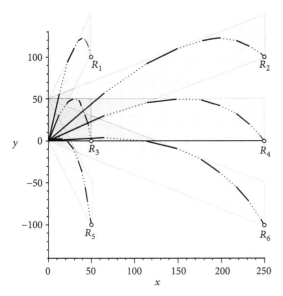

FIGURE 14: Planning trajectories through six different Rs, all with an arc height of 50.

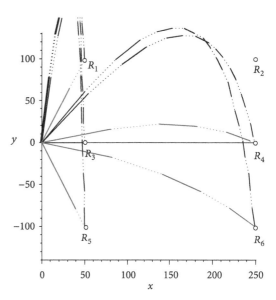

FIGURE 16: Planning trajectories through six different Rs, all starting at 100 m/s. Each of the five reachable targets has a trajectory with a (red) low arc and a (black) high arc.

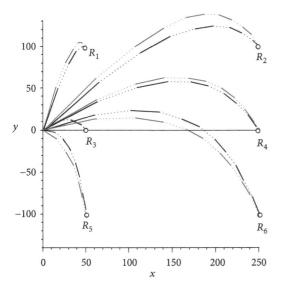

FIGURE 15: Planning trajectories through six different Rs while minimizing the initial velocity using the exact method (in black) and the approximate $h = 1/4$ method (in red) in a medium-fiction scenario.

between the exact method and the approximation becomes quite noticeable. To get an idea of the size of the error for a medium friction scenario, the trajectories resulting from the exact method and the approximation are shown side by side in Figure 15 for the case of $g = 9.81$ m/s^2 and $v_\infty = 25$ m/s.

6.7. Hitting a Target Given the Initial Speed. The last planning algorithm covered in this paper solves for the time t_r required to hit the target $[r_x, r_y]$ given the projectile's exact initial speed s. The solution is found by solving $v_{0,x}^2 + v_{0,y}^2 = s^2$ for the positive time t_r to position $[r_x, r_y]$, where $v_{0,x}$ and $v_{0,y}$ are once again defined by (21) and (22), respectively.

This particular equation may be expanded into the following quartic function:

$$\left(k^2 v_\infty^2\right) t_r^4 + \left(2k^2 v_\infty r_y\right) t_r^3 + \left(k^2 r_x^2 + k^2 r_y^2 + 2k v_\infty r_y - s^2\right) t_r^2$$
$$+ 2k \left(r_x^2 + r_y^2\right) t_r + \left(r_x^2 + r_y^2\right) = 0.$$

$$(30)$$

Note that when s is smaller than the minimal initial speed to hit $[r_x, r_y]$ (i.e., the sought solution of (29)), the problem has no valid solutions. But when s is larger than that, it will always have exactly two valid solutions. In that case, the smaller of the two t_r values represents the time to hit the target with a low arc, while the larger t_r root is the solution for a high arc. See Figure 16 for an example.

Using a similar approach as in the previous section, a specialized iterative solver can be implemented to solve this particular quartic function. The C++ function *GetTimeToTargetRGivenInitialSpeedS()* in Algorithm 2 solves the equation for either the high or low arc root and returns the resulting t_r or returns 0 if no solution exists. This implementation has also been written with robustness, efficiency, and accuracy for a wide range of parameters in mind. Tests showed that the procedure typically requires about six (modified) Newton's method iterations in total to converge to almost full *float* precision.

7. Future work

As already hinted at in Section 4, planning to hit moving targets can sometimes be done using a feedback loop between a target position prediction formula and a planner for a static target, together converging to a solution over multiple iterations. More research is necessary to explore the exact boundary conditions for this convergence to occur or alternatively to look for ways to solve these problems analytically.

Additionally, it is likely that the model presented in this paper can also be used for efficient exact collision detection between a trajectory and an arbitrary polygonal mesh by testing the trajectory in principal space against the intersection of the mesh and the principal plane. This algorithm might even be combined with the planners from Sections 6.1 and 6.2 to allow for efficient planning of the most optimal trajectory above or below a given polygonal mesh, respectively. These possibilities have not been investigated in depth for this paper but might be covered in future work.

8. Conclusion

A novel analytic approximation of ballistic trajectories with air resistance has been presented that was designed to balance physical accuracy and performance in a way that makes sense in the field of computer games.

The approximation's linearity in velocity has been used to define a special principal frame of reference, which makes it possible to always work with these trajectories in a simplified 2D space, even though the original problem can be in 3D with wind coming from any direction. The combined result is that the proposed model is able to produce trajectories that are complex enough to be physically plausible, while keeping the math simple enough to also allow for many different ways of efficient trajectory planning that otherwise might be too impractical for use in computer games.

Conflict of Interests

The author declares that there is no conflict of interests regarding the publication of this paper.

References

[1] G. M. Gregorek, *Aerodynamic Drag of Model Rockets*, Estes Industries, Penrose, Colo, USA, 1970.

[2] R. G. Watts and R. Ferrer, "The lateral force on a spinning sphere: aerodynamics of a curveball," *American Journal of Physics*, vol. 55, no. 1, pp. 40–44, 1987.

[3] H. D. Curtis, *Orbital Mechanics for Engineering Students*, ch 1–5, Elsevier Butterworth-Heinemann, Burlington, Mass, USA, 1st edition, 2005.

[4] S. T. Thornton and J. B. Marion, *Classical Dynamics of Particles and Systems*, Brooks/Cole, Belmont, Calif, USA, 2005.

[5] P. A. Karkantzakos, "Time of flight and range of the motion of a projectile in a constant gravitational field under the influence of a retarding force proportional to the velocity," *Journal of Engineering Science and Technology Review*, vol. 2, no. 1, pp. 76–81, 2009.

[6] R. D. H. Warburton, J. Wang, and J. Burgdöfer, "Analytic approximations of projectile motion with quadratic air resistance," *Journal Service Science & Management*, no. 3, pp. 98–105, 2010.

[7] P. S. Chudinov, "Approximate analytical investigation of projectile motion in a medium with quadratic drag force," *International Journal of Sports Science and Engineering*, vol. 5, no. 1, pp. 27–42, 2011.

[8] G. W. Parker, "Projectile motion with air resistance quadratic in the speed," *American Journal of Physics*, vol. 45, no. 7, pp. 606–610, 1997.

[9] D. M. Bourg, *Physics for Game Developers*, O'Reilly Media, 2002.

[10] D. Herbison-Evans, "Solving quartics and cubics for graphics," Tech. Rep. TR94-487, Basser Department of Computer Science, University of Sydney, 1994.

[11] W. H. Press, S. A. Teukolsky, W. T. Vetterling, and B. P. Flannery, *Numerical Recipes in C: The Art of Scientific Computing*, Ch 9, Cambridge University Press, 2nd edition, 1992.

16

Unifying Rigid and Soft Bodies Representation: The Sulfur Physics Engine

Dario Maggiorini, Laura Anna Ripamonti, and Federico Sauro

Department of Computer Science, University of Milan, Via Comelico 39, 20135 Milan, Italy

Correspondence should be addressed to Laura Anna Ripamonti; ripamonti@di.unimi.it

Academic Editor: Ali Arya

Video games are (also) real-time interactive graphic simulations: hence, providing a convincing physics simulation for each specific game environment is of paramount importance in the process of achieving a satisfying player experience. While the existing game engines appropriately address many aspects of physics simulation, some others are still in need of improvements. In particular, several specific physics properties of bodies not usually involved in the main game mechanics (e.g., properties useful to represent systems composed by soft bodies), are often poorly rendered by general-purpose engines. This issue may limit game designers when imagining innovative and compelling video games and game mechanics. For this reason, we dug into the problem of appropriately representing soft bodies. Subsequently, we have extended the approach developed for soft bodies to rigid ones, proposing and developing a unified approach in a game engine: Sulfur. To test the engine, we have also designed and developed "Escape from Quaoar," a prototypal video game whose main game mechanic exploits an elastic rope, and a level editor for the game.

1. Introduction

A physics simulation framework is generally conceived as a middleware application. Physics simulators can be classified into two main groups: *scientific* simulators and *real-time* simulators (also called "physics engines" or simply "engines" by game developers—see, e.g., [1, 2]). A scientific simulator focuses on the accuracy of the simulation, disregarding the optimization of computational time, and its major application fields include fluid dynamics, engineering simulations, weather forecasts, and movies. On the other hand, real-time simulators (or physics engines) aim at computing as fast as possible the simulation; generally, this result is obtained by simplifying the underlying mathematical model of the simulated phenomenon. Therefore, the resulting simulation loses some accuracy. While a less accurate result could become a relevant problem in a scientific application, it becomes a by far less cumbersome issue in the area of video games. Actually, the first and main reason for a video game to exist is to provide *fun* to its players [3], which is achieved not only through alluring game mechanics, but also by providing an environment that fosters *immersivity* [4–6].

To enhance immersion in their game, designers should know everything about the physics that applies to the world they have created, in order to mimic it in the most appropriate and convincing way [7, 8]. This knowledge includes at least two synergic aspects: on the one hand, players have "a sense of how real-world works," and, on the other hand, many games include some elements of "ultraphysics," such as teleport, magic, gods intervention, faster-than-light travel, and hyperdimensionality. The physics simulated by the engine should implement all the laws that the game requires and no more, and both physics and ultraphysics laws must adhere to players' naïve physics understanding [7]. At the same time, the simulated physics—even if simplified—should guarantee that no evident discrepancies from the expected behaviours will suddenly pop up, destroying the illusion of the players.

The history of real-time engine for physics simulation is quite recent. This is due mainly to two constraints: on one hand, till the last decade, CPUs processing power was not enough to handle the heavy burden of mathematical models underpinning physics simulation, and, on the other hand, developers' attention was focused primarily on the enhancement of graphic engines that lead to the creation of graphic accelerators and graphics processing units (GPUs) and fostered the rush toward high quality rendering and photorealism. Until 1998, the only games focusing on physics were driving simulations (one title for all: Gran Turismo [9], whose franchise reached its sixth chapter in 2013). From that year on, several engines focusing on physics started to appear, among which is the well-known Havok [10]. At the moment, a quite significant number of other engines have entered the market, among which are PhysX, Euphoria, Digital Molecular Matter, Bullet, ODE, CryEngine, Unreal Development Kit (UDK), Unity3D, and many others. Nonetheless, the interest in the improvement of engines is still high, because a good simulation increases both players' commitment in the game and the exploitation of completely new gameplays.

1.1. Structure of a Physics Engine for Video Games. Engines work on discrete intervals of time and are generally composed of three main subsystems: one aimed at calculating new positions of physical entities, one focused on detecting collisions among entities, and the last one in charge of managing collisions (see Figure 1).

The first component is a numerical integrator in charge of solving some differential equations representing movement and determining, for each frame, the new position of the moving objects. The collision detection subsystem generally implements a hierarchical data structure to simplify the search for collisions (all the pairs of objects too far to collide are excluded *a priori* from the collision detection process). The remaining objects are then tested from a geometrical point of view to verify if any intersection is taking place. The final goal is to generate a list of colliding objects, which specifies their contact points and relative velocities. This list is passed on to the collision resolution subsystem that manages the physics of the collisions (e.g., by making colliding objects bounce away or shatter). From the engine perspective, generally, in-game objects can belong to three different types: *particles*, *particles systems* (free or also connected among them), and *rigid bodies*. In this approach, soft bodies are—generally—rendered as systems of particles connected by spring joints [1, 11]. Rigid bodies are more complex than particles to represent: a (system of) particle(s) has just a *position*, while a rigid body can be seen like a particle, which has both a *position* and an *orientation* (hence, also rotation mechanics is involved). Both kinematic and dynamic can be applied to (systems of) particles and rigid bodies (see, e.g., [12]).

1.2. Simulating Rigid Bodies as Particles Systems. The most diffused approach implemented into physics engines, based on the distinction among particles and rigid bodies, has several drawbacks. As easily imaginable, the physics of (systems of) rigid bodies is quite complex, from both implementative and mathematical points of view, since it requires selecting the most effective way to manage: center of mass, momentum, and moment of inertia. To lower this complexity, we propose an innovative and unified approach rooted into the idea of representing rigid bodies through particles systems. Besides providing a simpler representation, this approach would also

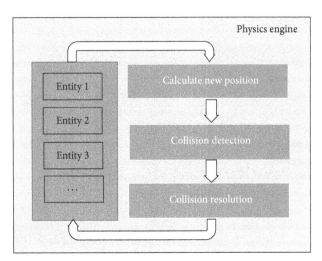

FIGURE 1: Structure of a general-purpose physics engine for video games.

offer the possibility to simulate in an easier way *destructible* objects (see Figure 2). These entities present several peculiarities because they start out in an undamaged state (they appear like one single cohesive object), but they must be able to break into many pieces according to different behaviours (i.e., a piece of glass shatters in a different way from a piece of wood). Anyway, as we will see, using particles systems to represent rigid bodies is not an easy task since it requires integrating impulsive forces generated by springs, a process that frequently presents problems of instability (see Section 2).

The approach we propose provides two types of joints among particles: *elastic* and *semirigid* joints. The elastic joint is a classical spring joint with a spring able to reach a good level of stiffness thanks to an opportune integration method and a high refreshing rate. The semirigid connection is assured by maintaining constant the distance among the particles in the system and by adopting the Verlet approach to integration [13–15]. We have developed and tested this new approach for games in 2D, in order to limit complexity, implementation, and testing time. Nonetheless, we have designed all the components of the engine keeping in mind the possibility to extend it quite easily to the third dimension. In particular, we have developed the following.

(i) Atlax. It is a framework designed to manage all the low-level tasks typically required by a real-time graphic application, such as interfacing the operating system for managing audiovisual input and output, windows and rendering context management, data compression, and 3D models. Particular emphasis has been put on the design of the timing system, in order to guarantee the possibility of decoupling the rendering refreshing rate from physics processing rate (that can rise up to 10 KHz). In particular, the timestamp selected for the physics simulation remains fixed for the whole simulation run. This choice has been made in order to avoid unexpected behaviors (such as objects exploding for no apparent reason). As

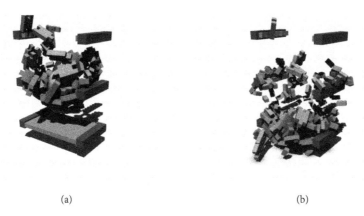

(a)   (b)

FIGURE 2: Example of destructible objects: a series of walls crumbling.

a consequence, when the simulated system is very complex and the required computational time cannot cope with the predefined time interval, the simulation will only slow down, without getting unstable.

(ii) Sulfur. It is a static library that implements the physics engine. Sulfur contains several classes, implementing particles and particles systems, elastic and rigid joints, collision detection, and resolution. It is a middleware software application; hence, it is completely separated from Atlax.

(iii) SulfurChamber. It is a sandbox application aimed at providing a graphical user interface (GUI) for Sulfur, where it is possible to create and to modify physic entities.

(iv) Escape from Quaoar [16]. It is a video game based on mechanics aimed at exploiting the peculiarities of Sulfur.

The remainder of this paper is organized as follows: in Section 2, we briefly examine the state of the art in physics simulation, also digging into the main characteristics of the more diffused off-the-shelves engines. In Section 3, we will describe how the Sulfur game engine has been designed, while in Section 4 we describe the applications we have developed to implement and test our approach. Namely, they include Atlax, a low-level framework that interacts with the operating system, Sulfur, the physics engine, SulfurChamber, a sandbox aimed at experiencing and experimenting with Sulfur, and Escape from Quaoar, a complete video game based on Sulfur. Finally, in Section 5, we summarize the main results we have obtained so far and present some closing remarks and some future development for the engine.

2. State of the Art in Physics Simulation

The final goal of the majority of the game engines is the simulation of a limited number of physic phenomena, among which the most important are the kinematics and dynamics of rigid and soft bodies, represented through Newton's laws of motion and Hooke's law. The literature on these issues in the field of gaming is quite limited and more often oriented to practitioners or to teaching activities (see, e.g., [1, 2, 8, 11, 17, 18], etc.). Also, we want to point out that it is out of the main scope of the present work to simulate the dynamics of fluids, since it would imply addressing several more physics phenomena, not included in our research focus—at least for now. Fluid motion is governed by the Navier-Stokes equations, and its simulation typically requires a computational mesh of the fluid domain. Problems arise when the geometry of the fluid takes complex shapes, since mesh generation may become a major bottleneck. Moreover, exterior flow problems (like, e.g., the flow around an airfoil) require special handling. To tackle these issues, different techniques have been proposed and developed, and they are continuously improved, among which it is worth remembering at least the *smoothed particle hydrodynamics* (SPH) and the *vortex particle methods* (see, e.g., [19]). In particular, SPH has been created to simulate nonaxisymmetric phenomena in astrophysics, and it was proposed for the first time by Monaghan [20]. Since its creation, SPH has evolved into other fields, among which are fluid simulation (see, e.g., [21, 22]) and solid mechanics (see, e.g., [23–25], etc.). It has also been improved in order to support interactive simulations [26]; thus, it is frequently adopted to simulate fluid dynamics in 2D video games, even for mobile devices. Both SPH and vortex particle methods are mesh-free interpolation techniques, which use "particles" to represent parcels of fluid. Their main difference lies in the fact that SPH solves the momentum equation, while vortex methods solve the vorticity equation. Furthermore, in contrast to vortex methods, each particle in SPH shows only a local influence, thus making it easier to handle collisions with, for example, the boundaries of a container. Nonetheless, their main application field is fluids simulation or—at most—the simulation of fractures of rigid bodies; in both cases, accuracy of the simulation is more important than its velocity.

The game objects managed by an interactive physics simulation engine are, as we already saw (Section 1), of different types and natures (generally particles or rigid bodies) and belong to different categories, which require specific interactions with the engine. In particular, it is important to distinguish between *physics-driven* and *game-driven* objects. Physics-driven objects completely depend on the simulator (e.g., a stone rolling down from a slide), while game-driven objects are not subject to the simulation, because they are usually controlled by the player (e.g., a sword wielded by a character); nonetheless, they may have physics interactions with the environment (e.g., the player uses the sword to break a chest). Last but not least, the environment usually contains a certain number of "fixed" objects (e.g., the floor) that will interact only with the collision management system. It is important to notice that the collision management system should be present in whichever game engine, even if the physics is not applied, in order to determine superimposition and interaction among game objects. For this reason, the collision management system is usually separated from the remainder of the engine.

The adoption of a physics engine may have some relevant implications. The user should be well aware of these implications, starting from the moment she is starting designing a new game. In particular, the presence of the engine introduces *unpredictability, emerging behaviours,* and the necessity to *balance the values assumed by several variables* [2]. As a matter of fact, an object whose behavior is governed by some approximated physics law may, from time to time, show a behavior that is not desired or that is unexpected. In these cases, the best solution is to "overwrite" the simulation with predefined animation. In the same vein, players may exploit some physic phenomena to their advantage, bending the gameplay in ways not foreseeable by the game designer (an example for all is the following: players may aim a rocket launcher at the floor to get a boost for achieving a higher jump). Finally, yet importantly, in a physics simulation, there are many variables (e.g., friction, gravity, etc.) whose values may affect in many ways the overall game system. It is of paramount importance that, during the design and testing phases of the game, these values are properly balanced in order to produce an environment that matches the perception of physics laws that the player has for that specific game.

As we saw, the main purpose of a physics engine is to approximate bodies dynamics, that is to say, how they behave when they are subjects to a system of forces. Hence, we need, on the one hand, to determine, for each instant of time, position, velocity, and rotation for each body, and, on the other hand, to detect and resolve possible collisions among bodies. To obtain these goals, a real-time physics simulation is based on appropriate numerical resolution techniques for motion laws aimed at refreshing, at each interaction, position, velocity, and orientation in space of an object starting on its previous state and on the forces applied on it. Actually, it is important to underline that, since game engines are interactive simulators, it is not possible to foresee how the system of forces applied to each in-game object will evolve in time. For this reason, it is necessary to approximate the future state by applying numerical methods to the integration of differential equations representing motion laws. There is a certain number of different possible approaches to numerical integration, and each method shows different qualities and drawbacks. Digging deeply into the numerical integration issue is out of the scope of the present work. Nonetheless, we will now briefly go through the most diffused approaches adopted in the field of physics simulators for video games, highlighting the main features of each approach. Numerical

methods are all based on Taylor's polynomial evidenced in Taylor's theorem. They can be classified on the basis of their *order, convergence,* and *stability* (for a detailed description of numerical integration methods, see, e.g., [17]).

The simplest numerical integrator is the *Euler* method (also called *Explicit Euler* method), a first order method usually adopted by programmers that are tackling for the first time physics simulation. In spite of its simplicity and execution velocity, this method is highly inaccurate, since it focuses on velocity to determine the next position of an object.

The *SUVAT* (displacement S, initial velocity U, final velocity V, acceleration A, and time T) method is another first order method, slightly more accurate than the previous one, since it takes into consideration also acceleration. Nonetheless, it is quite unstable and it works well only when acceleration is constant along the integration interval.

The *symplectic Euler* method (also called *semi-implicit Euler* method or *Newton-Størmer-Verlet* (NSV) method) is another first order method, quick and simple, but—due to the fact that it is a symplectic method—by far more stable than the previous approaches. This method behaves quite well also when simulating oscillatory behaviours (like in the case of springs).

The *Runge-Kutta 2* method (or *Midpoint* method) is more accurate than its predecessors (it is a second order integrator), but it is also slower.

The Runge-Kutta 4 method is a fourth order integrator; hence, it becomes useful only when execution velocity is not a constraint, but accuracy is very relevant.

Finally, yet importantly, the class of the *implicit* methods guarantees a pretty good stability, even when rigid springs are involved, but sacrifices simplicity of implementation and velocity of computation.

2.1. Characteristics of the More Diffused Off-the-Shelves Engines. Before diving into the design and development from scratch of a real-time interactive physic simulator, we have taken into account the existing frameworks used for physics simulation in the video games industry. We have compared the characteristics of the more diffused ones among them, with the aim of verifying if at least one of them could match our specific requirements. The requirements we were looking for can be summarized as follows:

(1) efficient support to *physics simulation in 2D* (eventually easily extensible to 3D);

(2) *support for both rigid and soft bodies*, with a seamless gamma of stiffness;

(3) *two-way interaction between rigid and soft bodies.*, that is to say, the capability of soft bodies to both collide and exert forces on rigid bodies and vice versa;

(4) *affordability for a small indie team* with low budget. This requirement mirrors the fact that big players in the video game industry usually develop and maintain their own solutions for physics simulation or buy third party software applications.

All the off-the-shelves engines we have examined are unable to satisfy the whole range of constraints we have set, even the most renowned applications (such as Unity3D), as Table 1 sums up (the requirements listed above have been put in columns). Here, below, we list their major characteristics.

Box2D [27] is free to use and is tailored for 2D, but it is lacking soft-body simulation.

Bullet [28] is a widely used open-source physics simulation library, and it has been used for many games. It recently added support to soft bodies, and it is a good candidate to compare our results with. There is also limited support to 2D environments, but only for rigid bodies. Although with some tricks and some new code it could be possible to use it anyway, it would not satisfy our requirement (1): efficient and native support to 2D soft-body simulation.

CryEngine 3/BeamNG [29] is an extremely powerful game engine, one of the market leaders. It has a pretty new soft-body physics simulator provided by the team of Rigs of Rods (BeamNG). Unfortunately, the licensing system for indie developers is not completely clear, and it is very likely that it does not provide the full features set that the paid version offers. Moreover, it would be absolutely overdimensioned and cumbersome to use for a 2D game.

Digital Molecular Matter (DMM) [30] is different from the previous engines, because it is based on a simulation method called finite element analysis [31–34], which is far more accurate than the ones usually adopted in game engines. It aims to achieve realistic results and supports a wide range of platforms. It matches part of our requirements, but, unfortunately, it is not free to use and again does not support 2D environments.

Havok [10] is one of the market leaders. It runs on every platform (mobiles as well) and provides an excellent combination of performance and accuracy. The core system handles rigid-body dynamics, and it can be augmented with a set of subsystems, like the recently added *Cloth* module, which is aimed at simulating character's clothes and hair. It is not very affordable, and it does not satisfy both requirements (1) and (2): there is a clear separation between rigid and soft bodies and it can be applied only to 3D environments.

Newton Game Dynamics [35] is another open-source library, not supporting soft bodies. It is a bit outdated one also.

Open Dynamics Engine (ODE) [36] is free to use, but it is outdated and only supports rigid bodies.

PhysX [37] is another market leader. It does not support as many platforms as Havok, and its main feature—GPU acceleration—is currently only available using Nvidia video cards. The features set we are looking for seems to be more than fully implemented in an upcoming extension called *FLEX*, which promises unified rigid-body, soft-body, and fluid simulation, but—unfortunately—it is not available on the market yet, and it does not seem to cover 2D simulations. Moreover, the product is free only when it is used to develop for the Windows operating systems.

Unreal Development Kit (UDK) [38] is another powerful and widely used game engine that supports our required features. Unfortunately, although it offers a license tailored for indie developers, it is not as cheap as several other solutions and it is known to be quite cumbersome to use. Again, it is not targeted at 2D.

Unity3D [39] is one of the most popular game development frameworks currently around. It supports every platform and provides a cheap license for independent developers. It provides a basic physics module that does not include any kind of soft-body simulation.

3. Designing the Sulfur Real-Time Interactive Physics Engine

As we saw, the spikiest issues in physics simulation for video games are the management of the rotation component in the motion of rigid bodies, the accurate detection of collisions (especially when complex nonconvex objects are involved [40]), and a convincing visual representation of collisions among rigid bodies.

The purpose of a physics engine is to approximate the dynamic behaviours of objects subject to a set of forces. The main idea behind Sulfur is to deploy an alternative approach to rigid bodies simulation by extending the methodology commonly applied to soft bodies, in order to avoid calculating the rotation component of motion. Actually, this effect would emerge spontaneously from a particle system, in which each particle is linked to some others and translates when subject to forces.

3.1. Simulating Soft Bodies with Sulfur. A particle is described by its *mass*, *position*, and *velocity* (the latter two are represented by bidimensional vectors in the 2D case). Moreover, when a particle is connected to some others, topological information is needed too. To represent a deformable or soft body (like, e.g., some jelly), we need a set of particles connected by some elastic joint. To describe the constraints linking two particles connected by an elastic (spring) joint, we can use Hooke's law that is corrected with the damping. The resulting equation is

$$F\left(t, x\left(t\right), \dot{x}\left(t\right)\right) = -k\left(|d| - l_0\right)\vec{d} + b\left(\dot{x}\left(t\right) - \dot{x}_p\left(t\right)\right), \quad (1)$$

where

$F = -k(|d| - l_0)\vec{d}$ is Hooke's law;

$F(t, \dot{x}(t)) = -b\dot{x}(t)$ is the damper;

$\dot{x}_p(t)$ is the velocity of the other particle connected to the joint;

t is time;

k is the elastic constant;

l_0 is the length of the spring;

d is the variation in the length of the spring;

b is the damping constant.

Adding the damper is extremely useful, not only because it increases the realism of the resulting simulated behavior, but also—and perhaps mainly—because it helps mitigate oscillations intensity and duration. Since it is our aim to simulate also rigid bodies using particle systems, it is of

TABLE 1: Comparison of the more diffused game engines based on the requirements we have defined.

	Requirements			
	1	2	3	4
Box2D	Yes	No	No	Yes
Bullet	Partial	Yes in 3D	Yes in 3D	Yes
CryEngine 3/BeamNG	No	Yes	Yes	Partial
Digital Molecular Matter (DMM)	No	Yes	Yes	No
Havok	No	No	No	No
Newton Game Dynamics	Yes	No	No	Yes
Open Dynamics Engine (ODE)	Yes	No	No	Yes
PhysX	No	Upcoming	Upcoming	Only Windows
Unreal Development Kit (UDK)	No	Yes	Yes	Partial
Unity3D	Yes	No	No	Yes

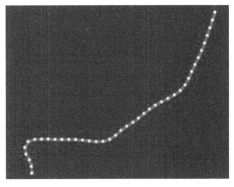

FIGURE 3: The rope is composed of 40 particles used to tune damping and refreshing rate in its starting state.

fundamental importance to be sure that the simulation will behave appropriately in a large interval of possible values for the elastic constant. For this reason, it has been necessary to balance damping, to define the most appropriate refreshing rate for the simulator, and to select the best possible numeric integrator, that is to say, the one that guarantees the most correct behavior while, at the same time, presenting good performances in terms of calculation time (we are dealing with real-time systems). To obtain these goals, we have tested different configurations of damping and refreshing rate on a linear configuration composed of a system of 40 particles, which simulates a rope (dots in Figure 3), connected by elastic joints (dashes in Figure 3). The starting state of the rope is horizontal and at rest (the spring between two consecutive particles is at rest; hence, the distance between the particles coincides with the length of the joint). When the simulation is started, both gravity and air friction start to affect the system (Figure 4). In particular, the air friction constant value has been set to 0.02, the length of the spring to 0.05 m, and the mass of the particles to 0.05 kg. It is quite easy to spot the moment in which the system loses stability: the rope vibrations get uncontrollable and the rope explodes due to growing elastic snaps (Figure 5). Table 2 summarizes the maximum values for the elastic constant when the refreshing rate is set to 500 Hz, while Table 3 summarizes the same values when the damping constant is set to 0.2. It is possible to notice that the values smaller than 50.0 (for the elastic constant) are not included, since, in such cases, the spring is too weak and its simulation loses any significance.

From Table 2, it is possible to notice that the accuracy of the integrator does not imply stability; for example, Runge-Kutta 4 (RK4) is a fourth order integrator, but it is quite ineffective with a high stiffness. In the same vein, NSV and inverse Euler (IE) are by far more effective than RK4, even if they both are only first order integrators. When the refreshing rate is taken into consideration (Table 3), it becomes clear that

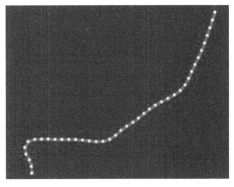

FIGURE 4: The rope oscillates correctly under the effects of friction and gravity.

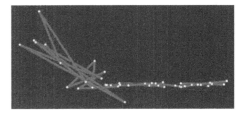

FIGURE 5: The rope explodes because the system has become instable.

semi-implicit integrators behave by far better than explicit integrators: in the first case, it is possible even to raise the value of the elastic constant six times without losing stability, while in the latter case that value can be—at most—doubled.

For these reasons, we have chosen to set the default refreshing rate at 500 Hz and the damping constant to 0.2 and to implement the symplectic Euler integrator (NSV).

Last but not least, it is important to underline that, for both soft and rigid bodies represented by means of a particles system, it is necessary to introduce some "internal" joint that will guarantee that the object will not collapse on itself after a collision. This phenomenon is depicted in Figure 6: the deformable square on the left of the figure has collided with the floor, but it has no internal joint among the particles, while

TABLE 2: Maximum values of the elastic constant with variable damping and fixed refreshing rate (500 Hz).

		Damping			
	0.0	0.1	0.2	0.3	0.4
Eulero	—	50	100	150	200
SUVAT/RK2	—	100	200	300	400
RK4	—	150	300	450	600
NSV/IE	50	8500	9000	9500	11000

TABLE 3: Maximum values of the elastic constant with variable refresh rate and fixed damping (0.2).

		Frequency (refresh rate—Hz)			
	60	100	250	500	1000
Eulero	—	—	50	100	1000
SUVAT/RK2	—	—	100	200	400
RK4	—	60	150	300	600
NSV/IE	150	450	2700	8000	47500

the deformable square on the right has—correctly—bounced away after the collision.

3.2. Simulating Rigid Bodies with Sulfur. Increasing the stiffness of the elastic joint alone is not enough to simulate effectively rigid bodies by means of a particles system. Actually, not only the stiffness should be enough to avoid deformation of objects during collisions, but also the simulation should behave properly when the system includes particles with a very different mass. In this latter case, the lighter particles will accelerate more than the heavier ones, even if they are all subject to the same force. Consequently, the system will unbalance and become instable. To avoid these undesirable effects, we are forced to introduce a new type of joint and, subsequently, to select an integrator that is able to handle it adequately. In particular, the new joint is a spring with infinite stiffness. In this case, the distance of two particles situated at the two ends of a joint is always constant, and Hooke's law is no longer useful. This particular joint will not generate a force (like in the case of the soft body), but an instantaneous change in velocity, thus modifying particles positions. Therefore, the integrator we have applied to soft bodies is no longer useful. As a matter of fact, traditional integrators are based on the assumption that the instantaneous acceleration is enough to describe completely the particle movement; in the case of this new joint, these integrators will lose the kinetic energy produced by the stiff spring, bringing highly inaccurate results.

A valid choice for an alternative integrator is the *Verlet* method [14, 15], a symplectic integrator of the second order, that is able to calculate the new position $x(t + \Delta t)$ of a particle after a certain interval of time has passed. The Verlet method is based on Taylor's theorem; it is applied two times: the

first time forward (in time) and then backward (in time), as described by the following formulae:

$$x(t + \Delta t)$$
$$= x(t) + \dot{x}(t)\Delta t + \frac{1}{2}\ddot{x}(t)\Delta t^2 + \frac{1}{6}x^{(3)}(t)\Delta t^3 + O\left(\Delta t^4\right),$$

$$x(t - \Delta t)$$
$$= x(t) - \dot{x}(t)\Delta t + \frac{1}{2}\ddot{x}(t)\Delta t^2 - \frac{1}{6}x^{(3)}(t)\Delta t^3 + O\left(\Delta t^4\right).$$
$$(2)$$

Hence,

$$x(t + \Delta t) = 2x(t) - x(t - \Delta t) + \ddot{x}(t)\Delta t^2 + O\left(\Delta t^4\right). \quad (3)$$

In (3), velocity does not appear explicitly; if needed, it can be derived from the difference between the starting and final positions of the particle(s). It is precisely for this reason that the Verlet method works well with our rigid joint: the integrator takes into account both forces and variations in particles positions without losing any kinetic energy. The *Velocity Verlet* and *Leapfrog* integrators are more accurate versions of the Verlet integrator [17], but they are more demanding from a computational point of view, without supplying any significant improvement to the stability of the system. For these reasons, the Sulfur engine is based on the Verlet method.

3.3. Managing Collisions with Sulfur. Even if we have chosen to create an engine aimed at 2D environments, the idea to simulate any type of body using only particles systems requires a careful analysis of all the possible implications and consequences on the collision management system. In particular, our approach allows the creation of particles aggregates with arbitrary shapes (linear, concave, and convex). Moreover, we intend to exploit the intrinsic modular nature of these aggregates to simulate fractures. Therefore, we need to apply a collision detection system that is able to track even the smallest possible aggregate: two particles connected by a joint. It is possible to notice that a single particle is an immaterial point with infinitesimal size; hence, it is not subject to collisions. These peculiarities imply that applying the most diffused techniques for collision detection (such as *Bounding Volume Hierarchy (BVH), Sweep And Prune (SAP), Separating Axis Theorem (SAT), and Gilbert-Johnson-Keerthi (GJK) distance algorithm*; see, e.g., [41–48]) is not a viable way. In the same vein, the *Bentley-Ottmann* algorithm, also called *Sweep-Plane* algorithm [49], which is aimed at finding intersections between segments on a plane, is not adaptable to our specific case. In particular, it considers only one-dimensional segments that cannot cope with some extreme case, such as those depicted in Figure 7. The segment on the left of the figure would pass through the floor unnoticed, unless we release the constraint of one dimensionality. Similarly, the segment on the right would cross, unnoticed, the joint in the floor.

Since no standard method to manage collision detection seems to be able to support our approach to rigid-body

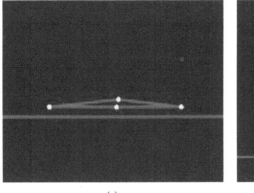
(a)

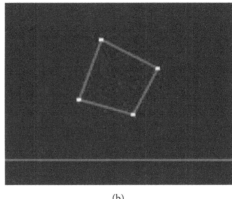
(b)

FIGURE 6: A deformable soft square—with and without internal joint—collides with the floor.

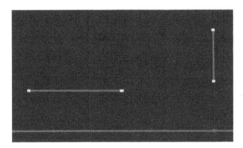

FIGURE 7: Two segments that should collide with the floor.

representation, we have developed an original approach, which preserves the two "canonical" phases: *broad* and *narrow* phases of collision detection.

The first—*broad*—phase of collision detection is aimed at detecting the objects potentially superimposing. To avoid the trap of one-dimensional segments, we include each segment in a "capsule" (see Figure 8(a)), which simulates thickness. We then subdivide the plane with a uniform grid and keep track of the cells crossed by each segment in each moment (see Figure 8(b)). When a cell registers a collision, the capsules are superimposing and they are selected and included in a list of objects that will be further processed during the following *narrow* phase. To guarantee that the broad phase is executed in the shortest possible time, we have implemented the *Bresenham Line* algorithm [50], which supplies good performances, with an execution time which depends linearly from the number of capsules present on the grid.

The subsequent *narrow* phase of collision detection takes as input the cells selected during the broad phase and verifies whether or not the couple of segments is really in contact and, in case, determines the contact point.

Finally, the *reaction* to the collision is calculated according to a projection approach: the bodies are moved away from each other the minimum distance necessary to separate them. The joint among the particles will guarantee that the whole object will move away in a convincing way.

To add realism to the simulation of collisions, we have also added a simplified version of a friction model. We take into account only sliding friction, without any distinction between

static and dynamic frictions. The main idea is to apply to the particles a force that is tangent to the direction of the collision and proportional to the projection of velocity on this tangent, but in the opposite direction. This is only a first attempt to include friction in our simulator, and it is under improvement for further developments.

4. Atlax, Sulfur, SulfurChamber, and Escape from Quaoar

Both Atlax and Sulfur have been developed in C++, which is the most diffused language for computational intensive applications and for interactive physics simulations. All the libraries we have adopted are independent of the operating system in order to provide the maximum possible portability. All the codes we have developed have been tested on both Windows and Linux.

Atlax is a framework application aimed at supporting the development of interactive graphic applications. Its most relevant feature is to be based transparently on two low-level different libraries: *wxWidgets* [51], a cross-platform graphical user interface (GUI) library, and *Simple DirectMedia Layer* [52], a cross-platform library designed to provide low-level access to audio, keyboard, mouse, joystick, and graphics hardware via OpenGL [53] and DirectX [54]. The first library is used when we need to create applications with a GUI, such as a sandbox for the physics engine. The second library is specifically aimed at video games. Therefore, this approach made it possible to create an engine that can be used both for the real game and for the editor, just by switching the underpinning library.

Sulfur is the library of the physics engine. It is strongly linked to Atlax, since the two share some classes (notably to execute calculus and to dynamically manage particles and joints). It implements the approach we have summarized in Section 3.

Based on Atlax and Sulfur, we have developed two applications aimed at testing the effectiveness of the approach: SulfurChamber and Escape from Quaoar.

SulfurChamber is the sandbox software application for the Sulfur physics engine, and it is based on the Atlax-wxWidgets

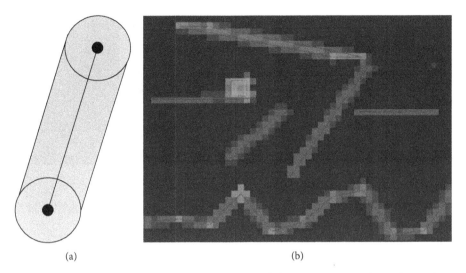

FIGURE 8: A single capsule surrounding a segment (a) and the representation of capsules on the grid.

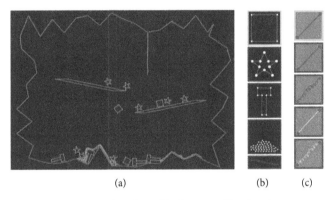

FIGURE 9: Soft and rigid bodies in SulfurChamber.

version. Its main purpose is to allow the experimenting of different configurations of particles with varying elasticity, gravity, sliding friction, and air friction (Figure 9(a)). In particular, it is possible to create objects starting from a predefined set (Figure 9(b)) or by designing them from scratch by combining sets of particles and joints (Figure 9(c)). We have tested the performances of SulfurChamber on several different combinations of hardware and operating system, that is to say, AMD Atlon64 3200 with Windows XP, Intel Core2Duo T7700 with Windows 7, and Intel Core-i7 930 with Linux-Ubuntu. The simulation has been run by simulating an increasing number of identical squared boxes (each of which is composed of four particles: four main rigid joints and two internal structural joints). Couples of boxes were dropping from above continuously; hence, no box was in a state of rest (this would have the consequence of excluding the box from the physics simulation). The values of friction, mass, and gravity were set to the same values for the whole simulation. Table 4 summarizes the percentage of consumption of the CPU time dedicated to executing calculations to refresh the physics simulation. From the data emerges that the maximum numbers of boxes for which the system remains stable and reactive are around 60 or less, depending on the combination

TABLE 4: Performance of Sulfur with different hardware and software configurations.

	Number of dropping boxes per second						
	20	40	60	80	100	150	200
Athlon64—Win XP	12%	30%	45%	65%	83%	100%	100%
Core2Duo—Win 7	10%	22%	42%	55%	72%	95%	100%
i7-930—Ubuntu	5%	10%	20%	25%	35%	50%	75%

hardware-operating system (when the CPU consumption reaches 80%–90%, the simulation obviously starts to slow down, till getting irremediably stuck). Even if this maximum number of objects was enough for the video game we have developed to test the opportunities offered by Sulfur, it is evident that the physics engine would benefit a lot from some improvements aimed at optimizing code and performances.

Escape from Quaoar [16] is a side-scroller platform video game that has been designed and developed to test the performances of Sulfur in a real application. For this reason, the gameplay explicitly exploits and stresses the whole range of features provided by the physics simulator. The core mechanic is based on an elastic rope (see Figure 10(b)), that

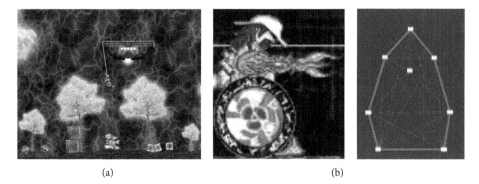

FIGURE 10: Screenshots from Escape from Quaoar: example of a level (a) and the main character texture and underpinning particle system (b).

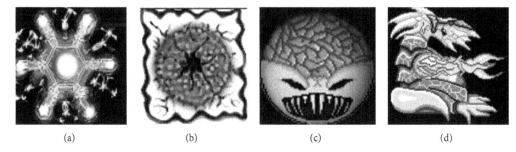

FIGURE 11: The first three objects have been modeled by elastic aggregates of particles, while the latter one is a rigid body, which stays fixed on the floor.

is, the only locomotion mean at disposal of the player. All the in-game objects are physics-driven (except for the main character arm that is moved by the player to fire the rope towards specific points). Monster and objects encountered in the levels are—soft or rigid—particles systems masked by appropriate textures (see Figure 11(a)). The overall behavior of the game is very satisfying, and the game has participated in the 13th Independent Game Festival (IGF) [55].

5. Conclusion and Future Work

The main goals of our work have been to design and create a physics simulator for video games that are able to unify rigid and soft bodies simulation, endowed with effective and reactive collision detection and resolution system. The Sulfur physics engine has reached this goal, overcoming the stiffness problem intrinsic to traditional approaches by using the Verlet integrator coupled with the adoption of particles systems to simulate not only soft bodies, but also rigid ones. This approach has an interesting side effect: it does not mess up with angles and rotations. In the same vein, we have obtained a sound approach to collision management by coupling a static grid with Bresenham algorithm. Hence, with a relatively small effort, we are able to manage a relevant number of dynamic objects. Last but not least, we have extensively tested the proposed solution by developing 26 levels for a side-scroller video game, whose mechanics is based on elastic bodies, obtaining satisfying results.

Nonetheless, we are well aware that Sulfur is still in its infancy. It needs improvements and developments from several points of view, such as the following:

(i) increasing accuracy of simulation for friction;

(ii) creating an efficient and effective approach to manage curve and circular objects (at present they can only be simulated with a huge number of particles and joints);

(iii) optimizing calculation-intensive code section, by moving the workload to the GPU;

(iv) introducing angular joints, to decrease the number of particles used to represent a single object;

(v) introducing a more sophisticated simulation of fractures (at the moment, fractures are obtained by removing some joints);

(vi) extending Sulfur to 3D simulation;

(vii) extending Sulfur to simulate fluids motion;

(viii) finally, yet importantly, reducing the refreshing rate (whose value at present is around 500 Hz), without scarifying stability while—possibly—increasing performances. This goal could be reached by selecting an appropriate, but more complex, integrator that could reduce the number of iterations.

Conflict of Interests

The authors declare that there is no conflict of interests regarding the publication of this paper.

References

[1] D. H. Eberly, *3D Game Engine Design: A Practical Approach to Real-Time Computer Graphics*, Morgan Kaufmann, San Francisco, Calif, USA, 2001.

[2] J. Gregory, Ed., *Game Engine Architecture*, Taylor and Francis, 2009.

[3] R. Koster, *A Theory of Fun for Game Design*, Paraglyph Press, 2005.

[4] M. Csikszentmihalyi, *Flow: The Psychology of Optimal Experience*, Harper Perennial, 1991.

[5] T. Fullerton, *Game Design Workshop: A Playcentric Approach to Creating Innovative Games*, Elsevier, 2008.

[6] E. Zimmerman and K. Salen, *Rules of Play: Game Design Fundamentals*, The MIT Press, 2004.

[7] R. Bartle, *Designing Virtual Worlds*, New Riders Pub, 2003.

[8] I. Millington, *Game Physics Engine Development*, Morgan Kaufmann, San Francisco, Calif, USA, 2007.

[9] Gran Turismo, http://www.gran-turismo.com/.

[10] Havok, http://www.havok.com/.

[11] D. H. Eberly, *3D Game Engine Architecture: Engineering Real-Time Applications with Wild Magic*, Morgan Kaufmann, San Francisco, Calif, USA, 2005.

[12] A. Witkin and D. Baraff, "Physically based modeling: principles and practice," in *Proceedings of the Association for Computing Machinery Special Interest Group on Graphics (SIGGRAPH '97)*, Los Angeles, Calif, USA, 1997.

[13] T. Jakobsen, "Advanced Character Physics," 2003, http://www.pagines.ma1.upc.edu/~susin/files/AdvancedCharacterPhysics.pdf.

[14] M. Mcguire and O. C. Jenkins, *Creating Games: Mechanics, Content, and Technology*, A K Peters, 2008.

[15] L. Verlet, "Computer "experiments" on classical fluids. I. Thermodynamic properties of Lennard-Jones molecules," *Physical Review*, vol. 159, no. 1, pp. 98–103, 1967.

[16] Escape from Quaoar, http://www.escapefromquaoar.com/.

[17] D. H. Eberly, *Game Physics*, Morgan Kaufmann, San Francisco, Calif, USA, 2003.

[18] D. Kodicek, *Mathematics and Physics for Game Programmers*, Charles River Media, Hingham, Mass, USA, 2005.

[19] G. H. Cottet and P. D. Koumoutsakos, *Vortex Methods. Theory and Practice*, Cambridge University Press, 2000.

[20] J. J. Monaghan, "Smoothed particle hydrodynamics," *Annual Review of Astronomy and Astrophysics*, vol. 30, no. 1, pp. 543–574, 1992.

[21] A. Hérault, G. Bilotta, A. Vicari, E. Rustico, and C. del Negro, "Numerical simulation of lava flow using a GPU SPH model," *Annals of Geophysics*, vol. 54, no. 5, pp. 600–620, 2011.

[22] E. Rustico, G. Bilotta, A. Hérault, C. Del Negro, and G. Gallo, "Smoothed particle hydrodynamics simulations on multi-GPU systems," in *Proceedings of the 20th Euromicro International Conference on Parallel, Distributed and Network-Based Computing, Special Session on GPU Computing and Hybrid Computing*, Munich, Germany, 2012.

[23] J. Bonet and S. Kulasegaram, "Correction and stabilization of smooth particle hydrodynamics methods with applications in metal forming simulations," *International Journal for Numerical Methods in Engineering*, vol. 47, no. 6, pp. 1189–1214, 2000.

[24] M. I. Herreros and M. Mabssout, "A two-steps time discretization scheme using the SPH method for shock wave propagation," *Computer Methods in Applied Mechanics and Engineering*, vol. 200, no. 21-22, pp. 1833–1845, 2011.

[25] T. Rabczuk and J. Eibl, "Simulation of high velocity concrete fragmentation using SPH/MLSPH," *International Journal for Numerical Methods in Engineering*, vol. 56, no. 10, pp. 1421–1444, 2003.

[26] M. Muller, D. Charypar, and M. Gross, "Particle-based fluid simulation for interactive applications," in *Proceeding of the ACM SIGGRAPH/Eurographics Symposium on Computer Animation*, pp. 154–159, Eurographics Association, 2003.

[27] Box2D, http://box2d.org/.

[28] Bullet, http://bulletphysics.org/wordpress.

[29] Cryengine, http://www.crytek.com/cryengine.

[30] "Digital Molecular Matter—Pixelux," http://www.pixelux.com/.

[31] I. Babuška, U. Banerjee, and J. E. Osborn, "Generalized finite element methods: main ideas, results, and perspective," *International Journal of Computational Methods*, vol. 1, no. 1, pp. 67–103, 2004.

[32] K. J. Bathe, *Finite Element Procedures*, Klaus-Jürgen Bathe, Cambridge, Mass, USA, 2006.

[33] J. N. Reddy, *An Introduction to the Finite Element Method*, McGraw-Hill, New York, NY, USA, 3rd edition, 2005.

[34] O. C. Zienkiewicz, R. L. Taylor, and J. Z. Zhu, *The Finite Element Method: Its Basis and Fundamentals*, Butterworth-Heinemann, 6th edition, 2005.

[35] Newton Game Dynamics, http://newtondynamics.com/forum/newton.php.

[36] Open Dynamics Engine—ODE, http://www.ode.org/.

[37] PhysX, http://developer.nvidia.com/object/physx.html.

[38] "Unreal Development Kit—UDK," http://www.unrealengine.com/en/udk/.

[39] Unity3D, http://unity3d.com/.

[40] I. Millington and J. Funge, *Artificial Intelligence for Games*, Morgan Kaufmann, 2nd edition, 2009.

[41] D. Baraff, *Dynamic simulation of non-penetrating rigid bodies [Ph.D. thesis]*, Computer Science Department, Cornell University, 1992.

[42] J. D. Cohen, M. C. Lin, D. Manocha, and M. Ponamgi, "I-COLLIDE: an interactive and exact collision detection system for large-scale environments," in *Proceedings of the Symposium on Interactive 3D Graphics*, pp. 189–196, Monterey, Calif, USA, April 1995.

[43] E. Christer, *Real-TimeCollision Detection*, Morgan Kaufmann series in interactive 3D technology, Elsevier, Amsterdam, The Netherlands, 2005.

[44] E. G. Gilbert, D. W. Johnson, and S. S. Keerthi, "A fast procedure for computing the distance between complex objects in three-dimensional space," *IEEE Journal of Robotics and Automation*, vol. 4, no. 2, pp. 193–203, 1988.

[45] Golshtein and E. G. Tretyakov, *Modified Lagrangians and Monotone Maps in Optimization*, Wiley, New York, NY, USA, 1996, translated by N. V. Tretyakov.

[46] J. Günther, S. Popov, H.-P. Seidel, and P. Slusallek, "Realtime ray tracing on GPU with BVH-based packet traversal," in *Proceedings of the IEEE/Eurographics Interactive Ray Tracing Symposium (IRT '07)*, pp. 113–118, September 2007.

[47] K. Shimizu, Y. Ishizuka, and J. F. Bard, *Nondifferentiable and Two-Level Mathematical Programming*, Kluwer Academic Publishers, Boston, Mass, USA, 1997.

[48] G. van den Bergen, *Collision Detection in Interactive 3D Environments*, Morgan Kaufmann, San Francisco, Calif, USA, 2003.

[49] U. Bartuschka, K. Mehlhorn, and S. Naher, "A robust and efficient implementation of a sweep line algorithm for the straight-line segment intersection problem," in *Proceedings of the Workshop on Algorithm Engineering*, S. Orlando, Ed., 1997.

[50] J. E. Bresenham, "Algorithm for computer control of a digital plotter," *IBM Systems Journal*, vol. 4, no. 1, pp. 25–30, 1965.

[51] wxWidgets, http://www.wxwidgets.org/.

[52] SDL, 2013, http://www.libsdl.org/.

[53] OpenGL, http://www.opengl.org/.

[54] Direct3D, http://www.microsoft.com/en-us/download/details.aspx?id=23803.

[55] "IGF—Independent Games Festival," http://www.igf.com/.

Neural Network to Solve Concave Games

Zixin Liu[1,2] and Nengfa Wang[2]

[1] College of Computer Science and Information, GuiZhou University, Guiyang 550025, China
[2] Department of Mathematics and Statistics, Guizhou University of Finance and Economics, Guiyang 550004, China

Correspondence should be addressed to Zixin Liu; xinxin905@163.com

Academic Editor: Daniel Thalmann

The issue on neural network method to solve concave games is concerned. Combined with variational inequality, Ky Fan inequality, and projection equation, concave games are transformed into a neural network model. On the basis of the Lyapunov stable theory, some stability results are also given. Finally, two classic games' simulation results are given to illustrate the theoretical results.

1. Introduction

Recently, game theory has attracted considerable attention due to its extensive applications in economics, political science, and psychology, as well as logic and biology [1–5]. It has been widely recognized as an important tool in many fields.

For game theory, the existence and stability of Nash equilibrium point are the most concerned problems. In past decades, these problems have been widely researched. Up to now, many excellent papers and monographs can be found, such as [6–11]. However, most previously established theory results are difficult to be adopted in practical applications, since the existence results only tell us that, for a given game, the Nash equilibrium point exists, but they do not tell us what it is or how we can calculate it.

As is well known, the solving problem of Nash equilibrium point is as important as the existence and stability problems. In order to compute the Nash equilibrium point for a given game, all kinds of optimal algorithms and experiments have been derived in [12–15]. Among these methods, computer technique is one of the most popular ones. For a given game, by utilizing a computer programme to simulate the players, Nash equilibrium point can be approximately solved through computer logic calculation. However, when the quantity of players is large, the computation complexity and converge analysis must be considered.

Conversely, projection neural network for solving optimization problems has its distinctly superior. This point is

elaborated in [16–18]. The first is that it has parallel computing ability. The second is that the solution naturally exists. The last is that it can be implemented by circuits easily. One natural question is, for a given game, whether we can compute the Nash equilibrium point by neural network. This idea motivates this study.

Combined with concave game theory, projection equation theory, variational inequality, Ky Fan inequality, and neural network method, we first established the relationship between neural network and concave games and pointed out that the equilibrium point of the constructed neural network is the Nash equilibrium point of our concerned game. Then, by using the Lyapunov stable theory, we analyzed the stability of the established neural network. Finally, two classic games are presented to illustrate the validity of the main results.

2. N-Person Noncooperative Games

Consider a typical n-person noncooperative game as follows: let $N = \{1, 2, \ldots, n\}$ be the set of players. For each $i \in N$, X_i, a metric space, denotes the strategy set and $f_i : X = \Pi_{i=1}^{n} X_i \to \mathbb{R}$ is the payoff function of ith player, respectively.

For each $i \in N$, denote $\hat{i} = N \setminus \{i\}$. For n-person noncooperative games, one of the most important problem is to research whether there exists $x^* = (x_1^*, x_2^*, \ldots, x_n^*) \in X$ such that, $\forall i \in N$, $f_i(x_i^*, x_{\hat{i}}^*) = \max_{u_i \in X_i} f_i(u_i, x_{\hat{i}}^*)$, where x^* is called the Nash equilibrium point. And another problem is, if x^* exists, what it is. To further discussion, the following basic assumptions, definitions, and lemmas are needed.

Assumptions. We have

(1) $\forall i \in N$, strategy set $X_i \in \mathbb{R}^{m_i}$ is nonempty, closed, and convex.

(2) $\forall i \in N$, payoff function $f_i : X = \Pi_{i=1}^n X_i \to \mathbb{R}$ is continuously differentiable, and, $\forall x_{\hat{i}} \in X_{\hat{i}}, u_i \to f_i(u_i, x_{\hat{i}})$ is concave on X_i.

Definition 1. Let C be a convex subset of linear space $\mathbb{E}$, $\forall x_1, x_2 \in C, \forall \lambda \in (0, 1)$; if function $f : C \to \mathbb{R}$ satisfies

$$f\left(\lambda x_1 + (1 - \lambda) x_2\right) \geq \min\left\{f\left(x_1\right), f\left(x_2\right)\right\}, \qquad (1)$$

then f is said to be quasiconcave.

Definition 2. Let X be a Hausdorff topological space, $f : X \to \mathbb{R}$ is a functional, $x \in X$, and if, $\forall \varepsilon > 0$, there exists open neighborhood $U(x)$ of x such that $\forall x' \in U(x)$,

$$f(x) < f\left(x'\right) + \varepsilon, \qquad (2)$$

then functional f is said to be lower semicontinuous.

Remark 3. Obviously, function f being concave means that it is quasiconcave; functional f being continuous means that it is lower semicontinuous.

Lemma 4 (Ky Fan inequality). *Let X be a nonempty convex compact subset of Hausdorff linear topological space $\mathbb{E}$; $f : X \times X \to \mathbb{R}$ satisfies the following.*

(1) $\forall x \in X, y \to f(x, y)$ *is lower semicontinuous on X.*

(2) $\forall y \in X, x \to f(x, y)$ *is quasiconcave on X.*

(3) $\forall x \in X, f(x, x) \leq 0$.

Then, there exists $y^* \in X$ such that, $\forall x \in X, f(x, y^*) \leq 0$.

Lemma 5. *Let $X \in \mathbb{R}^n$ be a nonempty, closed, and convex subset of $\mathbb{R}^n$, and function $f : X \to \mathbb{R}$ is continuously differentiable and concave; then, $\forall x, y \in X$,*

$$f(y) \leq f(x) + \langle \nabla f(x), y - x \rangle, \qquad (3)$$

where $\nabla f(x) = (\partial f/\partial x_1, \partial f/\partial x_2, \partial f/\partial x_n)$.

From Lemma 5, the following results are obvious.

Lemma 6. *Let $X \in \mathbb{R}^n$ be a nonempty, closed, and convex subset of $\mathbb{R}^n$, and function $f : X \to \mathbb{R}$ is continuously differentiable and concave, $x^* \in X$; then, $f(x^*) = \max_{x \in X} f(x)$ if and only if $\forall x \in X$ the following variational inequality holds:*

$$\langle \nabla f\left(x^*\right), x - x^* \rangle \leq 0. \qquad (4)$$

Remark 7. N-person noncooperative game is called a concave one if the payoff function $f_i : X \to \mathbb{R}$ is continuous, and, $\forall x_{\hat{i}} \in X_{\hat{i}}, u_i \to f_i(u_i, x_{\hat{i}})$ is concave on X_i. For concave game, there exists a special equivalence relation among the Brouwer fixed-point theory and variational inequality problem [19]; this relationship provides the theoretical basis to solve the Nash equilibrium point for concave game by neural networks.

3. The Equivalence between Concave Games and Variational Inequalities

In this section, we will point out that any concave game can be transformed into a variational inequality problem equivalently, and we will utilize Ky Fan inequality to prove the existence of the Nash equilibrium point.

Theorem 8. *$\forall i \in N$, strategy set $X_i \in \mathbb{R}^{m_i}$ is nonempty, closed, and convex, payoff function $f_i : X = \Pi_{i=1}^n X_i \to \mathbb{R}$ is continuously differentiable, and, $\forall x_{\hat{i}} \in X_{\hat{i}}, u_i \to f_i(u_i, x_{\hat{i}})$ is concave on X_i. Then, $x^* = (x_1^*, x_2^*, \ldots, x_n^*) \in X$ is the Nash equilibrium point of concave game if and only if x^* is a solution of the following variational inequality, namely:*

$$\forall x \in X, \quad \langle \nabla f\left(x^*\right), x - x^* \rangle \leq 0. \qquad (5)$$

Proof. $\forall i \in N, \forall x_i \in X_i$, set $\overline{x} = (x_i, x_{\hat{i}}^*)$, and then $\overline{x} \in X$, since $\langle \nabla f(x^*), x - x^* \rangle \leq 0$; from Lemma 6, we have $f_i(x_i^*, x_{\hat{i}}^*) = \max_{x \in X} f_i(x, x_{\hat{i}}^*)$. Conversely, if $x^* = (x_1^*, x_2^*, \ldots, x_n^*) \in X$ is the Nash equilibrium of concave game, then, $\forall i \in N, f_i(x_i^*, x_{\hat{i}}^*) = \max_{x \in X} f_i(x, x_{\hat{i}}^*)$; from Lemma 6, we have, $\forall x \in X, \langle \nabla f(x^*), x - x^* \rangle \leq 0$. This completes the proof.

Remark 9. This proof is similar to the convex situation in [20]. In fact, from [20], one can obtain this result directly. Here, for the readability, we still give out the proof details.

Remark 10. From Theorem 8, one can see that the Nash equilibrium point problem of a concave game is equivalent to a variational inequality problem. In order to solve the Nash equilibrium point of a concave game, we only need to solve the related variational inequality.

Theorem 11. *$\forall i \in N$, strategy set $X_i \in \mathbb{R}^{m_i}$ is nonempty, closed, and convex, payoff function $f_i : X = \Pi_{i=1}^n X_i \to \mathbb{R}$ is continuously differentiable, and, $\forall x_{\hat{i}} \in X_{\hat{i}}, u_i \to f_i(u_i, x_{\hat{i}})$ is concave on X_i. Then, there exists $x^* = (x_1^*, x_2^*, \ldots, x_n^*) \in X$, such that,*

$$\forall x \in X, \quad \langle \nabla f\left(x^*\right), x - x^* \rangle \leq 0. \qquad (6)$$

Namely, the Nash equilibrium point of the concerned concave game exists.

Proof. $\forall x, y \in X$, define

$$\varphi(x, y) = \langle -\nabla f(x), x - y \rangle. \qquad (7)$$

Since $f_i : X = \Pi_{i=1}^n X_i \to \mathbb{R}$ is continuously differentiable, then it is easy to check that,

(1) $\forall y \in X, x \to \varphi(x, y) = \langle -\nabla f(x), x - y \rangle$ is continuous on X;

(2) $\forall x \in X, y \to \varphi(x, y) = \langle -\nabla f(x), x - y \rangle$ is concave on X;

(3) $\forall x \in X, \varphi(x, x) = \langle -\nabla f(x), 0 \rangle = 0$.

From Lemma 4, there exist $x^* = (x_1^*, x_2^*, \ldots, x_n^*) \in X$ such that, $\forall x \in X$, we have $\varphi(x^*, x) = \langle -\nabla f(x^*), x^* - x \rangle \leq 0$;

namely, $\forall x \in X$, $\langle \nabla f(x^*), x - x^* \rangle \leq 0$, and this completes the proof.

Remark 12. From Theorem 11, one can see that if X_i and f_i satisfy assumptions (1) and (2), the solution of the variational inequality in Theorem 11 exists, which means that the Nash equilibrium point of our concerned concave game exists. Combined with Theorems 8 and 11, we can construct neural network model to solve concave game problems.

4. Neural Network Model for Concave Games

4.1. Neural Network Model Construction. To proceed, we first introduce an important lemma as follows.

Lemma 13 (see [21]). *Let $f : \mathbb{R}^n \to \mathbb{R}^n$ be continuous function, and Ω is subset of $\mathbb{R}^n$; then x^* satisfies $\langle f(x^*), x - x^* \rangle \geq 0$ for all $x \in \mathbb{R}^n$ if and only if x^* is the fixed point of equation $x = P_\Omega(x - \alpha f(x))$, where α is arbitrary positive constant and $P_\Omega(x - \alpha f(x))$ is projection operator defined by*

$$P_\Omega(u) = \arg \min_{v \in \Omega} \|u - v\|. \tag{8}$$

On the basis of Theorems 8 and 11 and Lemma 13, we can construct the following neural network to solve the Nash equilibrium point of our concerned concave game:

$$\frac{dx(t)}{dt} = -x(t) + P_X(x(t) + \alpha \nabla f(x(t))), \tag{9}$$

where $x(t) \in \mathbb{R}^n$ is the state vector, $X = \prod_{i=1}^n X_i$, $\nabla f(x(t)) = (\nabla_{x_1(t)} f_1(x(t)), \nabla_{x_2(t)} f_2(x(t)), \ldots, \nabla_{x_n(t)} f_n(x(t)))$, and $f_i : X \to \mathbb{R}$ is the payoff function of ith player.

Remark 14. From Lemma 13, one can see that x^* is an equilibrium point of system (9) if and only if it is a Nash equilibrium point of our concerned concave games; notice Theorem 11; one can obtain that the equilibrium point of system (9) exists. Thus, if the equilibrium point of system (9) is asymptotically stable, we can solve the Nash equilibrium point through neural network (9), which can be implemented by electric circuit. This means that Nash equilibrium point can be solved by electric circuit.

Remark 15. If function f is convex and $\alpha < 0$, system (9) becomes a typical projection neural network model, which is widely researched in [22–25]. Similar to [24], we will give the stability analysis as follows.

4.2. Stability Analysis. Set x^* as the equilibrium point (also the Nash equilibrium point) of system (9), and let $y(t) = x(t) - x^*$; then system (9) can be transformed into

$$\frac{dy(t)}{dt} = -y(t) + P_X(y(t) + x^* + \alpha \nabla f(y(t) + x^*))$$

$$- P_X(x^* + \alpha \nabla f(x^*)). \tag{10}$$

Lemma 16 (see [21]). *Let Ω be a closed convex set of $\mathbb{R}^n$; then projection operator satisfies*

$$(v - P_\Omega(v))^T (P_\Omega(v) - x) \geq 0, \quad v \in \mathbb{R}^n, \ x \in \Omega,$$

$$\|P_\Omega(u) - P_\Omega(v)\| \leq \|u - v\|, \quad u, v \in \mathbb{R}^n, \tag{11}$$

where $\|\cdot\|$ denotes $L^2(\mathbb{R}^n)$ norm.

Theorem 17. *Under assumptions (1) and (2), the state vector of system (9) globally asymptotically converges to the Nash equilibrium point.*

Proof. Set X^* as the equilibrium point set of system (9); obviously, $X^* \subset X$. If state vector $x(t) = x^* \in X^*$, then the conclusion holds naturally. Without loss of generality, we assume that $x(t) \notin X^*$. In this case, construct the Lyapunov function as follows:

$$V(y(t)) = \alpha (f(x^*) - f(y(t) + x^*)). \tag{12}$$

Since, $\forall i \in N$, $f_i(x_i^*, x_{\hat{i}}^*) = \max_{x \in X} f_i(x, x_{\hat{i}}^*)$, we have $V(y(t)) \geq 0$, $V(0) = 0$. The time derivative of $V(y(t))$ along the trajectory of system (10) is given as

$$\dot{V}(y(t)) = \left\langle -\alpha \nabla f(y(t) + x^*), \frac{dy(t)}{dt} \right\rangle. \tag{13}$$

Notice that $x^* = P_X(x^* + \alpha \nabla f(x^*))$; it follows that

$$\dot{V}(y(t)) = \left\langle -\alpha \nabla f(y(t) + x^*), \frac{dy(t)}{dt} \right\rangle$$

$$= \left\langle -\alpha \nabla f(y(t) + x^*), -y(t) - x^* \right.$$

$$\left. + P_X(y(t) + x^* + \alpha \nabla f(y(t) + x^*)) \right\rangle. \tag{14}$$

Since $x(t) = y(t) + x^* \in X$, denote $P_X(y(t) + x^* + \alpha \nabla f(y(t) + x^*)) = P_X(u(t))$, where $u = y(t) + x^* + \alpha \nabla f(y(t) + x^*)$, (14) can be rewritten as

$$\dot{V}(y(t)) = \left\langle -\alpha \nabla f(y(t) + x^*), \frac{dy(t)}{dt} \right\rangle$$

$$= \left\langle -\alpha \nabla f(y(t) + x^*), P_X(u(t)) - x(t) \right\rangle$$

$$= \left\langle -u(t) + x(t), P_X(u(t)) - x(t) \right\rangle \tag{15}$$

$$= -\left\langle u(t) - P_X(u(t)), P_X(u(t)) - x(t) \right\rangle$$

$$- \left\langle P_X(u(t)) - x(t), P_X(u(t)) - x(t) \right\rangle.$$

Notice that $x(t) \notin X^*$; we have $-\langle P_X(u(t)) - x(t), P_X(u(t)) - x(t) \rangle < 0$, and additionally, from Lemma 16, we have $-\langle u(t) - P_X(u(t)), P_X(u(t)) - x(t) \rangle < 0$; thus, $\dot{V}(y(t)) < 0$. On the basis of the Lyapunov stable theory, one can obtain that the state vector of system (9) globally asymptotically converges to the Nash equilibrium point. This completes the proof. □

Remark 18. For convex optimization problems, projection neural network has similar property. Compared with previous work, our Lyapunov function sufficiently uses the property of Nash equilibrium point; thus, it is more simple and the proof is more concise. The reason is that, in our proof, the value of v in Lemma 13 is set more appropriately.

Remark 19. Similar to the proof of [23], we can obtain the following propositions.

Proposition 20. *For any initial value $x_0 \in X$, the solution $x(t, x_0)$ of system (9) is unique, bounded, and $x(t, x_0) \in X$.*

Proposition 21. *If the domain of payoff function f is $\mathbb{R}^n$ and continuous, under assumptions (1) and (2), for any initial value $x_0 \notin X \subset \mathbb{R}^n$, there exists $T > 0$ such that for all $t > T$, the solution $x(t, x_0)$ of system (9) satisfies $x(t, x_0) \in X$.*

Remark 22. Proposition 20 means that, for any initial value in the strategy set X, the solution through this initial value is unique and bounded, and the strategy set X is an invariant set. Proposition 21 means that the strategy set X is attractive.

Remark 23. On the basis of Propositions 20 and 21, we can further show that the equilibrium point of system (9) is not only globally asymptotically stable but also approximately exponentially stable.

Theorem 24. *If the domain of payoff function f is $\mathbb{R}^n$ and continuous, under assumptions (1) and (2), when $\alpha > 0$ is sufficiently small, then the state vector of system (9) approximately exponentially converges to the Nash equilibrium point, and the approximate convergence exponent is 1.*

Proof. From system (9), one can obtain

$$\frac{d\left(x(t) - x^*\right)}{dt} = \left(x^* - x(t)\right) + P_X\left(x(t) + \alpha \nabla f(x(t))\right) \tag{16}$$
$$- P_X\left(x^* + \alpha \nabla f(x^*)\right).$$

Set the initial value of system (9) as x_0, and by differential theory and Lemma 13, we have

$$\left\|x(t) - x^*\right\|$$
$$\le e^{-(t-t_0)} \left\|x_0 - x^*\right\|$$
$$+ \int_{t_0}^{t} e^{-(t-s)} \left\|P_X\left(x(s) + \alpha \nabla f(x(s))\right) - P_X\left(x^* + \alpha \nabla f(x(s))\right)\right\| ds$$
$$\le e^{-(t-t_0)} \left\|x_0 - x^*\right\|$$
$$+ \int_{t_0}^{t} e^{-(t-s)} \left\|P_X\left(x(s) + \alpha \nabla f(x(s))\right) - P_X\left(x^* + \alpha \nabla f(x(s))\right)\right\| ds$$

$$+ \int_{t_0}^{t} e^{-(t-s)} \left\|P_X\left(x^* + \alpha \nabla f(x(s))\right) - P_X\left(x^* + \alpha \nabla f(x^*)\right)\right\| ds$$
$$\le e^{-(t-t_0)} \left\|x_0 - x^*\right\|$$
$$+ \int_{t_0}^{t} e^{-(t-s)} \left\|x(s) - x^*\right\| ds$$
$$+ \alpha \int_{t_0}^{t} e^{-(t-s)} \left\|\nabla f(x(s)) - \nabla f(x^*)\right\| ds. \tag{17}$$

If $x_0 \in X$, from Proposition 20, we have $x(t) \in X$. Notice assumptions (1) and (2); one can obtain that $\|\nabla f(x(s)) - \nabla f(x^*)\|$ is bounded, which can be assumed as M. In this case, we have

$$\left\|x(t) - x^*\right\| \le e^{-(t-t_0)} \left\|x_0 - x^*\right\| + \alpha M$$
$$+ \int_{t_0}^{t} e^{-(t-s)} \left\|x(s) - x^*\right\| ds. \tag{18}$$

By Gronwall-Bellman inequality, when α is sufficiently small, one can obtain that

$$\left\|x(t) - x^*\right\| \le e^{-(t-t_0)} \left\|x_0 - x^*\right\| e + \alpha e M$$
$$\approx e \left\|x_0 - x^*\right\| e^{-(t-t_0)}, \tag{19}$$

which means that, when $x_0 \in X$ and α is sufficiently small, the state vector of system (9) approximately exponentially converges to the Nash equilibrium point, and the approximate convergence exponent is 1.

If $x_0 \notin X$, from Proposition 21, there exists $T > 0$ such that, $\forall t > T$, $x(t) \in X$. In this case, we have

$$\left\|x(t) - x^*\right\| \le e^{-(t-t_0)} \left\|x_0 - x^*\right\|$$
$$+ \int_{t_0}^{t} e^{-(t-s)} \left\|x(s) - x^*\right\| ds$$
$$+ \int_{t_0}^{T} \alpha e^{-(t-s)} \left\|\nabla f(x(s)) - \nabla f(x^*)\right\| ds$$
$$+ \int_{T}^{t} \alpha e^{-(t-s)} \left\|\nabla f(x(s)) - \nabla f(x^*)\right\| ds. \tag{20}$$

Since f is continuous on $\mathbb{R}^n$, under assumptions (1) and (2), by Proposition 21, there exist positive constants M_1, M_2 such that $\int_{t_0}^{T} \alpha e^{-(t-s)} \|\nabla f(x(s)) - \nabla f(x^*)\| ds \le \alpha M_1$, $\int_{T}^{t} \alpha e^{-(t-s)} \|\nabla f(x(s)) - \nabla f(x^*)\| ds \le \alpha M_2$. Thus, we have

$$\left\|x(t) - x^*\right\| \le e^{-(t-t_0)} \left\|x_0 - x^*\right\| + \alpha\left(M_1 + M_2\right)$$
$$+ \int_{t_0}^{t} e^{-(t-s)} \left\|x(s) - x^*\right\| ds. \tag{21}$$

By Gronwall-Bellman inequality, when α is sufficiently small, one can obtain that

$$\|x(t) - x^*\| \leq e^{-(t-t_0)} \|x_0 - x^*\| e + \alpha e (M_1 + M_2)$$
$$\approx e \|x_0 - x^*\| e^{-(t-t_0)}, \tag{22}$$

which means that, when $x_0 \notin X$ and α is sufficiently small, the state vector of system (9) still approximately exponentially converges to the Nash equilibrium point, and the approximate convergence exponent is 1. This completes the proof.

Remark 25. For system (9), when it is used to convex optimization problem, Theorem 24 does not require that $\nabla^2 f$ exists, and $\nabla^2 f > 0$ and $\|\nabla^2 f\|$ local bounded. Thus, the conditions of Theorem 24 are weaker than those derived in literature [24].

5. Numerical Examples

In order to show the effectiveness of the technique proposed in this paper, we revisit two classic games as follows.

Example 26 (Cournot competition). Consider an industry comprised of two firms, and they choose output levels q_i, $i = 1, 2$, and have cost function $C_i(q_i)$, $i = 1, 2$. The firms' products are assumed to be perfect substitutes (the homogeneous-goods case). Let $Q = q_1 + q_2$ denote the aggregate industry output level; market demand for the perfect-substitutes case is a function of aggregate output and its inverse is denoted as $P(Q)$. Thus, the firms' profit functions can be written as

$$\pi_1(q_1, q_2) = q_1 P(Q) - C_1(q_1),$$
$$\pi_2(q_1, q_2) = q_2 P(Q) - C_2(q_2). \tag{23}$$

A Cournot equilibrium (q_1^*, q_2^*) means that

$$q_1^* \in \arg\max \pi_1(q_1, q_2^*) = q_1 P(q_1 + q_2^*) - C_1(q_1),$$
$$q_2^* \in \arg\max \pi_2(q_1^*, q_2) = q_2 P(q_1^* + q_2) - C_2(q_2). \tag{24}$$

For this game, the existence, uniqueness, and stability problems about the Cournot equilibrium have been deeply researched by many authors. Here, we are only concerned about how to calculate it when the special profit functions and parameters are given. In order to verify the technique established in this paper, we assume that $P(Q) = a - (q_1 + q_2)$, $C_1(q_1) = q_1 c$, $C_2(q_2) = q_2 c$, where $a > c > 0$ are given positive constants and $P(Q) > 0$. In this case, as is well known, the Nash equilibrium point is $q_1^* = q_2^* = (1/3)(a - c)$ [26]. Obviously, the strategy set $X = \Pi_{i=1}^2 X_i$, $X_i = \{q_i : 0 \leq q_i \leq a\}$, $i = 1, 2$, is nonempty, closed, and convex, and profit functions $\pi_i(q_1, q_2)$, $i = 1, 2$, satisfy assumption (2). By Section 4, we can construct the following neural network to solve the Nash equilibrium:

$$\frac{dq(t)}{dt} = -q(t) + P_X(q(t) + \alpha \nabla \pi(q(t))), \tag{25}$$

where $q(t) = [q_1(t), q_2(t)]^T$ is the state vector; $P_X(q(t) + \alpha \nabla \pi(q(t))) = [P_X^1, P_X^2]^T$, where

$$P_X^1 = 0.5 \left| (1 - 2\alpha) q_1(t) - \alpha q_2(t) + \alpha(a - c) \right| + \frac{a}{2}$$
$$- 0.5 \left| (1 - 2\alpha) q_1(t) - \alpha q_2(t) + \alpha(a - c) - a \right|,$$

$$P_X^2 = 0.5 \left| (1 - 2\alpha) \alpha q_2(t) - \alpha q_1(t) + \alpha(a - c) \right| + \frac{a}{2}$$
$$- 0.5 \left| (1 - 2\alpha) \alpha q_2(t) - \alpha q_1(t) + \alpha(a - c) - a \right|. \tag{26}$$

If $a = 100$, $c = 4$, from $q_1^* = q_2^* = (1/3)(a - c)$, we know that $q_1^* = q_2^* = 32$. In what follows, we will show that for initial value $q_0 \in X$ or $q_0 \notin X$, neural network (25) approximately exponentially converges to the Nash equilibrium point. Set $\alpha = 0.005$, $q_0 = [1, 5]^T \in X$; by simulation tool box, the simulation result is in Figure 1. From Figure 1, one can see that the state vector of neural network approximately exponentially converges to the Nash equilibrium point. Set $q_0 = [-5, -3]^T \notin X$; by simulation tool box, the simulation result is in Figure 2. From Figure 2, one can see that the state vector of neural network also approximately exponentially converges to the Nash equilibrium point.

Additionally, if $P(Q)$, $C_i(q_i)$ are given general nonlinear functions such that $\pi_i(q_1, q_2)$ satisfies assumptions (1) and (2), in this case, to calculate the Nash equilibrium point directly is difficult. However, by using the technique established in this paper, we still can get one Nash equilibrium point through simulation tool box.

Example 27 (Hotelling competition). Consider the typical Hotelling game with two firms and a continuum of consumers. These consumers are distributed on a linear city of unit length according to a uniform density function. Each consumer is entitled to buy at most one unit of the commodity. Set p_i, $D_i(p_1, p_2)$, $i = 1, 2$, which are the firm i's pricing strategy and demand function, respectively. x is the distance between the location of the consumer and store and t is the transportation cost coefficient. The production cost is assumed to be identical and equal to c per unit for both firms. Thus, the firms' profit functions can be written as

$$\pi_1(p_1, p_2) = (p_1 - c) D_1(p_1, p_2),$$
$$\pi_2(p_1, p_2) = (p_2 - c) D_2(p_1, p_2). \tag{27}$$

A Hotelling equilibrium (p_1^*, p_2^*) means that

$$p_1^* \in \arg\max \pi_1(p_1, p_2^*) = (p_1 - c) D_1(p_1, p_2^*),$$
$$p_2^* \in \arg\max \pi_2(p_1^*, p_2) = (p_2 - c) D_2(p_1^*, p_2). \tag{28}$$

As is well known, if

$$D_1(p_1, p_2) = \frac{p_2 - p_1 + t}{2t}, \qquad D_2(p_1, p_2) = \frac{p_1 - p_2 + t}{2t}, \tag{29}$$

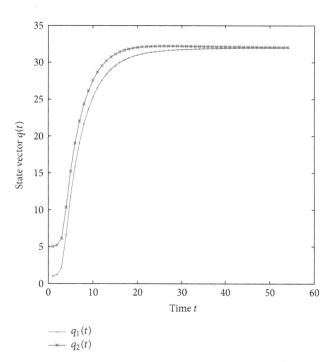

FIGURE 1: The state vector of system (25) with $q_0 = [1, 5]^T \in X$.

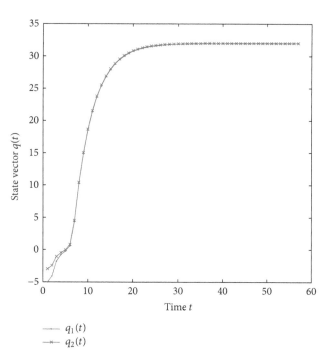

FIGURE 2: The state vector of system (25) with $q_0 = [-5, -3]^T \notin X$.

the Nash equilibrium point is $p_1^* = p_2^* = c+t$ [27]. Obviously, the strategy set $X = \Pi_{i=1}^2 X_i$, $X_i = \{p_i : c \le p_i \le c + t\}$, $i = 1, 2$, is nonempty, closed, and convex, and profit functions $\pi_i(p_1, p_2)$, $i = 1, 2$, satisfy assumption (2). By Section 4, we can construct the following neural network to solve the Nash equilibrium point:

$$\frac{dp(t)}{dt} = -p(t) + P_X(p(t) + \alpha \nabla \pi(p(t))), \qquad (30)$$

where $p(t) = [p_1(t), p_2(t)]^T$ is the state vector; $P_X(p(t) + \alpha \nabla \pi(p(t))) = [P_X^1, P_X^2]^T$, where

$$P_X^1 = 0.5 \left| (1 - 2\alpha) p_1(t) + \alpha p_2(t) + \alpha(c + t) - c \right|$$
$$- 0.5 \left| (1 - 2\alpha) p_1(t) + \alpha p_2(t) + (\alpha - 1)(c + t) \right|$$
$$+ \frac{2c + t}{2},$$

$$P_X^2 = 0.5 \left| \alpha p_1(t) + (1 - 2\alpha) p_2(t) + \alpha(c + t) - c \right|$$
$$- 0.5 \left| \alpha p_1(t) + (1 - 2\alpha) p_2(t) + (\alpha - 1)(c + t) \right|$$
$$+ \frac{2c + t}{2}.$$

$$(31)$$

Set $\alpha = 0.005$, $c = 2$, $t = 5$; from $p_1^* = p_2^* = c + t$, we know that $p_1^* = p_2^* = 7$. Similar to Example 26, when initial value $p_0 \in X$ or $p_0 \notin X$, neural network (30) still approximately exponentially converges to the Nash equilibrium point $(p_1^*, p_2^*)^T$. The simulation results can be seen in Figures 3 and 4. From Figures 3 and 4, one can

see that the state vector of neural network approximately exponentially converges to the Nash equilibrium point.

Similarly, if $D_i(p_1, p_2)$, $i = 1, 2$, are given general nonlinear functions such that $\pi_i(q_1, q_2)$ satisfies assumptions (1) and (2), in this case, to calculate the Nash equilibrium directly is difficult. However, by using the technique established in this paper, we still can get one Nash equilibrium point through simulation tool box.

Remark 28. The numerical simulation examples show that the results established in this paper are both valid from theoretical and practical points of view. These results provide us a new technique to solve the Nash equilibrium point of concave game. This new technique establishes a bridge between the neural network method and game theory and expands the scientific applications area of neural network.

Remark 29. It is worth to be pointed out that, by using the neural network technique derived in this paper to solve the Nash equilibrium point, the initial strategy value can be out of the strategy set; this phenomenon can provide us a new computer algorithm to solve the Nash equilibrium point. This new method is different from the traditional computer logic calculation and simulation method, which requires that every step's strategy values must be in the strategy set. And the new technique can reduce computation complexity significantly.

Remark 30. The results obtained in this paper show that, theoretically, the Nash equilibrium points of all kinds of concave game can be solved by neural network technique. However, when the payoff function does not satisfy assumption (2), for example, when the payoff function is only lower semicontinuous, upper semicontinuous, or quasi-continuous, how to use

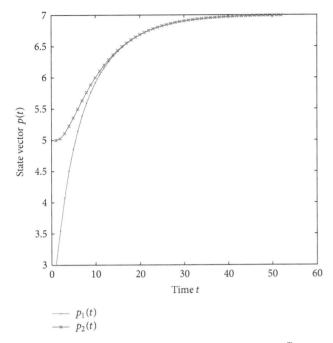

FIGURE 3: The state vector of system (30) with $q_0 = [3, 5]^T \in X$.

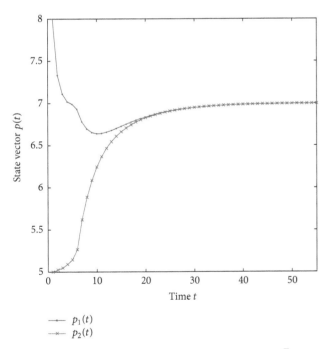

FIGURE 4: The state vector of system (30) with $q_0 = [5, 8]^T \notin X$.

neural network technique to solve the Nash equilibrium point still needs to be deeply researched. And this is our future research direction.

6. Conclusion

The analysis results obtained in this paper imply that every concave game satisfying assumptions (1) and (2) can be equivalently transformed into a neural network model. There exists equivalence between the equilibrium point of neural network and the Nash equilibrium point of concave games. And the equilibrium point's convergence is independent whether the initial value is in the strategy set or not. This means that concave games can be implemented by neural network, or even by hardware. Two classic games' simulation results show that the results established in this paper are valid.

Conflict of Interests

The authors declare that there is no conflict of interests regarding the publication of this paper.

Acknowledgments

This work was supported by the China Postdoctoral Science Foundation Grant (2012 M521718) and the Soft Science Research Project in Guizhou Province ([2011]LKC2004).

References

[1] E. Rasmusen, *Games and Information: An Introduction to Game Theory*, Blackwell Publishers, Oxford, UK, 2000.

[2] N. McCarrty and A. Meirkowitze, *Political Game Theory*, Cambridge University Press, Cambridge, UK, 2007.

[3] C. F. Camerer, *Behavioral Game Theory: Experiments in Strategic Interaction*, Princeton University Press, Princeton, NJ, USA, 2006.

[4] W. Hodges, "Logic and Games," in *The Stanford Encyclopedia of Philosophy*, E. N. Zalta, Ed., 2013.

[5] T. L. Vincent and J. S. Brown, *Evolutionary Game Theory, Natural Selection, and Darwinian Dynamics*, Cambridge University Press, Cambridge, UK, 2005.

[6] G. Carmona, *Existence and Stability of Nash Equilibrium*, World Scientific, River Edge, NJ, USA, 2013.

[7] Y. H. Zhou, J. Yu, and S. W. Xiang, "Essential stability in games with infinitely many pure strategies," *International Journal of Game Theory*, vol. 35, no. 4, pp. 493–503, 2007.

[8] J. Yu, H. Yang, and C. Yu, "Structural stability and robustness to bounded rationality for non-compact cases," *Journal of Global Optimization*, vol. 44, no. 1, pp. 149–157, 2009.

[9] Z. Lin, "On existence of vector equilibrium flows with capacity constraints of arcs," *Nonlinear Analysis: Theory, Methods & Applications*, vol. 72, no. 3-4, pp. 2076–2079, 2010.

[10] S. W. Xiang and Y. H. Zhou, "On essential sets and essential components of efficient solutions for vector optimization problems," *Journal of Mathematical Analysis and Applications*, vol. 315, no. 1, pp. 317–326, 2006.

[11] Z. Yang and Y. J. Pu, "Existence and stability of solutions for maximal element theorem on Hadamard manifolds with applications," *Nonlinear Analysis: Theory, Methods & Applications*, vol. 75, no. 2, pp. 516–525, 2012.

[12] J. Y. Halpern and R. Pass, "Algorithmic rationality: adding cost of computation to game theory," *ACM SIGecom Exchanges*, vol. 10, no. 2, pp. 9–15, 2011.

[13] S. Özyildirim and N. M. Alemdar, "Learning the optimum as a Nash equilibrium," *Journal of Economic Dynamics and Control*, vol. 24, no. 4, pp. 483–499, 2000.

[14] N. G. Pavlidis, K. E. Parsopoulos, and M. N. Vrahatis, "Computing Nash equilibria through computational intelligence methods," *Journal of Computational and Applied Mathematics*, vol. 175, no. 1, pp. 113–136, 2005.

[15] R. Porter, E. Nudelman, and Y. Shoham, "Simple search methods for finding a Nash equilibrium," *Games and Economic Behavior*, vol. 63, no. 2, pp. 642–662, 2008.

[16] X. L. Hu, "Dynamic system methods for solving mixed linear matrix inequalities and linear vector inequalities and equalities," *Applied Mathematics and Computation*, vol. 216, no. 4, pp. 1181–1193, 2010.

[17] D. Wang, D. Liu, D. Zhao, Y. Huang, and D. Zhang, "A neural-network-based iterative GDHP approach for solving a class of nonlinear optimal control problems with control constraints," *Neural Computing and Applications*, vol. 22, no. 2, pp. 219–227, 2013.

[18] W. Bian and X. P. Xue, "Neural network for solving constrained convex optimization problems with global attractivity," *IEEE Transactions on Circuits and Systems I*, vol. 60, no. 3, pp. 710–723, 2013.

[19] J. Yu, *Game Theory and Nonlinear Analysis*, Science Press, Beijing, China, 2008.

[20] J. Yu, *Game Theory and Nonlinear Analysis*, Science Press, Beijing, China, 2nd edition, 2011.

[21] D. Kinderlehrer and G. Stampcchia, *An Introduction to Variational Inequalities and Their Applications*, Academic Press, New York, NY, USA, 1980.

[22] X. B. Liang and J. Wang, "A recurrent neural network for nonlinear optimization with a continuously differentiable objective function and bound constraints," *IEEE Transactions on Neural Networks*, vol. 11, no. 6, pp. 1251–1262, 2000.

[23] Y. S. Xia and J. Wang, "On the stability of globally projected dynamical systems," *Journal of Optimization Theory and Applications*, vol. 100, no. 2, pp. 129–150, 1999.

[24] Y. M. Li, J. Z. Shen, and Z. B. Xu, "Global convergence analysis on projection-type neural networks," *Chinese Journal of Computers*, vol. 28, no. 7, pp. 1178–1184, 2005.

[25] Y. Q. Yang, J. Cao, X. Xu, and J. Liu, "A generalized neural network for solving a class of minimax optimization problems with linear constraints," *Applied Mathematics and Computation*, vol. 218, no. 14, pp. 7528–7537, 2012.

[26] A. Cournot, *Researches into the Mathematical Principles of the Theory of Wealth*, Macmillan, New York, NY, USA, 1987.

[27] H. Hotelling, "Stability in competition," *Economic Journal*, vol. 39, no. 153, pp. 41–57, 1929.

Permissions

The contributors of this book come from diverse backgrounds, making this book a truly international effort. This book will bring forth new frontiers with its revolutionizing research information and detailed analysis of the nascent developments around the world.

We would like to thank all the contributing authors for lending their expertise to make the book truly unique. They have played a crucial role in the development of this book. Without their invaluable contributions this book wouldn't have been possible. They have made vital efforts to compile up to date information on the varied aspects of this subject to make this book a valuable addition to the collection of many professionals and students.

This book was conceptualized with the vision of imparting up-to-date information and advanced data in this field. To ensure the same, a matchless editorial board was set up. Every individual on the board went through rigorous rounds of assessment to prove their worth. After which they invested a large part of their time researching and compiling the most relevant data for our readers. Conferences and sessions were held from time to time between the editorial board and the contributing authors to present the data in the most comprehensible form. The editorial team has worked tirelessly to provide valuable and valid information to help people across the globe.

Every chapter published in this book has been scrutinized by our experts. Their significance has been extensively debated. The topics covered herein carry significant findings which will fuel the growth of the discipline. They may even be implemented as practical applications or may be referred to as a beginning point for another development. Chapters in this book were first published by Hindawi Publishing Corporation; hereby published with permission under the Creative Commons Attribution License or equivalent.

The editorial board has been involved in producing this book since its inception. They have spent rigorous hours researching and exploring the diverse topics which have resulted in the successful publishing of this book. They have passed on their knowledge of decades through this book. To expedite this challenging task, the publisher supported the team at every step. A small team of assistant editors was also appointed to further simplify the editing procedure and attain best results for the readers.

Our editorial team has been hand-picked from every corner of the world. Their multi-ethnicity adds dynamic inputs to the discussions which result in innovative outcomes. These outcomes are then further discussed with the researchers and contributors who give their valuable feedback and opinion regarding the same. The feedback is then collaborated with the researches and they are edited in a comprehensive manner to aid the understanding of the subject.

Apart from the editorial board, the designing team has also invested a significant amount of their time in understanding the subject and creating the most relevant covers. They scrutinized every image to scout for the most suitable representation of the subject and create an appropriate cover for the book.

The publishing team has been involved in this book since its early stages. They were actively engaged in every process, be it collecting the data, connecting with the contributors or procuring relevant information. The team has been an ardent support to the editorial, designing and production team. Their endless efforts to recruit the best for this project, has resulted in the accomplishment of this book. They are a veteran in the field of academics and their pool of knowledge is as vast as their experience in printing. Their expertise and guidance has proved useful at every step. Their uncompromising quality standards have made this book an exceptional effort. Their encouragement from time to time has been an inspiration for everyone.

The publisher and the editorial board hope that this book will prove to be a valuable piece of knowledge for researchers, students, practitioners and scholars across the globe.

List of Contributors

Tse Guan Tan, Jason Teo and Kim On Chin
Evolutionary Computing Laboratory, School of Engineering and Information Technology, Universiti Malaysia, Jalan (UMS), 88400 Kota Kinabalu, Sabah, Malaysia

Ryan McDaniel and Roman V. Yampolskiy
Computer Engineering and Computer Science, University of Louisville, Louisville, KY 40292, USA

Bian Wu and Alf Inge Wang
Department of Computer Science, Norwegian University of Science and Technology, 7491 Trondheim, Norway

Jacco Bikker and Jeroen van Schijndel
ADE/IGAD, NHTV Breda University of Applied Sciences, Monseigneur Hopmansstraat 1, 4817 JT Breda, The Netherlands

Yusuke Yoshiyasu
School of Science and Technology, Keio University, Kanagawa 223-8522, Japan

Nobutoshi Yamazaki
Department of Mechanical Engineering, Keio University, Kanagawa 223-8522, Japan

Alasdair G. Thin, Craig Brown and Paul Meenan
School of Life Sciences, Heriot-Watt University, Edinburgh EH14 4AS, UK

Guy Hawkins and Scott Brown
School of Psychology, Newcastle Cognition Laboratory, University of Newcastle, Callaghan, NSW 2308, Australia

Keith Nesbitt
School of Design Communication and IT, University of Newcastle, Callaghan, NSW 2308, Australia

Marcel Toshio Omori and Alan Salvany Felinto
Computer Sciences Department, State University of Londrina, Londrina, PR 86051-980, Brazil

Ching-I Teng and Han-Chung Huang
Graduate Institute of Business and Management, Chang Gung University, Taoyuan 333, Taiwan

Mochamad Hariadi and Mauridhi Hery Purnomo
Electrical Department, Faculty of Industrial Technology, Institut Teknologi Sepuluh Nopember, Kampus ITS Keputih, Sukolilo, Jawa Timur, Surabaya 60111, Indonesia

Moh. Aries Syufagi
Multimedia Studies Program, Public Vocational High School 1, Jl. Tongkol No. 03, Jawa Timur, Bangil 67153, Indonesia
Department of Information, STMIK Yadika, Jl. Bader No. 7, Kalirejo, Jawa Timur, Bangil 67153, Indonesia

Anthony Savidis
Human-Computer Interaction Laboratory, Institute of Computer Science, Foundation for Research and Technology Hellas, N. Plastira 100, Vassilika Vouton, 70013 Heraklion, Crete, Greece
Department of Computer Science, University of Crete, Knossou Avenue, 71409 Heraklion, Crete, Greece

Effie Karouzaki
Human-Computer Interaction Laboratory, Institute of Computer Science, Foundation for Research and Technology Hellas, N. Plastira 100, Vassilika Vouton, 70013 Heraklion, Crete, Greece

George Adam, Christos Bouras, Vaggelis Kapoula and Andreas Papazois
Computer Technology Institute & Press "Diophantus" and Computer Engineering & Informatics Department, University of Patras, N. Kazantzaki, Panepistimioupoli, 26504 Rion, Greece

Angelo C. Loula
Intelligent and Cognitive Systems Lab, State University of Feira de Santana, 44036-900 Feira de Santana, BA, Brazil

Leandro N. de Castro
Natural Computing Laboratory, Mackenzie Presbyterian University, 01302-090 Sao Paulo, SP, Brazil

Antônio L. Apolinário Jr.
Computer Science Department, Federal University of Bahia, 40170-290 Salvador, BA, Brazil

Pedro L. B. da Rocha
Laboratory of Terrestrial Vertebrates, Institute of Biology, Federal University of Bahia, 40170-290 Salvador, BA, Brazil

Maria da Conceição L. Carneiro and Vanessa Perpétua G. S. Reis
Institute of Education Gast~ao Guimar~aes, 44026010 Feira de Santana, BA, Brazil

Ricardo F. Machado
Graduate Studies Program in History, Philosophy and Science Teaching, Federal University of Bahia and State University of Feira de Santana, 44036-900 Feira de Santana, BA, Brazil

Claudia Sepulveda
Department of Education, State University of Feira de Santana, 44036-900 Feira de Santana, BA, Brazil

Charbel N. El-Hani
Institute of Biology, Federal University of Bahia, 40170-290 Salvador, BA, Brazil

Giliam J. P. de Carpentier
Linnaeusstraat 32 bis, 3553 CE Utrecht, The Netherlands

Dario Maggiorini, Laura Anna Ripamonti and Federico Sauro
Department of Computer Science, University of Milan, Via Comelico 39, 20135 Milan, Italy

Zixin Liu
College of Computer Science and Information, GuiZhou University, Guiyang 550025, China
Department of Mathematics and Statistics, Guizhou University of Finance and Economics, Guiyang 550004, China

Nengfa Wang
Department of Mathematics and Statistics, Guizhou University of Finance and Economics, Guiyang 550004, China

Printed in the USA
CPSIA information can be obtained
at www.ICGtesting.com
JSHW051442221024
72173JS00006B/1554

9 781632 402608